LOVE UNITES US

LOVE UNITES US

WINNING THE FREEDOM TO MARRY IN AMERICA

Edited by

KEVIN M. CATHCART and LESLIE J. GABEL-BRETT

THE NEW PRESS

NEW YORK
LONDON

"Gay Marriage: A Must or a Bust?" originally appeared in *Out/Look* 6, Fall 1989, and included "Why Gay People Should Seek the Right to Marry" by Thomas B. Stoddard and "Since When Is Marriage a Path to Liberation?" by Paula L. Ettelbrick.

"The Hawai'i Marriage Case Launches the U.S. Freedom-to-Marry Movement for Equality" by Evan Wolfson is reprinted with permission from *Legal Recognition of Same-Sex Partnerships: A Study of National, European and International Law*, edited by Robert Wintemute and Mads Andenaes. Portland, Oregon: Hart Publishing, 2001.

"Gender Identity Defines Sex: Updating the Law to Reflect Modern Medical Science Is Key to Transgender Rights" by M. Dru Levasseur is reprinted from *Vermont Law Review* with permission from the author.

Requests for permission to reproduce selections from this book should be mailed to: Permissions Department, The New Press, 120 Wall Street, 31st floor, New York, NY 10005.

Published in the United States by The New Press, New York, 2016
Distributed by Perseus Distribution

ISBN 978-1-59558-550-9 (hc)
ISBN 978-1-62097-177-2 (e-book)
CIP data is available

The New Press publishes books that promote and enrich public discussion and understanding of the issues vital to our democracy and to a more equitable world. These books are made possible by the enthusiasm of our readers; the support of a committed group of donors, large and small; the collaboration of our many partners in the independent media and the not-for-profit sector; booksellers, who often hand-sell New Press books; librarians; and above all by our authors.

www.thenewpress.com

Book design and composition by Bookbright Media
This book was set in Sabon and Berkeley Oldstyle

Printed in the United States of America
10 9 8 7 6 5 4 3 2 1

CONTENTS

ACKNOWLEDGMENTS

A movement for social change consists of thousands of activists, plaintiffs, allies, and donors. This book is for all the named and unnamed people who did and still do the work of fighting for equality, with our admiration and gratitude.

We are especially grateful for the editorial talents and dedication of our Lambda Legal colleagues—Angelo Ragaza, content and editorial director, and Alberto Galindo, associate editor and Spanish content specialist—for their careful reading, editing, and counsel throughout this project, and Edwin Tablada, Education and Public Affairs associate, for his valuable assistance. Thank you also to Julie Enszer, our wonderful editor from The New Press who has guided us with wisdom and good humor.

This story is all about love and fighting for justice—two things we each are fortunate to share, in abundance, with our spouses Mayo Schrieber and Carolyn Gabel-Brett. We thank them for all they bring to our lives.

INTRODUCTION: LOVE UNITES US

LESLIE J. GABEL-BRETT AND KEVIN M. CATHCART

—⟨∞⟩—

Leslie J. Gabel-Brett is the director of Education and Public Affairs for Lambda Legal.

Kevin M. Cathcart was the executive director of Gay & Lesbian Advocates & Defenders from 1984 to 1992 and the executive director of Lambda Legal from 1992 to 2016.

Fighting for marriage equality was neither an obvious nor uncontested choice for the lesbian, gay, bisexual, and transgender (LGBT) civil rights movement. When we each started out as activists in the 1970s, marriage for same-sex couples was not a topic that we or anybody with whom we worked even discussed. A lesbian and a gay man, we identified as feminists and saw marriage as an institution that often oppressed women, reified gender roles, and maintained the power of straight men. We also viewed it as an institution that, in general, limited sexual expression and freedom. If we thought about it at all, seeking the freedom to marry seemed far-fetched and far less likely to succeed than a fight for equal rights at work—an issue we thought was not threatening and was easy for the public to understand.

Sometimes, it's good to be wrong.

We were not wrong about all of it—patriarchal marriage is a limiting and often harmful institution. But, as the title of this book suggests and the chapters that follow make clear, we learned something powerful about the strategy for ending stigma, prejudice, and antipathy toward LGBT people: talking about love, human connections, and the shared experiences of life illuminated our common humanity. Sharing stories about courtship, commitment, children, illness, and loss led more swiftly to understanding and compassion than all our talk about equality and rights. Love unites us.

Over time, many of us began to understand the intersections between the arguments about love and those about equal rights. Some believed deeply in marriage and the transformative power of fighting for it. Others felt that, while we might not all wish to get married, equality required that same-sex couples have the same choice to marry as different-sex couples. We knew it would not be easy to win, but if we secured the freedom to marry, it would make other measures like antidiscrimination laws seem like moderate demands; it would help change people's perceptions of who lesbians, bisexuals, and gay men are; and it would (for those who married) solve hundreds of different legal problems.

Of course, our different messages were often intermingled, and our strategies did not proceed in a straight line. Some of the first significant legislative victories for our civil rights movement were passage of state and local antidiscrimination statutes that we won by arguing for equal rights. We started down that strategic path and secured our first victory in Wisconsin in 1982. However, in 2016, we still do not have a federal law explicitly prohibiting discrimination on the basis of sexual orientation and gender identity and expression, and less than half the states in the country have state laws providing such protections. When we began fighting for family protections, we started with parental rights (including custody and visitation), then began building the case for domestic partnership protections. In the early stages of that work, we used the language of rights and responsibilities and teased apart the concept of civil marriage—a relationship sanctioned by the government that structured a large bundle of obligations and protections with respect to children, property, and decision-making—from the more commonplace concept of marriage bound up with romantic and sexual love and religion.

In fact, we talked about rights all the time. A well-known advocate for marriage equality in Connecticut would carry around a two-foot-high stack of statutes and pile them in front of an audience to illustrate the number of laws that included benefits or obligations associated with marriage. By decoding civil marriage and enumerating some of its protections and obligations, we began to make the case for equality. Should someone in a same-sex relationship be prohibited from making decisions and visiting a dying partner in the ICU? Should a non-biological lesbian, gay, or bisexual parent be unable to get medical care for her or his child? Should a parent living with HIV be denied custody or visitation of a child? Should aging same-sex partners be separated in the nursing home, or be denied the ability to bury their partners when they die? Shouldn't both same-sex parents be equally obligated to pay child support?

The bridge between rights and protections and "common humanity" was articulated plainly in 1999 in the Vermont Supreme Court's decision in *Baker v. Vermont*. This was the second important legal victory on the path to winning marriage equality, following the 1996 ruling in Hawai'i. Vermont Chief Justice Amestoy wrote:

> The extension of the Common Benefits Clause [of the Vermont State Constitution] to acknowledge plaintiffs as Vermonters who seek nothing more, nor less, than legal protection and security for their avowed commitment to an intimate and lasting human relationship is simply, when all is said and done, a recognition of our common humanity.

The landmark ruling in Vermont led to passage of civil unions rather than marriage equality. As we progressed from the first fights for domestic partnerships, "reciprocal beneficiary" statuses, civil unions, and other alternatives to marriage, we came to understand the degree to which these bundles of rights, packaged as anything but marriage, were unmistakable expressions of exclusion and painful markers of inferiority. While they ameliorated many of the concrete harms that same-sex couples faced, they made the harm to human dignity even plainer. We started talking less about rights and more about love and respect.

The movement for the freedom to marry was a slice of the LGBT civil rights movement. It grew from the seeds of other struggles for equality for LGBT people and people living with HIV, progressed alongside these continuing fights—sometimes dwarfing them in attention and resources—and shaped their future. The ultimate Supreme Court marriage victory came in 2015, a year in which at least twelve transgender women were known to have been murdered in the first six months, most of them women of color. It was decided in a country where thirty-nine states still had statutes specifically criminalizing the transmission of HIV or where HIV-related criminal charges recently had been brought. And it came in a society where LGBTQ youth represented 40 percent of young people experiencing homelessness due, in large part, to family rejection. Within four weeks of the *Obergefell* decision, the "Equality Act," a new comprehensive civil rights bill to provide explicit protections against discrimination in employment, housing, public accommodations, credit, and jury service, was introduced in Congress. Marriage equality was neither the beginning nor the end of the story.

Social justice movements are complex and messy, shaped by a combination of strategy, chance, and the opposition these movements face. They are propelled forward by thousands of activists and strategists, allies, and funders, all of whom are passionate and motivated by visions of success. There are varied strategies including litigation, communications and public education, electoral advocacy, and grassroots mobilization. When a movement is at its best, these elements reinforce each other, forming a giant engine with many moving parts. There are also differences of opinion, compromises and betrayals, victories and setbacks. Organizations are formed, plans developed, and funds raised. Then unexpected things happen.

For the early modern lesbian and gay rights movement (not yet explicitly inclusive of bisexual or transgender rights), three things happened to push questions of family and marriage more urgently into our thoughts and higher on our priority lists. First, the agonizing AIDS epidemic forced gay men out and highlighted our legal and personal vulnerability. It taught us painful lessons about our needs for personal connections and care, on the one hand, and the harms that come from exclusion from government protections, on the other. Second, individual couples across the country, from Minnesota to Hawai'i, yearned for and demanded access to marriage. They may or may not have represented the majority of LGBT people in the early days, but they were brave, outspoken, and compelling. Third, as is often the case, backlash, or an attack, defines a fight: once the Defense of Marriage Act was passed in 1996 in reaction to the state court decisions in Hawai'i, the fight was on, and we were determined not to lose.

The Epidemic

It is painful to remember and impossible to explain the fear and anger of the early AIDS epidemic, which surfaced in the United States in 1981 and exploded, growing rapidly year by year. Legions of gay men, many of them quite young, died terrible and painful deaths, often quickly after diagnosis. Others who did not get sick or did not get sick until much later lived in terror and mourning, losing lovers, friends, and community and not knowing who would be next. From a handful of cases diagnosed in 1981, in 1982 there were sixteen hundred cases, and six hundred people died. By 1988 there were 107,000 cases in the United States, with 62,000 deaths, and four years later, 335,000 cases and 198,000 dead. Worldwide the numbers are even more staggering, as the epidemic has grown: In 2015, nearly 37 million people around the world were living with HIV, with more than two-thirds of them in sub-Saharan Africa. In 2014, 1.2 million people died from AIDS.[1]

In a country that did not much care about AIDS—as government responses ranged from nonexistent to painfully slow, and in which gay and bisexual men lacked basic legal protections—the effects of the epidemic were devastating.

Gay and bisexual men were not the only group hit by the epidemic, but they were hit hardest from the start. Men lost their jobs when their illnesses became evident, and sometimes just for being or being presumed to be gay and therefore considered to be high risk, often losing critical health insurance at the same time. Mistreatment by medical professionals and institutions was not uncommon, including by doctors, nurses, dentists, hospitals, and EMTs. Landlords tried to evict people; the first AIDS discrimination lawsuit in the United States was Lambda Legal's case on behalf of a doctor whose landlord tried to evict his medical practice because he treated people with what later became known as HIV.

Rejection by families was not uncommon, nor was cowardice from political and religious leaders. With no possible legal recognition of our relationships, men faced terrible challenges in trying to take care of their partners, not being allowed to make medical decisions or even funeral arrangements, and losing homes and property to the biological families of those who died. There were legal battles over all of these issues, including poignant lawsuits over who had the right to possession of the ashes of the cremated deceased. The legal resources available were overwhelmed by the need for them, and many people did not have the stamina for lawsuits while sick or caring for sick partners and friends.

The epidemic highlighted our medical and legal vulnerabilities. It shed light on active gay sexual cultures as well as what had often been invisible to the world at large: committed and long-term gay relationships. It was a time of both terror and heroism. It underscored the LGBT community's lack of political power, and led to people coming out, organizing, creating new community organizations, and strengthening existing ones, completely shifting the course of the LGBT civil rights movement. Being sick forced many gay men, from those with the most ordinary lives to the most famous, out of their closets, and many who weren't physically ill but knew they were at risk and were angry about how their brothers were treated came out as well. Groups like ACT UP and Gay Men's Health Crisis (GMHC) were created, and organizations like Lambda Legal saw their funding increase as more and more people joined in the fight for treatment and a cure, for recognition of their families, and for an end to invisibility and discrimination.

While we have come a long way since those bleak early days, we are still fighting many of the same battles. Important treatment breakthroughs in the 1990s led to a rapid decrease in deaths from AIDS, but about fifty thousand people a year still seroconvert in the United States, the majority of them gay or bisexual men, and the majority of those African American, young, and poor. The Affordable Care Act and the access to treatment it can provide give us our best shot at ending the epidemic, but it is still politically contested, and many people with HIV in America today are not in treatment. While in the 1990s and the first decade of this century LGBT civil rights groups and HIV groups gradually became disconnected from each other and often went down separate paths, we are proud that all of our community's legal groups kept doing critical HIV-related litigation and policy work, which helped inform and shape our broader LGBT rights work.

Knocking on the Courthouse Door

We will never know how many same-sex couples in the United States declared themselves married, held private ceremonies, considered themselves "common law" husbands or wives, and lived together in long-term committed relationships. By the early 1980s, scholars published groundbreaking works describing the rich history of long-term same-sex relationships in Western cultures—some that resembled or took the form of marriages, and others that did not but were lasting relationships of mutual love and dependence.[2] In 1987 and again in 1993, mass weddings were held at the historic marches on Washington where thousands of same-sex couples exchanged non-legal vows. In a heartbreaking evocation of the emotions and yearning arising from the growing power of our movement and the aching grief of the AIDS epidemic, Michael Callen, in one of the last performances before his death, sang "Love Don't Need a Reason" from the main stage of the march: "Love don't need a reason / Love's never a crime / And love is all we have for now / What we don't have is time."[3]

While some members of the lesbian and gay community were extolling the virtues of sexual liberation or criticizing the failings of marriage as an institution, others yearned for the validation, romance, and equality offered by it. By 1970, very soon after the Stonewall Rebellion, some couples began knocking on the courthouse door. William Eskridge (see page 21) tells the story of Mike McConnell and Jack Baker, who applied for a marriage license in 1970 in Hennepin County, Minnesota. Their early legal challenge resulted in the infamous refusal of the U.S. Supreme Court to consider their appeal for want of a "substantial federal question" (*Baker v. Nelson*). Eskridge also recounts the legal challenges brought in the early 1970s by a lesbian couple in Wisconsin and another in Kentucky. These were not cases strategically brought by LGBT activists and organizations in the big cities where activism was growing; these were cases brought by determined couples who believed they should have had the right to get married.

Immigration rules also prompted legal challenges by same-sex binational couples who were not permitted to live together in the United States as married couples can. Tony Sullivan and Richard Adams got a marriage license in Boulder, Colorado, in 1975. When they applied for an extended visa for Sullivan who was Australian and faced deportation, the U.S. Immigration and Naturalization Service denied their request, writing: "You have failed to establish that a bona fide marital relationship can exist between two faggots." In response to their protest, they received an amended letter without the offensive language, but the INS continued to deny the validity of their marriage and refused to grant Sullivan a visa. The federal judge who authored the final denial of their application in 1985 was Anthony Kennedy, then a judge on the U.S. Ninth Circuit Court of Appeals (*Adams v. Howerton*; *Sullivan v. INS*).

The debate within the LGBT movement about the value and meaning of seeking the right to marry grew more serious and contentious through the 1980s, with Thomas B. Stoddard, then the executive director of Lambda Legal, publicly debating the organization's legal director, Paula Ettelbrick. He wrote in 1989 that " . . . the issue is not the desirability of marriage, but rather the desirability of the right to marry." He explained further that marriage is "the political issue that most fully tests the dedication of people who are not gay to full equality for gay people." (See pages 32–33.) At the same time, Ettelbrick argued " . . . marriage will not liberate us as lesbians and gay men. In fact, it will constrain us, make us more invisible, force our assimilation into the mainstream, and undermine the goals of gay liberation." (See page 35.) The debate continued for years—and continues still. Activists and scholars fully explained their opposition to seeking entry into marriage in a document widely published in 2006 entitled "Beyond Same-Sex Marriage," writing:

> We . . . seek to offer . . . a new vision for securing governmental and private institutional recognition of diverse kinds of partnerships, households, kinship relationships and families. In so doing, we hope to move beyond the narrow confines of marriage politics as they exist in the United States today.
>
> We seek access to a flexible set of economic benefits and options regardless of sexual orientation, race, gender/gender identity, class, or citizenship status.
>
> We reflect and honor the diverse ways in which people find and practice love, form relationships, create communities and networks of caring and support, establish households, bring families into being, and build innovative structures to support and sustain community.[4]

Notwithstanding this debate, there were same-sex couples who wanted the freedom to marry, and they saw no reason to wait. Throughout this book, individual plaintiffs and their loved ones—including Annie Goodridge (see page 90), Kris Perry (see page 176), Pat Ewert (see page 207), Amy Sandler (see page 244), and Maritza López Avilés and Iris Delia Rivera Rivera—tell their stories and describe what it meant to them to fight for the dignity of marriage. In Hawai'i in 1990, three same-sex couples, including Ninia Baehr and Genora Dancel, applied for marriage licenses (see page 45). Evan Wolfson, who was at Lambda Legal at the time and went on to found the national group Freedom to Marry, recounts on page 40 how their legal case "rocked the world." Although not initiated by Lambda Legal and not universally embraced, Wolfson persuaded Lambda Legal (by then led by Executive Director Kevin M. Cathcart) to join the case. The Hawai'i Supreme Court was the first ever to rule that excluding same-sex couples from marriage was discrimination. It sent the case back to the trial court to determine whether the state could justify this discrimination. In 1996, the trial judge rejected all the arguments the state offered for excluding same-sex couples from marriage. Before the legal process concluded, however, antigay forces succeeded in 1998 in persuading Hawai'i voters to support the first constitutional amendment specifically targeting same-sex relationships—effectively reversing the legal victory and temporarily ending the fight for the freedom to marry in Hawai'i.

Backlash Helps to Define the Fight

If the story in Hawai'i was a wake-up call for the LGBT rights movement, it appears to have been a three-alarm fire for the opponents of gay rights, leading to a backlash not only in that state but in Congress and states around the country. The trial court decision in Hawai'i was not issued until December 3, 1996. But Congress had already passed the so-called Defense of Marriage Act (DOMA) by September 21 of that year. Marriage equality panic had set in.

On September 10, 1996, the U.S. Senate voted overwhelmingly in favor of DOMA (85–14), and also defeated an employment non-discrimination bill that day by a single vote (50–49). The discriminatory law, signed by President Clinton, explicitly prohibited the federal government from recognizing the validity of the marriages of same-sex couples and from providing any protections or benefits of marriage to them. It also included a provision allowing states to refuse to recognize the marriages of same-sex couples from other jurisdictions. The *New York Times* quoted Senator Trent Lott, the Republican majority leader from Mississippi, as explicitly describing the measure as a defensive response to legal actions in Hawai'i: "It is a pre-emptive measure to make sure that a handful of judges, in a single state, cannot impose a radical social agenda upon the entire nation." The *Times* also quoted Democratic Senator Robert C. Byrd making the argument against marriage equality that would be heard over and over again:

"The drive for same-sex marriage," he said, "is, in effect, an effort to make a sneak attack on society by encoding this aberrant behavior in legal form before society itself has decided it should be legal. . . . Let us defend the oldest institution, the institution of marriage between male and female as set forth in the Holy Bible."[5]

Wolfson notes in his chapter about the fight in Hawai'i that anti-marriage bills were introduced in three state legislatures in 1995, even before the trial court decision a year later. By 1997, only one year after the Hawai'i decision and passage of the federal bill, as many as twenty-six states had some form of ban against marriage for same-sex couples by executive order, statute, or constitutional amendment. The number of states kept climbing after that, notwithstanding the fact that same-sex couples were not allowed to marry anywhere in the country.

In his chapter (see page 100) on the development in 2005 of a national strategy to win marriage equality, Matt Coles of the ACLU cites two "disasters": passage of the federal DOMA and state mini-DOMAs, and the declaration by President George W. Bush, in his bid for reelection, of support for a U.S. constitutional amendment barring marriage for same-sex couples. The amendment resolution garnered a majority—though not a sufficient super-majority—in the House of Representatives, and voters in thirteen states approved discriminatory state constitutional amendments on Election Day that year. As Coles concludes, "It wasn't a pretty picture."

Yet, progress was made. As Mary L. Bonauto recounts (see page 73), a case for the freedom to marry was filed by local attorneys and Gay & Lesbian Advocates & Defenders (GLAD) in Vermont in 1997, with a court victory in 1999. As recounted by Kevin M. Cathcart (see page 51), Suzanne B. Goldberg (see page 56), and Paul Smith (see page 66), LGBT legal groups met to devise coordinated strategies, and in 1999 Lambda Legal challenged the remaining states' sodomy laws in a landmark case that led to the transformational U.S. Supreme Court victory in *Lawrence v. Texas* in 2003. With the victory in *Lawrence*, being lesbian or gay was finally decriminalized, and the legal path to marriage opened up when, as Goldberg writes, the Court "as never before . . . gave its constitutional embrace and protection to the basic humanity of lesbians and gay men." GLAD's historic marriage case, *Goodridge v. Department of Public Health*, which had been filed in Massachusetts in 2001, was won four months later in November 2003, and for the first time in our nation's history, same-sex couples could legally marry within the borders of the United States.

While there were still passionate dissenters about whether or not the fight for marriage equality was in the best interests of LGBT people or our movement for equality, it had become very clear that the fight against the freedom to marry had become a very powerful and effective strategy for conveying hatred and prejudice against LGBT people and for seeking to codify our status as inferior members of society under the law. With anti-sodomy laws eliminated, same-sex couples could no longer be treated as criminals under the law for simply having sexual relations. Antigay activists needed a new vehicle to enforce segregation and discrimination against us. Whether we all liked it or not, the fight for marriage was on.

The Contest to Define Marriage and Family

Who has the right to marry? What is the meaning of marriage and family? These questions have always been contested ground in the history of our country. As long as slavery was legal, slaves were not allowed to marry. After emancipation and until 1968, people of different races were barred from marrying one another in many states. Women's rights within marriage with respect to owning property and participating in public life were absent or strictly limited until a series of reforms swept the country in the latter half of the nineteenth century. Over the course of our history, violence within families has been treated differently under the law than violence outside the family.

Indeed, as the American Historical Association and a long list of distinguished historians of marriage explained in their amicus brief in the *Obergefell* case before the U.S. Supreme Court:

> Marriage is a capacious and complex institution. Though religion, sentiment, and custom may color an individual's understanding of marriage, marriage as a civil institution in the United States has served a number of complementary purposes—political, social, economic, legal, and personal. Over this Nation's history, states have recognized that marriage serves to facilitate the state's regulation of the population; to create stable households; to foster social order; to increase economic welfare and minimize public support of the indigent or vulnerable; to legitimate children; to assign providers to care for dependents; to facilitate the ownership and transmission of property; and to compose the body politic . . .
>
> Equally devoid of credence is the notion that civil marriage is so deeply entrenched in tradition that it resists competing constitutional imperatives. To the contrary, marriage has remained a vital institution because it is not static.[6]

Opponents of marriage equality argued in court and in the court of public opinion that the very definition of marriage precluded same-sex couples from entering into it. Their arguments came down to these: 1) Marriage is a universal human institution that has always been defined as between one man and one woman; 2) this definition is rooted in religious teachings that are universal and should govern civil marriage; and 3) allowing civil marriage between people of the same sex is bad for children in two ways: a) children need a mother and a father; and b) allowing same-sex couples to join the institution of civil marriage will reduce its meaning and authority for different-sex couples, leading them to engage in more "irresponsible procreation" outside of marriage. All of these claims were wrong.

At first, these arguments succeeded. In 2006 and 2007, courts in New York, Washington State, and Maryland delivered defeats. Jeffrey S. Trachtman (see page 127) described the illogic of the 4–2 ruling upholding the marriage ban in the New York case (*Hernandez v. Robles*): "The Court remarkably suggested that 'unstable relationships between people of the opposite sex present a greater danger that children will be born into or grow up in unstable homes than is the case with same-sex couples.' In other words, because same-sex couples procreate more responsibly . . . and are more likely to provide a stable home, they (and their children) are denied the benefits and protections of civil marriage." Chief Justice Judith Kaye, writing for the minority, lamented that "future generations will look back on today's decision as an unfortunate misstep."

Such arguments were initially persuasive not only in court, but also in the public debate about marriage. According to Gallup, Americans opposed marriage for same-sex couples in 2005 by a 59 percent to 37 percent margin. The consequences were evident, as all but six states had enacted some type of prohibition against the freedom to marry either by statute or constitutional amendment by 2007.

Each of these arguments was false and unsupported by the evidence. It took about a decade of strategic and persistent legal, community education, and organizing work to reach the day, on June 26, 2015, when the U.S. Supreme Court declared that the U.S. Constitution required that same-sex couples be allowed the freedom to marry across the country. The distance traveled in judicial reasoning—between the articulation of "irresponsible procreation" as a justification to deny same-sex couples the freedom to marry in 2006 in *Hernandez*, and the incredulous rejection of that theory eight years later in a 2014 federal appeals court ruling allowing same-sex couples to marry in Indiana and Wisconsin—was remarkable. Well-known moderate Judge Richard Posner wrote in the Seventh Circuit decision in *Baskin v. Bogan*:

The challenged laws discriminate against a minority defined by an immutable characteristic, and the only rationale that the states put forth with any conviction—that same-sex couples and their children don't need marriage because same-sex couples can't produce children intended or unintended—is so full of holes that it cannot be taken seriously. To the extent that children are better off in families in which the parents are married, they are better off whether they are raised by their biological parents or by adoptive parents.

As Coles (see page 100) and Wolfson (see page 108) describe, the movement had a plan to move forward and win the argument for love and equality. And as the many chapters that follow demonstrate, the plan worked. Our plan was to strategically and methodically win marriage in states where that goal was judged reasonably achievable; to increase protections for LGBT people in other states where that goal was achievable; to persistently and creatively tell the stories of same-sex couples and their families in order to hold up our common humanity and illustrate the harms suffered by the denial of marriage; to hold the government accountable for treating same-sex couples differently than others; to reach a tipping point in public opinion and in the number of places where we had the freedom to marry; and then, finally, to win nationwide.

Soon after the California Supreme Court ruled in favor of marriage in 2008, nine national LGBT legal and advocacy organizations[7] made public the strategy that previously had been confidential. Controversy followed. In a document entitled "Make Change, Not Lawsuits," the nine national organizations urged same-sex couples, attorneys, and advocates to wait before bringing a federal lawsuit for marriage. We believed it prudent to allow a state-based strategy for winning marriage to proceed first. In the widely circulated and posted document, the organizations explained:

> The fastest way to win the freedom to marry throughout America is by getting marriage through state courts (to show that fairness requires it) and state legislatures (to show that people support it). We need to start with states where we have the best odds of winning. When we've won in a critical mass of states, we can turn to Congress and the federal courts. At that point, we'll ask that the U.S. government treat all marriages equally. And we'll ask that all states give equal treatment to all marriages and civil unions that are celebrated in other states.
>
> But one thing couples shouldn't do is just sue the federal government or, if they are from other states, go sue their home state or their

employer to recognize their marriage or open up the health plan. Pushing the federal government before we have a critical mass of states recognizing same-sex relationships or suing in states where the courts aren't ready is likely to get us bad rulings. . . . Bad rulings will make it much more difficult for us to win marriage, and will certainly make it take much longer.

That same year, after the freedom to marry was taken away from same-sex couples by a popular vote in California, the newly formed American Foundation for Equal Rights filed its federal lawsuit (then called *Perry v. Schwarzenegger*) to overturn Proposition 8 and secure a federal court ruling establishing a constitutional right for same-sex couples to marry anywhere in the country. Heated statements were exchanged, in private and public, about the disagreements. LGBT media reported a struggle within the movement that was characterized, by some, as a battle between "Gay, Inc." and new leaders.

The differences of opinions were always about strategy, not goals. When the document was released in the spring of 2008, marriage was legal in only Massachusetts and California. History showed that the U.S. Supreme Court rarely, if ever, moved far faster than an overwhelming majority of states. Caught up in the excitement and optimism created by the California court victory, couples and attorneys from around the country called Lambda Legal with questions and plans to bring marriage cases in state and federal courts. We believed that some courts were more likely to deliver victories than others. Many of the leaders in the LGBT organizations who published the cautionary document had lived through the devastating 1986 U.S. Supreme Court loss in *Bowers v. Hardwick*, when the Court upheld sodomy laws; they had fought tirelessly for seventeen long years to get that decision reversed in *Lawrence v. Texas* in 2003. For these leaders, the risks of an adverse decision prompted by premature federal court challenges were clear.

In fact, nearly all of the strategies for success worked just as predicted, while none of the feared losses or setbacks transpired. In less than a year, GLAD won a state marriage victory in Connecticut and Lambda Legal won marriage in Iowa. President Obama's position on the freedom to marry "evolved," making it possible for other leaders to support marriage equality. By 2012, after years of public education and political advocacy, LGBT advocates secured the right to marry in a number of state legislatures across the country. Attorneys Ted Olson and David Boies, hired by AFER, skillfully litigated the Proposition 8 case, winning the first federal trial court decision declaring a marriage ban unconstitutional. (See Perry, page 176.) The case took several years to reach the U.S. Supreme Court; once there, the high court avoided ruling on the constitutionality of all bans on marriage while delivering an important victory by restoring the freedom to marry in California.

Only one part of the strategy worked differently than originally predicted: instead of holding the federal government accountable for respecting marriages through legislative repeal of the federal Defense of Marriage Act (DOMA), GLAD, Lambda Legal, and the ACLU (which was co-counsel with private attorney Roberta Kaplan) each decided that federal court challenges to DOMA could pave the way to subsequent victories for the right to marry. They brought separate DOMA challenges, winning several important rulings in the lower courts. In 2013, one of the DOMA challenges (*United States v. Windsor*) reached the Supreme Court. (See Esseks, page 210.) Kaplan argued the case, and on June 26, 2013, the Court struck down the core provision of DOMA that barred federal recognition of same-sex couples' marriages. *Lawrence v. Texas* had unlocked the door; the *Windsor* victory threw it wide open. Court after court subsequently ruled marriage bans unconstitutional.

Winning Marriage

Chapters by Camilla Taylor (see page 131), Hayley Gorenberg (see page 218), Peggy A. Tomsic (see page 227), and Paul D. Castillo (see page 235) describe the legal victories that followed in Iowa, New Jersey, Utah, and Indiana—a sample of the states where courts rejected the flawed arguments that had previously prevailed. As Shannon Minter (see page 145), Kate Kendell (see page 168), Lisa Hardaway (see page 176), and Kris Perry (see page 176) explain about the fight for marriage in California, the journey included thrilling victories, heartbreaking setbacks, and the determination to keep fighting back. Chapters by Nadine Smith (see page 248); Sharon Lettman-Hicks (see page 200); Mary L. Bonauto, Gary D. Buseck, and Janson Wu (see page 183); Anne Stanback (see page 92); Francisco Dueñas (see page 161); and Marc Solomon and Thalia Zepatos (see page 195) describe the work we did, in state after state, to inform, educate, and persuade our neighbors, co-workers, and elected leaders to support our struggle for love, dignity, and equality under the law and to win the freedom to marry through ballot measures and state legislation. We did the hard work of a movement, holding meetings in town halls and houses of worship; forming alliances in schools and workplaces; meeting with legislators; and writing, talking, and telling our stories.

We had many allies and partners. Dueñas describes his work to build partnerships with LGBT people in the Latina/o community and with Latina/o civil rights organizations (see page 161). Karin Wang (see page 157) recounts the decisions and actions taken by the Asian Americans Advancing Justice to support the struggle for marriage equality. The growing number and breadth of amici in cases across the country and consistently rising poll numbers showing support for marriage equality were clear indicators that we were making steady progress. Victories in courts and legislatures led not only to greater freedom for same-sex couples in the states where marriage was affirmed under the law, but also to the growing number of happy, loving couples and families whose very lives demonstrated the truth of our arguments.

The country appeared ready for marriage equality, and we believed the courts were too—but our freedom was no less contested than it had ever been. As victory followed victory, the opposition grew more ugly and fierce. Anti-LGBT elected officials railed against "activist" judges and courts. As Jennifer C. Pizer describes in "Shields Not into Swords" (see page 323), state legislatures raised and enacted laws to allow individuals and businesses to continue to discriminate against same-sex couples in the name of religion.

By the start of the 2015 Supreme Court term, there were petitions before the Court seeking review of seven separate cases brought in various combinations by Lambda Legal, the ACLU, NCLR, and the team of Ted Olson and David Boies, as well as other private counsel in three judicial circuits where federal appeals courts had struck down marriage bans and state officials were appealing. Most observers believed this would be the long-awaited moment when the Court would take up one or more marriage cases and finally render a decision. At Lambda Legal, we had six different press releases prepared to respond to every combination we could imagine about cases taken, rejected, or set aside. Not one of our press releases was accurate. On October 6, 2014, the Supreme Court denied review of all seven cases. Surprise and jubilation swept through our movement.

The decision to deny review in these pending cases meant that same-sex couples would now be allowed to marry in Indiana, Oklahoma, Utah, Virginia, and Wisconsin—in these states, game over. Moreover, other states within the Fourth, Seventh, and Tenth Circuits where cases were pending would now be quickly resolved in favor of marriage equality because the now-final circuit court rulings established binding precedent within those circuits. Attorneys from all the LGBT organizations and private firms worked feverishly through nights and weekends to file the necessary papers. The very next day, Tuesday, October 7, the Ninth Circuit Court of Appeals struck down marriage bans in Idaho and Nevada. The number of marriage equality states jumped from nineteen to thirty-two (plus the District of Columbia) in less than two weeks, and soon thereafter increased to thirty-five. At LGBT rights organizations across the country, we were exhausted and thrilled.

What did it all mean? The plain answer was that the Court needed a "controversy" or split among circuits in order to grant review, and all the pending cases had reached the same result: in favor of the freedom to marry for same-sex couples. But would the Court have allowed marriages to go forward in so many states, only to rule later that the other states could continue to discriminate? Was this the signal that we had five votes on the Court in favor of marriage equality? Or was this some kind of compromise or maneuver that would ultimately lead to defeat and disappointment?

We did not have long to wait. On November 16, 2014, the Sixth Circuit Court of Appeals delivered the first appellate ruling post-*Windsor* to uphold bans against marriage for same-sex couples in six different cases from Michigan, Ohio, Kentucky, and Tennessee. All the plaintiff parties quickly sought Supreme Court review. Although now late in the term, the Court finally had the controversy it needed to grant review. It consolidated all the cases, and on January 12, 2015, granted review in what jointly became known as *Obergefell v. Hodges*. When *Obergefell* reached the Supreme Court in 2015, the "tipping point" predicted ten years earlier in the national strategy memo had been reached: a majority of states and the public were on the side of marriage equality. Notwithstanding the stormy disagreements, each person and organization had risen to the call of history, found common ground, and had done what needed to be done.

Closing Arguments

Bringing and winning the cases that led to the U.S. Supreme Court victory for the freedom to marry on June 26, 2015, as described by Susan Sommer (see page 268), Alphonse Gerhardstein (see page 265), and Mary L. Bonauto (see page 261), was a "leap of love." The six consolidated cases included individuals, couples, and families as plaintiffs whose lives illustrated all our lives; they were seeking marriage licenses, birth and death certificates, and government recognition of their families. Their stories were about commitment, birth and adoption, illness and loss—about our common humanity.

The configuration of lawyers and organizations working together to secure this final victory included all the LGBT legal rights organizations that had led this fight for so many years: the ACLU, GLAD, the National Center for Lesbian Rights, and Lambda Legal, working shoulder to shoulder with private attorneys from firms large and small who had stepped up, taken risks, and pursued a vision of fairness and justice for their clients. Private attorneys were often the ones who had first filed these marriage equality cases. Fittingly, private attorney Douglas Hallward-Driemeier argued before the Supreme Court for marriage recognition

(Question 2). The movement attorney who stood up in court and delivered the closing arguments for the freedom to marry, on behalf of all of us, was Mary L. Bonauto, the visionary who had won the freedom to marry in Massachusetts thirteen years earlier. Victory could not have been sweeter.

The Story Is Not Over

When the decision was rendered on June 26, 2015, one of us (Kevin) was sitting in the courtroom with other lawyers, plaintiffs, and leaders, and one of us (Leslie) was in the Lambda Legal office in New York City. The strict decorum of the U.S. Supreme Court prohibits audible reactions to decisions. But white knuckles quickly turned to clasped hands, and sobs of joy were heard as Justice Kennedy read the decision aloud. In New York, we cheered, applauded, and hugged as the enormity of the news sank in: after decades of struggle, the freedom to marry had finally been won.

Yet June 26, 2015, was a complicated day in our nation. President Obama appeared in the Rose Garden at the White House to praise the decision, saying, "Progress on this journey often comes in small increments, sometimes two steps forward, one step back, propelled by the persistent effort of dedicated citizens. And then sometimes, there are days like this when that slow, steady effort is rewarded with justice that arrives like a thunderbolt." He called the lead plaintiff, Jim Obergefell, to congratulate him as he stood on the steps of the Court.

Then the president flew to Charleston, South Carolina, to deliver a eulogy for Reverend Clementa Pinckney, who had been murdered the week before along with eight other parishioners of an historic African American church in an act of racist violence. Many of us at Lambda Legal joined millions of others across the country to watch the president's passionate remarks, late in the afternoon. It was a day of both profound celebration and sorrow. We witnessed as clear a representation as ever there could be of our imperfect union, pressing forward in pursuit of our highest values and mourning our failure to always live by them.

No single Supreme Court decision solves every problem nor brings an end to a movement for justice. The victory in *Obergefell* has brought both concrete and symbolic benefits to LGBT people across the country. But, as Jon W. Davidson argues (see page 291), "the glass is only half full." Just as DOMA had been the angry backlash to the early marriage victory in Hawai'i, and Proposition 8 had been the backlash to marriage equality in California, new, deceptive and discriminatory versions of the so-called "Religious Freedom Restoration Act" were (and are) the backlash to the marriage victories that followed *Windsor* and *Obergefell*. In the final chapters, Davidson, Beverly Tillery (see page 302),

M. Dru Levasseur (see page 306), Gautam Raghavan (see page 310), Scott A. Schoettes (see page 314), Andrea J. Ritchie (see page 318), and Jennifer C. Pizer (see page 323) discuss a sample of the many challenges we still face, including racism, the struggle for the rights of people who are transgender and for people living with HIV, the fight for federal laws explicitly protecting LGBT people from discrimination, the challenges of police violence and discrimination against LGBT and gender-nonconforming people, and the misuse of religion as a justification for discrimination. Our movement, like every other civil rights movement, keeps moving forward by seeing and naming the barriers to justice and using every available strategy to overcome them. We move forward, also, by joining the work of others at the intersections of discrimination, where we can embrace a shared vision of fairness and celebrate our common humanity.

As Justice Kennedy wrote in his majority opinion in *Obergefell*, the Constitution's principle of equal protection allows us to see that "new insights and societal understandings can reveal unjustified inequality within our most fundamental institutions that once passed unnoticed and unchallenged." As a nation, we will continue the work of noticing, challenging, and working together to secure justice.

I. OPENING ARGUMENTS, 1970–98

THE FIRST MARRIAGE CASES, 1970–74

WILLIAM N. ESKRIDGE JR.

———— ✸ ————

William N. Eskridge Jr. is the John A. Garver Professor of Jurisprudence at Yale Law School.

Born in 1942, James Michael McConnell grew up in Norman, Oklahoma, in a closely-knit mom-and-dad family with three sisters and an older brother. As early as second grade, Mike knew he was "different," and later he realized he was homosexual. In the late 1950s, while working as a cashier at his dad's barbershop, Mike developed crushes on the engineering and ROTC students at the University of Oklahoma (OU) who regularly needed their crew cuts updated. When Mike himself became a student at the university, he met and fell in love with Bob Gaylor, who was his partner for about four years. After they broke up, Mike was devastated but returned to the university, where he secured a bachelor's degree in library science.[1]

Hailing from Chicago, Richard John Baker, also born in 1942, was the last of ten children. Before age six, he had lost both parents. Jack was enrolled in a Catholic boarding school, where he spent most of his childhood and where he, too, realized he had erotic feelings for other boys. In 1965, while serving in the U.S. Air Force and assigned to the Airman Education Commissioning Program at OU, Jack earned a degree in industrial engineering. His military career was cut short, however, when it was discovered he had previously accepted an invitation to share sex with an enlisted man, and had been exchanging letters with other gay men while on active duty. Afterward, Jack returned to Norman, Oklahoma.

Dominated by Oklahoma's Baptist culture, Norman was officially intolerant of homosexuality—but, as a college town, it hosted a thriving homosexual subculture.[2] Among its stars was Mike McConnell, nicknamed the "Masked Mother" because of his supportive attitude toward his friends. Still recovering from his failed relationship, Mike ran into Jack at a "barn party" (a social event held in a barn) organized by a mutual friend on Halloween night, 1966. For Jack, it was love at first sight: the brilliant library science student with the incandescent smile was the soul mate he had been searching for.[3]

Mike was not so sure. Even though the dashing, crew-cut veteran reminded him of the men he had crushed on in the 1950s, Mike took several months to realize Jack was his soul mate. As in all things, Jack was persistent. On March 10, 1967, Jack's twenty-fifth birthday, "Jack asked me to be his lover. I was now ready to state what I wanted as a commitment: love openly and not repeat the mistakes of previous relationships. I was in it for the long haul, whatever that took. I wanted *marriage*—not just 'secret' rings recognized by a circle of mostly closeted friends. Jack agreed to make it happen."[4]

For that reason, Jack entered law school at the University of Minnesota in September 1969. Having earned a master's degree in library science and working as a librarian in a private college, Mike joined him there in April 1970 after the university offered him a job as head of cataloguing at its St. Paul campus. Most first-year law students spend the year competing for grades that will earn them top law firm jobs. Not Jack. As an ardent activist, he joined the campus group Fight Repression of Erotic Expression (FREE), which sought to liberate people from repressive regulations of sexual and gender-nonconformity. Under Jack's leadership, FREE successfully pressured the university to advance a new policy barring discrimination against lesbian and gay persons. Not forgetting his promise to Mike, Jack found time to research Minnesota marriage law, which explained how two "persons" could apply for a marriage license.[5] Were two gay men not "persons"?

Jack brought Mike to religious services at the university's Newman Center Chapel. One Sunday, they asked the priest, Reverend William Hunt, "Do you feel that if two people give themselves in love to each other and want to grow together with mutual understanding, that Jesus would be open to such a union if the people were of the same sex?" Reverend Hunt said, "Yes, in my opinion, Christ would be open." Elated, the couple planned a religious ceremony. But they realized they needed a marriage license for the Reverend to legally marry them.

Accompanied by several colleagues from FREE, Jack Baker and Mike McConnell appeared at the Hennepin County Courthouse on May 18, 1970, to apply for a marriage license. Clerk of the Court Gerald Nelson had no idea what to do with this couple. On May 22, County Attorney George Scott advised Nelson that Minnesota law did not authorize a marriage license for a same-sex couple. The common law treated marriage as only pertaining to different-sex couples, and Minnesota's divorce and other marriage-related laws explicitly regulated only relations between a "husband" and a "wife." To approve the license, Scott concluded, "would be to result in an undermining or destruction of the entire legal concept of our family structure in all areas of law."[6]

Most Minnesotans agreed with Scott. Only a handful of Americans could even conceive of, much less endorse, marriage between two men in 1970. Most devout Catholics, fundamentalist Protestants, and orthodox Jews found *homosexual* marriage an affront to their religious beliefs because they understood the Bible as promoting marriage as the socially valuable institution in which procreative sex serves God's purposes for humankind. Coming from a different point of view, many radical feminists and gay liberationists were highly critical of *marriage* of any kind. Why should lesbians and gay men join an essentially patriarchal, heterosexist institution?[7] Even the leading progressive organizations, such as the national ACLU and the Kinsey Institute (both of which declined Baker and McConnell's requests for help on their petition), felt the idea of gay marriage was not a viable civil rights issue in 1970–72.[8]

Some of Baker and McConnell's close gay friends were fearful: "I must say, unfortunately, that I wouldn't fight with or for you in person or otherwise publicly because I value my family, friends (gay and straight), job, and happiness far above some man-made laws, which in the end are meaningless."[9] Indeed, the decision to seek a marriage license was costly to this first couple in many ways. The Baker family was bitterly divided when Jack told them, at Thanksgiving dinner, that he and Mike planned to get married.[10]

Over objections from its library administrators, the University Board of Regents vetoed Mike McConnell's job offer. Although the university's librarians needed McConnell's services to update their obsolete cataloguing system, the board recoiled from the publicity surrounding the marriage lawsuit. And though the state was penalizing McConnell for exercising his First Amendment rights to speak and petition the government, federal appellate judges justified this censorship as a reasonable response to his alleged effort "to foist tacit approval of this socially repugnant concept [equal treatment of 'homosexuals'] upon his employer."[11]

None of this deterred McConnell and Baker from pursuing civil marriage. In December 1970, with the assistance of the local ACLU, they filed a lawsuit challenging the discrimination on both statutory and constitutional grounds. Trial judges summarily dismissed the complaint in *Baker v. Nelson*, the

Minnesota Supreme Court affirmed with little discussion, and the U.S. Supreme Court dismissed their appeal for lack of a "substantial federal question."[12] Notwithstanding these rebuffs, the plucky couple did secure a marriage license from Blue Earth County, Minnesota, on August 16, 1971. The county clerk did not realize that McConnell and Baker (under a legally changed name) were a same-sex couple.

Reverend Roger Lynn performed their marriage ceremony on September 3, 1971, where Mike and Jack exchanged gold wedding rings designed by their friend Terry Vanderplas.[13] When placed side by side, the elegant rings spell out "Jack/Loves/Mike." Local officials not only refused to recognize this marriage, but even threatened the minister and the couple with criminal prosecution for marriage fraud.[14]

So why did Baker and McConnell persist in this quest for marriage recognition? They felt a profound romantic and personal connection just like the ideal marriage, such as the loving relationships their own parents had enjoyed. Jack and Mike were personally indignant that they should be treated any differently than childless straight couples. (Like many such couples, they sought to adopt a child in 1974, but their petition was stonewalled because their relationship was not properly gendered.) Jack observed that his and Mike's commitment was more robust than that of some of his own siblings' marriages.[15]

Schooled in the NAACP's inspiring campaign against racial discrimination, the generation that came of age in the 1960s was hostile to all forms of arbitrary status-based treatment. Indeed, Baker, McConnell, and their lawyer and former roommate, Michael Wetherbee, compared discrimination based on sexual orientation to that based on race and illegitimacy, two status-based categories widely considered arbitrary grounds for state discrimination.[16] A year after Baker and McConnell's Hennepin County application, two African American lesbians, Donna Burkett and Mononia Evans, applied for a marriage license in Milwaukee County, Wisconsin. Like Baker and McConnell, this couple maintained that theirs was a matter of "civil rights," requiring strictly equal treatment, and they filed a federal lawsuit to enforce their constitutional civil rights.[17] Also like Baker and McConnell, Burkett and Evans had a religious wedding ceremony, with Burkett dressed in a tuxedo and Evans in a wedding gown.[18]

In addition, Baker and McConnell believed that the exclusion of same-sex couples from civil marriage was discrimination because of sex, another fishy basis for state exclusions. Not only was the classification sex-based—Baker's marriage application was denied *solely* because of the sex of his partner, McConnell—but the ideology undergirding the exclusion was sexism and patriarchy. By defining marriage only in terms of procreation, the state was insisting upon a definition that was long associated with gendered roles, where husbands worked outside the home and wives raised the children. The sex discrimination argument was also made, prominently, by John Singer and Paul Barwick, a Seattle, Washington, couple whose application for a marriage license was made and declined on September 10, 1971. Like Baker and McConnell, they sued in state court. Even though the Washington Constitution contained an Equal Rights Amendment barring sex discrimination, the state appellate judges ruled that its intended protections did not extend to "homosexuals."[19]

There was also a strategic political element to the Baker and McConnell marriage license application. Both men had "come out" in the 1960s. Running as an openly gay candidate, and with a much-admired poster displaying the air force veteran in women's dress shoes, Jack Baker won consecutive terms as the student body president at the University of Minnesota in 1971 and 1972. His and Mike's view was that coming out in public was not only essential for the mental and emotional health of any lesbian or gay person, but was an important strategy for advancing the cause of equal treatment more generally. To this day, Mike is adamant that almost anyone of goodwill can support complete equality, including marriage equality, if only that person can listen to and learn about gay people.[20]

Accordingly, Baker and McConnell held hands on campus, kissed each other in public, danced together at the Barrister's Ball, were featured in a widely read *Look* magazine article on "the homosexual couple," and made their application for a marriage license into a public event.[21] In these and other performances, Baker and McConnell sought "confrontation," in order to "[m]ake our presence felt by the straight society, make them face the issue" of fair treatment of gays.[22] In 1970, there were few actions that were more confrontational than a "homosexual" couple's demanding the right to civil marriage, an institution that the Minnesota Supreme Court traced back to the Genesis account of Adam and Eve.[23]

In-your-face gay pride and gay-is-good activism were critically important motivations for other early marriage equality lawsuits, including the first lawsuit to follow Baker and McConnell's application. On June 6, 1970, Marjorie (Margie) Jones and Tracy Knight applied for a marriage license in Jefferson County, Kentucky (Louisville): "The boys had just applied, and we couldn't let the boys get ahead of us," cracked Jones.[24] Like Singer and Barwick, Jones, a twice-divorced mother of three children, and Knight were not completely committed to a lifetime together. Instead, these lesbians were "fighters" motivated by a strategy of confronting both straights and closeted homosexuals with lesbian and gay pride.[25] Like "the boys," Jones and Knight were rebuffed by the legal process: the Jefferson County clerk denied their marriage application, the Circuit Court dismissed their lawsuit challenging the constitutionality of the discrimination (comparing their "perverted lust" with "thievery and chicanery"), and the Kentucky Court of Appeals affirmed in a dismissive opinion.[26]

Although judges rejected every one of these early lawsuits, they were harbingers for the future—and not just because they put the issue of marriage equality on the nation's public law agenda. Starting with their trial court memorandum and continuing through their jurisdictional statement to the U.S. Supreme Court, Mike Wetherbee, assisted by Jack Baker, laid out the case for marriage for same-sex couples that anticipates the arguments still made today.[27] Their central claim was that the state was denying two gay men a fundamental right to marry, with all the legal rights and duties associated with it, for reasons that were arbitrary, whether that reason be the sex of the partners or their sexual orientation. The plaintiffs challenged the state to explain why all the benefits and duties of marriage are routinely extended to childless different-sex couples, but not to same-sex couples, many of whom are raising children. There is no policy reason, and religion-based morality is not a sufficient justification for the government.

This exclusion is a core violation of *both* the Due Process Clause (protecting liberty and the right to marry) *and* the Equal Protection Clause of the Fourteenth Amendment, similar to the analysis that invalidated different-race marriage bans in *Loving v. Virginia*.[28] "In a sense, the analysis presented here involves a mixing of both due process and equal protection doctrines. As applied to the government disability at issue in this case, however, they tend to merge."[29]

Likewise, the central argument made by supporters of traditional marriage was made by County Attorney George Scott and David Mikkelson, the assistant representing the government in *Baker v. Nelson*. They contended that including same-sex couples would be a fundamental *redefinition* of marriage. Because marriage has universally been limited to one man and one woman throughout biblical and Western history, every state's family law was organized around that precept. This traditional understanding of marriage has proven workable—and changing it would open a Pandora's box of unpredictable consequences.[30] Judges lack the legitimacy and the expertise to figure out or manage these consequences, and so constitutional litigation is not the way to redefine the longstanding, treasured institution.

Almost forty-five years after Baker and McConnell's application for a marriage license, the Supreme Court, on April 28, 2015, heard argument in *Obergefell v. Hodges*, the Marriage Equality Cases. Led by the chief justice, the Court viewed the redefinition of marriage argument as the core defense of the traditional exclusion of same-sex couples. How can unelected judges legitimately redefine an institution that no culture in world history had understood to include same-sex couples?[31]

Ironically, no one on argument day articulated the response to the redefinition point as well as Jack Baker, Mike McConnell, and Mike Wetherbee did forty-five years ago. It is *the state* (and *not* "the gays") that has redefined marriage, to meet the needs of adults who love one another. In a society where marriage licenses are routinely given to elderly couples, to couples choosing contraception, and to couples preferring to adopt children, same-sex couples are similarly situated and, hence, ought to be treated the same. Indeed, the analogy is closer still, for "[t]here is nothing in the nature of single-sex marriage that precludes procreation and child rearing,"[32] as hundreds of thousands of same-sex couples have demonstrated over the years.

GAY MARRIAGE: A MUST OR A BUST?

REPRINTED FROM OUT/LOOK, 1989

—— ✸✸✸ ——

In 1989, *Out/Look* magazine published two essays by leading attorneys from Lambda Legal that framed the arguments for and against the fight for marriage for same-sex couples. Below is the *Out/Look* introduction, followed by essays by Thomas B. Stoddard and Paula L. Ettelbrick.

Most of us have probably shouted, "But gay people can't get married!" while explaining why we were less than thrilled to have to attend a cousin's wedding. Lesbians and gay men can't get married; 57 percent of straight people in the U.S. disapprove of two people of the same sex living together as a married couple (according to a recent poll conducted by the San Francisco Examiner); *and until recently, the odds of winning the right to marry have seemed impossible.*

But slowly, the prospect of legal lesbian and gay marriages have [sic] become less of a fairytale. This year, Denmark changed its laws to allow them. And in the U.S., the Board of Directors of the Bar Association in San Francisco called for a change in the California laws that make marriage the sole province of heterosexuals. Legislation that extends minimal benefits to unmarried "domestic partners" recently was enacted in San Francisco and West Hollywood, which now join the ranks of Berkeley and Santa Cruz, California, and Madison, Wisconsin, where domestic partners have been granted even more partial benefits.

If the popularity of The Wedding (the event at the 1987 March on Washington for Lesbian and Gay Rights at which thousands of men and women "married" their partners of the same sex) is any indication of popular sentiment in our communities, many lesbians and gay men across the country would get hitched in a second, if we actually could.

But how big of a priority should the lesbian and gay movement place on seeking that right? While few would begrudge any couple the right to publicly celebrate their relationship, there is less consensus about how much energy we should expend to get the government to sanction those same relationships.

Lesbian and gay civil rights organizations across the country, including the New York-based Lambda Legal Defense and Education Fund, have been debating this question. In the pages that follow, two Lambda staff members share some of the arguments that have surfaced as their organization has evaluated what kinds of precedent-setting cases it should take on.

WHY GAY PEOPLE SHOULD SEEK THE RIGHT TO MARRY

Thomas B. Stoddard

———❦———

Thomas B. Stoddard (1949–97) was executive director of the Lambda Legal Defense and Education Fund in New York from 1986 to 1992.

Even though, these days, few lesbians and gay men enter into marriages recognized by law, absolutely every gay person has an opinion on marriage as an "institution." (The word "institution" brings to mind, perhaps appropriately, museums.) After all, we all know quite a bit about the subject. Most of us grew up in marital households. Virtually all of us, regardless of race, creed, gender, and culture, have received lectures on the propriety, if not the sanctity, of marriage—which usually suggests that those who choose not to marry are both unhappy and unhealthy. We all have been witnesses, willing or not, to a lifelong parade of other people's marriages, from Uncle Harry and Aunt Bernice to the Prince and Princess of Wales. And at one point or another, some nosy relative has inevitably inquired of every gay person when he or she will finally "tie the knot" (an intriguing and probably apt cliché).

I must confess at the outset that I am no fan of the "institution" of marriage as currently constructed and practiced. I may simply be unlucky, but I have seen preciously few marriages over the course of my forty years that invite admiration and emulation. All too often, marriage appears to petrify rather than satisfy and enrich, even for couples in their twenties and thirties who have had a chance to learn the lessons of feminism. Almost inevitably, the partners seem to fall into a "husband" role and a "wife" role, with such latter-day modifications as the wife who works in addition to raising the children and managing the household.

Let me be blunt: in its traditional form, marriage has been oppressive, especially (although not entirely) to women. Indeed, until the middle of the last century, marriage was, at its legal and social essence, an extension of the husband and his paternal family. Under the English common law, wives were among the husband's "chattel"—personal property—and could not, among other things, hold property in their own names. The common law crime of adultery demonstrates the unequal treatment accorded to husbands and wives: while a woman who slept with a man who wasn't her husband committed adultery, a man who slept with a woman not his wife committed fornication. A man was legally incapable of committing adultery, except as an accomplice to an errant wife. The underlying offense of adultery was not the sexual betrayal of one partner by the other, but the wife's engaging in conduct capable of tainting the husband's bloodlines. (I swear on my Black's Law Dictionary that I have not made this up!)

Nevertheless, despite the oppressive nature of marriage historically, and in spite of the general absence of edifying examples of modern heterosexual marriage, I believe very strongly that every lesbian and gay man should have the right to marry the same-sex partner of his or her choice, and that the gay rights movement should aggressively seek full legal recognition for same-sex marriages. To those who might not agree, I respectfully offer three explanations, one practical, one political, and one philosophical.

The Practical Explanation

The legal status of marriage rewards the two individuals who travel to the altar (or its secular equivalent) with substantial economic and practical advantages. Married couples may reduce their tax liability by filing a joint return. They are entitled to special government benefits, such as those given surviving spouses and dependents through the Social Security program. They can inherit from one another even when there is no will. They are immune from subpoenas requiring testimony against the other spouse. And marriage to an American citizen gives a foreigner a right to residency in the United States.

Other advantages have arisen not by law but by custom. Most employers offer health insurance to their employees, and many will include an employee's spouse in the benefits package, usually at the employer's expense. Virtually no employer will include a partner who is not married to an employee, whether of the same sex or not. Indeed, very few insurance companies even offer the possibility of a group health plan covering "domestic partners" who are not married to one another. Two years ago, I tried to find such a policy for Lambda, and discovered that not one insurance company authorized to do business in New York—the second-largest state in the country with more than 17 million residents—would accommodate us. (Lambda has tried to make do by paying for individual insurance policies for the same-sex partners of its employees who otherwise would go uninsured, but these individual policies are usually narrower in scope than group policies, often require applicants to furnish individual medical information not required under most group plans, and are typically much more expensive per person.)

In short, the law generally presumes in favor of every marital relationship, and acts to preserve and foster it, and to enhance the rights of the individuals who enter into it. It is usually possible, with enough money and the right advice, to replicate some of the benefits conferred by the legal status of marriage through the use of documents like wills and power of attorney forms, but that protection will inevitably, under current circumstances, be incomplete.

The law (as I suspect will come as no surprise to the readers of this journal) still looks upon lesbians and gay men with suspicion; suspicion casts a shadow over the documents they execute in recognition of a same-sex relationship. If a lesbian leaves to her lover, her will may be invalidated on the grounds that it was executed under the "undue influence" of the would-be beneficiary. A property agreement may be denied validity because the underlying relationship is "meretricious"—akin to prostitution. (Astonishingly, until the mid-seventies, the law throughout the United States deemed "meretricious" virtually any formal economic arrangement between two people not married to one another, on the theory that an exchange of property between them was probably payment for sexual services; the Supreme Court of California helped unravel this quaint legal fantasy in its 1976 ruling in the first famous "palimony" case, *Marvin v. Marvin*.) The law has progressed considerably beyond the uniformly oppressive state of affairs before 1969, but it is still far from enthusiastic about gay people and their relationships—to put it mildly.

Moreover, there are some barriers one simply cannot transcend outside of a formal marriage. When the Internal Revenue Code or the Immigration and Naturalization Act say "married," they mean "married" by definition of state statute. When the employer's group health plan says "spouse," it means "spouse" in the eyes of the law, not the eyes of the loving couple.

But there is another drawback. Couples seeking to protect their relationship through wills and other documents need knowledge, determination, and—most importantly—money. No money, no lawyer. And no lawyer, no protection. Those who lack the sophistication or the wherewithal to retain a lawyer are simply stuck in most circumstances. Extending the right to marry to gay couples would assure that those at the bottom of the economic ladder have a chance to secure their relationship rights, too.

The Political Explanation

The claim that gay couples ought to be able to marry is not a new one. In the seventies, same-sex couples in three states—Minnesota, Kentucky, and Washington—brought constitutional challenges to the marriage statutes, and in all three instances they failed. In each of the three, the court offered two basic justifications for limiting marriage to male–female couples: history and procreation. Witness this passage from the Supreme Court of Minnesota's 1971 opinion in *Baker v. Nelson*: "The institution of marriage as a union of man and woman, uniquely involving the procreation and rearing of children within a family, is as old as the book of Genesis. . . . This historic institution manifestly is more deeply founded than the asserted contemporary concept of marriage and societal interests for which petitioners contend."

Today no American jurisdiction recognizes the right of two women or two men to marry one another, although several nations in Northern Europe do. Even more telling, until earlier this year [1989], there was little discussion within the gay rights movement about whether such a right should exist. As far as I can tell, no gay organization of any size, local or national, has yet declared the right to marry as one of its goals.

With all due respect to my colleagues and friends who take a different view, I believe it is time to renew the effort to overturn the existing marriage laws, and to do so in earnest, with a commitment of money and energy, through both the courts and the state legislatures. I am not naive about the likelihood of imminent victory. There is none. Nonetheless—and here I will not mince words—I would like to see the issue rise to the top of the agenda of every gay organization, including my own (although that judgment is hardly mine alone).

Why give it such prominence? Why devote resources to such a distant goal? Because marriage is, I believe, the political issue that most fully tests the dedication of people who are not gay to full equality for gay people, and also the issue most likely to lead ultimately to a world free from discrimination against lesbians and gay men.

Marriage is much more than a relationship sanctioned by law. It is the centerpiece of our entire social structure, the core of the traditional notion of "family."

Even in its present tarnished state, the marital relationship inspires sentiments suggesting that it is something almost suprahuman. The Supreme Court, in striking down an anti-contraception statute in 1965, called marriage "noble" and "intimate to the degree of being sacred." The Roman Catholic Church and the Moral Majority would go—and have gone—considerably further.

Lesbians and gay men are now denied entry to this "noble" and "sacred" institution. The implicit message is this: two men or two women are incapable of achieving such an exalted domestic state. Gay relationships are somehow less significant, less valuable. Such relationships may, from time to time and from couple to couple, give the appearance of a marriage, but they can never be of the same quality or importance.

I resent—indeed, I loathe—that conception of same-sex relationships. And I am convinced that ultimately the only way to overturn it is to remove the barrier to marriage that now limits the freedom of every gay man and lesbian.

That is not to deny the value of domestic partnership ordinances, statutes that prohibit discrimination based on marital status, and other legal advances that can enhance the rights (as well as the dignity) of gay couples. Without question, such advances move us further along the path to equality. But their value can only be partial. (The recently enacted San Francisco "domestic partnership" ordinance, for example, will have practical value only for gay people who happen to be employed by the City of San Francisco and want to include their non-marital spouses in part of the city's fringe benefit package; the vast majority of gay San Franciscans—those employed by someone other than the city—have only a symbolic victory to savor.) Measures of this kind can never assure equality. Gay relationships will continue to be accorded a subsidiary status until the day that gay couples have exactly the same rights as their heterosexual counterparts. To my mind, that means either that the right to marry be extended to us, or that marriage be polished in its present form for all couples, presumably to be replaced by some new legal entity—an unlikely alternative.

The Philosophical Explanation

I confessed at the outset that I personally found marriage in its present avatar rather, well, unattractive. Nonetheless, even from a philosophical perspective, I believe the right to marry should become a stated goal of the gay rights movement.

First, and most basically, the issue is not the desirability of marriage, but rather the desirability of the right to marry. That I think two lesbians or two gay men should be entitled to a marriage license does not mean that I think all gay people should find appropriate partners and exercise the right, should it eventually exist. I actually rather doubt that I, myself, would want to marry, even though I share a household with another man who is exceedingly dear to me. There are others who feel differently, for economic, symbolic, or romantic reasons. They should, to my mind, unquestionably have the opportunity to marry if they wish and otherwise meet the requirements of the state (like being old enough).

Furthermore, marriage may be unattractive and even oppressive as it is currently structured and practiced, but enlarging the concept to embrace same-sex couples would necessarily transform it into something new. If two women can marry, or two men, marriage—even for heterosexuals—need not be a union of a "husband" and a "wife." Extending the right to marry to gay people—that is, abolishing the traditional gender requirements of marriage—can be one of the means, perhaps the principal one, through which the institution divests itself of the sexist trappings of the past.

Some of my colleagues disagree with me. I welcome their thoughts and the debates and discussions our different perspectives will trigger. The movement for equality for lesbians and gay men can only be enriched through this collective exploration of the question of marriage. But I do believe many thousands of gay people want the right to marry. And I think, too, they will earn that right for themselves sooner than most of us imagine.

SINCE WHEN IS MARRIAGE A PATH TO LIBERATION?

Paula L. Ettelbrick

———— ⚬⚬⚬ ————

Paula L. Ettelbrick (1955–2011) was legal director at Lambda Legal from 1988 to 1993.

"Marriage is a great institution . . . if you like living in institutions," according to a bit of T-shirt philosophy I saw recently. Certainly, marriage is an institution. It is one of the most venerable, impenetrable institutions in modern society. Marriage provides the ultimate form of acceptance for personal intimate relationships in our society, and gives those who marry an insider status of the most powerful kind.

Steeped in a patriarchal system that looks to ownership, property, and dominance of men over women as its basis, the institution of marriage long has been the focus of radical feminist revolution. Marriage defines certain relationships as more valid than all others. Lesbian and gay relationships, being neither sanctioned or commingled by blood, are always at the bottom of the heap of social acceptance and importance.

Given the imprimatur of social and personal approval which marriage provides, it is not surprising that some lesbians and gay men among us would look to legal marriage for self-affirmation. After all, those who marry can be instantaneously transformed from "outsiders" to "insiders," and we have a desperate need to become insiders. It could make us feel OK about ourselves, perhaps even relieve some of the internalized homophobia that we all know so well.

Society will then celebrate the birth of our children and mourn the death of our spouses. It would be easier to get health insurance for our spouses, family memberships to the local museum, and a right to inherit our spouse's cherished collection of lesbian mystery novels even if she failed to draft a will. Never again would we have to go to a family reunion and debate about the correct term for introducing our lover / partner / significant other to Aunt Flora. Everything would be quite easy and very nice.

So why does this unlikely event so deeply disturb me? For two major reasons. First, marriage will not liberate us as lesbians and gay men. In fact, it will constrain us, make us more invisible, force our assimilation into the mainstream, and undermine the goals of gay liberation. Second, attaining the right to marry will not transform our society from one that makes narrow, but dramatic, distinctions between those who are married and those who are not married to one that respects and encourages choice of relationships and family diversity. Marriage runs contrary to two of the primary goals of the lesbian and gay movement: the affirmation of gay identity and culture; and the validation of many forms of relationships.

When analyzed from the standpoint of civil rights, certainly lesbians and gay men should have a right to marry. But obtaining a right does not always result in justice. White male firefighters in Birmingham, Alabama, have been fighting for their "rights" to retain their jobs by overturning the city's affirmative action guidelines. If their "rights" prevail, the courts will have failed in rendering justice. The "right" fought for by the white male firefighters, as well as those who advocate strongly for the "rights" to legal marriage for gay people, will result, at best, in limited or narrowed "justice" for those closest to power at the expense of those who have been historically marginalized.

The fight for justice has as its goal the realignment of power imbalances among individuals and classes of people in society. A pure "rights" analysis often fails to incorporate a broader understanding of the underlying inequities that operate to deny justice to a fuller range of people and groups. In setting our priorities as a community, we must combine the concept of both rights and justice. At this point in time, making legal marriage for lesbian and gay couples a priority would set an agenda of gaining rights for a few, but would do nothing to correct the power imbalances between those who are married (whether gay or straight) and those who are not. Thus, justice would not be gained.

Justice for gay men and lesbians will be achieved only when we are accepted and supported in this society despite our differences from the dominant culture and the choices we make regarding our relationships. Being queer is more than setting up house, sleeping with a person of the same gender, and seeking state approval for doing so. It is an identity, a culture with many variations. It is a way of dealing with the world by diminishing the constraints of gender roles, which have for so long kept women and gay people oppressed and invisible. Being queer means pushing the parameters of sex, sexuality, and family, and in the process transforming the very fabric of society. Gay liberation is inexorably linked to women's liberation. Each is essential to the other.

The moment we argue, as some among us insist on doing, that we should be treated as equals because we are really just like married couples and hold the same values to be true, we undermine the very purpose of our movement and begin the dangerous process of silencing our different voices. As a lesbian, I am fundamentally different from non-lesbian women. That's the point. Marriage, as it exists today, is antithetical to my liberation as a lesbian and as a woman because it mainstreams my life and voice. I do not want be known as "Mrs. Attached-To-Somebody-Else." Nor do I want to give the state the power to regulate my primary relationship.

Yet, the concept of equality in our legal system does not support differences; it only supports sameness. The very standard for equal protection is that people who are similarly situated must be treated equally. To make an argument for equal protection, we will be required to claim that gay and lesbian relationships are the same as straight relationships. To gain the right, we must compare ourselves to married couples. The law looks to the insiders as the norm, regardless of how flawed or unjust their institutions, and requires that those seeking the law's equal protection situate themselves in a similar posture to those who are already protected. In arguing for the right to legal marriage, lesbian and gay men would be forced to claim that we are just like heterosexual couples, have the same goals and purposes, and vow to structure our lives similarly. The law provides no room to argue that we are different, but are nonetheless entitled to equal protection.

The thought of emphasizing our sameness to married heterosexuals in order to obtain this "right" terrifies me. It rips away the very heart and soul of what I believe it is to be a lesbian in this world. It robs me of the opportunity to make a difference. We end up mimicking all that is bad about the institution of marriage in our effort to appear to be the same as straight couples.

By looking to our sameness and de-emphasizing our differences, we don't even place ourselves in a position of power that would allow us to transform marriage from an institution that emphasizes property and state regulation of relationships to an institution which recognizes one of many types of valid and respected relationships. Until the constitution is interpreted to respect and encourage differences, pursuing the legalization of same-sex marriage would be leading our movement into a trap; we would be demanding access to the very institution which, in its current form, would undermine our movement to recognize many different kinds of relationships. We would be perpetuating the elevation of married relationships and of "couples" in general, and further eclipsing other relationships of choice.

Ironically, gay marriage, instead of liberating gay sex and sexuality, would further outlaw all gay and lesbian sex which is not performed in a marital context. Just as sexually active non-married women face stigma and double standards around sex and sexual activity, so too would non-married gay people. The only legitimate gay sex would be that which is cloaked in and regulated by marriage. Its legitimacy would stem not from an acceptance of gay sexuality, but because the Supreme Court and society in general fiercely protect the privacy of marital relationships. Lesbians and gay men who do not seek the state's stamp of approval would clearly face increased sexual oppression.

Undoubtedly, whether we admit it or not, we all need to be accepted by the broader society. That motivation fuels our work to eliminate discrimination in the workplace and elsewhere, fight for custody of our children, create our own families, and so on. The growing discussion about the right to marry may be explained in part by this need for acceptance. Those closer to the norm or to power in this country are more likely to see marriage as a principle of freedom and equality. Those who are more acceptable to the mainstream because of race, gender, and economic status are more likely to want the right to marry. It is the final acceptance, the ultimate affirmation of identity.

On the other hand, more marginal members of the lesbian and gay community (women, people of color, working class, and poor) are less likely to see marriage as having relevance to our struggles for survival. After all, what good is the affirmation of our relationships (that is, marital relationships) if we are rejected as women, black, or working class?

The path to acceptance is much more complicated for many of us. For instance, if we choose legal marriage, we may enjoy the right to add our spouse to our health insurance policy at work, since most employment policies are defined by one's marital status, not family relationship. However, that choice assumes that we have a job and that our employer provides us with health benefits. For women, particularly women of color who tend to occupy the low-paying jobs that do not provide health care benefits at all, it will not matter one bit if they are able to marry their woman partners. The opportunity to marry will neither get them the health benefits nor transform them from outsider to insider.

Of course, a white man who marries another white man who has a full-time job with benefits will certainly be able to share in those benefits and overcome the only obstacle left to full societal assimilation—the goal of many in his class. In other words, gay marriage will not topple the system that allows only the privileged few to obtain decent health care. Nor will it close the privilege gap between those who are married and those who are not.

Marriage creates a two-tier system that allows the state to regulate relationships. It has become a facile mechanism for employers to dole out benefits, for businesses to provide special deals and incentives, and for the law to make distinctions in distributing meager public funds. None of these entities bothers to consider the relationship among people, the love, respect, and need to protect that exists among all kinds of family members. Rather, a simple certificate of the state, regardless of whether the spouses love, respect, or even see each other on a regular basis, dominates and is supported. None of this dynamic will change if gay men and lesbians are given the option of marriage.

Gay marriage will not help us address the systemic abuses inherent in a society that does not provide decent health care to all of its citizens, a right that should not depend on whether the individual 1) has sufficient resources to afford health care or health insurance, 2) is working and receives health insurance as part of compensation, or 3) is married to a partner who is working and has health coverage which is extended to spouses. It will not address the underlying unfairness that allows businesses to provide discounted services or goods to families and couples—who are defined to include straight, married people and their children, but not domestic partners.

Nor will it address the pain and anguish of the unmarried lesbian who receives word of her partner's accident, rushes to the hospital, and is prohibited from entering the intensive care unit solely because she is not a spouse or family member. Likewise, marriage will not help the gay victim of domestic violence, who, because he chose not to marry, finds no protection under the law to keep his violent lover away.

If the laws change tomorrow and lesbians and gay men were allowed to marry, where would we find the incentive to continue the progressive movement we have started that is pushing for societal and legal recognition of all kinds of family relationship? To find a place in the law for the elderly couple who, for companionship and economic reasons, live together but do not marry? To recognize the right of a longtime, but unmarried, gay partner to stay in his rent-controlled apartment after the death of his lover, the only named tenant on the lease? To recognize the family relationship of the lesbian couple and two gay men who are jointly sharing child-raising responsibilities? To get the law to acknowledge that we may have more than one relationship worthy of legal protection?

Marriage for lesbians and gay men still will not provide a real choice unless we continue the work our community has begun to spread the privilege around to other relationships. We must first break the tradition of piling benefits and privileges on to those who are married, while ignoring the real life needs of those who are not. Only when we de-institutionalize marriage and bridge the economic and privilege gap between the married and the unmarried will each of us have a true choice. Otherwise, our choice not to marry will continue to lack legal protection and societal respect.

The lesbian and gay community has laid the groundwork for revolutionizing society's views of family. The domestic partnership movement has been an important part of this progress insofar as it validates non-marital relationships. Because it is not limited to sexual or romantic relationships, domestic partnership provides an important opportunity for many who are not related by blood or marriage to claim certain minimal protections.

It is crucial, though, that we avoid the pitfall of framing the push for legal recognition of domestic partners (those who share a primary residence and financial responsibilities for each other) as a stepping stone to marriage. We must keep our eyes on the goals of providing true alternatives to marriage and of radically reordering society's view of family.

The goals of lesbian and gay liberation must simply be broader than the right to marry. Gay and lesbian marriages may minimally transform the institution of marriage by diluting its traditional patriarchal dynamic, but they will not transform society. They will not demolish the two-tier system of the "haves" and the "have nots." We must not fool ourselves into believing that marriage will make it acceptable to be gay or lesbian. We will be liberated only when we are respected and accepted for our differences and the diversity we provide to this society. Marriage is not a path to that liberation.

THE HAWAI'I MARRIAGE CASE LAUNCHES THE U.S. FREEDOM-TO-MARRY MOVEMENT FOR EQUALITY[1]

EVAN WOLFSON

———— ∞ ————

Reprinted from *Legal Recognition of Same-Sex Partnerships: A Study of National, European and International Law,* edited by Robert Wintemute and Mads Andenaes

Evan Wolfson is founder and president of Freedom to Marry.

Although same-sex couples had sought the freedom to marry from the very beginning of the modern gay rights movement, American courts in the 1970s were willing to rubberstamp antigay discrimination.[2] Couples were routinely denied civil marriage licenses—no matter how long they had been together, no matter how committed their relationships, and no matter how much they (and their children) needed the legal, economic, and social support that comes with civil marriage.[3] Lesbian and gay movement organizations did little to challenge the continuing exclusion of same-sex couples from the basic human right, the important personal choice, and the legal protections, responsibilities, and commitment that civil marriage represents. All that changed in the early 1990s, with a groundbreaking case in Hawai'i.[4]

In December 1990, three same-sex couples in Hawai'i asked for civil marriage licenses, which were denied in April 1991. Their attorney, Dan Foley of the Honolulu law firm of Partington & Foley, filed a legal case that rocked the world. The lower court rebuffed the couples, but on May 5, 1993, the Hawai'i Supreme Court ruled that the denial of licenses constituted prima facie sex discrimination, in violation of the state constitutional guarantee of equal protection.[5] For the first time ever, a court declared that lesbian and gay couples in love were entitled to a day in court, to challenge their exclusion from the central social and legal institution of marriage.

From the moment the Hawai'i Supreme Court issued its landmark ruling in 1993, the challenges and opportunities loomed large.[6] Gay legal groups began beating the drum, urging other national gay organizations, state and local groups, and allies to seize the moment to educate the public, organize against right-wing attacks, and do the necessary cultural and political work that must accompany legal advances for true social change. For the first time ever, a broad swath of the gay national and local groups came together around a single statement of belief, the Marriage Resolution,[7] and began meeting regularly to coordinate and promote efforts through the National Freedom to Marry Coalition.

Of course, the 1993 ruling did not order the issuance of marriage licenses or strike down the marriage law. All the Hawai'i Supreme Court did was what courts are supposed to do: turn to the government and say, if you are going to discriminate, you have to have a reason. The Court sent the case back to the lower court to give the government a chance to show that "reason" (a "compelling state interest") or stop discriminating.

Despite this measured judicial step, right-wing antigay groups went on the attack. The backlash began even before anyone had lashed, that is, before any court had examined the government's reason, indeed, before any state had permitted same-sex couples to wed. In 1995, anti-marriage bills were introduced in three state legislatures to codify the de facto reality that, in all fifty states, same-sex couples were denied marriage licenses; and to declare the radical proposition that the prospective lawful marriages of same-sex couples would be denied equal treatment under law, should they cross the wrong state border. With waves of anti-marriage legislation introduced across the country every year since 1995, these anti-marriage activists sought to make America a "house divided" in which couples could be legally married in some states but no more than roommates in the eyes of the law if they traveled through, worked in, or visited another state.[8]

In February 1996, most of the "usual suspects" in the right-wing antigay set gathered in Iowa, shortly before the presidential caucuses, to announce an all-out state-by-state campaign against gay people's freedom to marry. These right-wing opponents decided to inject the question of civil rights for lesbians and gay men into presidential election-year politics. They sought thereby to whip up their troops and scare politicians who had just begun to experience the emerging public discussion of how the denial of civil marriage harms real-life families.

In addition to a spate of state-by-state anti-marriage bills, these antigay groups prompted Republican legislators in Congress to introduce a federal anti-marriage measure, the so-called "Defense of Marriage Act" or DOMA.[9] Inserting the federal government into marriage for the first time in U.S. history, the so-called DOMA created a radical federal caste system of first-class and second-class marriages.[10] Under DOMA, if the federal government likes whom you marry, your first-class marriage gets a vast array of legal and economic protections and recognition from federal statutes.[11] But if the federal government does not like whom you marry, your second-class marriage is denied federal recognition, protection, and benefits in all circumstances. Additionally, DOMA purported to authorize states to discriminate against the lawful marriages of same-sex couples validly celebrated in other states—an unprecedented attempt to transform the Constitution's full faith and credit clause[12] into a "some faith and credit" clause at the whim of Congress. For all its radical sweep and dubious constitutionality, however, DOMA did not "ban" same-sex couples from marrying; rather, it represented a concession by our enemies that gay people seem likely to win the freedom to marry, and thus they wish to discriminate against the soon-to-be lawful marriages.

In America, we should not have second-class citizens, and we should not have second-class marriages. Hearkening back to the not-so-long-ago ugly days of discrimination against those who chose to marry the "wrong" kind of person (such as interracial or interfaith couples) and the days when Americans had to "go to Reno" (Nevada) just to get a civil divorce, these state and federal anti-marriage bills are unconstitutional, divisive, wrong, and cruel. They will be challenged once couples are allowed to legally marry in some state, as the civil rights struggle to win the freedom to marry advances.[13]

Unsurprisingly, anti-marriage measures, such as DOMA, those adopted by state legislatures, and the ballot initiatives (referendums) launched by right-wing groups when some state legislatures rejected their discriminatory bills, have been used to attack gay individuals and families far beyond the domain of marriage itself.[14] Even more significantly, the anti-marriage measures are not just an attempt to erect additional legal barriers against equality; they represent the right-wing's effort to squelch the emerging and vital discussion about gay people's freedom to marry and the meaning of equality. In that, they have failed. As religious denominations, politicians, news media, community leaders, and the public continue to debate civil marriage, civil unions, and gay inclusion, a *Wall Street Journal/NBC* poll reported in September 1999 that two-thirds of all Americans now believe that gay people will win the freedom to marry (and the sky will not fall).[15] The latest Associated Press poll showed only 51 percent opposed.[16]

Meanwhile, in Hawai'i, the Supreme Court's 1993 ruling led to a full trial on the justifications for discrimination. After extensive testimony and briefing, Judge Kevin Chang held that the state had failed to show even a single valid reason for denying lesbian and gay couples the opportunity to make the legal commitment of marriage.[17] That historic ruling represented the first, and still the only, time that a court has recognized that same-sex couples, too, have the freedom to marry, and ordered *full* equality for lesbians and gay men.[18]

The judge stayed his order that the licenses be issued pending an appeal to the State Supreme Court.

Knowing that they had failed to show a good reason for discrimination, the opponents of equality remained unrelentingly determined to thwart an independent judiciary's review of the exclusion from marriage. They poured millions of dollars into the state to pressure the legislature and the electorate into adopting a constitutional amendment that had the radical aim of removing the marriage law (and its discriminatory different-sex restriction) from judicial review under the equal protection guarantees of the Hawai'i Constitution.[19] The Hawai'i Supreme Court subsequently ruled that its hands were tied, because the amendment "[took] the statute out of the ambit of the equal protection clause of the Hawaii [sic] Constitution," at least as regards marriage licenses, and dismissed the case.[20] Thus ended the famous "Hawai'i marriage case" that had once seemed the likeliest vehicle for ending sex discrimination in civil marriage, much

Lambda Legal's Kevin Cathcart and Hawai'i plaintiffs Ninia Baehr and Genora Dancel following Washington press conference about Hawai'i and DOMA. Photo Credit: COURTESY OF LAMBDA LEGAL

as *Pere* *v. Lippold* in California had begun the nation's journey toward ending race discrimination in civil marriage.[21]

Even though the Hawai'i case failed to bring us all the way to the break-through we still hope to see soon, it served as an historical vehicle that launched an important, necessary, and continuing national discussion. It laid the foundations for the next major affirmative freedom-to-marry case and the ensuing civil union legislation in Vermont, as well as for states to come, pushed mainstream politicians and others into an "all but marriage" position in support of gay inclusion and rights, and left us far ahead of where we were when it started. Thanks to the Hawai'i case and the ongoing freedom-to-marry movement it sparked, the idea of gay people getting married has gone from an "oxymoron" ridiculed by our opponents, or a dream undiscussed by non-gay people (and most gay people, too), to a reality waiting to happen.

Within just seven years of the Hawai'i Supreme Court's initial ruling, we have seen the creation of civil unions, that is "gay marriages," on U.S. soil. While "gay marriage" is not good enough (we want "marriage," full equality, not two lines at the clerk's office segregating couples by sexual orientation), the progress and possibilities remain astonishing. Full equality and inclusion shimmer within reach. Now it is up to us—gay and non-gay alike—to do the reaching, and the reaching out.

"NEITHER THE FIRST NOR THE LAST"

HAWAI'I PLAINTIFFS NINIA BAEHR AND GENORA DANCEL

Ninia Baehr and Genora Dancel, along with two other couples,
sued the director of the Department of Health in Hawai'i in
1990, after they applied for a marriage license and were denied.

We were not the first same-sex couple in the United States suing for marriage equality, nor were we the last. What set us apart was that we were named plaintiffs in the first marriage equality case to receive a positive ruling, *Baehr v. Lewin.*

"We" are Genora Dancel and Ninia Baehr. Along with two other couples, we applied for a marriage license in Hawai'i in 1990, when marriage was not legal for same-sex couples anywhere in the world. Marriage equality is now the law of the land.

We would not have thought to apply for a marriage license had we not, by chance, talked with Bill Woods, a local activist who believed the Hawai'i Constitution allowed for same-sex couples to marry. Bill asked us if we wanted to make a case for equality. Genora's life flashed before her eyes—all her history feeling like a second-class citizen, and all she had to lose by standing up for equality. She was working two full-time jobs to pay the mortgage on the house where her parents lived with her, and she ran the risk of being fired twice over—not only because she was a lesbian, but because she was now suing for her right to marry. Ninia asked Genora to make the final decision, and the day we applied for a marriage license was the day Genora came out—on television! From then on, even though she had little informal or formal support—she had never been to a gay community center, bar, or church, and never talked much with family or friends about her sexual orientation—Genora spoke out. With her big smile, brown skin, and understanding of local kids, Genora was a

Evan Wolfson with Genora Dancel, Ninia Baehr, Del Martin, and Phyllis Lyon
at Lambda Legal "Rights of Spring" event in San Francisco, 1996. Photo Credit:
COURTESY OF EVAN WOLFSON

hit with K–12 and even college students. She used up her vacation time
to promote equality.

Back then, no organization wanted to take our case. Attorney Dan
Foley became our first hero: he agreed to represent this rag-tag group of
people who, along with us, simply wanted their love to be recognized as
equal under the law. For years, marriage equality money came from our
paychecks and from small fundraisers. Ninia cooked food, found door
prizes, and organized events. Our first financial supporters were drag
queens and bar patrons. We paid Dan only a small fraction of what we
owed him, but he earned a special place in our hearts and in history.

Early on, the ACLU submitted an amicus brief in our favor. As it
began to seem that we might win, additional individuals, foundations,
and organizations offered support. Evan Wolfson, then an attorney with
Lambda Legal and later the founder of Freedom to Marry, persuaded
Lambda Legal to support our lawsuit. We appeared at many Lambda
Legal fundraising events, and we are eternally grateful that Evan became
co-counsel on our case. It took millions of LGBTQ people and our allies
to win marriage equality. Without Dan, Evan, and even Bill, however, we
might not be where we are today.

We are now married—just not to each other! Although it isn't the relationship we envisioned when we applied for a marriage license, we have a lifelong, loving partnership. And when it comes to speaking about marriage equality, we still speak out together.

II. SEX BEFORE MARRIAGE: STRIKING DOWN SODOMY LAWS

THE SODOMY ROUNDTABLE

KEVIN M. CATHCART

Kevin M. Cathcart was executive director of Gay & Lesbian Advocates & Defenders from 1984 to 1992 and executive director of Lambda Legal from 1992 to 2016.

It is difficult to overstate the harms done to gay and lesbian people by sodomy laws. Until 1961, every state in the United States had sodomy laws on the books. Arrests and prosecutions of gay men were common. In many places, police entrapment of gay men was rampant, and the reach of the laws went even further, associating all lesbians and gay men with criminal sexual activity. All too often police officers, judges, and other people involved in the criminal justice system targeted and harassed gay men, lesbians, bisexual, and transgender people even though they had never been arrested nor convicted of any crime. Sodomy laws were also used to justify other forms of discrimination, including employment and custody and visitation rights.

In 1955 the American Law Institute, an independent organization devoted to studying and improving the law, proposed a Model Penal Code that did not include sodomy laws; when Illinois adopted the model code in 1961, it became the first state in the country to decriminalize sodomy. Legal challenges to sodomy laws were brought in the 1950s and 1960s, generally by desperate men facing criminal charges, but none succeeded. In 1971, as the women's and reproductive rights movements changed laws and attitudes about sexuality and the lesbian and gay rights movement began to grow, Connecticut became the second state in the

Evan Wolfson and plaintiff Michael Hardwick (*Bowers v. Hardwick*) in 1986. Photo Credit:
COURTESY OF EVAN WOLFSON

country to decriminalize consensual sex between same-sex partners, followed by
another eighteen states by the end of that decade. The reach of sodomy laws was
still so great, however, that many courts and members of the public continued to
consider all lesbians and gay men as criminals.

   As the pace of legislative repeal began to slow, civil rights lawyers were on the
lookout for cases in which they could bring constitutional challenges to sodomy
laws, hoping for the U.S. Supreme Court to strike down the laws in all states.
In 1982, the American Civil Liberties Union (ACLU) of Georgia found such a
case: Michael Hardwick, a gay man living in Atlanta, had been arrested in his
own home for private, consensual, non-commercial adult sexual activity; he was
willing to fight back. Even though, after his arrest, the local district attorney
declined to prosecute the case, Hardwick went to court to argue that the law had

unfairly targeted him as a gay man. As this challenge began in federal court, it became clear to Abby Rubenfeld, then–legal director of Lambda Legal, that the organizations fighting sodomy laws needed to coordinate their efforts. She called a meeting, hosted by Lambda Legal and the ACLU in late 1983, that led to the formation of what was then called the Ad Hoc Sodomy Law Task Force. Among its purposes were to coordinate, to plan strategy, and to work out difficult questions about the risks of trying to get a case to the Supreme Court. Once Michael Hardwick's case was on its way to the Court in 1986, the Ad Hoc Task Force also worked to create amicus support.

The well-known Harvard law professor and civil rights lawyer Laurence Tribe argued the case on behalf of Hardwick before the Supreme Court. Despite the courage of Hardwick and the efforts of the LGBT and other civil rights advocates, the Supreme Court upheld sodomy laws by a 5–4 vote. The tone of the majority opinion and concurrence were ugly and dismissive. Writing for the majority, Justice Byron White declared:

> The issue presented is whether the Federal Constitution confers a fundamental right upon homosexuals to engage in sodomy, and hence invalidates the laws of the many States that still make such conduct illegal, and have done so for a very long time. . . . Proscriptions against that conduct have ancient roots. . . . Against this background, to claim that a right to engage in such conduct is "deeply rooted in this Nation's history and tradition" or "implicit in the concept of ordered liberty" is, at best, facetious.

After leaving the Court, Justice Powell later told an audience of students at New York University Law School that he probably made a mistake with his vote, but went on to call the case frivolous. What could have been a one-vote victory became a one-vote loss.

The Supreme Court decision was a terrible blow to the movement. The Court had made it clear that it did not see gay people as worthy of constitutional protections. Coming as it did in the early years of the AIDS epidemic, it provoked fear of renewed antigay legislation, including the risk of recriminalization of sodomy in the twenty-four states that no longer had such laws on the books. Thankfully, this did not come to pass—no state recriminalized sodomy, and while public reaction to the Supreme Court's decision was mixed, many editorial writers and political cartoonists took the Court to task for its interference in people's private lives. Still, the combination of the disdain of the Court and the growth of the AIDS epidemic also led to significant increases in support for lesbian and gay civil rights organizations, which, in turn, enabled growth in the work of Lambda

Legal and other groups. Both litigation, now under state constitutions, and legislative work against sodomy laws continued, and there was a steady chipping
away at the number of states with sodomy laws on the books.

The Ad Hoc Sodomy Law Task Force continued to meet, gradually expanding its focus to include other antigay legal issues, including family law, HIV,
employment, and, in time, transgender issues, while keeping sodomy law reform
in the mix. The four main lesbian and gay legal organizations—Lambda Legal;
Gay & Lesbian Advocates & Defenders (GLAD); The National Center for Lesbian Rights (NCLR), which had earlier been called the Lesbian Rights Project;
and the ACLU, which in 1986 created its Lesbian and Gay Rights Project—were
now meeting together, generally twice a year. They shared their thinking, coordinated strategy, and sometimes divided up cases on which to focus. This work
created a much stronger legal movement, as the Ad Hoc Task Force evolved into
the LGBT Litigators' Roundtable.

As a participant in these meetings since 1984, first as a representative of GLAD
and later of Lambda Legal, I saw first-hand the positive impacts of getting people
from organizations that were both collegial and competitive to talk to each other
regularly, work together, and get to know one another, and I often wished we
could have created a similar roundtable for the LGBT organizations that focus
on legislative or political advocacy. I won't say there weren't disagreements—
and sometimes strong ones on everything from legal theories to case selection
to geography to media positioning—but people behave better with people they
know. Often when people have to sit across the table on a regular basis, they
come to like and respect one another.

These meetings have grown from a few people from a handful of organizations to now about a hundred invitees from close to two dozen groups—the
core litigation groups named above plus legal staff from a much broader range of
LGBT groups. The Roundtable, as it is generally known, was a key forum beginning in the early 1990s for discussion, arguments, and planning around marriage litigation. It is impossible to imagine all the progress the litigation groups
have achieved without the Roundtable as a key and central forum.

Meanwhile, through the late 1980s and 1990s, these groups continued to
spearhead litigation against sodomy laws, while political efforts to repeal the
laws continued as well. By 2003, when *Lawrence v. Texas* went to the Supreme
Court, only seventeen years after the decision in *Bowers v. Hardwick*, LGBT activists and our allies had cut the number of states with sodomy laws on the books
from twenty-six to thirteen. When I say "only seventeen years," I do not make
light of the tremendous harm that sodomy laws continued to do in that period,
but it was unusual, in Supreme Court time, for the Court to revisit an issue and
reverse itself in less than two decades. Moving from a bare majority of states to

a minority with such laws on the books was critical to the success of *Lawrence*. Winning *Lawrence*, in turn, was critical to the success of every marriage equality case that followed. A persistent, coordinated campaign of public education and impact litigation had set the stage for the next big steps forward.

"NOT TONIGHT, DEAR—IT'S A FELONY": *LAWRENCE V. TEXAS* AND THE PATH TO MARRIAGE EQUALITY

SUZANNE B. GOLDBERG

———⊷∞∞⊷———

Suzanne B. Goldberg is the Herbert and Doris Wechsler Clinical Professor of Law at Columbia Law School.

I was in my office at Lambda Legal one fall afternoon in 1998 when I got a call from Mitchell Katine, a lawyer I knew in Texas. Two men had been arrested and held by the police overnight for violating the state's "Homosexual Conduct" law. Would Lambda Legal be interested in getting involved, he asked.

That was an easy question to answer. Absolutely, yes. Advocates for lesbian, gay, bisexual, and transgender (LGBT) rights had long been looking for a path to challenge the dozen or so criminal sodomy laws that remained in the United States. These were the laws that imposed criminal penalties on adults for engaging in sexual relations—typically oral or anal sex—either in same-sex couples or different-sex couples. Not only did the laws themselves cause harm, but so, too, did the leading antigay Supreme Court ruling from 1986, *Bowers v. Hardwick*, which said it was "at best, facetious" for a gay man to argue that the U.S. Constitution protected his right to have consensual sex with another man.[1] Making things worse, the Court added that the public's moral disapproval of homosexuality was reason enough to uphold the law.

As much as sodomy laws were a problem on their own, the *Hardwick* decision's ripple effects caused even more widespread harm. Lesbian moms and gay dads were losing custody of their children because they were "criminals in the eyes of the law." In one case, the Virginia Supreme Court even gave a grandmother custody because the mother was a lesbian, saying, "[c]onduct inherent in lesbianism is punishable as a Class 6 felony in the Commonwealth, . . . thus, that conduct is another important consideration in determining custody."[2]

Gay and lesbian employees were losing their jobs for the same reason. Notoriously, the Cracker Barrel restaurant chain enacted a policy to discourage hiring of gay and lesbian employees at its restaurants.[3] Teachers, too, for example, faced significant discrimination as a result of "moral fitness" tests in state licensing.[4]

In court, judges regularly allowed these forms of discrimination to continue. We will not forbid states from discriminating in family or employment decisions, they wrote in decision after decision, when the Constitution allows states to criminalize the "conduct that defines the class" of gay people.[5]

Bowers v. Hardwick was thus not a one-off Supreme Court ruling but instead a serious barrier to gay people's equality in nearly all domains, certainly including marriage. Even if few states actually enforced their sodomy laws against consenting adults, the decision packed a powerful atmospheric punch. Opponents of gay people's equality in courts, legislatures, and public debates about antidiscrimination laws rested comfortably on moral disapproval as a legitimate basis for government action, with the support of the nation's basic charter and the highest court in the land.

Some years earlier, LGBT advocates had focused on challenging another serious barrier to equality: the classification of homosexuality as a psychiatric disorder. To the extent homosexuality was seen as a mental illness, they knew it would be near-impossible to advocate broadly for equal treatment. After significant effort by researchers, analysts, and advocates, the American Psychiatric Association removed homosexuality from the list of mental disorders in its Diagnostic and Statistical Manual ("the DSM") in 1973.

Yet sodomy laws had stuck around. In fact, even though nearly half the states repealed their sodomy laws altogether during the 1970s, others adopted laws that permitted oral and anal sex for different-sex partners while criminalizing those acts for same-sex couples. Even the laws that criminalized these sex acts for anyone—"equal opportunity" laws, as we called them at the time—were often used to justify antigay discrimination because neither employers nor family court judges spent much time looking into the sex acts of heterosexuals.

In the early 1980s, after a string of high court rulings protecting individuals' intimate decision making regarding contraception and reproduction, it seemed that these unequal criminal laws would soon fall, enabling advocacy for equality in other domains. When that did not happen and the Court upheld Georgia's deployment of its equal-opportunity sodomy law in Michael Hardwick's bedroom, it was clear that challenging sodomy laws would have to remain a very high priority for advocates.

But going back to the Supreme Court right away was neither possible nor advisable, and efforts focused mainly on state legislatures and courts, with considerable success. During this time, I traveled to Montana to speak at Missoula's first lesbian and gay pride weekend, where a popular button read, "Not tonight, dear. It's a felony." That was in 1994; Montana's state supreme court struck down the law three years later.

Still, plenty of sodomy laws remained, and the laws' defenders cited everything from moral disapproval to preventing the spread of AIDS as reasons to keep the status quo. In addition to flat-out hostility, there were more technical obstacles to deal with, as in Texas where courts had said that the only way to challenge the "Homosexual Conduct" law would be if someone was actually prosecuted by the state for violating it. This had been happening, but those arrested would quickly enter a plea deal to avoid publicity and the trouble that was bound to follow when they were outed to family, friends, and co-workers.

That is why it was so easy to say yes when Mitchell Katine asked if Lambda Legal would take on the case for John Lawrence and Tyron Garner. John and Tyron were two gay men living in Houston who had been friends for some time. John was a nurse, and Tyron worked at an assortment of jobs. One evening, while they were in John's home, the Houston police barged in after receiving a false crime report. They arrested both men, dragged them out in their underwear, and charged them with violating the "Homosexual Conduct" law. The police then held them overnight even though the violation carried no jail time.[6]

Soon after hearing these facts from Mitchell, I headed to Houston to meet John and Tyron and talk with them about what would be involved in fighting back against their prosecution. In particular, I wanted to make sure they were comfortable with being identified publicly as gay, since the legal challenge would put that fact out in the open for all of their friends, family, and co-workers to see.

Yet even though we knew the case might gain some attention, the media quickly exploded with interest in the case. Still, John and Tyron were strong in their view that they did not want what had happened to them—being arrested on charges of consensual sex—to happen to others, and they took up the mantle of their case with courage and determination.

At Lambda Legal, we also knew, as I shared with John and Tyron, that this was perhaps our best shot at asking the Supreme Court to revisit and reverse its ruling in *Bowers v. Hardwick*. The facts were good in the sense that the police had actually arrested them inside of John's home, showing starkly how sodomy laws authorized the state to enter an adult's bedroom and punish consensual sexual decision making between adults with the force of criminal law.

The timing was good, too. In 1996, in a case called *Romer v. Evans*, the Supreme Court struck down a Colorado state constitutional amendment banning the state and local governments from protecting gay people against discrimination.[7] I had worked on that case since shortly after my arrival at Lambda in 1991; the amendment had passed in 1992. Together with many colleagues—including Matt Coles at the ACLU and our lead counsel, former Colorado Supreme Court Justice Jean Dubofsky, who had been brought into the case by colleagues at the Colorado Legal Initiative Project—we logged countless hours developing

From left to right: Plaintiff Tyron Garner, attorney Suzanne B. Goldberg, and plaintiff John Lawrence. Photo Credit: COURTESY OF LAMBDA LEGAL

arguments for why the Court should not allow moral disapproval of homosexuality to extend to this case and justify Colorado's legal barricade against gay people's civil rights.

Romer was a terrific win—the first-ever opinion from the Supreme Court that endorsed the Constitution's protections for gay people.[8] Importantly, the Court concluded that the amendment's singular ban on legal protections for gay people could be explained only by antigay animus and not by the state's asserted interest in protecting its scarce resources or its constituents' freedom of association. On behalf of six of the Court's nine members, Justice Kennedy wrote, "We must conclude that Amendment 2 classifies homosexuals not to further a proper legislative end but to make them unequal to everyone else. This Colorado cannot do. A State cannot so deem a class of persons a stranger to its laws."[9]

The Court did not take on the question of sodomy laws in this decision, and, in dissent, Justice Scalia was furious. Citing *Bowers v. Hardwick,* he wrote: "In holding that homosexuality cannot be singled out for disfavorable treatment, the Court contradicts a decision, unchallenged here, pronounced only ten years ago . . . , and places the prestige of this institution behind the proposition that opposition to homosexuality is as reprehensible as racial or religious bias."

Romer seemed, then, to signal a new openness on the Court's part to gay rights claims, though Congress was at the same time working fervently to shut down gay people's equality claims in the military and in marriage. By passing "Don't Ask, Don't Tell" in 1994, a ban on gay people serving openly in the military became the law of the land. Two years later, Congress enacted the "Defense of Marriage Act," which banned the federal government from recognizing same-sex couples' marriages, even though there was not a single state at the time that allowed same-sex couples to marry.

As harsh as these laws were, they also energized public debates and private conversations about the place of gay people in American society. Some of these discussions had begun when the AIDS epidemic prompted increased attention to the harsh effects of discrimination and violence on gay people. This renewed national attention in the mid-1990s, in the context of military service and marriage, prompted more roiling debates over the contributions gay people were making to American society and the justifications for continuing discrimination.

Against this backdrop, *Lawrence v. Texas* began to move through the Texas state courts. The first stop for the "Homosexual Conduct" law violations in this case was on November 20, 1998, in a courtroom in a Houston office park. Because the maximum penalty was a fine rather than jail time, these prosecutions began in the same justice-of-the-peace court where nearly everyone else was there to deal with a traffic ticket. Although we had prepared a submission to highlight our objections to the law, this was a court of "no record," meaning that the constitutional case would really begin in the state criminal court. John and Tyron pled "no contest" to the charges, paid a fine, and we indicated our intention to move the case along.

Being in court that day produced a sense of simultaneous disbelief and outrage. Here was the criminal law of Texas calling these men to account in public for allegedly engaging in consensual sex inside John's home and then treating their "crime" as it would treat a speeding ticket. It was as though the state knew this was not really criminal conduct but wanted to use its symbolic power to humiliate gay people and send a broad and degrading message about gay people to the general public. In some ways, the experience reminded me of what I had read about bar raids during the 1950s and 1960s, including raids that prompted the Stonewall Rebellion in 1969, where the police wielded their authority to make a point about the lesser social status of LGBT people. Fortunately, John and Tyron were willing to fight back. We drew fortitude from one another and from our collective sense of justice to get through the day.

Next stop, a few weeks later, was the Texas Criminal Court. There, the proceeding consisted of the prosecutor reading the police officer's arrest report and the judge accepting "no contest" pleas again from Tyron and John. Although it still felt absurd to have our clients prosecuted under a law that criminalized consensual sex, the Texas Criminal Court with its columns outside and formality inside at least felt like a proper forum.

At this point in the case, Lambda Legal was able to submit our written arguments explaining why Texas's sodomy law was unconstitutional. Though the arguments were made more elaborately when we reached later stages in the case, the basic points remained the same. The "Homosexual Conduct" law, we said, violated the U.S. Constitution's guarantees of equality and privacy. In other words, the law invaded gay people's private decision making and physical space and did so unequally because it left non-gay people free to engage in the very same acts. We knew the judge would have to reject our privacy argument because *Bowers v. Hardwick* was the law of the land, but we had to make it anyway to "preserve" it for the appeal.

As expected, the judge denied our request to dismiss the charges on the ground that the law was unconstitutional. He knew, as did we, that this case needed to get to a higher-level court if the permissibility of the Texas law was to be decided once and for all.

Quite amazingly, in June 2000, a three-judge panel of the mid-level appeals court declared the law unconstitutional after Ruth Harlow, then Lambda Legal's deputy legal director and subsequently Lambda Legal's legal director, argued the case there, holding that it discriminated based on sex in violation of the Texas Equal Rights Amendment. But in March 2001, the full appeals court took hold of the case and, in a 7–2 vote, reversed that decision and declared the "Homosexual Conduct" law valid.

Still, there was some dissent that held promise—not only for the sodomy prohibition but also for marriage arguments to come. Justice John S. Anderson offered this scenario to highlight how the law discriminated based on sex by penalizing only same-sex couples:

> There are three people in a room: Alice, Bob, and Cathy. Bob approaches Alice, and with her consent, engages with her in several varieties of "deviate sexual intercourse," the conduct at issue here. Bob then leaves the room. Cathy approaches Alice, and with her consent, engages with her in several kinds of "deviate sexual intercourse." Cathy is promptly arrested for violating section 21.06.[10]

The judge explained that he "indulged in this tableau to demonstrate one important point: one person simply committed a sex act, while another committed a crime. While the acts were exactly the same, the gender of the actors was different, and it was this difference alone that determined the criminal nature of the conduct."[11]

Notwithstanding the power of that argument, the appeals court upheld the law, and Lambda Legal appealed to the state's highest criminal court. For a year, that court did not act; instead, it left advocates and John and Tyron waiting. Finally, in April 2002, the Texas Court of Criminal Appeals announced it would not hear the case. This meant that the "Homosexual Conduct" law was still available for Texas law enforcement to use against same-sex partners at any time.

Although lawyers usually prefer to win, losing in the Texas courts was actually a good thing because Lambda Legal could ask the U.S. Supreme Court to take the case, strike down the Texas statute, and reverse *Bowers v. Hardwick*. This, in turn, would remove the profound barrier to gay equality claims that *Bowers* continued to impose.

In July 2002, Lambda's lawyers and cooperating attorneys filed a *cert*. petition seeking review by the U.S. Supreme Court. The petition identified the questions raised by the case and urged the high court to exercise its discretion to take the case and revisit the Texas court's ruling. It presented three questions. Did the "Homosexual Conduct" law violate the U.S. Constitution's equality guarantee? Did the law violate the Constitution's right to privacy? Should *Bowers v. Hardwick* be overruled?

On December 2, 2002, the Supreme Court agreed to hear the case. Advocates were optimistic, reasoning that the Court would not have wanted to take the case if it was going to uphold the Texas law, since the Texas court had already done that. Of course, no one outside the Court ever really knows in advance what the Court intends to do; still, excitement began to mount that the LGBT community might finally be free of the burden of *Bowers*.

With broad-based efforts, advocates from around the country filed friend-of-the-court briefs to support the challenge. Groups including historians, the American Psychological Association, faith-based and civil rights organizations, and more weighed in on the grave harms caused by sodomy laws and the compelling need for constitutional protection of the intimate, personal decision making that had been criminalized by the Texas law. Some associations and civil rights groups took what was then a significant risk to publically support gay rights in court for the first time.

In March 2003, having been asked to argue the case by Lambda Legal, experienced Supreme Court litigator Paul Smith from the firm Jenner & Block stood before the Supreme Court and presented the case for why the Court's 1986 *Bowers* ruling should no longer be considered good law. Tough questioning ensued from the justices, both for Smith and the lawyer for Texas who sought, weakly by all accounts, to defend the state law (see page 66).

Just three months later, on June 26, 2003, a majority of the Court declared that "*Bowers* was not correct when it was decided, and it is not correct today. It ought not to remain binding precedent. *Bowers v. Hardwick* should be and now is overruled."[12] Importantly, Justice Kennedy's opinion for the Court also recognized that the Constitution protects "personal decisions relating to marriage, procreation, contraception, family relationships, [and] child rearing" and that "persons in a homosexual relationship may seek autonomy for these purposes, just as heterosexual persons do."[13]

Justice Kennedy did not address what his opinion might mean for marriage, but it was clear that a new door had now been opened for marriage equality, and other justices responded in kind. Justice O'Connor, who wrote a separate opinion, agreed the Texas law should be struck down, but relied on the Constitution's equality protections instead of privacy, adding that the decision did not mean the end to marriage discrimination. She wrote: "Unlike the moral disapproval of same-sex relations—the asserted state interest in this case—other reasons exist to promote the institution of marriage beyond mere moral disapproval of an excluded group."[14]

Justice Scalia, in a characteristically scathing dissent, connected the dots directly between the Constitution's protection for sexual intimacy and its protection for marriage equality. "Today's opinion dismantles the structure of constitutional law that has permitted a distinction to be made between heterosexual and homosexual unions, insofar as formal recognition in marriage is concerned," he wrote.[15] He added, with sarcasm resonating almost audibly from the written words: "If moral disapprobation of homosexual conduct is 'no legitimate state interest' for purposes of proscribing that conduct, . . . what justification could there possibly be for denying the benefits of marriage to homosexual couples exercising '[t]he liberty protected by the Constitution . . . ?'"[16]

But after *Lawrence*, there was no going back. By early November of that year, the Massachusetts Supreme Judicial Court agreed that there was no permissible reason to exclude same-sex couples from marriage, though it relied on its own constitution rather than the federal guarantees when it required the state to grant marriage equality.[17] This thrilling victory, in a case brought by Gay & Lesbian Advocates & Defenders, delivered the freedom to marry to same-sex couples for the first time in the United States. And while the Supreme Court's *Lawrence* decision did not mandate the Massachusetts result, it had surely paved the way. By reversing its earlier condemnation of gay people in *Bowers*, the nation's highest court had, in some sense, pulled back from its jurisprudential hostility.

Many state and federal courts followed suit in the following years, citing *Lawrence* as they ruled in favor of the freedom to marry. A decade later, the Supreme Court took its first direct look at what *Lawrence* meant for marriage when it considered Edie Windsor's challenge to the federal Defense of Marriage Act (DOMA). Striking down DOMA, Justice Kennedy cited *Lawrence* as essential support for the decision. The federal law's refusal to recognize same-sex couples' marriages, he wrote, "demeans the couple, whose moral and sexual choices the Constitution protects, . . . and whose relationship the State has sought to dignify."[18]

In dissent, Chief Justice Roberts ignored *Lawrence* and tried to set out a path that would allow states to exclude same-sex couples from marriage even if the federal DOMA was invalid.[19] But Justice Scalia took up where he had left off ten years earlier, arguing in a separate, furious dissent that *Lawrence*'s rejection of moral disapproval as grounds for government-sponsored distinctions meant that state "defense of marriage" acts would also likely fall.

Precisely two years later, *Lawrence* did indeed lead to marriage equality in the United States. In *Obergefell v. Hodges*, issued a dozen years to the day after *Lawrence*, the U.S. Supreme Court ruled that the Constitution requires every American state to allow same-sex couples to marry and to recognize same-sex couples' valid marriages.[20]

Lawrence threads throughout Justice Kennedy's opinion, appearing more than a dozen times. At the beginning, Justice Kennedy invoked *Lawrence* while recounting the Court's changed approach to the rights of gay people,[21] and then to make clear that history and tradition are important but not definitive in determining which rights the Constitution protects as fundamental.[22] Next, *Lawrence* is the lead precedent to support the Constitution's protection for intimacy "inherent in" the marital bond.[23] And following that comes citation after citation to *Lawrence*, all adding up to the proposition that the U.S. Constitution's protection of liberty and equality protects same-sex couples' right to marry throughout the United States.

Surely when John Lawrence and Tyron Garner were arrested and thrown in jail overnight for "homosexual conduct" in 1998, they were not thinking about marriage equality. Likewise, when we started planning their litigation strategy at Lambda Legal, foremost in our minds were sodomy laws, not marriage. At that point, winning marriage nationwide seemed like a distant pipe dream, even if an important one. Neither man lived to see how his courage and the legal victory they secured together helped to win the freedom to marry for so many others.

Yet, as is the nature of social change, each step toward equality creates new possibilities. Winning *Lawrence* meant that the scourge of *Bowers v. Hardwick* was gone from the law books, with the Court apologizing, in effect, for its earlier constitutional disdain. Lower courts, state legislatures, and elected officials took this to heart as they created new options for recognizing same-sex couples' relationships through civil unions and ultimately marriage.

The Supreme Court also did not shrink from the meaning of *Lawrence*. Instead, and over time, as the nation moved toward greater equality, so too did the Court, following the path it had begun in 2003 when, as never before, it gave its constitutional embrace and protection to the basic humanity of lesbians and gay men.

ARGUING *LAWRENCE V. TEXAS* AT THE SUPREME COURT

PAUL SMITH

—⊗⊗⊘—

Paul Smith is chair of the Appellate and Supreme Court Practice, and co-chair of the Media and First Amendment and Election Law and Redistricting Practices at the law firm Jenner & Block.

Lawrence v. Texas, the case that overturned *Bowers v. Hardwick* and decriminalized sex between two consenting adults of the same sex, was one of many Supreme Court cases that I have worked on over the years. In one sense the case was like many of the others. We filed a petition asking the Court to review the case, and we were thrilled when the Court agreed to do so. We wrote "merits briefs" explaining to the Court why it should rule that the Constitution does not permit the government to criminalize private, adult, consensual sexual intimacy involving two people of the same sex. And I argued the case before the Court one March morning in 2003 for an hour.

But in reality, working on *Lawrence* was an experience unlike any I've had before or since. There was a sense throughout that we were making history, changing in a fundamental way the relationship between the LGBT community and the U.S. legal system. The extraordinary lawyers at Lambda Legal and other lawyers active in the movement for LGBT equality had spent seventeen years preparing for a case in which the Court could overrule its odious decision in *Bowers v. Hardwick*. There, the Court had labeled "at best, facetious" any claim that the Constitution prevented a state from putting people in jail for engaging in sexual behavior with another person of the same sex. That ruling, in turn, stood as a huge barrier to progress toward greater equality for LGBT people. And it sent a message that gay men and lesbians were, at best, second-class citizens in their own country.

It is hard to overstate what was at stake in *Lawrence*. The first question Lambda Legal raised with me and my colleagues was whether it was too risky to go back to the Supreme Court with such an important case at that stage of history. We concluded that the Court would not grant review unless there was a good chance it would overturn *Bowers*. And that is how it worked out. The Court did grant review, and that day we knew we had a very good shot at eliminating *Bowers* from American law once and for all.

The argument day came after weeks of intensive preparation, including at least three "moot courts" where lawyers played the role of justices asking the hardest questions that might be asked in the real courtroom. After each moot session, I met with the core team members—Ruth Harlow, Pat Logue, and Susan Sommer from Lambda Legal, and Bill Hohengarten from my firm—to go over every answer and refine each of them. When the day came for the real thing, the audience in the Supreme Court courtroom included members of the public who had camped out overnight to be sure to get in to watch. Up front, the lawyers seating section right behind the podium was filled with veterans of gay rights fights over the past two decades—many probably questioning the decision to give responsibility for the argument to a relative newcomer to the movement (even though I was a veteran Supreme Court litigator).

I went first, and the justices we knew would be against us—principally Chief Justice Rehnquist and Justice Antonin Scalia—asked the kinds of questions we had expected and prepared for. Occasionally, they surprised us. Perhaps the most memorable surprise was the chief justice asking, if we won the case, whether that would mean schools could not prefer straight people over gay people as kindergarten teachers. Consistent with our basic approach, I answered that they would need some concrete reason for doing so and that mere moral disapproval of homosexuality would not be such a justification. Justice Scalia pushed back saying that the justification would be concern that contact with gay teachers would make children more likely to grow up gay. As some members of the audience hissed a little, I had one of those split seconds when several thoughts pass through your mind simultaneously. First, I thought such a concern was absurd factually, and reflected old and hateful stereotypes about gay men preying on children and seeking to "convert" them. I worried that not confronting such a remarkable comment would cause the LGBT community to feel poorly represented at this critical moment. On the other hand, I knew that allowing the argument to take such a detour would do nothing to help us win THIS case, which had to do with the right to be left alone from government interference in choices about sexual and life partners. So I dismissed the concern as unpersuasive and quickly moved back to the mission at hand.

The friendly justices predictably did not ask many questions except for an occasional softball. Justice Ruth Bader Ginsburg, for example, asked whether we were in fact asking the Court to overturn *Bowers*. I said that was exactly what we were asking for.

Two other justices—Justices Sandra Day O'Connor and Anthony Kennedy—were considered the "swing justices" most likely to cast decisive votes. They were even quieter. This was unusual for them. Justice O'Connor was famous for asking a first question that made clear what she thought about the case. But given the historic importance of the case and the intense scrutiny of every word they said, Justices O'Connor and Kennedy chose to remain largely mum.

We nevertheless left that day very hopeful that a majority of the justices would vote our way. As it turned out, we had to wait until the very last day of the term in June 2003 to find out for sure. Because we knew the term was ending, everyone involved in the case made the trip to the Court that morning to see the justices take the bench and deliver their opinions orally. The suspense was tremendous, as other cases were announced first. Eventually the chief justice announced that Justice Kennedy would deliver the majority opinion in *Lawrence v. Texas*. He proceeded to talk for quite a while before giving any hint about which way the Court was going to rule. But eventually he started to discuss all the things the Court majority had misunderstood when it issued the decision in *Bowers*. That's when we began to realize what was in store.

As Justice Kennedy explained, what the *Bowers* Court had failed to appreciate that day was that sex for same-sex couples could serve as the foundation for a family relationship, just as it does for straight people. As he put it from the bench, to "say the issue in *Bowers* was simply the right to engage in certain sexual conduct demeans the claim put forward, just as it would demean a married couple were it to be said that marriage is simply about the right to have sexual intercourse." And in fact, sodomy laws "seek to control a personal relationship that is within the liberty of persons to choose without being punished as criminals."

Ultimately, he got to the words that still ring in my ears: "*Bowers* was not correct when it was decided, and it is not correct today. It ought not to remain binding precedent. *Bowers versus Hardwick* should be and now is overruled." Many tears flowed in that courtroom, for we knew something historic and wonderful had just happened.

But before we could celebrate, we had to endure listening to Justice Scalia read his dissent out loud (a practice that is done only once or twice each Supreme Court term). He did not hold back in fully expressing how outraged he was. As he put it:

Lambda Legal attorneys Susan Sommer, Patricia Logue, and Ruth Harlow with co-counsel Paul Smith and William Hohengarten, who successfully argued *Lawrence v. Texas*, and plaintiff John Lawrence (center) at the U.S. Supreme Court, 2003. Photo Credit: COURTESY OF LAMBDA LEGAL

It is clear from this that the Court has taken sides in the culture war and in particular in that battle of the culture war that concerns whether there should be any moral opprobrium attached to homosexual conduct. For many Americans do not want persons who openly engage in homosexual conduct to be partners in their business, scoutmasters for their children, teachers in their children's schools, or boarders in their home. They view this as protecting themselves and their families against a lifestyle they believe to be immoral and destructive.

It was tough to listen to this kind of extreme commentary with a stone face. But Justice Scalia said something else that was interesting. He pointed out that, in light of the majority's ruling, there was no logical stopping point on the road to a constitutional right to marry for same-sex couples. As he put it:

At the end of its opinion, the Court says that the present case "does not involve whether the government must give formal recognition to any relationship that homosexual persons may seek to enter." Don't believe it. Today's opinion dismantles the structure of constitutional law that has permitted a distinction to be made between heterosexual and homosexual unions. If moral disapprobation of homosexual conduct is as the Court says, "no legitimate state interest," and if as the Court says casting aside all pretense at neutrality "when sexuality finds overt expression in intimate conduct with another person, the conduct can be but one element in a personal bond that is more enduring," what justification could there possibly be for denying the benefits of marriage to homosexual couples . . . ?

He has proved to be quite prophetic.

III. VICTORIES, DEFEATS, AND A PLAN
TO WIN MARRIAGE, 1996–2009

THE LITIGATION: FIRST JUDICIAL VICTORIES IN VERMONT, MASSACHUSETTS, AND CONNECTICUT

MARY L. BONAUTO

Mary L. Bonauto is director of the Civil Rights Project at Gay & Lesbian Advocates & Defenders (GLAD).

Vermont

The first convening of lawyers and activists in the New England region organized by Gay & Lesbian Advocates & Defenders (GLAD) to discuss marriage advocacy happened in 1994 in Boston, Massachusetts. The agenda was to discuss the road forward from the Hawai'i Supreme Court's preliminary ruling, in favor of marriage equality in May 1993.

GLAD's message at that meeting was startling to some: we can win marriage in Hawai'i, and we can do legal, political, and public education work now to ensure those marriages are respected when couples return home. Susan Murray and Beth Robinson, attorneys at Langrock, Sperry & Wool, a highly regarded plaintiffs' firm in Vermont, were present and ready for action to enlist the support of LGB Vermonters and straight allies, including members of the clergy and lawmakers. They would soon form the Vermont Freedom to Marry Task Force.

GLAD's thinking at that time was to file state constitutional claims, since cases decided on independent state grounds are not reviewable by the U.S. Supreme Court. In addition, strategically, a direct marriage challenge in Vermont made sense. Vermont's State Constitution promised "common benefits" to all members of the community, substantively similar yet also distinct from more modern equal protection provisions; and the Vermont Supreme Court interpreted the Constitution as a living document not bound by so-called original intent. In 1993, the Court had authorized second-parent adoption for same-sex and other unmarried couples, acknowledging that same-sex couples and families exist and deserve the law's cognizance. The legislature subsequently codified that good result in a new adoption statute and had also included sexual orientation in its non-discrimination and hate crimes laws.

It was also quite difficult to amend the Vermont Constitution. Amendments could only be proposed every four years and required two-thirds of the State Senate and a majority of the House to agree. After approval, a new legislature had to re-approve the measure before it would go to voters for possible ratification.

At a meeting on a snowy December day at Beth Robinson's home in 1996, Beth, Susan, myself, and then-GLAD Executive Director Amelia Craig all agreed GLAD would join as co-counsel in the first freedom-to-marry case after the preliminary win in Hawai'i. This was just six months after the U.S. Congress passed the federal Defense of Marriage Act, and states had begun to pass discriminatory public policies about "same-sex marriage." In July 1997, with a trove of marriage and legal research memos, plaintiff and spokesperson training and heads-up meetings, we announced the filing of *Baker v. State of Vermont* in Burlington on behalf of Stan Baker and Peter Harrigan, Lois Farnham and Holly Puterbaugh, and Nina Beck and Stacy Jolles. All three couples lived in the greater Burlington area. Two of the three couples were parents.

From the outset, we were determined to keep the focus on real people rather than allow an abstract debate. We wanted to show that the marriage laws mattered in the day-to-day lives of Vermonters. Nina and Stacy described how, during their son Noah's birth, hospital agents had challenged Stacy's right to be there even with her documents in hand. Holly and Lois and Stan and Peter repeatedly shared their lives throughout the litigation. Tragically, early in the litigation, Noah's heart failed and a donor heart never came in time. After a period of grieving, Nina and Stacy returned, determined to make this a case for the benefit of all children of LGB parents.

Our claims were like the claims that have followed since: the exclusion of same-sex couples from the freedom to marry denies the fundamental right to marry and also fails equal protection review, whether the close scrutiny required of laws discriminating against people based on sex and sexual orientation or even rational basis scrutiny.

The State of Vermont came back at us with the now familiar arguments: the fundamental right is limited to different-sex couples; marriage is inherently a different-sex institution linked to procreation; the state can place no limits on who may marry if it cannot bar same-sex couples from marrying. On the equality claims, Vermont offered seven reasons for the exclusion and argued heightened review was not required in any event. The Trial Court, without oral argument, accepted one reason: the notion that the State had an interest in "furthering the link between procreation and child rearing." By December 1997, we had appealed to the Vermont Supreme Court.

Clearly we needed to help the Supreme Court understand that procreation is not a requirement for marriage, and that discriminatory marriage laws undermined the State's interest in protecting children (including those of Nina and Stacy and Holly and Lois). We argued: "There is no basis for the implicit assumption that marriage is a zero sum game such that allowing same-sex couples to marry will somehow harm different-sex marriages or result in a decrease in the number of such marriages. . . . [N]or can the State logically explain how the exclusion of same-gender couples . . . helps different-sex marriages or results in more such marriages involving procreation and parenting." This was the first time these arguments were made in court, and they would be made over and over again for nearly two decades.

In response, Vermont relied on arguments very much alive in the public square and on people's minds—don't children need both a male and a female parent; indeed, doesn't marriage itself require male–female complementarity; can we risk "destabilizing change" in marriage; and would marriage make Vermont too different from all the other states.

Beth presented our arguments to the Vermont Supreme Court in November 1998, about two weeks after Hawai'i and Alaska voters amended their constitutions to effectively ban marriage to same-sex couples. The mood was tense. Was the hope for marriage for same-sex couples just a flash in the pan? Beth, up first, began her argument by invoking the California Supreme Court's first-ever ruling in 1948 striking down a ban on marriage between people of different races. She said the decision was "controversial, courageous, and correct." She drew out the parallels between the arguments used to justify race-based bans and those here—children, tradition, moral disapproval, the feared slippery slope. Justice Denise Johnson commented that "someone has to go first" with regard to the freedom to marry. Chief Justice Amestoy asked whether we believed that the State could constitutionally eliminate the institution of civil marriage for everyone, providing legal benefits some other way. The State's arguments rested heavily on its assertion that the state didn't need particularly strong reasons to justify its exclusion of same-sex couples.

We waited thirteen months for the Court's decision, and Vermont Freedom to Marry put that time to good use: speaking opportunities, house parties, and neighborhood meetings, along with continued outreach to legislators to forestall the possibility of an adverse constitutional amendment.

On December 20, 1999, the Court ruled that same-sex couples were entitled to the same benefits and protections of marriage as different-sex couples as a matter of the Common Benefits Clause. "[N]one" of the State's asserted interests "provides a reasonable and just basis for the continued exclusion of same-sex couples from the benefits incident to a civil marriage license under Vermont law." Reflecting our efforts to tie the law to people's lives, the Court wrote in a concluding paragraph that its ruling acknowledging "plaintiffs as Vermonters who seek nothing more, nor less, than legal protection and security for their avowed commitment to an intimate and lasting human relationship is simply, when all is said and done, a recognition of our common humanity."

This was an historic and powerful ruling, and a genuine breakthrough. But some bitter came with the sweet. The Court left implementation to the legislature, which could pass marriage legislation or some alternative that provided the same material benefits.

We were obviously disappointed by that aspect of the Court's decision. None of us had imagined an artificial splitting of "marriage" into two components, tangible benefits on the one hand, and the dignity and status of marriage on the other. The dignity of married status was itself one of the benefits of marriage. Justice Johnson was the only justice to concur but dissent as to remedy, believing the judiciary was compelled to provide marriage once the Court found a constitutional violation. To our further disappointment, within moments of the decision's release, Governor Howard Dean assured the public that the legislature would explore an alternative legal status rather than require marriage licensing. With the legislature opening on January 4, 2000, there was no time for delay. The first legislative campaign for marriage had begun.

The House Judiciary Committee, led by Chair Thomas Little and Vice Chair Bill Lippert, who was an openly gay man, announced it would study the issue; and, over the next six weeks, it effectively conducted a teach-in on marriage and relationship recognition led by Vermonters and experts across the spectrum. For example, among the Vermont and other law professor witnesses testifying for us was Yale historian Nancy Cott, author of *Public Vows: A History of Marriage and the Nation* (2000). Nancy eventually became the go-to expert on the history of marriage and an author of amicus briefs for historians in state and federal appellate courts.

State House hearings in Montpelier, almost invariably held on bitterly cold nights with snow or ice storms, featured Vermonters who very publicly came out in telling legislators about their love for their partners. The power of gay people identifying themselves and their families, as well as extended family members speaking up for the gay people in their lives, cannot be overstated. Of course, opposition demonstrators were there as well: a newly formed group calling itself "Take It to the People," or TIP, which argued the people should decide the issue; "Operation Rescue" founder Randall Terry; and, yes, the Westboro Baptist Church.

In mid-February, the Committee chose its path: it would craft a law providing the same benefits, protections, and responsibilities of marriage but through a separate system. This was both a blow and a crisis: after all of its marriage advocacy, would Vermont Freedom to Marry help craft, or support, a bill that was not marriage, or should advocates walk away and go back to court? A meeting of core volunteers and supporters was hastily called on a weekend morning. The group agreed to support only a marriage bill. Yet the pressure continued to mount as the committee crafted a bill. At a later meeting, with heavy hearts but with the eyes of the nation on them, the group decided to back "civil unions" as the most protective law for same-sex couples anywhere in the country. I attended this meeting and backed that approach. It seems like a significant compromise now—and it was—but at the time, it was also a big step forward in bringing same-sex couples and their children out of the shadows of discrimination and under the protection of Vermont law.

Opponents did not want civil unions or any recognition of same-sex relationships. They argued that several pairs of people who cannot marry, such as "two maiden aunts," could benefit from state recognition, and so why should same-sex couples receive these protections. In response to these stated concerns, the legislature enacted an additional "reciprocal beneficiary" law to allow some other people who could not marry to achieve a limited set of legal protections.

Along with the civil union bill itself, the Vermont Senate considered two constitutional amendments. One would constitutionalize a limitation on marriage, while the other would deny both marriage and other measures like the civil union bill under consideration. Over the course of two days of debate and voting, I saw how a court's affirmation of constitutional protections made it so much more difficult for legislators to take those protections away. We had opponents, of course, but a number of senators explained why they opposed taking away protections for same-sex couples by connecting the dots to discrimination experienced in their own families, such as anti-Catholic prejudice, or describing soulful conversations with their own children. One senator read a constituent letter from a woman later identified as Helena Blair, a seventy-eight-year-old mother of eight from a Vermont farm family who had a gay son. Should she "cast him out or accept him instantly? . . . God blessed us with eight children. And God made no mistake when he gave us our gay son." Like Mrs. Blair, the senators embraced LGB Vermonters and rejected both amendments.

The Senate handily passed the civil union bill, but it was tense in the House. Representative Lippert, vice chair of the House Judiciary Committee and the only openly gay representative, took to the House floor to speak as a gay man about his own life and the rights others "take for granted" but which he and other gay people are categorically denied. Another Committee member, Republican Representative John Edwards, a retired state trooper who had worked through his own discomfort with homosexuality during the committee process, spoke in favor of the bill and voted for it. He knew it might cost him his reelection, but he believed he was making Vermont a better place for all citizens. On March 15, 2000, the House approved the bill by a vote of 76–69.

Civil unions commenced on July 1, 2000—the first comprehensive relationship recognition status for same-sex couples anywhere in the United States. There was great happiness and great power in legal acknowledgment of same-sex couples' committed relationships. People from around the nation flocked to Vermont to join in civil union, with over fifteen hundred couples joining in civil union in the first six months, 78 percent of whom were from out of state. In 2001, 1,875 couples joined in civil union, and in 2002, another 1,707 couples followed.

But the fight was far from over. The "Take Back Vermont" movement, fomented by Republican gubernatorial candidate Ruth Dwyer, engulfed the state, the 2000 election cycle, and eventually, the marriage debate in Vermont for the next decade. This level of vitriol was new to Vermont. The Vermont Freedom to Marry Task Force—again pioneered by Beth and Susan—formed an electoral arm and went to work fundraising and volunteering for Democratic and Republican supporters of civil unions. Many longtime state representatives who had supported the civil union bill were suddenly outcasts in their own communities. In the end, the vast majority of our legislative supporters were reelected. But the losses were enough that Democrats lost control of the House.

In the 2001–2 legislative session, the newly elected House majority passed a measure to repeal civil unions and make the limited reciprocal-beneficiary status available to same-sex couples. The newly elected Republican Speaker cast the tie-breaking vote in favor of the bill, but the measure died in the Senate. Although such bills would return in future years, the civil union law had survived its biggest acid test.

In the end, we had a signal achievement but also faced a certain chill and a lack of political will to do more, despite marriage being our goal. Our only choice was to continue making the case in the political and electoral processes and in our own community, however long it might take. It took another nine years to win marriage in the legislature.

Massachusetts

After Vermont enacted its civil union law in 2000, people in other New England states regularly asked, "Why can't we do something here?" At GLAD, we agreed Massachusetts should be next. Massachusetts had passed a comprehensive non-discrimination law in 1989, and later enacted laws addressing equal educational access and hate crimes. All the same, domestic partner laws, whether statewide or local, had been thwarted.

Looking at the justices of the Supreme Judicial Court (SJC), our highest court, we were convinced they would be fair and that we could win. The SJC had a long and generally good track record in addressing issues relevant to LGB people's lives. As far back as 1980, the SJC ruled that a parent's sexual orientation said nothing about parental fitness. By the 1990s, we had turned the tide on parenting, winning both second-parent adoption and de facto parenting protections. The Court also sensitively handled matters including same-sex sexual harassment on the job, limiting the reach of criminal laws involving consensual "sex offenses," and municipal authority for enacting domestic partners ordinances.

The grassroots movement had also been building with Freedom to Marry Boston. The group went state-wide, with leaders like Josh Friedes (later of Equal Rights Washington), Valerie and Jackie Fein-Zachary, Vickie Henry (later of GLAD), and Marc Solomon (later of MassEquality and Freedom to Marry) building out the Freedom to Marry Coalition to focus on personal stories, faith communities, and, with GLAD, outreach to the LGB communities about what it means to be denied marriage.

Although many of our political friends were hesitant about a lawsuit, we believed a win was more likely than not. Massachusetts' State Constitution, penned by John Adams, offered guarantees for individual equality and liberty beyond those protected at the federal level. The visibility and integration of LGB people and families across Massachusetts was simply obvious. We felt an imperative to move forward rather than squander an opportunity.

The battle was coming in any event. A newly formed and richly funded anti-gay group was already preparing to move forward with a constitutional amendment to bar marriage and civil unions. We wanted to engage affirmatively and with the voices of real couples and families, not defensively. Strategically, if we won the case and the amendment proceeded to the ballot, voters would know what it looked like when same-sex couples married before casting their vote. Likewise, if we lost the case, we would minimize any perceived "need" to amend the constitution, thus keeping the door open for a legislative change to the marriage laws.

We decided to find plaintiffs from across Massachusetts and bring the issue closer to more people in more communities than we had in Vermont: Hillary and Julie Goodridge (with daughter Annie) of Boston; David Wilson and Robert Compton of Boston; Michael Horgan and Ed Balmelli of Boston; Maureen Brodoff and Ellen Wade (with daughter Kate) of Newton; Gary Chalmers and Richard Linnell (with daughter Paige) of Northbridge near Worcester; Heidi Norton and Gina Smith (now Nortonsmith) (with sons Avery and Quinn) of Northampton; and Linda Davies and Gloria Bailey (now Bailey-Davies) from Cape Cod.

When we announced the filing of *Goodridge v. Dept. of Public Health* on April 11, 2001, at three press conferences across the state, we ensured there would be no mistaking our intentions. We were seeking marriage for same-sex couples as required by the Massachusetts Constitution, not civil unions.

Before filing suit, we knew we needed a strategic, coordinated media strategy. We brought in Mary Breslauer, who went on to help marriage efforts in many other states, to work with the plaintiffs with their "job" of telling their own authentic stories, and to be proactive with regional and national press. We wanted others to understand they were "real people" and "real families" with concerns and lives like others. There were kitchen table scenes and family gatherings—pictures that spoke universally and built empathy and were the stories and images that appeared repeatedly over the years.

This complemented an overall legal and communications strategy of growing support from (then) unlikely sources like businesses, Republicans, and clergy, with the latter being particularly important given the vocal opposition of the Catholic Church and, initially, much of the black clergy.

My GLAD colleague Jennifer Levi argued our case to the trial court while I was on parenting leave in 2002. The Commonwealth's stance disappointed us. They saw a request for a "radical change" in a "controversial area" that they argued belonged solely with the legislature and not the courts. And they clung to the notion that the central purpose of marriage was procreation, while asserting "real and statistically significant differences" in child outcomes between same-sex and different-sex parents—a position not only disrespectful of gay and lesbian parents but also at odds with the Commonwealth's consistent efforts to remove sexual orientation as a factor in parenting considerations.

By May 2002, the Superior Court ruled for the Commonwealth, disclaiming a role for the courts. We appealed and headed to the SJC. There, in early November 2002, we filed our opening brief. Since the attorney general would clearly urge the Court to stay its hand, we emphasized how passing the buck to the legislature would have consequences for our plaintiffs and other couples. We emphasized how personally profound the stakes were, beginning: "The right to marry the person you love and with whom you share your life is one of the most fundamental of all of our human and civil rights. The desire to marry is grounded in the intangibles of love, an enduring commitment, and a shared journey through life." Given all that marriage is and represents, we continued, denying marriage is "a denial of the equal citizenship of gay and lesbian people who make their homes in communities across this Commonwealth" and "enshrines a second-class status" upon "the plaintiffs, their families, and their children." At the end, we focused on the profound harms at stake since "[i]t takes no citation to acknowledge that the opportunity to marry one's soulmate, one's closest confidante and steadfast ally, easily ranks as one of the most joyous experiences in many people's lives."

And we responded to all of the State's arguments, particularly the notion that regulating heterosexual procreation was the *raison d'être* for civil marriage, amplifying our arguments from Vermont and also urging the leading authors of a well-respected family law treatise to weigh in with a friend-of-the-court brief.

This amicus brief, along with ten others, brought to the court voices of experts that many probably assumed would not support same-sex couples' claims. The names of some of the largest firms in the state were on briefs submitted by state constitutional law scholars, social workers and pediatricians, civil rights groups, historians of marriage and the family, and both the Massachusetts and Boston Bar Associations. This was an unprecedented show of support for marriage at the time.

On the morning of oral arguments, March 4, 2003, I went to the courthouse library to gather my thoughts and give myself a pep talk: "We're right, we're right, we're right." Before the Court, I began: "The Plaintiffs stand before this court seeking nothing more and nothing less than the same respect under our laws and Constitution as all other people enjoy; the same liberty to marry the person of their choice and the same equal right to marry on the same terms applied to other people. Love and commitment infuses the relationships of these seven couples. They are locked out of a precious right." The questions came steadily: Why should the Court decide this rather than the legislature? Why should the court do something virtually no other Court had done? When could this issue reach the voters? Had the Vermont situation "set off a firestorm through the rest of the country?" Was the ban on interracial couples marrying deeply rooted in our country's history? Why wouldn't polygamy be next?

Counsel for the Commonwealth received tough questioning as well. Arguing for "fostering the link between procreation and marriage" and "childrearing," some members of the Court pushed back: where same-sex couples can adopt and the legislature has left that decision in place, is that "not powerful recognition that childrearing of single-sex couples is optimal for certain children?" Doesn't a procreation-only purpose for marriage eliminate other aspects of the right?

We waited over eight months for a decision. During that time, legal marriage for same-sex couples came to Canada; and, with its historic opinion in *Lawrence v. Texas*, the Supreme Court overturned any remaining sodomy laws, firmly establishing that gay people, too, share in the promises of liberty and equality under the U.S. Constitution. These developments did not speak to the Massachusetts Constitution, but they could only help.

On November 18, 2003, as I was driving to a legislative hearing in Connecticut, I learned that the opinion would be issued that morning. I drove to Boston and walked to the courthouse to secure a copy of a very thick ruling. The first paragraph of the majority opinion, authored by Chief Justice Margaret H. Marshall, broke an historic barrier:

> Marriage is a vital social institution. The exclusive commitment of two individuals to each other nurtures love and mutual support; it brings stability to our society. For those who marry, and for their children, marriage provides an abundance of legal, financial, and social benefits. In return, it imposes weighty legal, financial, and social obligations. . . . The Massachusetts Constitution affirms the dignity and equality of all individuals. It forbids the creation of second-class citizens. . . . [The Commonwealth] has failed to identify any constitutionally adequate reason for denying civil marriage to same-sex couples.

I was ecstatic. In a 4–3 ruling relying on both equality and liberty principles, the Court held that there was no rational basis for denying marriage. The government's justifications were either illegitimate, unrelated to the exclusion of same-sex couples, or contradicted by Massachusetts law, and so the "deep and scarring hardship" effectuated by the marriage exclusion must end.

The Court described marriage as a "wholly secular institution" and a "licensing law" in which the State defines the entry and exit terms as well as the rights and duties of marriage, thereby "order[ing] society" and "encouraging stable relationships over transient ones." The Court also acknowledged the personal and cultural significance of marriage: "Civil marriage is at once a deeply personal commitment to another human being and a highly public celebration of the ideals of mutuality, companionship, intimacy, fidelity, and family." Connected to and expressing our human yearnings for "security, safe haven, and connection . . . the decision whether and whom to marry is among life's momentous acts of self-definition." Likewise important, with marriage comes "enormous" legal protections "touching nearly every aspect of life and death" that also assists children by easing their parents' way to family-based protections. Noting that "civil marriage has long been termed a 'civil right,'" the Court reasoned that "the right to marry means little if it does not include the right to marry the person of one's choice," subject to "appropriate government restrictions." The history of exclusion "must yield to a more fully developed understanding of the invidious quality of the discrimination."

Applying the individual liberty and equality safeguards of the Massachusetts Constitution to the common law exclusion of same-sex couples from marriage, the Court spoke of "'freedom from' unwarranted government intrusion" into the "decision of whether and whom to marry, how to express sexual intimacy, and whether and how to establish a family," as well as "'freedom to' partake in benefits created by the State for the common good."

I ran back to the office to share hugs with colleagues and our clients. But the reveling was cut short. An Associated Press story, out to wire outlets all over the world, reported that we had won civil unions, not marriage. Reporters were clamoring for an answer. The battle to undo *Goodridge* had begun.

At our mobbed press conference with our plaintiffs on stage, I was firm. We won marriage. Yes, there was a six-month delay before the ruling would go into effect, but that was to allow the legislature to make any necessary changes to laws and for local officials to get their staff and paperwork in order.

That very day, we learned the attorney general's office had advised the press about our supposedly limited victory. They insisted there was ambiguity because the Court had ordered the "protections, benefits, and obligations" of marriage but not marriage licensing. As if on cue, the State Senate crafted a civil union bill with an explicit marriage ban and on December 11, 2003, requested an advisory opinion from the SJC about whether the bill complied with *Goodridge*. Opinion polls in the State showed about 50 percent support, but storm clouds were gathering with the apocalyptic rhetoric and President George W. Bush's support of a federal marriage amendment. National support for marriage dipped to a low of 29 percent.

On the advisory opinion question, GLAD briefed as an "interested party," arguing that "a civil union regime cannot satisfy" the Constitution. "Nothing but marriage can provide the same protections, benefits, and obligations as marriage." Amici flocked to our position. Civil rights groups had seen this kind of retrenchment before. Harvard Law School Professor Laurence Tribe authored a brief on behalf of our nation's leading constitutional law professors.

On February 3, 2004, with the same 4–3 split of justices, the *Opinions of the Justices to the Senate* stated unequivocally: "For no rational reason the marriage laws of the Commonwealth discriminate against a defined class; no amount of tinkering with language will eradicate that stain. . . . The bill maintains an unconstitutional, inferior, and discriminatory status for same-sex couples" and thus does not comply with *Goodridge*.

Principle, and the Court, held firm in delivering the first judicial blow to civil unions as separate and unequal. But the dissents were pointed, even accusing the *Goodridge* majority of "judicial activism." Word had it that legislative leadership was furious. And the senate president was set to convene a joint session of the legislature to consider the pending marriage amendment in a week's time.

Each long day until May 17, 2004, when *Goodridge* would go into effect, brought new challenges, new firsts, and a few triumphs as well. After the advisory opinion, we faced more lawsuits. Several claimed the Court lacked power or authority to hear or decide *Goodridge* and that implementation of the ruling should be stayed until the constitutional amendment process had run its course. A federal lawsuit filed by the antigay legal group Liberty Counsel claimed that the Court had violated the constitutional guarantee of a republican form of government. Their request to halt the upcoming issuance of marriage licenses moved to the First Circuit and then the full Supreme Court before being denied on Friday evening, May 14, 2004.

The state constitutional convention proceedings commenced on February 11, 2004, and continued on February 12 and for two days in March. Those of us on the ground in Massachusetts realized we needed a strong coalition that would bring local groups and partners together in a full-fledged campaign operation to fight the amendment, one that would and could be financially sustained by individual donors as well as national organizations like the National Gay and Lesbian Task Force (NGLTF) and the Human Rights Campaign (HRC). Marty Rouse and Jeremy Pittman, now both at HRC, took the (thankless) leadership spots at MassEquality to coordinate and oversee lobbying, field, political, communications, and fundraising in conjunction with a strong advisory committee of all participants.

Before the first day of convention proceedings, MassEquality organized a candlelight vigil on a bitterly cold night where thousands of people came to say they agreed with the SJC. I challenged the crowd to keep this "beacon of equality burning bright" throughout our land. Legislators were barraged with constituent contacts, and the statehouse teemed with people. Large, boisterous demonstrations were not only outside the building; our supporters sang patriotic songs at top volume to encourage our legislative allies in the House chamber. The *Goodridge* plaintiffs staged their own event after Governor Romney penned an opinion editorial to the *Wall Street Journal* comparing *Goodridge* to *Dred Scott* and calling for a federal amendment to overrule it. The plaintiffs, whose repeated requests for a meeting had been ignored, converged on his office to ask for a face-to-face meeting. After the media showed up, we were admitted to the governor's office. He was stone cold. I explained why we were there and turned it over to the plaintiffs, several of whom talked about why marriage mattered to them and how it would protect their families. "I didn't know you had families," the governor replied, with no feeling. When each had finished, he said, "Is that all?" and began to usher us out. Before he could, Julie Goodridge confronted him, asking what she should say to the couple's eight-year-old daughter about why the governor didn't want them to marry. "I don't care what you tell her," he replied. "Tell her whatever you've been telling her for the last eight years."

These examples are among the many personal acts of courage that framed and infused the debate. Thousands of people reached out to their legislators, something new to many of them, and others spoke up in their daily lives at work, in church, at the dinner table, and with neighbors. We cannot overstate the importance of these personal conversations, and owe much of our progress to those many people, gay and non-gay, who we will never fully account for but who made our humanity their struggle.

Supportive legislators, along with GLAD, the Massachusetts Freedom to Marry Coalition, the newly formed MassEquality, and lobbying groups like the ACLU and local LGBT advocate Arline Isaacson, worked together day and night with a deeply involved grassroots coalition to keep us alive to fight another day and defeat the passage of an amendment. Despite predictions that our opponents would quickly pass a marriage ban, we were alive at the end of the first day of proceedings. Two proposed amendments had been defeated: both had banned marriage, but one created civil unions, and the other made civil unions possible. On the second day, our allies defeated a stand-alone marriage ban without mention of civil unions. Our opponents were flummoxed and furious. The lessons of Vermont were coming to fruition: it's difficult to take away basic rights for a group of people once they have been vindicated. In the February and March sessions alike, we were buoyed by unexpected support from Republicans, from socially conservative Democrats, and from our allies all explaining why they would not vote to take away our rights.

After two more days of wrangling in March, most of the people on our team and most of our legislative allies went along with a strategic approach of banning marriage but creating civil unions in the Constitution. The thinking was that this measure would be unpalatable to both opponents for the second vote in the next legislative session and that we would win more opposition to a marriage ban after we had marriage in effect. It wasn't pretty, but without a doubt, it kept us alive to fight another day.

More obstacles and surprises arose. In light of the convention's approval of an amendment proposal, Governor Romney announced he would go to Court and seek to stay the issuance of marriage licenses. The attorney general refused to represent the governor in that venture.

At long last, the stay expired. On the evening of May 16, the City of Cambridge hosted a celebration and opened its doors at midnight to begin issuing licenses. Ten thousand people were there to revel and support the city staff and couples.

All of the plaintiff couples planned to marry on May 17. They wanted to, and national and international media were clamoring for those very first marriages. We had assigned GLAD or volunteer lawyers to all of them. I was with the three Boston couples. We had an amazing ally in Boston Mayor Tom Menino. He wanted that morning to be special, to have it recorded as an historic moment in the city's history. The plaintiffs were welcomed and applauded at City Hall, both at the clerk's window where they had once been denied licenses, and also when he introduced them to the media phalanx recording the historic marriage licensing. We went out to City Hall Plaza for the short walk to the courthouse so we could seek a waiver of the three-day waiting period. There were happy people everywhere, police sharpshooters on the roof, and a lonely band of protestors from Kansas. Two officers, Javier Pagan and Wanda Treadway, cleared a path through the mob and escorted us to the courthouse. I made the motion to Judge Nancy Gould, arguing that each of the plaintiffs had waited long enough. The judge granted all of the motions.

For all of the anticipation and political wrangling that had preceded May 17, the real drama of that day was the outpouring of pure joy. It was mind boggling when we heard the clergy member state: "By the power vested in me by the Commonwealth of Massachusetts, I pronounce you legally married." The joy, the reality, the justice in it, changed everything. People had expected *something* to happen once same-sex couples started marrying. But no one could fully appreciate the continued outpourings of joy that changed the debate forever more. That joy sustained us for the long road ahead, including the targeting of pro-marriage legislators in the 2004 elections and the looming next phase of the constitutional amendment fight.

Connecticut

Connecticut was a strong choice for an early win on marriage under a state constitution. It had so much going for it, including the General Assembly's long track record in addressing discrimination against gay and lesbian people. It decriminalized sodomy in 1969. In 1991, it made Connecticut the third state in the country to pass a comprehensive law prohibiting sexual orientation discrimination. It had also added enhanced penalties for antigay and other hate crimes.

But we were still assessing the state Supreme Court. There was a robust state constitutional jurisprudence, and the Court had issued an excellent sex discrimination opinion as well as a nuanced opinion holding that the military could not recruit at the state law school because of its antigay policies. However, the Court had refused to allow second-parent adoption in 1999.

The advocacy group Love Makes a Family (LMF), the coalition led by Anne Stanback, took on marriage in 2000. LMF and GLAD worked closely together, with LMF working on public education goals and GLAD on legal analysis. (See page 92 on LMF's work.)

Knowing the Massachusetts SJC would rule at some point in 2003, we met with local attorney Maureen Murphy and agreed to reach out to attorneys Kenneth Bartschi and Karen Dowd at Horton, Shields & Knox, a well-regarded appellate firm, to work with us on an anticipated marriage case. Between LMF and Maureen, we located terrific plaintiffs throughout the state: Beth Kerrigan and Jody Mock; Janet Peck and Carol Conklin; Geraldine and Suzanne Artis; Jeffrey Busch and Stephen Davis; J.E. Martin and Denise Howard; John Anderson and Garrett Stack; Barbara and Robin Levine-Ritterman; and Damaris Navarro and Gloria Searson. We assumed the State would carry most of the defense, but we wanted the plaintiffs to seek marriage licenses in a town where local officials would rely on their own counsel rather than that of the anti-marriage groups we assumed would offer assistance.

We filed *Kerrigan v. Commissioner of Pub. Health* on August 24, 2004, naming the State and Town of Madison as defendants. We were waylaid when the Family Institute of Connecticut (FIC) and a group of objecting clerks sought to intervene as defendants and then appealed a ruling against them.

In the next legislative session, while the case was still pending in the trial court, the Judiciary Committee of the state legislature heard extensive testimony in support of and in opposition to a marriage bill. To our surprise—and in the face of strenuous objections from Love Makes a Family—the committee replaced the text of the marriage bill with a civil union measure replicating the language crafted in Vermont, which then passed and was signed by the governor. Passage of the law made Connecticut the second in the nation to adopt a civil union regime, and the first to do so without the judiciary requiring the legislature to act.

Again, something to celebrate but also a dilemma. Even generally supportive individuals told us that the legislature had addressed our concerns and that the case was dead. When we were able to brief our case in late summer 2005, we focused on the same types of arguments supporting the freedom to marry we had made before; and we used the civil unions law *offensively* as "the strongest possible legislative declaration that same-sex couples and their children need and are worthy of the very same rights and protections as married different-sex couples." Yet same-sex couples were kept separate from marriage by a deeply felt sense that marriage was inherently an institution between a man and a woman. The State used the civil union law offensively, too, as evidence of adequate protections, political clout, and political progress that undercut our claims.

In July 2006, the Superior Court judge ruled for the State. She declined to conduct a constitutional analysis because there was "no harm" in light of the civil union law's creation of "an identical set of legal rights in Connecticut for same-sex couples and opposite-sex couples." In her view, the legislature's enactment of the civil union law was "courageous and historic," and their view as to how to remedy social problems merited deference from the judiciary. To our arguments about the imposition of an inferior status, the judge wrote: "Although the plaintiffs may feel themselves to be relegated to a second-class status, there is nothing in the text of the Connecticut statutes that can be read to place the plaintiffs there."

Our appeal to the Connecticut Supreme Court was looking inauspicious— particularly in the national context, where we had just faced stinging court losses on marriage from the highest courts of New York, Washington, New Jersey, Maryland, Arkansas, and Indiana—even as New Jersey provided a path to civil unions. We did not want to be drawn into attacking civil unions, but we wanted to highlight the impact of the continued exclusion from marriage even if, as some thought, the civil union law was an acceptable compromise. With LMF, we agreed our key messages would focus on the value of marriage as compared to civil unions. As we boiled it down, we came to this:

> Marriage is more than a collection of legal rights. It tells the community that two people love each other and are a family. Since everyone understands and respects this, it makes being married something important, something we aspire to, and something that protects us in daily life as well as times of crisis. Civil unions provide some legal benefits, but they do not come close to these other, broader protections of marriage.

Our November 2006 brief to the Court led off with a "Statement of Facts" echoing these themes in the words of the plaintiffs themselves. Jody Mock, for example, said a civil union would devalue her relationship with Elizabeth Kerrigan because it "would only call to everyone's attention that we can't really get 'married.'"

We focused the Court on the key questions: is it permissible to deny the right to marry to these plaintiffs, with all the prestige, dignity, respect, familiarity, and personal meaning it provides? "Is it constitutional for the legislature to deny marriage where it also creates only for gay people a separate legal system, with a different name, and deems them eligible for all state-based rights available to married spouses?"

Even with the "remarkable" journey of Connecticut lawmakers in "confronting and eliminating aspects of discrimination against lesbian and gay people," we believed they had "failed with respect to ending marriage discrimination." Other than a reflexive sense of difference, what could justify "an explicit policy judgment that same-sex couples deserve and squarely fit within the existing structure of marriage" but then relegation to a different status? We expanded briefing on the history of discrimination and oppression visited on gay people in our culture over the last century, which allowed us to show that the different types of relationship recognition maintained the gay–straight distinction that our nation was beginning to leave behind.

GLAD attorney Ben Klein argued for the plaintiffs in May 2007. Unexpectedly, he received a bevy of questions about heightened scrutiny for sexual orientation classifications. We had been making this argument consistently, but had been urged by some attorneys to "save our pages" since this argument had no chance. We stayed the course because it was correct and because it reflected the real bias at the root of the marriage exclusion.

The Court ruled in favor of the plaintiffs in October 2008—with a thrilling result. It became the second state high court after California to identify sexual orientation as a "quasi-suspect" or "suspect" classification, thus triggering closer review. (California's June 2008 ruling in the *Marriage Cases* was the first.) Its insightful and nuanced legal and political analysis particularly compared the respective legal journeys of women and LGB people. The heightened scrutiny analysis also allowed the Court to contextualize the civil union law in a landscape of historical and ongoing discrimination against gay people and same-sex couples. The harm was evident, it ruled, when read "in light of the pernicious history of discrimination faced by gay men and lesbians," and because marriage is "an institution of transcendent historical, cultural, and social significance, whereas [civil union] is not." Even though designed to benefit same-sex couples, its "intended effect" was to "treat politically unpopular or historically disfavored minorities differently from persons in the majority."

To great joy in another state, Connecticut couples began obtaining marriage licenses in November. After the devastating defeat in the Prop 8 vote in California in that same month, Connecticut was another beacon of hope. It also showed the country that marriage equality could be implemented without political or popular opposition. And to its credit, in 2009, the General Assembly passed the first statute codifying a favorable marriage ruling, and providing a system for transitioning the State to marriage.

MY MOTHERS SAID "I DO"

ANNIE GOODRIDGE

Annie Goodridge is the daughter of Julie and Hillary Goodridge, plaintiffs in Goodridge v. Department of Public Health.

On the morning of November 18, 2003, I was eight years old and in third grade gym class when my mothers heard the news. They, along with six other plaintiff couples, had legally won the right to marry as same-sex partners in Massachusetts. They quickly left home and drove the short distance to my school. Running into the gym, they screamed, "We won! We won!" and I ran over to them, overjoyed. After they left, I went right back to gym class, but I couldn't wipe the smile off my face.

While I knew then that the case, *Goodridge v. Department of Public Health*, was a monumental triumph, I wouldn't see the impact of the case until later on in life.

On my parents' wedding day, May 17, 2004, my mothers and I walked from Boston City Hall to the courthouse, marriage license in hand. Flanked by police, we were completely surrounded by well-wishers and protesters, both for and against the freedom to marry. I had never felt so supported and scared in my life. With us was our lawyer, Mary Bonauto, whose bravery and genius was one of the main reasons the case was won. Later that day, I saw my two mothers say, "I do," in front of family, friends and international media. We drove away in our blue VW beetle, metal cans bouncing behind us, with "Just Married" written on our car. It was one of the happiest days of my life.

When I was a freshman in high school, I was sitting in the library one day when friends showed me a picture of my mothers in our U.S. History textbook. I immediately burst into tears. It had never occurred to me that

Annie Goodridge with her mothers on May 17, 2004. Photo Credit: PHOTOGRAPHY BY SUSAN R. SYMONDS, USED WITH PERMISSION.

one day, children would learn about us in American History class, let alone have that "one day" be just seven years later.

On June 26, 2013, section 3 of the Defense of Marriage Act was struck down in *United States v. Windsor*, allowing state-sanctioned marriages to receive federal benefits. This was an historic decision. Before our case was filed, it felt as if same-sex couples would never win the right to marry in our liberal state; later we were nervous that no other state would follow our lead. But little by little, freedom was sweeping the country.

By the tenth anniversary of equal marriage in Massachusetts, nineteen states had officially legalized the right of same-sex couples to marry. I, along with my family, watched that number grow at an almost exponential rate.

On the morning of June 26, 2015, I was at work. My mom called the office, and my co-workers brought me to the phone. When I heard the news that marriage was now legal for same-sex couples throughout the entire country, tears erupted from my body. I have never been more proud of my family and of our amazing lawyer, Mary Bonauto. While the country still has a long way to go in terms of equality, I'm glad to see it's taking an important step toward progress. And I couldn't be happier to have been a part of it.

LOVE MAKES A FAMILY IN CONNECTICUT

ANNE STANBACK

──ⴲ──

Anne Stanback is director of strategic partnerships for the Equality Federation. She was founding executive director of Love Makes a Family.

In October 2008, same-sex couples won the right to marry in Connecticut. Less than a month later, California voters passed Proposition 8, temporarily ending marriages in that state. Connecticut advocates had made clear that civil unions, which our legislature passed in 2005, were no substitute for marriage, and we had now won that argument in court. At one of the most devastating moments in our movement, Connecticut's win became critical. It helped create a bulwark against the tide of opposition.

Love Makes a Family formed as an informal coalition in January 1999 to lobby for a second-parent adoption bill. Our state Supreme Court had just handed down an unfavorable decision on the issue. After a narrow defeat in the first year, the bill allowing second-parent adoptions passed in the spring of 2000. The coalition shifted focus to the next obvious issue impacting same-sex couples and their families: marriage.

Many of us were surprised at how supportive legislators were of second-parent adoption. That support, however, did not extend to marriage. This was true of some of our coalition partners as well. Nevertheless, as we officially incorporated Love Makes a Family as the state marriage campaign, we maintained a strong core of groups who served on the founding governing board: ACLU of

Connecticut, the Connecticut Coalition for LGBT Civil Rights, the Connecticut Women's Education and Legal Fund, the Connecticut Conference of the United Church of Christ, and Connecticut PFLAG.

Love Makes a Family benefited from activist leaders who had developed strong personal relationships working together for decades on a range of issues, and collaborative working relationships among regional, state, and national LGBT players, most importantly Gay & Lesbian Advocates & Defenders (GLAD). We also benefited from the work of several key individuals involved with the marriage fight from the very beginning.

Betty Gallo, with whom many of us had worked closely in the late 1980s and early 1990s on the passage of the state's non-discrimination law and later on the second-parent adoption bill, served as the organization's lobbyist and a key strategist. Maureen Murphy, an attorney in private practice who had provided legal assistance to more same-sex couples than any other lawyer in the state, was an early advisor and leader in the organization. Senator Andrew McDonald and Representative Michael Lawlor, whose positions as co-chairs of the Judiciary Committee were essential to the campaign's success, were critical champions in the legislature.

By the time same-sex couples began marrying in 2008, Love Makes a Family was recognized as one of the largest and most effective grassroots networks in Connecticut. But in the fall of 2000, the organization had no budget and operated out of my kitchen.

We kicked off our public campaign with an educational forum in January 2001, inviting three of the best known marriage advocates in the movement—Mary Bonauto from GLAD; Beth Robinson, the attorney who helped win the marriage victory in Vermont; and Evan Wolfson, then at Lambda Legal. Less than two months later, the legislature's Judiciary Committee held an initial hearing on legal recognition of same-sex couples, giving the issue its first widespread visibility.

In 2002, legislators introduced Connecticut's first marriage bill. Although we did not have the votes to move the bill to the full legislature—and had not expected to—we won a small, but symbolically significant victory: the passage of a law granting same-sex couples certain rights related to serious illness and death. Equally important was a section that required the legislature's Judiciary Committee to hold special hearings in the fall on the public policy implications of marriage and civil union for same-sex couples.

During this time, before Massachusetts opened marriage to same-sex couples, the idea of making it legal for same-sex couples to marry was still an unfamiliar concept, even to many longtime allies of the LGBT community. We had learned in passing the sexual orientation non-discrimination bill in 1991 that the most effective way to change hearts and minds was to tell our personal stories. For many, this involved coming out for the first time.

Love Makes a Family became known for this storytelling. We spent a great deal of time identifying and training effective messengers to tell their stories in emotionally compelling ways. We carefully planned legislative hearings and spent countless hours identifying and connecting local couples and clergy with reporters in their regions so that legislators and others would realize that loving, committed same-sex couples were their neighbors and constituents. We recognized that the issue was new to many, so we met people where they were, understanding that the more they engaged in the marriage conversation, the more accepting they would become.

Love Makes a Family also became well known for our legislative advocacy. In 2002, two years before the launch of Facebook and long before the digital component of marriage campaigns became a centerpiece, Love Makes a Family became one of the first Connecticut advocacy groups to effectively use online activism to reach legislators, a revolutionary lobbying tool in those early years.

It was our use of in-district house meetings, however, that legislators most often credited with making them rethink their positions. As with public hearings, we carefully choreographed these gatherings. We learned early on that it was most effective to hold them in constituents' homes, to invite a diverse mix of gay and straight constituents to attend, and to provide all of them with proper training. The tone was non-confrontational and always personal. Over eight years, nothing proved more powerful in changing the hearts and minds of elected officials.

The 2003 legislative session ended in June without any action on the raised marriage bill. Days later, marriage history was made in Ontario, Canada, when the first same-sex couples in North America legally wed. Less than two weeks later, the U.S. Supreme Court ruled in *Lawrence v. Texas* that state sodomy laws were unconstitutional. Then in November, the Supreme Judicial Court of Massachusetts ruled in *Goodridge v. Department of Public Health* that there was no legal basis under the state Constitution to prohibit same-sex couples from marrying (see page 82). As elsewhere around the country, these events, particularly the ruling in *Goodridge*, had a significant impact on the work and strategies of Love Makes a Family.

More national funding, including a grant from the newly formed Civil Marriage Collaborative, began to flow to state marriage work, which allowed Love Makes a Family to hire two early staff members, Adam Nicholson and Carol Buckheit. We made the strategic decision not to introduce a bill in the 2004 legislative session while we waited on the response to the temporarily stayed *Go-*

odridge decision. We also had begun conversations with GLAD and knew that a Connecticut lawsuit would be filed later in the year.

As we celebrated with the couples marrying in Massachusetts, we continued to organize new constituencies, like Latino/as for Marriage Equality, to grow our base with a new door-to-door canvassing program, to ramp up our electoral work in support of pro-equality candidates, and to highlight key stories, which now included stories of Connecticut couples who had married across the state line in Massachusetts.

In August, GLAD filed *Kerrigan & Mock v. CT Department of Public Health*. Thus began a two-track effort to win the freedom to marry in Connecticut.

In the fall of 2004, legislative leadership began conversations about moving a civil union bill in the 2005 session. GLAD, Freedom to Marry, and other national LGBT leaders urged Love Makes a Family not to support a civil union compromise. They argued, and many of us agreed, that for the state's marriage organization to champion a second-class marital status when full marriage equality was now legal next door in Massachusetts was a strategic misstep. The strong momentum we had worked so hard to create would likely disappear. The new lawsuit could be hurt. Our PAC would be in a position of supporting anti-gay candidates who supported civil union as a way to avoid marriage. And the national landscape—with one civil union state and one marriage state—would tilt in favor of second-class status.

After a great deal of discussion and heated debate, Love Makes a Family's board voted to oppose a civil union compromise and to fight hard in the 2005 legislative session for full marriage equality. Our decision to forgo certain protections in order to stand firmly for equality was grueling—tears were shed, and many relationships were strained.

Our board's vote was not unanimous. Our lobbyist and legislative champions strongly disagreed with the decision; many of our members and donors were angry. It was the most challenging time in our organization's existence.

It quickly became clear that few people in 2005 could articulate the difference between civil unions and marriage. If civil unions conferred all of the rights and protections of marriage—and if we had no access to federal rights anyway, given the federal Defense of Marriage Act—what was the real difference between the two?

For obvious reasons, we had begun by focusing on the critical legal protections that marriage conferred and the harm caused from the denial of access to those protections. However, with civil unions created to replicate all of those state rights, it became clear that our messaging and framing needed to change. While the rights were unquestionably important, that was not why heterosexual couples got married, and it wasn't why same-sex couples wanted to marry.

During that legislative session, we worked hard to focus our messaging on love, family, and commitment. We argued that we should not be forced to choose between having access to critical legal protections and having equality under the law. In the end, the language of the marriage bill was stripped out, and civil union language was inserted. Making another difficult decision, Love Makes a Family chose not to stand in the way of the enactment of significant legal protections for couples and families, and withdrew its opposition to the bill. But we continued to urge legislators to speak out on the floor in support of marriage.

The bill passed with strong bipartisan support. It was signed by Republican Governor Jodi Rell that same day and went into effect on October 1, 2005. Because Love Makes a Family had drawn a line in the sand, we forced others to see that civil unions and marriage were not the same. Powerful new endorsements were issued by groups like the AFL-CIO, and first-time pro-marriage editorials were written. One of the most memorable lines later came from the state's newspaper of record, *The Hartford Courant*. In an editorial urging Connecticut's legislature to move past civil unions to full marriage equality, and quoting one of the capital city's most famous residents, the *Courant* wrote: "Mark Twain famously illustrated the difference between the right word and the almost right word by using as an example the difference between 'lightning' and 'lightning bug.' . . . What's in a word? For those who want to marry and can't, plenty."

Love Makes a Family's challenge as an organization shifted once the civil union bill passed. We needed to walk the fine line of acknowledging the excitement of the new law (and, in fact, leading the celebrations), while at the same time keeping up the drumbeat that same-sex couples deserved the equality, respect, and dignity that only come with marriage. We also knew we had a responsibility to educate our community about civil unions. At forums around the state, we educated people about the nuts and bolts and the dos and don'ts for entering into a civil union.

In June 2006, a lower court ruled against the plaintiffs in the *Kerrigan* case, maintaining that civil unions provided adequate rights. GLAD appealed, and the case soon moved to the state Supreme Court.

Love Makes a Family saw 2007 as our best chance to win in the legislature and perhaps the last chance before the Supreme Court ruled in *Kerrigan*. Our base of support had skyrocketed, our faith network and allied coalitions had grown and diversified, and, perhaps most importantly, a Quinnipiac Poll reported for the first time that a majority of Connecticut voters supported marriage over civil unions. After an emotional twelve-hour public hearing, the Judiciary Committee voted to support a marriage bill, but, heartbreakingly, no bill emerged from the full General Assembly, and no victory was to come from the legislature that year.

Attention shifted to the Supreme Court. The *Kerrigan* decision was unusually late. For months we began each week reviewing and revising our Decision Day action plan. We worked alongside GLAD, doing all we could to make the case for marriage equality in the court of public opinion, which we hoped would have an impact on the Court.

Early on Friday morning, October 10, I packed my car for an annual Cape Cod weekend with friends. As I loaded my bike on the rack, my phone rang. It was Ben Klein, GLAD's lead attorney on the *Kerrigan* case. He had just gotten word that the decision would be handed down later that morning.

By 9 a.m., Carol Buckheit (Love Makes a Family associate director) and I were in the office, ticking off the items on our Decision Day plan. We made scores of calls to key people, from elected officials to state and national partners; from our rally speakers to the downtown Hartford hotel that had been on alert since the summer. Robo calls we had recorded months before began to run, and multiple versions of prepared emails and website text were readied to go live for the moment the outcome of the decision was revealed.

At 11 a.m., we had a crowd of people piled into the office, watching on several computer screens for the decision to appear. I had an excited but slightly sick feeling. I knew that with a win nearly a decade of work would be ending. But I also recognized that with a loss the campaign would return to the legislature the next year.

At a few minutes after the hour, cheers went up and champagne corks popped as we saw the result of GLAD's brilliant lawyering and years of public education and grassroots organizing on the screen. Writing for the Court majority, Justice Richard Palmer stated, "Although marriage and civil unions do embody the same legal rights under our law, they are by no means equal. As we have explained, the former is an institution of transcendent historical, cultural, and social significance, whereas the latter most surely is not."

Media calls began immediately. Students showed up to make signs in our parking lot. Staff and volunteers made phone calls throughout the day. And on a glorious fall afternoon, a huge crowd gathered near the steps of the state capitol building and cheered speaker after speaker on into the evening. The celebration moved to the Hartford Hilton where we relished the sweet victory just a little longer.

The work to get from decision day to marriage day with its celebrations and media frenzy was enormous. As a result of unfortunate timing, we had one more fight to get through before we could breathe a sigh of relief that the freedom to marry was secure.

Connecticut's state Constitution requires that every twenty years a question appear on the ballot asking voters if there should be a constitutional convention.

To our dismay, we had realized that the twenty-year mark was going to land in the same year that the state Supreme Court would likely rule. We knew our opponents would use this as a last ditch measure to subvert a marriage win. We never dreamed the vote would take place a mere eight days before the first marriages occurred.

Love Makes a Family alerted key partners and took the lead in creating a ballot committee to defeat the calling of a constitutional convention. Polling showed that the two issues we had all worried might be problematic—marriage equality and abortion rights—were two that actually polled well with Connecticut voters. Rather than needing to downplay them, we were able to highlight those issues to our advantage.

Across the country, LGBT people were focused on the 2008 election and the candidacy of Barack Obama and Proposition 8. In Connecticut we had the added concern of this little-noticed ballot question with the potential of stripping us of a victory that so many had fought for over so many years.

On election night, after nearly a year of organizing, we celebrated the decisive 59.4 percent to 40 percent defeat of the ballot question. With the thrill of electing our nation's first African American president and the heartbreak of the loss in California, we knew that the defeat of our constitutional convention question would not be news. But for Love Makes a Family, GLAD, and our many partners, the election results allowed us to fully savor the first marriages that began a little more than a week later.

On April 22, 2009, the Connecticut legislature codified the language of the *Kerrigan* decision into statute, including the automatic conversion of civil unions into marriages by October 2010. Governor Rell signed the bill into law the following day. With that, Love Makes a Family's mission was complete.

Surprising some of our supporters, we made the decision to close our doors, transitioning out of business at the end of 2009. This was not a decision we made lightly. We had begun one-on-one interviews and focus groups with members and key stakeholders shortly after the *Kerrigan* decision in October 2008. We did not believe success on marriage meant the work for the LGBT community was over. We recognized that we had strong partners in the state and beyond doing the remaining work. However, after nearly a decade of intensive effort, we needed to step back.

As part of our transition, we encouraged our members to support partner organizations and gave grants to smaller groups. We split the bulk of our remaining assets between GLAD for their DOMA repeal work and the Connecticut Women's Education and Legal Fund to hire an organizer for the coalition effort to add gender identity and expression to the state non-discrimination laws. We archived our materials at Yale University, and with hundreds of supporters and activists from across the state, we threw a party to celebrate the success we had achieved.

At the end of 2009, Love Makes a Family closed its doors, leaving only our PAC operating in order to protect legislators facing backlash from their vote to codify the *Kerrigan* decision. No such backlash ever materialized.

THE PLAN TO WIN MARRIAGE

MATT COLES

———⌗———

Matt Coles is the ACLU's deputy legal director and director of its Center for Equality.

There actually was a plan to win marriage. It was an eleven-and-a-half page, single-spaced strategic outline, endorsed by all the major groups working on LGBT rights. And while it had at least two crucial ideas (though the one for which it was most often cited may not have been one of them), the fact that it existed when it did may have been almost as important as those ideas.

Whether you are enthusiastic about marriage for same-sex couples, think it's a sad switch from the sexual revolution to patriarchy, or are mostly indifferent about it, marriage was, for LGBT rights across the board, the right issue at the right moment (more about that later). To understand the importance of the plan—"Winning Marriage" was its name—it's important to understand the time, not so long ago in years but ages ago in culture, when it was hatched.

It Was the Worst of Times

The work that led to the plan started in the winter of 2005. In hindsight today, marriage for same-sex couples looks like an inevitability. It didn't look inevitable then. To many it looked impossible.

There were three major waves in the campaign to get recognition of LGBT relationships. The first began in 1970 with *Baker v. Nelson,* an ACLU-sponsored case that asked the courts in Minnesota to rule that it was unconstitutional to deny marriage to same-sex couples. The courts declined, and the U.S. Supreme Court refused to take up the case, saying there was no real federal constitutional issue. *Baker* was followed by four or five other cases, all with the same result. The last, *Adams v. Howerton,* an immigration case, came to a bad end at the federal court of appeals in San Francisco in 1982.

In the meantime, the second wave began. This was an effort, aimed at first at local governments and private companies, to get health and pension benefits for same-sex partners of employees. Maybe more important, the local "domestic partnership" laws created local "registries" designed more than anything else to get couples visibility. Throughout the 1980s and early 1990s, that work slowly racked up wins in city councils and local legislatures across the country, and made strong inroads in the film, tech, and banking industries.

While the domestic partnership wave was underway, a new attempt to get marriage for same-sex couples began, with lawsuits first in Hawai'i in 1990 and then in Alaska in 1995. The first results were encouraging. Although the Hawai'i case was thrown out by the first level court, the Hawai'i Supreme Court ruled in 1993, in what subsequently became Lambda Legal's case, that keeping same-sex couples from marriage was sex discrimination. Therefore it was unconstitutional under the state constitution, unless the state could provide a most compelling need to do it. In 1996, a lower court judge ruled that the state hadn't come close, and so the state appealed. In 1998, a lower court judge in Alaska ruled that the state's ban on marriage for same-sex couples was likely unconstitutional under Alaska's Constitution. (The cases were brought under state constitutions because a win could not be appealed to the U.S. Supreme Court, and the U.S. Court did not look very hospitable at the time.)

Two Disasters

Then disaster struck. In 1998, the voters in Hawai'i changed the state Constitution and took away the state high court's power to decide the case and gave the issue to the legislature, which had no desire to make a change. The voters in Alaska went further by putting an absolute ban on marriage for same-sex couples into the state Constitution.

Congress had gotten into the act two years earlier, with the so-called Defense of Marriage Act (DOMA). It said that even if a state did allow a same-sex couple to marry, the federal government would not follow its usual practice of recognizing the marriage. It went on to say that states would also have the power to refuse to recognize marriages of same-sex couples from other states. DOMA passed overwhelmingly, and President Bill Clinton signed it into law. In the years following, over two-thirds of states passed "mini DOMAs," most of them declaring both that the state would not marry same-sex couples and would not recognize the marriages of same-sex couples from other states.

The picture wasn't entirely grim. In 1999, the Vermont Supreme Court ruled that, while the state didn't necessarily have to allow same-sex couples to marry, it had to give them the same legal rights and benefits it gave married couples. That victory won by Gay & Lesbian Advocates & Defenders (GLAD) led to the historic Vermont Civil Union Law. And in 2003, the Massachusetts Supreme Court, in another case brought by GLAD, finally broke the ice. The Massachusetts Constitution, the Court ruled, did not allow the state to refuse to marry same-sex couples (see page 82).

Then the real disaster hit with the elections in November 2004. It started when President George W. Bush, running for reelection, announced he would support an amendment to the United States Constitution to ban marriage for same-sex couples. Not quite five weeks before the 2004 national election, the House of Representatives voted on a resolution to put the ban into the Constitution. The resolution failed, not because it couldn't get a majority. The vote was 236 to 187 in favor, but that was 84 short of the two-thirds it needed to pass. Not quite five weeks later, in thirteen states voters passed state constitutional amendments taking away the power of state courts and state legislatures to allow marriage for same-sex couples. Nine of those amendments also banned civil unions, and one banned *any* form of recognition for same-sex relationships.

The State of the (Marriage) Union

So this was the state of the marriage union in early 2005. On one hand, one state allowed same-sex couples to marry, and three others had either full civil union or some other strong recognition system. On the other hand, the President of the United States supported amending the federal Constitution to ban marriage for same-sex couples. He had just been reelected by a comfortable margin. In the House of Representatives, about 54 percent of the members supported the amendment to ban marriage, and close to half the Senate did. Maybe worse, with thirteen states passing new state constitutional bans on marriage, there were now seventeen states with bans in their state constitutions, many also banning civil unions. And it was already clear that more bans would be proposed and would likely pass in 2005 and 2006. Ominously, there was a serious effort underway to end marriage in Massachusetts, and it had succeeded in the first of two votes in the state's constitutional convention.

It wasn't a pretty picture. There were several ways to read the trends, but the momentum at both the state and federal level didn't necessarily seem to be going our way.

Deep Divisions and an Unexpected Experiment

The creation of Winning Marriage started at a meeting in Denver, called by the Gill Foundation, a major supporter of the LGBT movement. The funders were trying to get some of the groups working on LGBT rights to work better together. But partway through the meeting, attention turned to the hardest issue facing the organizations: Was it possible to buck the tide of constitutional amendments and start making progress again on marriage? If so, how could it be done?

The groups at the meeting, all of the major groups working on LGBT rights, took an unusual step. They agreed to form a working group to examine the question. The group would, for the most part, not consist of executive directors or CEOs, and no group would automatically have a seat at the table. That decision was critically important. Executive directors have responsibilities to act in the best interests of the organizations they head. That doesn't always make for the kind of tough thinking and forthright expression the problem needed.

The working group would instead be made up of experienced legal and political operatives. However, nothing the group produced would be binding on the organizations unless they approved it. The groups left it to a couple of their members to pick the members of the working group and get it to work. (The membership of the group is listed at the end of this chapter.)

Once it got going, the experiment moved with breathtaking speed. The meeting organizer circulated an email proposing one path to marriage twelve days before the meeting. The group met for two days in Jersey City on May 10 and 11, 2005. The group's scribe circulated the first draft of a "concept paper" summarizing the working group's conclusions six days later. The final was ready and went to the organizations on May 24. After comments, it was finished on June 20.

However, when the working group met, it was far from clear that any paper or plan for going forward would emerge. Its membership reflected the deep divisions in the organized LGBT community on where to go on marriage. Some folks felt the cases had unleashed a backlash so powerful that the only thing to do was play defense on state and federal anti-marriage amendments and slowly try to shift the focus of the work and the public discussion to laws against discrimination.

Other folks felt that relationships were the right issue—and in any case one that could not be avoided. They thought the movement should focus on equal legal rights, through things like civil unions and domestic partnerships, at least in the near term. Most of the folks in these two groups didn't see how marriage could be won in any foreseeable time frame.

A third group felt the focus of the work should be mainly, perhaps exclusively, on marriage. To these folks, lack of focus and resources were the main reasons the movement was getting beat up. To many in this group, working on civil unions or domestic partnerships was a trap that would only delay marriage, perhaps for many years.

Two Lightbulb Moments

One of the things with which the plan was credited was articulating a clear pathway to winning marriage. The effort should start in the courts, the plan said, in the states where the odds of winning were strongest and the odds of a repeal by initiative smallest. As we began to win, we should move to the next most-likely-to-win states. At the same time, we should start trying to get marriage through state legislatures, since legislatures arguably have more social and political legitimacy. Ultimately, when there was a sufficient "critical mass" of states with marriage, the movement would turn toward the federal government, either Congress or more likely the Courts, to bring recalcitrant states into line.

Though some later saw this pathway as a crucial step forward, it was hardly new. It essentially followed the script the public interest legal groups (though not many private lawyers) had been following for almost ten years. It had been articulated in the pre-meeting email from the organizer, and several of the legal groups had put the ideas in writing even earlier.

All of which is not to say the pathway part of the plan was unimportant. Not all of the political groups were aware of the ideas it embodied. And for everyone, having it written plainly and ultimately agreed to by all the groups was helpful. It was a modest step forward.

But while it seemed fairly easy to get agreement—that this was the way it would be done if it was done—it was still hardly clear to many that it could be done at all.

That a plan ever emerged was in large part the result of two lightbulb moments in the conversation. Near the middle of the first day, those who thought marriage could not be done in any foreseeable time frame and those who thought it could be done fairly quickly with the right effort were deadlocked in a fairly unproductive conversation about who had the best crystal ball. Then, someone (no one remembers exactly)—who did not think marriage was possible in any foreseeable time frame—suggested a thought experiment. He proposed that we have a conversation about what we thought we could accomplish in particular states over the next ten to fifteen years. As that conversation progressed, the group refined the issue and asked itself what proved to be a crucial question: could we, in ten to fifteen years, get ten states with marriage, ten will full civil union, ten with some less comprehensive form of relationship recognition like limited domestic partnerships, and twenty with either non-discrimination laws or significant cultural climate change?

To make the thought experiment work, the group decided to name the states its members thought could go into each bucket. While the discussion was lively, there was surprisingly little disagreement about what could be done where. And in an hour or so, there was virtual unanimity on the question posed by the experiment: we could get ten/ten/ten/twenty in ten to fifteen.

The second lightbulb came on within moments as everyone in the room began to see the problem a bit differently than they had before. Because if we could get to ten/ten/ten/twenty, virtually everyone agreed, we could start stepping states up, moving from civil union to marriage, from domestic partnership to civil union, and from there to marriage. In that way, we could get to that essential critical mass, maybe in five more years, or maybe in ten.

A Strategy Emerges

And at that moment, there was a strategy for winning marriage. For those who didn't think marriage was realistic, there was now a practical path. Those who thought we should only concentrate on marriage now saw that civil unions, domestic partnerships, and other work might help, not hinder, the road to marriage.

To be sure, one of the virtues of the ten/ten/ten/twenty scheme was that it allowed everyone to agree while harboring private reservations. Those who thought marriage itself should be the focus of most work were happy that everyone agreed that, in some places, we should go straight to marriage. It was possible, some of them thought, that, with a few marriage wins, civil union and lesser steps would quickly be discarded. Some of those who thought marriage was still too big an ask for most of the country thought it was possible that as we got more civil unions and domestic partnerships work would focus there until the country was better prepared.

But that cheat—if that's what it was—may have been the real virtue of this part of the plan. It knitted together all the strategic approaches into one that valued the principle work of each. So it allowed each group to do the work it thought most important, all the while respecting the fact that the different approaches could, when coordinated, be a critical part of getting the ultimate goal. The plan grasped a critical but not-much-noticed principle of effective politics. Success often depends not on complete agreement but on a shared goal and strategic compromises—maybe accommodations is a better way to put it—that allow people to follow their own best judgment and work alongside others following different approaches.

The Big Picture, the Public, and the Process

The paper made three other contributions to the battle for marriage. First, it opened with a big-picture analysis that made a couple of crucial points. The LGBT movement as a whole, the paper said, despite the recent bad patch, was making tremendous progress. More important, marriage was now an unavoidable battleground, as the opposition was already using it to try to stop progress on all LGBT issues—for example, by banning adoption by those who weren't married or who couldn't marry. The movement needed the perspective, and a better understanding of the stakes.

Second, in three short paragraphs the paper argued that winning the public would be essential. Changing the rules, the paper said, is not enough. For change in a republic to be real and to endure, the people have to accept it. That insight, not universally shared at the time, was central to the ultimate winning strategy.

The paper also said that it was essential that a real campaign for marriage, with national communications and field capacities, needed to be created. That didn't happen for over five years, when Freedom to Marry was created by Evan Wolfson.

But something else did happen right away. The meetings forged a bond of deep trust among the participants. And that bond seemed to go back with them to their organizations. With greater trust and with everyone more or less working off the same page, the organizations did work better together. Still, not everyone always agreed on what was the best next move, but the days when moves would be made without consultation and conversation were over.

There's a popular myth creeping into the history of LGBT rights and marriage that the leadership of the LGBT movement embraced marriage and forced the community to support the decision. But the Hawai'i case, the Alaska case, and many others were cases rejected by leadership and embraced instead by some parts of the grassroots community. In any case, the plan was right about this: once anti-LGBT forces seized on marriage as a way to roll back the LGBT movement on relationships and everything else, there was no choice but to fight for marriage.

It is clear to me now, as one who didn't see it at first, that marriage was the right issue to take to America. For years, the primary underlying justification for all forms of antigay discrimination was essentially this: gay people are psychologically flawed, incapable of deep, lasting emotional commitment. The fight over marriage let us shine a bright light on that lie. Once it was clear to America that it was a lie, that in our capacity for love and commitment we are no different, neither better nor worse than the rest of humanity, the rationale for treating gay people differently began its long-deserved collapse.

After Note

The unexpected Jersey City crew included:

Michael Adams, then at Lambda Legal, now at SAGE

Mary L. Bonauto, GLAD

Toni Broaddus, then at The Equality Federation, now at Compassion & Choices

Rea Carey, NGLTF, now but not then its executive director

Seth Kilbourn, then at HRC, now at Open House

Shannon Minter, NCLR

Alexander Robinson, then at NBJC, now at Creative Alliance

Roey Thorpe, then at Basic Rights Oregon, now at Equality Federation

Evan Wolfson, Freedom to Marry

Ellen Carton, Facilitator

Matt Coles, ACLU, group convener and scribe

MOVEMENT + STRATEGY + CAMPAIGN: THE FREEDOM TO MARRY WINNING COMBINATION

Evan Wolfson, with Adam Polaski

⸺◦◦◦⸺

Evan Wolfson is founder and president of Freedom to Marry.

Adam Polaski is deputy digital director for Freedom to Marry.

When people talk about social justice advances that move the country forward, they tend to emphasize either the moment they themselves tuned in or the thrill of the final showdown—the bill passed through Congress, the order signed by the president, the Supreme Court triumph. When we romanticize these moments, however, and hold them up as the turning point, the victory—as powerful and consequential as they are—we risk losing sight of the decades of struggle, sacrifice, and successes that lay the groundwork for the days like June 26, 2015, when, as President Obama put it, "that slow, steady effort is rewarded with justice that arrives like a thunderbolt."

The Supreme Court majority opinion affirming the freedom to marry nationwide underscored that the long-sought, hard-fought victory came, not just through litigation, but through the sustained application of all of the methodologies of social change, including public education, legislation, direct action, electoral work, and fundraising, alongside litigation. Going out of his way to recognize the history of struggle and debate, honor our movement, and acknowledge the millions of Americans to whom this victory belongs, Justice Anthony Kennedy wrote:

There may be an initial inclination in these cases to proceed with caution—to await further legislation, litigation, and debate. The respondents warn there has been insufficient democratic discourse before deciding an issue so basic as the definition of marriage. In its ruling on the cases now before this Court, the majority opinion for the Court of Appeals made a cogent argument that it would be appropriate for the respondents' States to await further public discussion and political measures before licensing same-sex marriages. . . .

Yet there has been far more deliberation than this argument acknowledges. There have been referenda, legislative debates, and grassroots campaigns, as well as countless studies, papers, books, and other popular and scholarly writings. There has been extensive litigation in state and federal courts. Judicial opinions addressing the issue have been informed by the contentions of parties and counsel, which, in turn, reflect the more general, societal discussion of same-sex marriage and its meaning that has occurred over the past decades. As more than 100 amici make clear in their filings, many of the central institutions in American life—state and local governments, the military, large and small businesses, labor unions, religious organizations, law enforcement, civic groups, professional organizations, and universities—have devoted substantial attention to the question. This has led to an enhanced understanding of the issue—an understanding reflected in the arguments now presented for resolution as a matter of constitutional law. . . .

The dynamic of our constitutional system is that individuals need not await legislative action before asserting a fundamental right.

The Supreme Court opinion thus reflects the work that hundreds of organizations and hundreds of thousands of people have devoted over many decades to this fight for dignity, equality, and the fundamental freedom to marry for all.

Out of the nearly seventy rulings in favor of the freedom to marry in the two years leading up to the final Supreme Court triumph, one of the most stirring passages came in the case—litigated by Salt Lake City law firm Magleby & Greenwood, with assistance from the National Center for Lesbian Rights—that brought the freedom to marry to ruby-red Utah. Kicking off a cascade of federal court wins following the Supreme Court's 2013 decision in *United States v. Windsor*—the successful challenge to the so-called Defense of Marriage Act argued by Roberta Kaplan of Paul, Weiss—Judge Robert Shelby of the federal district court in Utah wrote: "It is not the Constitution that has changed, but the knowledge of what it means to be gay or lesbian."

Much like Justice Kennedy's recounting of the history and context for the final victory, that passage encapsulated our movement's strategy. The Constitution was always there for LGBT people to invoke, but we had to help the country— the decision-makers, the judges, the American people—understand who we are and be willing to apply the command of the Constitution equally to us. By pursuing a rounded strategy of climate creation and engagement in the court of public opinion, not just the courts of law—using the powerful engine of change that the marriage conversation provided—the freedom to marry movement not only ended marriage discrimination but also dramatically changed societal attitudes about gay and lesbian people.

Winning, Losing, and Regrouping

It was clear early on that the freedom to marry could not be won by one organization, one individual, one court case, one methodology, or one battle alone. If it were possible to win simply with the correct legal argument and the weight of the Constitution on our side, then same-sex couples would have won in the first wave of litigation back in the 1970s, which included a case that reached the U.S. Supreme Court and was summarily dismissed. At that time, however, the country was not ready; gay and lesbian people did not win any of those early cases.

Same-sex couples weathered many challenges in these early years—including the AIDS cataclysm, which shattered the societal silence about gay people's lives. But in the midst of the intense discrimination and life-and-death horrors of that dark period, the second wave of marriage litigation—most importantly the pivotal 1993 ruling of the Hawai'i Supreme Court and the 1996 marriage win in the Hawai'i trial court, the world's first-ever ruling in favor of the freedom to marry for same-sex couples—wrought a tectonic shift, making marriage seem attainable and launching the ongoing global freedom to marry movement.

Ultimately, the Hawai'i trial court marriage win was appealed, and before the Hawai'i Supreme Court could even hear the case, antigay forces interfered by stampeding voters into passing a constitutional amendment that snatched away the freedom to marry shimmering within reach. At the same time, antigay activists and members of Congress pushed through the so-called Defense of Marriage Act (DOMA), a preemptive measure declaring that even if Hawai'i or other states began issuing marriage licenses to same-sex couples, these marriages would be denied all federal respect.

Shortly after these significant blows, the Vermont legislature fell short of delivering the freedom to marry, despite an order from the Vermont Supreme Court—in a case brought by local attorneys, Beth Robinson and Susan Murray, and Gay & Lesbian Advocates & Defenders (GLAD)—that held that the state must afford same-sex couples the same "benefits and protections" that different-sex couples could access through marriage. The legislature invented a new, lesser family status, "civil union," granting legal recognition to gay and lesbian couples in Vermont—but not marriage. It was a step forward, but it was not what we wanted.

After the destructive impact of DOMA, the stifling of same-sex couples' claims by the constitutional amendment in Hawai'i, and the unsatisfying establishment of civil unions in Vermont, movement leaders were again challenged to step up to what it would take to get the job done.

Thinking Anew, Developing the Strategy

In 2000, the Evelyn & Walter Haas Jr. Fund approached me while I was still at Lambda Legal, seeking advice. The foundation was interested in investing in gay rights as a key part of their broader focus on civil rights and wanted to know: how could they best support work to advance rights and dignity for gay people?

I told Haas that what I had written in 1983 as a law student, what I had worked on throughout the 1990s as counsel in the Hawai'i marriage case and leader of the National Freedom to Marry Coalition, remained, for me, the right answer: create a campaign to win the freedom to marry.

Haas Jr. made a big bet—and a $2.5 million challenge-grant—in 2001 to help start Freedom to Marry, the campaign to win marriage nationwide. This investment from a highly respected non-gay foundation was then the largest foundation award in the history of the gay movement. In Lincoln's words, it was time to "think anew" about what it would take to win—to engage in intense conversations with the brightest minds in our movement about the path forward.

I argued that the LGBT movement needed a smart, central campaign singularly committed to the goal of winning marriage for same-sex couples nationwide. That central campaign should have three elements. First, it should have a shared strategy, one that each group and person could contribute their piece to, a strategy that a central campaign would drive with relentless energy and laser-sharp focus. Second, it needed vehicles that put wins on the board and created momentum. And third, it needed concrete action steps—ways that Americans could get involved and be a part of the campaign. This approach— what I would later describe as the Ladder of Clarity[1]—would inform what the campaign wanted to do, what it could encourage others to do, and the bench-marks by which the campaign could be held accountable and work to fill in the gaps.

Developing a strategy was essential. I worked closely with longtime friends and colleagues such as GLAD's Mary Bonauto, the ACLU's Matt Coles, Lambda Legal's Jon Davidson, and several others, and spent time consulting with key organizations and funders. Drawing lessons from other civil rights movements and looking at the trajectory of our own marriage battles, it was clear what it would take to win marriage nationwide. One of the country's two national ac-tors, Congress or the U.S. Supreme Court—most likely the Court—would need to bring the country to national resolution. To create the climate necessary for this national resolution, the Freedom to Marry campaign needed to build a critical mass of states where same-sex couples could marry and a critical mass of public support.

Building the critical mass of states and support would empower and impel the Supreme Court or Congress to act. Working backward from the endgame of the Supreme Court case or the congressional action, we mapped out the middle game and the initial action. We didn't have to win every state, but we had to win enough states. We didn't have to persuade every American, but we had to per-suade enough Americans.

This strategy—later branded by Freedom to Marry as the "Roadmap to Victory"—became and remained the national strategy our movement and its organizations pursued, as leaders in other national and state groups pursued complementary work in furtherance of the shared goal. To drive this strategy with a blend of leadership and partnership, catalyzing and collaborating, Freedom to Marry became the central campaign entity. The Roadmap to Victory national strategy, the movement it rallied behind it, and the collective work of all the activists and organizations delivered our fifteen-year climb in success, building from 27 percent support among the American people (in 1993) to 63 percent (in 2015), from zero states to all of the states.

Freedom to Marry: The Central Campaign

I had long envisioned a campaign that would embody "the four multis."

The campaign needed to be multi-year, waking up every day, staying consis-tent through the ups and downs, devoted to propelling work along the Roadmap. It needed to be multi-state, able to engage the various battles on several fronts so as to build the critical mass needed (rather than see a Hawai'i then a Vermont show promise and get picked off by the opponents). It needed to be multi-partner, since no one organization or person would be able to single-handedly achieve this enormous a victory. Finally, it needed to operate multi-methodologically, meaning that it must combine litigation, legislation, public education, storytelling, direct action, fundraising, and, eventually, even electoral work.

Freedom to Marry was created to catalyze this sustained, central campaign—and eventually, as cobbling together the work of varied organizations failed to get us fully where we needed, morphed to become the central campaign itself.

From the get-go, we got buy-in by pledging that Freedom to Marry would be singularly focused on driving toward marriage nationwide, would be collaborative and generous, would fill in the gaps rather than duplicating or displacing what others were doing, and would go out of business when victory was at last in hand, even when many of the other partner organizations doing important pieces of the work would remain. Freedom to Marry could not do *everything* alone, but it could bring together all of the vital players by providing the space, mechanism, coordination, and the call to a common strategy—and then drive that strategy toward its bold and ambitious goal, sticking with it through defeats as well as progress.

The Unique, Critical Contributions of a National Campaign

For many of the early years, the Freedom to Marry campaign that is now seen as a model for effective organizing was often more of a muddle. In 2003, the movement celebrated a watershed win in Massachusetts as GLAD won the first state court ruling to fully deliver the freedom to marry, and groups and funders came together alongside MassEquality to successfully defend the victory in the legislature. The marriage movement then scrambled to regain footing when slammed by the Karl Rove-engineered loss of thirteen anti-marriage ballot measures in 2004. Disagreement on the best approach to winning marriage in a second state, and even whether to keep fighting, marked a low point in the struggle.

While there were wonderfully talented and dedicated people working across the country, they and their organizations were too often hampered by insufficient funding and lack of infrastructure. State efforts sometimes seemed to start from scratch and, lacking the means to communicate or meet together, too often repeated the mistakes of the past. Freedom to Marry focused on bringing together the pieces that many supplied into a more powerful whole, filling the gaps with crucial programming and keeping a growing—and eventually increasingly successful—movement's eyes on the prize.

Being able to stick through the tough periods—2004 and the ballot defeats, 2006 and a wave of court losses, 2008 and the blow of Prop 8 in California—was one of Freedom to Marry's key functions. Freedom to Marry rallied the effort forward even when it was difficult, brainstorming new ways to push ahead and staying the course when others wavered.

It is clear now, looking back, that the central campaign model helped the marriage movement take enormous strides forward, synthesizing many different parts and elements to create a stronger whole. When critical needs arose, Freedom to Marry, as a truly integrated, focused campaign, stepped in to elevate the marriage movement to something greater than the sum of its parts. Freedom to Marry worked to capitalize on every opportunity, applying every best practice we learned, avoiding previous mistakes, and driving forward tenaciously toward victory nationwide. Here are just a few examples of the successes delivered by this central capacity:

Making the Case: Message and Message Delivery

In 2009, all signs indicated that our movement needed to focus on bringing more people into the freedom to marry cause. Polling in the mid-2000s consistently illustrated that the country was divided into thirds: One third strongly supported equality for gay people, while another third was entirely opposed to gay people in general. But the middle third represented the reachable—but not yet reached—middle. These Americans genuinely wrestled with the question of marriage for same-sex couples, but the marriage movement had not yet provided them with what they needed to open their hearts and change their minds.

Following the painful passage of Prop 8 in 2008, Freedom to Marry sought to understand how we could persuade that "moveable middle." Freedom to Marry joined with colleague organizations such as Third Way, as well as funders, in a Marriage Research Consortium, pooling data and analysis to crack the code on how to pick up the next swath and solidify and grow the majority for marriage. Through this vehicle, we ensured that resources were spent toward solving common, movement-wide challenges, without duplication.

Step by step, we discovered that in talking so much about the legal consequences of being denied the freedom to marry, the movement was not connecting with a significant slice of people; they agreed in theory that gay people should not be treated unfairly, but they did not understand the importance of marriage to gay people. The result was a second messaging track that specifically discussed the love and commitment same-sex couples share.

Armed with these findings, Freedom to Marry initiated a national public education framework through which we deployed new messaging points, personal stories, cutting-edge research, and guidance for reshaping the national conversation and pushing forward to ultimately achieve supermajority support for the freedom to marry. Freedom to Marry's focus, not just on message but on message delivery, helped other movement organizations and ultimately political leaders and the media shift the emphasis on how the movement made the case for marriage, and succeeded in moving a large share of the not-yet-reached to join our majority.

Winning the Country: Creating a Majority for Marriage

In addition to the right messages, we needed powerful messengers to help build an emotionally resonate national narrative. We needed to show throughout the country that supporting the freedom to marry was consistent with a wide range of American values.

Enlisting and deploying third-party validators, Freedom to Marry launched several organizing programs to elevate voices within and from different constituencies and demographics. Through our Young Conservatives for the Freedom to Marry program, young Republicans and right-leaning Americans could bring their message of why marriage matters to conservative media outlets and political tables, invoking conservative values of limited government and individual freedom. Likewise, when the Hollywood-backed American Foundation for Equal Rights—created by Rob Reiner, Chad Griffin, and Dustin Lance Black—brought former George W. Bush Solicitor General Ted Olson together with attorney David Boies to mount a legal challenge to Prop 8, it helped amplify the conservative case and outreach.

Through Southerners for the Freedom to Marry, Freedom to Marry worked closely with partners on the ground (including the Campaign for Southern Equality and key state groups) to highlight the growing support for marriage in southern states and focus on compelling stories of Southerners, with many explaining how their support came because of their strong commitment to faith, not in spite of it. *Familia es Familia*, a robust partnership of dozens of Latino civil rights organizations, made the case for support specifically within and from Latino communities. The five hundred-strong Mayors for the Freedom to Marry campaign allowed mayors from American cities large and small to speak out with and on behalf of same-sex couples, while giving advocates in states we couldn't win outright an organizing target—their local mayors—that could get local business and media attention and be integrated into Freedom to Marry's national narrative.

Shifting the Political Center of Gravity: Winning States

For many years, LGBT communities saw our opponents aggressively work against our efforts to win the freedom to marry and push constitutional amendments that shut out same-sex couples from marriage. The LGBT movement lost at the ballot more than thirty times, fell short of achieving winning votes in several state legislatures, and failed to create the climate necessary for many state judges to rule in favor of the freedom to marry.

Too often in these battles, national and state leaders seemed to be in a "Groundhog Day" of starting each fight anew; cobbling together resources, strategy, and logistical components with each fight; and sometimes reinventing the wheel or duplicating efforts.

By 2011, with a path to victory emerging in the New York legislature under the leadership of new governor Andrew Cuomo, Freedom to Marry worked with Empire State Pride Agenda and others to pioneer a model for quickly and efficiently establishing a state campaign coalition, singularly focused on winning marriage in the state. Key state and national partners came together for a joint campaign, New Yorkers United for Marriage, binding the organizations to a shared set of goals, a daily work-plan, and joint staffing. Freedom to Marry then replicated that New York model in several more states in 2011 and 2012, in memoranda-of-understanding "X United for Marriage" campaigns. The campaigns were set up on a pay-to-play model, enforcing partnership and effective implementation of strategy, while Freedom to Marry staff provided hands-on consultation and technical support in research, message development, fieldwork, political and legal coordination, communications support, and digital expertise.

Freedom to Marry strove to ensure that the various players in these states built up a truly integrated campaign. For example, regional communications operatives—often funded by Freedom to Marry and embedded in state groups—worked closely with our state coalitions to develop content our central communications and digital teams could push out through classic and digital media both in the states and as part of our national narrative. Throughout we worked closely with various organizations, such as the American Civil Liberties Union, American Unity Fund, the Human Rights Campaign, Lambda Legal, and state groups, who were often part of the campaigns built in the various states.

Fueling the Machine

The Freedom to Marry national campaign also functioned as a funding engine, working hard to raise money for our own operations and campaign as well as for the various players and partners involved. Freedom to Marry ensured that no matter whose watering can the funding went through, the field received the water it needed. Money was strategically invested where it was needed most, based on the expertise of campaign operatives who together had decades of experience in winning ballot, legislative, and public education campaigns on marriage. Since donors were able to invest through a national campaign—and had credible vetting and benchmarks from Freedom to Marry—they knew their dollars would be spent strategically in key battlegrounds that fit within the national strategy.

In addition to attracting large individual donors and directing the funding where it needed to go, I worked with key early funders to create the Civil Marriage Collaborative and thereby funnel more foundation money into state-based work pursuant to the central strategy. The CMC set of funders stayed with the cause even during the tough, early times, and at crucial junctures were also instrumental in bringing together key grant makers and LGBT movement leaders to rearticulate and recommit to the goal of winning marriage nationwide.

Showing the Courts That America Is Ready and It's Time for National Resolution

As the U.S. Supreme Court considered arguments on the freedom to marry in 2015, it was vital that the national conversation, supported through earned media stories and social buzz, mirrored the momentum in the courts. While our hand-in-glove legal partners—ACLU, GLAD, Lambda Legal, and NCLR, along with local attorneys and firms—made the case in the courtroom, the role of the national campaign was to help make the case in the court of public opinion. Like Freedom to Marry, the litigators were telling the stories of the harms suffered by same-sex couples and their families in the courtroom and in the media. Freedom to Marry also sought out new and unexpected messengers and journey stories, driving national attention in the press and online to this powerful evidence of change.[2] Our goal was to drive home a consistent drumbeat on two narrative themes conveying reassurance and urgency: America is ready for the freedom to marry, and every day that the Supreme Court waits to end this discrimination in the remaining states, loving couples and their families face real injury, indignity, and injustice.

Likewise, Freedom to Marry worked with our legal colleagues to assemble a telling array of amici briefs to the U.S. Supreme Court, featuring thousands of voices of faith leaders, mayors, businesses, and leading figures in the Republican party. Our TV ads in key states highlighted support from unexpected messengers and provided air cover that spurred and supported the ground-game of personal conversations and persuasion. And through a communications machine that built on the work of colleagues and reached new heights online and through a wide range of local and national media, Freedom to Marry amplified stories of same-sex couples who could not wait one more day for the freedom to marry, and of the people who supported them.

As the marriage cases finally came before the U.S. Supreme Court in 2015, the momentum was irrefutable, and it was clear that, as Freedom to Marry's last ad before the ruling put it, "It's time." The national campaign had united all the pieces, all the conversations, all the battles, all the advances, all the cases, all the years into a movement. The country, as reflected in the courts, was ready.

Celebrating the Long-Sought Victory

Shortly after the Supreme Court's marriage ruling, Freedom to Marry hosted a victory celebration (and going-out-of-business party), attended by Vice President Joe Biden and gathering more than a thousand movement colleagues and supporters, including many of the leaders and frontline fighters from key organizations, cases, and battles. In my remarks and toast that night, I summed up what it had taken to achieve the transformation and triumph of winning marriage nationwide:

> It's fitting that we gather today to celebrate our victory, America's victory, because it was on this day, July 9, in 1868, that We the People ratified the Fourteenth Amendment to the Constitution. The Fourteenth Amendment recommitted our country to liberty and equality for all and gave us the legal structure within which we won the freedom to marry two weeks ago.
>
> We won under the Constitution, but, of course, the Constitution didn't just fulfill its own promise. It took a movement to do that— so much work, sacrifice, trust, and hope to achieve this transformation, this triumph. No one person alone, no one organization alone, no one state, no one case, no one methodology of social change, no one battle, no one decade alone did this. It took a whole movement to bring us to this victory. It took the Constitution, and it took the country, millions of conversations and many battles that changed hearts and minds and helped the American people rise to fairness.
>
> At the same time, this movement was not just a random series of episodes. There was a strategy that we stuck with, and there was a campaign built to drive that strategy and foster and leverage the movement. That campaign was Freedom to Marry.

It was the combination of all of that—America's promise, a decades-long movement, a successful strategy, a tenacious campaign—that delivered, through slow and steady successes and stumbles, as the President said, justice, that came like a thunderbolt.

That is, indeed, something to celebrate.

LOSING FORWARD: THE MARRIAGE CASE IN NEW YORK

JEFFREY S. TRACHTMAN

——— ✿✿✿ ———

Jeffrey S. Trachtman is a partner in the New York law firm Kramer Levin Naftalis & Frankel LLP.

After the exhilaration of the *Goodridge* decision in Massachusetts—but before same-sex couples could actually marry anywhere in the United States—events in early 2004 sparked a wave of new marriage equality cases. Several of these, including *Hernandez v. Robles* in New York and parallel cases in Maryland and Washington, ended in crushing defeat. The arc of the moral universe may bend toward justice, but it doesn't sweep forward with an unwavering trajectory. While these losses brought the movement to a low point by 2006, each bent the arc slightly by highlighting the flimsy justifications for harming the millions of families excluded from civil marriage. Each loss spurred statewide grassroots organizing and political action that led, within a few years, to enactment of marriage equality. These victories in turn built momentum that yielded complete victory less than a decade after the initial losses.

Hernandez was the most thrilling case in my first thirty years as a litigator, though it was a heartbreaking defeat and the only case that made me cry twice. Our role in *Hernandez* resulted from a combination of longstanding commitment and lucky timing. My firm, Kramer Levin Naftalis & Frankel LLP, already had a gay rights pedigree: our founder, Arthur Kramer, was the brother of playwright and activist Larry Kramer. As chronicled in Larry's play and film, *The Normal*

Heart, we incorporated Gay Men's Health Crisis in 1981 and had represented it for decades. We had an attorney on Lambda Legal's board in the 1980s and had collaborated on several pro bono projects, including filing amicus briefs in *Dale v. Boy Scouts* and *Lawrence v. Texas* when many major firms still hesitated to work openly for LGBT equality.

We were honored and semi-thrilled when Lambda Legal asked us, around the time *Lawrence* was decided in 2003, to be their pro bono "New York marriage firm." I say "semi-" because New York, with its majority-Republican high court, was not expected to be an early battleground state. Marriage cases were being filed in carefully selected state courts in a strategy to build momentum while avoiding the risk of a premature nationwide ruling. Our work therefore initially focused on researching the legal and procedural complexities of winning recognition within New York for lawful marriages entered into elsewhere—at that point, mainly Canada. This led to co-counseling with Lambda Legal on several cases, including *Lewis v. New York State Dept. of Social Services* and *Godfrey v. Spano*, that helped establish recognition and ensure, among other things, that Edie Windsor was treated as a surviving spouse under New York law with standing to challenge DOMA.

Then, early in 2004, everything changed. Bold mayors on opposite coasts, Gavin Newsom in San Francisco and Jason West in New Paltz, New York, began performing wedding ceremonies for same-sex couples—part of broader protests that sprung up following the *Goodridge* decision. The buzz around these events created the likelihood that unrepresented couples (or self-represented lawyers) would begin suing for the right to marry. These plaintiffs soon materialized. Concerned that cases litigated without adequate resources could make bad law, the major LGBT rights groups decided they couldn't wait any longer and prepared to bring their own litigation.

Things moved especially fast in New York. Early in the week of March 1, 2004 (just days after the New Paltz marriages began), I reached out to Lambda Legal to see if they were contemplating an affirmative suit. In a series of increasingly urgent return calls, they asked us to begin preparing a complaint and to get the firm's clearance to file it by that Friday. To their credit, Managing Partner Paul Pearlman and other firm leaders gave a quick thumbs-up—recognizing that marriage equality was mainstream civil rights and that our role would be respected and even celebrated by certain clients with major diversity commitments and gay in-house counsel.

Overnight, Kramer Levin went from perennial amicus bridesmaid to impact litigation bride: co-counsel in a major civil rights case. Nearly two dozen attorneys from all corners of the firm volunteered for the exciting new project—including, for the first time, a significant number of non-gay attorneys other than me. Although I had been involved with LGBT rights issues for years (driven by a blend of liberal zeal and sublimation), 2004 marked a turning point in the wider embrace of these issues as mainstream civil rights. The core litigation team ultimately consisted of me and Norman Simon, a senior associate who had externed at Lambda Legal and is now a partner and recent co-chair of Empire State Pride Agenda. It also included junior associates Aaron Frankel, Michael Sternhell, Tricia Seith, and countless others who assisted with research.

Our march down the aisle was accompanied by a change in co-counsel. David Buckel, the director of Lambda Legal's marriage project and our partner on the recognition work, shifted his focus to the New Jersey marriage litigation. The New York helm was assumed by Susan Sommer, a brilliant refugee from law firm practice who is now Lambda Legal's director of constitutional litigation. It didn't take long to see the warmth and wicked sense of humor beneath Susan's no-nonsense exterior and, I hope, for her to appreciate the seriousness behind my relentless wisecracks.

Wasting no time, we filed a complaint that Friday, March 5, in New York County Supreme Court (the main state trial court in Manhattan) with just two plaintiffs: Daniel Hernandez and Nevin Cohen, a long-term committed couple who happened to be friends of a Lambda Legal staffer. Later in March, we filed an amended complaint including four additional couples: Lauren Abrams and Donna Freeman-Tweed, Michael Elsasser and Douglas Robinson, Mary Jo Kennedy and Jo-Ann Shain, and Daniel Reyes and Curtis Woolbright. Collectively, these five couples gave a sense of the ethnic and socioeconomic diversity of New York's gay families. The plaintiffs were a true New York mix that included a doctor, an environmental planner, a nonprofit activist, a technology manager, a midwife, and an actor/waiter. Three of the five couples were interracial, and three were raising biological or adoptive children.

Around the same time, James Esseks of the ACLU and Roberta ("Robbie") Kaplan of the Paul, Weiss law firm filed *Samuels v. Department of Public Health* in Albany on behalf of a similarly diverse array of plaintiff couples. This case became the chief companion for *Hernandez* in the Court of Appeals. Although there was inevitably a bit of logistical and public relations jockeying (and we had to coordinate with several other cases), the main teams worked together in remarkable harmony, laying the groundwork for friendships and future collaborations.

Over the next several months, the Kramer Levin team (working with Susan and Alphonso David, another Lambda Legal attorney who later served as counsel to Governor Andrew Cuomo) dug into several projects to build our case, highlighting themes that would resonate years later in *Windsor* and *Obergefell*.

First, we interviewed each of the clients and crafted detailed affidavits to bring our plaintiff families to life for the courts that would be reviewing our record. Aaron, Michael, and Tricia led this effort with great sensitivity and skill. Next, we catalogued the myriad legal benefits and protections that society provides to married couples in areas like medical decision making, parental rights, support obligations, and property inheritance. We also demonstrated—in part through our clients' own words—the dignitary harm caused by exclusion from civil marriage: the inherent message of second-class citizenship. As Aliya Shain, Jo-Ann and Mary Jo's teenage daughter, put it in her affidavit: "We shouldn't be told by the state that we're not good enough. I've grown up with my parents, and I've seen that what they deserve is marriage. We deserve this as a family."

Finally, we briefed the two principal legal claims asserted in every marriage equality case, both flowing from *Loving v. Virginia*: the so-called "due process" argument (denial of the fundamental right to marry the person of one's choice) and the "equal protection" argument (based on sexual orientation and sex discrimination). We limited ourselves to state constitutional claims to shield any favorable ruling from Supreme Court review, although we could still cite federal cases like *Loving* because the U.S. Constitution sets the floor (but not the ceiling) for state constitutional rights.

One major issue was how to define the "right" at stake. Did "marriage" inherently mean one man and one woman (a definition supposedly unchanged for "millennia," as some justices put it at the *Obergefell* argument)? Were we inventing a new right to something called "gay marriage"? Or was there, as we argued, simply this thing called marriage, from which same-sex couples had improperly been excluded? This dispute was pivotal in our case—and eventually in *Obergefell* as well.

We backed up our fundamental right argument with historical materials showing that the institution of marriage has, in fact, evolved over time in several key ways. For example, under the concept of "coverture," which prevailed for centuries, wives lost their entire legal identity and were deemed merged into their husbands; racial purity and separation were once widely deemed integral to the definition of marriage; and, even in 2004, it simply was not true that marriage by definition was one man and one woman, since Massachusetts permitted same-sex couples to marry, as did Canada, the Netherlands, Spain, and Belgium.

The other key issue was whether the government had any legitimate reason to exclude same-sex couples from civil marriage. On this point, Mayor Bloomberg, the effective defendant in our suit against the city clerk, was in a bit of a bind. In a deft political move, he had announced his support for legislatively extending marriage to same-sex couples the evening before we filed *Hernandez*. With this stance, he couldn't very well embrace overtly homophobic arguments for marriage discrimination.

From the first round of trial court briefing, we and the plaintiffs in parallel cases confronted and responded to a series of vague and illogical purported justifications. Some defendants argued that same-sex couples could be excluded to preserve the "traditional" definition of marriage (a circular argument in which discrimination becomes its own justification). Others suggested that the government could seek to preserve "uniformity" in the law (which ignored the states' role in our federal system as laboratories of social change). Still others insisted that it was rational to limit marriage to different-sex couples to encourage "responsible procreation" within a socially stable institution (a goal in no way furthered by excluding same-sex couples, many of whom also procreate).

All these issues were framed in massive summary judgment papers submitted by both sides to our trial judge, Justice Doris Ling-Cohan. Once briefing was complete, we expected to be called in for oral argument, but the judge felt the issues were clear enough to rule on the papers alone. I still remember being pulled out of a meeting on February 4, 2005, to be told there was a decision— and that we had actually won.

Talk about justice that arrives like a thunderbolt. "Similar to different-sex couples," wrote Justice Ling-Cohan, "same-sex couples are entitled to the same fundamental right to follow their hearts and publicly commit to a lifetime partnership with the person of their choosing." She concluded that equal recognition of this fundamental right "cannot legitimately be said to harm anyone."

This was huge. At that point, gay people had been legally marrying in the United States only since the previous May, and only in Massachusetts. And no judge outside of that state had ever issued a decision actually ordering the government to grant marriage licenses to same-sex couples. Although it would take another decade for this ruling to become the law of the land, Justice Ling-Cohan's words rang true and blazed a trail.

This was the first time, in my twenty years as a lawyer, that a result achieved for a client reduced me to tears of joy. It felt like we were not only helping to make history but also potentially unleashing untold happiness for thousands of friends and neighbors.

But it was all downhill from there, at least for our case. Despite his policy support for marriage equality, Mayor Bloomberg directed the Corporation Counsel to appeal the decision. The mayor was in a tough position, which I understood but didn't like. Only one state had thus far recognized marriage rights for same-sex couples, making it harder to declare existing New York law completely indefensible (as President Obama later did with DOMA). The *New York Times*, while celebrating the decision, urged the mayor to appeal to avoid confusion that might ensue from issuing marriage licenses based on a single trial court ruling in one county.

Still, what might have happened if Mayor Bloomberg had taken a deep breath and declined to appeal? He had to know in his heart that the decision was right. Someone else would have stepped forward to challenge the decision, but, without the imprimatur of the city defending discrimination, the dynamics of the appeal would have been very different. Mayor Bloomberg is rightly hailed today as an ally, but he could have been a true hero.

The government sought a fast resolution by appealing Justice Ling-Cohan's ruling directly to the Court of Appeals (New York's Supreme Court), but the Court bounced it back to the Appellate Division—where, in December 2005, a panel dominated by conservative appointees of Governor George Pataki reversed our short-lived victory.

The majority judges were dismissive if not cruel. Justice Milton Williams' opinion for the Court chided Justice Ling-Cohan for inventing "a new constitutional right" and held that defining marriage as "the union between one man and one woman" was "based on innate, complementary, procreative roles, a function of biology, not mere legal rights." Adding insult to injury, Justice James Catterson's concurrence dismissed our reliance on *Loving* as "disingenuous" and accused us of disrespecting the civil rights movement and ignoring the history of race relations: "How could one consider the horror of the Civil War and the majesty of the Emancipation Proclamation in the same breath as same-sex unions?" But of course, no one ever sought to equate historical injustices—and indeed, it demeans the great civil rights decisions to suggest they are limited to their facts rather than embodying universal principles of freedom and equality for all.

Justice David Saxe, the lone dissenter from the First Department's reversal, is a forgotten hero of *Hernandez*. Justice Saxe got the fundamental rights analysis right and also shrewdly illuminated the government's bind in seeking to justify the marriage ban while avoiding any negative implications about same-sex couples.

It was a disappointing outcome, but the Appellate Division was always understood to be a mere way station. Now in the position of appellant, we refashioned and expanded our arguments into a hundred-page brief. Writing it was truly a labor of love. But the path to four votes on the seven-member Court of Appeals seemed doubtful, reminding us why New York had not originally been a favored forum.

We started with the assumption that we had two votes for equality (Chief Judge Judith Kaye and Judge Carmen Ciparick, liberal appointees of Governor Mario Cuomo) and probably three against (Judges Victoria Graffeo, Susan Read, and Robert Smith, all Pataki appointees). The two wild cards were Judge

George Bundy Smith, an independent-voting Cuomo appointee, and Judge Albert Rosenblatt, a Pataki appointee thought to be open-minded on civil rights issues.

Judge Smith, the Court's only African American member, had roots in the civil rights movement—which could cut either way, given the varying reactions to our invocation of *Loving*. If he proved hesitant to embrace our arguments fully, we hoped we might still win over Judge Rosenblatt, who in turn might persuade Judge Smith to join a bipartisan majority—if not for a full marriage victory, then possibly for an equal protection ruling requiring civil unions with the same rights and responsibilities as marriage.

Then came our bad bounce: Judge Rosenblatt, for reasons that were not officially explained, recused himself from participating in the *Hernandez* appeal. He did so, apparently, because his daughter's law firm had been involved in marriage equality litigation in other states—but insiders were puzzled since the facts did not appear to require recusal. This twist left us in a challenging position: to garner four votes now, we would likely have to win over both Judges Smith—or at least one of them, creating a 3–3 tie that would be resolved by bringing in a wild-card Appellate Division justice.

The May 2006 oral argument did not clarify the tea leaves. Susan and Robbie (representing the *Hernandez* and *Samuels* plaintiffs, respectively) made powerful presentations, and both Judges Smith gave our hopes some oxygen. Judge G. Smith repeatedly mentioned civil unions, raising the possibility of a limited victory; Judge R. Smith vigorously questioned both sides, suggesting that his vote might actually be in play.

But one moment made my blood boil. The city's Court of Appeals brief had embraced the "responsible procreation" rationale while walking a fine line by expressly disclaiming any suggestion that "children being raised by single or same-sex parents are being brought up in a less beneficial environment than children being raised by married parents." At oral argument, Judge R. Smith asked the city's lawyer, Leonard Koerner, whether the legislature could rationally "prefer that children be brought up in opposite-sex households." Based on the mayor's public stance and the city's own brief, Mr. Koerner should have said "no." Unfortunately, his litigator's instinct got the best of him, and he responded: "Do I think they could make that judgment based on a study? The answer is yes," although he quickly tried to change the subject back from child-rearing to procreation.

I cannot say this was the moment we lost the case, because it may not have been winnable in the first place. But it was certainly dispiriting.

After the argument, we waited. In early July, with the decision about to be issued, I drove down from Cape Cod with my daughter, then sixteen, so we could both be present for the potentially historic moment. On Thursday morning, July 6, I was at my desk when the clerk's office in Albany called to say that the Appellate Division decision had been affirmed. Though we had anticipated this outcome, the news hit like a punch to the stomach.

We quickly obtained a copy of the decision: 4–2 with opinion for the Court by Judge Robert Smith. Although it addressed a number of other issues, and like the Appellate Division found no "fundamental right" for same-sex couples to marry, the Court framed the "critical question" as "whether a rational legislature could decide that [the benefits of marriage] should be given to members of opposite-sex couples, but not same-sex couples." It answered in the affirmative on two grounds, one ridiculous and the other repellant.

First, the Court endorsed a variation on the "responsible procreation" argument—that marriage is intended to encourage different-sex couples, who may "become parents as a result of accident or impulse," to form stable families for the benefit of their children and society. The Court remarkably suggested that "unstable relationships between people of the opposite sex present a greater danger that children will be born into or grow up in unstable homes than is the case with same-sex couples." In other words, because same-sex couples procreate more responsibly—after all, they can't just get drunk and adopt in one night, as columnist Dan Savage put it—and are more likely to provide a stable home, they (and their children) are denied the benefits and protections of civil marriage.

Perhaps sensing how absurd this sounded, Judge Smith offered a second ground: that the legislature could "rationally believe that it is better, other things being equal, for children to grow up with both a mother and a father." He based this utterly unsupported conclusion on "intuition and experience" and the "common sense premise that children will do better with a mother and father in the home."

Chief Judge Judith Kaye, writing for herself and Judge Ciparick, demolished the Court's wrongheaded decision in a dissent for the ages. She noted that "plaintiffs represent a cross-section of New Yorkers who want only to live full lives, raise their children, better their communities, and be good neighbors" and that like many other New Yorkers they "grew up hoping to find that one person with whom they would share their future, eager to express their mutual lifetime pledge through civil marriage." She lamented that plaintiffs are excluded from civil marriage solely "because of who they love." Judge Kaye denounced the Court's failure to correct this injustice as a "retreat" from "a proud tradition of affording equal rights to all New Yorkers."

Anticipating Justice Kennedy's reasoning in *Obergefell*, Judge Kaye explained that plaintiffs were not seeking a new right. The Supreme Court, she said, had "rejected the notion that fundamental rights it had already identified could be restricted based on traditional assumptions about who could be permitted their protection." Judge Kaye also destroyed Judge Smith's casually bigoted conclusions on childrearing: "The state plainly has a legitimate interest in the welfare of children, but excluding same-sex couples from marriage in no way furthers its interest. In fact it undermines it." She stressed that the marriage ban harms thousands of children being raised by same-sex couples; that any policy of favoring straight parents over gay parents would itself be impermissible discrimination; and that the social science evidence in any event overwhelmingly refuted Judge Smith's archaic "intuition."

Judge Kaye took head-on the majority's assertion that the scope of the right to marry should be left to the legislature: "It is uniquely the function of the Judicial Branch to safeguard individual liberties guaranteed by the New York State Constitution, and to order redress for their violation. The Court's duty to protect constitutional rights is an imperative of the separation of powers, not its enemy." She concluded that "future generations will look back on today's decision as an unfortunate misstep."

Losing *Hernandez* may not have been surprising, but it was deeply frustrating and disappointing. Later that morning, I joined co-counsel and clients at a downbeat but determined midtown press conference at which advocates criticized the bias and illogic in the Court's decision and vowed to overturn it in the legislature. I then headed down to a large, angry rally in Sheridan Square—arriving just in time to hear Alan van Capelle of Empire State Pride Agenda declare to the crowd that the loss should not be blamed on the lawyers, because Lambda Legal, the ACLU, Paul, Weiss, and Kramer Levin had done a great job. My colleagues and I appreciated this credit and other expressions of gratitude from clients and community leaders, including the personal thank-you call I received the next day from City Council Speaker Christine Quinn. But overall I felt numb.

The next morning, my daughter and I drove back to Cape Cod, eager to return to a jurisdiction where gay people could actually marry. Toward the end of the five-hour ride, we played the entire intensely emotional score of the musical *Rent*. The final, echoing chant of "No Day but Today" faded to silence just as we pulled up to the house and my daughter hopped out of the car. The melodramatic timing pushed me over the edge, unleashing the torrent of tears I had been holding back for more than a day.

Mainstream media reaction to the *Hernandez* decision was gratifyingly derisive. The *New Republic* called it "a lousy decision," and the *New York Times* attacked the Court's "twisted legal reasoning" and urged marriage equality supporters to "quickly move past this week's disappointment and get energized" to push the issue in the legislature. Law professor Kenji Yoshino, writing in the *New York Times*, noted the irony of denying equal marriage rights to same-sex couples because they may make more stable parents, while in the same breath saying the legislature rationally could have preferred different-sex parents. He mused that the "reckless procreation" argument might be appealing because "it sounds nicer to gays." This reasoning may explain why it was the last argument left standing in *Obergefell*.

Unfortunately, *Hernandez* was not the only defeat for marriage equality in 2006. Later in July, the Washington Supreme Court upheld the state's marriage ban in a bitterly divided 5–4 decision. A few months later, the Maryland Supreme Court followed suit, reversing an earlier trial court victory. Both decisions relied heavily, in upholding their states' bans, on the mantra of procreation.

Dan Savage noted the "perverse cruelty" of both the Washington and New York decisions: "The Courts ruled, essentially, that making my child's life less secure somehow makes the life of a child with straight parents more secure." While recognizing that the recent defeats had "demoralized supporters of gay marriage," Savage detected a silver lining: "If heterosexual instability and the link between heterosexual sex and human reproduction are the best arguments opponents of same-sex marriage can muster, I can't help but feel that our side must be winning."

In calling attention to the weak, if not laughable, grounds for denying the freedom to marry, losses like ours helped shape public opinion and spur legislative action. Between 2004 (when we filed the suit) and 2006 (when it was finally decided), public support in New York for marriage equality increased from 47 to 53 percent. Less than a year later, a marriage bill passed in the State Assembly. Other factors were at play, including the positive impact of marriage in Massachusetts, but we certainly helped advance the ball.

Following our defeat, and the devastating 2008 loss on Proposition 8 in California, marriage equality advocates refined our messaging, aided by the national quarterbacking of Evan Wolfson's Freedom to Marry. We learned that stressing the unfairness of denying couples the right to commit to each other resonated more with the political center than arguments based on legal concepts of equality or laundry lists of benefits and burdens. Lambda Legal also won a groundbreaking unanimous state Supreme Court victory in Iowa in 2009, demonstrating that marriage equality was possible not only on the coasts but also in the heartland. The plaintiffs in the Iowa litigation included several children of same-sex couples—reflecting a decision to challenge head-on the absurd logic of *Hernandez*.

In New York, the basic theme of fairness was hammered home in a series of sophisticated public service announcements featuring celebrities and real-life couples (including *Hernandez* plaintiffs Jo-Ann Shain and Mary Jo Kennedy). With a highly coordinated effort strongly backed by Governor Cuomo (superbly chronicled in Marc Solomon's *Winning Marriage*), the marriage bill finally passed the dysfunctional State Senate in 2011, and ballot victories followed a year later in Washington, Maryland, and two other states.

How sweet and surreal it was, early in 2012, to watch Norm and his longtime partner Héctor Lozada tie the knot in New York before our very own Justice Ling-Cohan, in a ceremony drawn from her own groundbreaking marriage decision. Toasting the handsome grooms, we celebrated what then seemed remarkable progress—not anticipating the astonishing acceleration that would bring first *Windsor* a year later and then *Obergefell* in 2015.

The year 2013 marked not just Edie Windsor's triumph, but also a more personal milestone: my own belated coming out after a twenty-eight-year marriage and more than fifteen years as a visible "straight ally." It was a difficult summer. My marriage ended, and I had to set up my first solo household in three decades while tending to my father through his final decline and hospice care. Meanwhile, I was sharing my personal news in a series of lunches and phone calls. The process was scary but was cushioned by my significant remaining privileges and the love and support of countless wonderful friends, colleagues, and relatives. All over the gay world, I imagine, there was the sound of the other shoe dropping. But people generally kept any eye-rolling to themselves.

On the eve of the *Obergefell* argument in April 2015, Freedom to Marry hosted an extraordinary Washington, D.C., gathering of hundreds of marriage equality plaintiffs and counsel from cases spanning forty-five years. Arriving at the event, I ran into Jo-Ann and Mary Jo scrutinizing a giant poster listing every single marriage plaintiff since 1970. We gasped when we spotted our New York couples close to the top of the display. Certainly there were pioneers who came before us, but it was thrilling to be reminded that our part in the drama came relatively early in the litigation process, helping to lay the groundwork for so many others who later joined forces to confront, and ultimately defeat, a great legal and social injustice.

"OUR LIBERTIES WE PRIZE": WINNING MARRIAGE IN IOWA

CAMILLA TAYLOR

———— ⚭ ————

Camilla Taylor is counsel at Lambda Legal; she was the National Marriage Project director at Lambda Legal from 2010 through 2015.

On April 3, 2009, when the Iowa Supreme Court unanimously struck down Iowa's marriage ban as unconstitutional in *Varnum v. Brien*, making Iowa one of only three states that permitted same-sex couples to marry, many people around the country were thunderstruck. Iowa? Unanimous? How could same-sex couples marry in Iowa but not California or New York? On CNN and MSNBC, Anderson Cooper and Rachel Maddow reported about the case with tones of incredulity.

At Lambda Legal, we were elated but not surprised. We had been working toward this day for more than six years, when we first began exploring the possibility of bringing a lawsuit in the Midwest on behalf of same-sex couples seeking the freedom to marry.

My work on the case began within a year of joining Lambda Legal in July 2002. At that time, no state permitted same-sex couples to marry. Thirteen states still criminalized lesbian and gay people as a result of sodomy laws that prohibited intimacy between members of the same sex. Given that climate, a successful marriage case in a Midwest state seemed laughable.

In fact, my two colleagues actually did laugh when they tasked me, the newest hire, with researching Midwest states to determine whether any of them might be fertile ground for marriage litigation. We needed research for our files, of course, but none of us expected my efforts to result in a lawsuit anytime soon. However, three things happened within a year that changed our outlook.

First, the Supreme Court struck down all sodomy laws nationwide as unconstitutional in Lambda Legal's case *Lawrence v. Texas*; this opinion paved the way for same-sex couples to seek affirmative recognition of their relationships. Second, the Massachusetts Supreme Judicial Court, in a lawsuit brought by our sister group, Gay & Lesbian Advocates & Defenders (GLAD), ruled that the Massachusetts Constitution guaranteed the right of same-sex couples to marry. This galvanized same-sex couples everywhere to demand equality in their home states, and our help desk took calls from same-sex couples eager to wed in almost every state in the country.

Third, my research turned up results that made me optimistic about a victory in Iowa's state court. Iowa's judiciary has a long proud history of independence and civil rights leadership. From its first decision in 1839, refusing to return a former slave to Missouri under the Fugitive Slave Act, the Iowa Supreme Court took courageous stands on the civil rights questions of each generation, often long before public opinion caught up. For example, in the nineteenth century, Iowa courts desegregated schools and public accommodations and were the first in the nation to admit a woman to the practice of law. And we could draw upon Iowa courts' history of unusual rectitude in our lawsuit calling upon Iowa courts to be among the first in the nation to strike down a marriage ban.

Moreover, and just as important, the Iowa Supreme Court had held, in opinion after opinion, that Iowa's state Constitution provides broader due process and equal protection guarantees to individuals than equivalent provisions in the federal Constitution. This was compelling because we intended to file suit in state court based exclusively on state constitutional guarantees, and the federal courts in Iowa's circuit had a history of hostility to marriage-related claims by lesbian and gay people.

Perhaps the most important factor in my decision to zero in on Iowa was a political one. Even if we could win a lawsuit in the highest court of any state, we nevertheless could end up losing, and at enormous cost, if our lawsuit prompted voters to amend the state Constitution to ban same-sex couples from marrying. Such a constitutional amendment would not only reverse any victory we might obtain but embed antigay discrimination in the state's foundational document. By 2002, four states had added marriage bans to their state constitutions, and many more were in the process of doing so by late 2003. Iowa, however, had the most cumbersome constitutional amendment process of any Midwest state; a constitutional amendment must originate in Iowa's legislature, and pass both houses in two consecutive legislative sessions before it could go to the voters for approval. As I wrote in a memo to my colleagues, "If preventing passage of a state constitutional [marriage ban] is the strongest factor in our selection of a state for marriage litigation, then Iowa is the obvious Midwest choice."

I cold-called a well-respected Iowa lawyer named Dennis ("Denny") Johnson, a former solicitor general of Iowa. I had found him on the Web and asked my Iowa lawyer contacts about him, but I still did not know much about him except that he had served in a Democratic administration and was described as down-to-earth, highly intelligent, and beloved by Iowa juries. He was kind and respectful on the phone even though he had never heard of Lambda Legal, and my proposal must have sounded crazy to someone with little or no contact with the LGBT community. I crammed my legal research and thoughts on strategy into a fifteen-page, single-spaced memorandum. I sent it off to Denny and held my breath. I was vastly relieved when he called to say that he had agreed to co-counsel the case with us. He told me later that after he read my memo, he did not see how we could lose (although he did quibble with my prediction—inaccurate, as it turned out—that Iowans would elect a Republican governor the following year). Approaching Denny may have been the best decision we ever made. Denny was in every way our partner in the case as well as a brilliant oral advocate and strategist, and we leaned on him throughout the case.

My colleague, Communications Director Lisa Hardaway, a native Iowan, and I started interviewing all of the same-sex couples who had contacted us seeking representation for a lawsuit for the freedom to marry. With each couple, we explored their interest and preparedness with respect to participating in a high-profile test case. We crossed the state in rental cars, meeting with couples and their children in their homes. Ultimately, we selected six couples for the lawsuit.

Kate and Trish Varnum had a genuine manner and warmth that charmed us. Together for years and eager to bring a child into their family through reproductive technology or adoption, they spoke frankly about their love for each other and the hurt they felt when their bishop refused to allow them to hold a commitment ceremony in the church Kate had attended her entire life. Their families, however, supported their love for each other. Kate's father said to Trish during their commitment ceremony, "I cannot call you my daughter-in-law" under Iowa law, "so I shall always refer to you as my daughter-in-love."

Larry Hoch and David Twombley were seniors who had met each other late in life after each had struggled to come to terms with his sexual orientation. Gregarious and sweet, they wished to marry to take care of each other as they grew older, and feared being kept apart in a hospital because they were legal strangers to each other.

Jason Morgan and Chuck Swaggerty, both around the age of thirty-five, lived in Sioux City, the most conservative part of the state. High school sweethearts, they were foster parents and dreamed of adopting children together. Jason's voice broke as he told us of how his inability to marry Chuck had interfered with his ability to be present to comfort Chuck after the death of Chuck's mother. When Jason took a day off of work to attend the funeral with Chuck, Jason's employer put a negative mark on Jason's record and required him to work throughout that weekend to make up the time.

Bill Musser and Otter Dreaming, in rural Decorah, Iowa, also were foster parents. Their community embraced them. Bill was a taxi driver and known to practically everyone in town, and both men were musicians.

Ingrid Olson and Reva Evans were young and stoic, living in Council Bluffs, which was barely more hospitable to lesbian or gay people than Sioux City. They, too, had been a couple for years and proudly showed us photos of their commitment ceremony. When we interviewed them, they bravely asked to be part of the suit even though Reva was pregnant with their son, Jamison, and they worried how litigation would affect his life.

The last of our plaintiff couples, Jen and Dawn BarbouRoske, lived in Iowa City with their two daughters, McKinley and Breeanna. McKinley, age eight, was blonde, serious, and precocious, with an air of maturity far beyond her years. Breeanna, at four, was all smiles and energy. Jen and Dawn told us they wished to marry not just because of their love for each other, but for the sake of their daughters. A year or two earlier, McKinley had burst into tears upon overhearing Jen laughingly tell Dawn about a co-worker who had been unaware that lesbian couples were barred by law from marrying and had assumed erroneously that Jen and Dawn were legally married. McKinley, too, had assumed her parents were married. In tears, she asked if Jen and Dawn would always be together as a family. Painfully, Jen and Dawn had to explain to McKinley that Iowa law barred them from marrying, and reassure her that they would always stay together and would marry if they could.

The most powerful story Jen and Dawn told us, however, was the story of their search for a school for McKinley. They had visited a school that seemed perfect, and were ready to write a tuition check when they thought to ask the principal whether McKinley would be treated differently because she has two mothers. The principal thought for a moment and replied, "Well, she wouldn't be able to give a presentation during the unit on families because we wouldn't want to upset the other parents." Jen and Dawn imagined McKinley—forced in shame to watch silently as every other child stood up and talked about their own families—and found another school for her. For Jen and Dawn, this experience summed up why they wanted Iowa's marriage ban struck down as unconstitutional—because the state's law declaring their family unworthy of marriage sent a message even to the youngest children that there was something wrong and inferior about their family. The law invited discrimination and indignity. Jen and Dawn wanted their daughters to grow up with pride in themselves and free of the state-sanctioned message that they should be ashamed of their family. This story eventually became the crux of our case.

One Iowa City couple, Janelle Rettig and Robin Butler, made it their mission to educate me about their state, even though their prior marriage in Canada meant they were not going to be part of the case. We spent hours in Iowa City discussing Iowa's role in the presidential caucuses, the state's demographics and geography, and its political climate. Among the things Janelle and Robin taught me was the state motto: "Our liberties we prize and our rights we will maintain." For them, this statement was a battle cry. Sometimes Janelle would call me to leave messages consisting of little more than a recitation of Iowa's motto as a reminder of the need to believe in Iowa's promise of liberty and equality.

Janelle and Robin firmly believed the Iowa Supreme Court would rule in our favor. Well-connected and politically moderate, they also believed the state legislature would hold firm and refuse passage of a constitutional amendment. Despite their conviction, I still fretted. At that time, the Iowa Senate was equally divided between Republicans and Democrats. The Senate Democratic leader, Mike Gronstal, had pledged to block any effort to amend the Constitution. However, if Democrats lost even one senator, Gronstal would lose his ability to stop discriminatory legislation, and Republicans were certain to pass the amendment as soon as possible. We agreed to hold off on filing any lawsuit until after an anticipated vote on a proposed constitutional amendment in the spring of 2004. We knew if the legislature stood firm and rejected the amendment, Iowa's cumbersome process for amending the state Constitution would prevent passage of such an amendment until 2007, which would give us time, we hoped, to make progress in the courts and educate Iowans about lesbian and gay people and their need for the freedom to marry.

I also reached out to Iowa lesbian and gay community leaders such as Sharon Malheiro, our co-counsel in a number of prior cases in Iowa and the director of the Des Moines LGBT community center, and Rich Eychaner, a gay philanthropist who championed efforts to prevent bullying in Iowa schools. I nervously presented them with the plan to file a lawsuit. To my relief, they supported filing suit.

In a close vote, the Iowa legislature did block an attempt to amend its state Constitution in 2004. However, the events of November 2004, in which voters in eleven states enacted marriage bans, gave us pause. Many in the LGBT community blamed marriage litigants for stoking flames that led to those electoral losses, and we postponed filing our Iowa lawsuit for a year.

We filed our complaint with a press conference in December 2005. In the months that followed, Lisa encouraged Iowa papers to editorialize in favor of our plaintiffs' claims. Editorial boards around the state met with us and the couples and wrote words of encouragement—not a single paper predicted we would lose or expressed the view that we should.

Shortly after we filed the case, attorney Ken Upton joined our team. Although new to Lambda Legal, Ken was a seasoned litigator with decades of experience and a gift at outmaneuvering his opponents. We also gained Jim Bennett, the new regional director of the Chicago office. Jim had a deep religious background and took on the task of organizing Iowa churches and religious leaders to sign on to a friend-of-the-court brief supporting our case. Hector Vargas, in our New York office, oversaw our community education efforts. Ken, Denny, Lisa, Jim, Hector, and our legal assistants Cheryl Angelaccio, Sarah Groom, and Graciela Gonzalez became our Iowa team.

The defendant in our lawsuit, Polk County, was represented by a local attorney, Roger Kuhl, and assisted by an antigay organization based in Scottsdale, Arizona—the Alliance Defense Fund, or ADF (now renamed the Alliance Defending Freedom). Polk County, doubtless at the prompting of ADF, made clear in its first filing that it intended to make the most offensive arguments available—namely that Iowa's marriage ban was necessary because it served the purpose of channeling procreation into superior households, and lesbian and gay parents were inferior to non-gay parents.

Ken, Denny, and I responded by making two decisions that were controversial and hotly debated among the small group of lawyers and organizations around the country who were litigating marriage cases. First, we added the three children of our plaintiff couples as plaintiffs themselves. We did this because Polk County's argument rested upon the implicit assumption that marriage benefits children, but ignored the fact that same-sex couples also have children and that these children are no less deserving of benefits and protections. We wanted the lawyer for Polk County to have to look McKinley in the eyes and explain why she was unworthy of having married parents. Many lawyers in our movement felt strongly at the time that adding child plaintiffs was a mistake, and heatedly told us so, pointing to national and state-by-state polling data showing the public's discomfort with the notion of lesbian and gay people rearing children. These lawyers wanted us to downplay child welfare arguments. However, we held firm, believing that these polls—which asked only abstract questions about hypothetical lesbian or gay people—would not predict what judges would do when confronted with the indignity and pain caused by marriage bans to actual children such as McKinley.

Second, we decided to seek a trial on the social science concerning outcomes for children of lesbian and gay parents. Although the science was solidly in our favor as a result of dozens of well-regarded peer-reviewed studies, this was a risky decision because social science can be mischaracterized by opponents or hostile judges. If a court were to make adverse social science findings about the relative abilities of lesbian or gay parents or child outcomes, such a decision could doom not just our other marriage cases but also child custody, adoption, and foster care cases, and our legislative efforts in other states to repeal adoption and foster care bans. A victory in our case was by no means a foregone conclusion. After all, we had lost marriage cases within the last two years in state high courts in New York, Washington State, and Maryland. Colleagues at other organizations accused us of taking too great a risk, but Ken and I disagreed. Our previous strategy hadn't worked; we had lost elsewhere because courts had ignored scientific evidence in favor of biased assumptions masquerading as what the New York Court of Appeals, its highest court, described in *Hernandez* as a "common sense premise" that children fare better with different-sex parents. Expert witness testimony would make the scientific evidence harder for courts to discard.

We designated the most well-respected social scientists in the field as our experts in child welfare and the nature and longevity of same-sex relationships. We then spent months flying to London, Montreal, and numerous cities around the country to defend our experts in depositions and to depose opposing "experts" who were philosophers and hobbyists, for the most part, and who either had no background in the relevant social science discipline or revealed complete ignorance of the relevant body of research.

I remember one deposition particularly clearly. Weather caused me to miss my connecting flight to Charlottesville, where I was scheduled to depose economist Steven Rhoads at the University of Virginia the following morning. I rented a car and drove through the night, arriving at the deposition after only an hour and a half of sleep. Polk County had designated Dr. Rhoads as an expert in "the complementarity of men and women and the biological differences between the sexes," even though Dr. Rhoads had no experience in any physical or social science other than economics. He believed men's biological destiny caused them to stray from their families and abandon their children absent the legal tie provided by marriage. He also believed women were ill-suited to working outside the home and secretly preferred childrearing responsibilities to employment. I was eight months' pregnant at the time, and Dr. Rhoads pointed at my distended belly at the end of the deposition and said in an overly familiar tone, "You'll know exactly what I mean in just a couple short weeks, I expect." Sleep deprived and annoyed, I simply laughed. As it turns out, I never did come to "know exactly" what he meant. I was eager to return to work after six weeks of parental leave, especially because the trial court had ruled in favor of the plaintiffs in *Varnum v. Brien* the day before, striking down Iowa's marriage ban as unconstitutional. The judge found the vast majority of Polk County's "experts," including Dr.

Rhoads, unqualified to offer an expert opinion, and dismissed their testimony entirely.

The gambles that Ken, Denny, and I had taken in naming child plaintiffs and seeking social science findings paid off. The trial court found, based on our uncontested evidence (since the opposing experts had been disqualified based on their depositions), that same-sex couples are just as good parents as different-sex couples, and that their children fare just as well. The court also focused on the harm caused by the marriage ban to our plaintiffs' children. As expected, Polk County appealed directly to the Iowa Supreme Court.

The landscape changed over the next year and a half as we prepared for a Supreme Court argument. First, national organizations such as Gill Action prioritized Iowa and urged political donors around the country to support Iowa state legislators who opposed a state constitutional amendment. Although we did not participate in such efforts, of course, we began hearing from activists and donors eager to understand our prospects of success before the Iowa high court. We had allies in our efforts to change public opinion in anticipation of a court victory.

Jim Bennett ramped up his grassroots efforts to obtain faith allies. More than one hundred and sixty Iowa religious leaders and congregations signed a supportive brief. We also hired Matt Fender, an energetic young organizer who changed hearts and minds one house party at a time. Matt also organized conferences for same-sex couples with children, which served multiple purposes—training spokespeople (such as Zach Wahls, the son of two mothers whose testimony opposing a constitutional amendment a year later would go viral), and supporting families who felt isolated in such a rural state. By the time the Iowa Supreme Court held oral argument in December 2008, we had many allies in Iowa and around the country rooting for our success. We felt optimistic that we could preserve any victory we might obtain by preventing passage of an antigay constitutional amendment in the Iowa legislature.

Meanwhile, Denny had retired from his law firm in order to move with his family to Colorado for a simpler life. However, he remained in Des Moines for three months for the sole purpose of preparing for the oral argument. Denny was an ultra-marathon runner whose commitment to everything he did was absolute, and this case was no exception. He participated in countless moot oral arguments with Lambda Legal staff as the weeks ticked down.

On the day of the oral argument in December 2008, crowds jammed the courtroom and an overflow room. The Iowa Supreme Court justices filed in. Conscious of the unusual significance and impact of the case, the Court allowed advocates on both sides to speak far longer than was scheduled.

Denny's oral argument was masterful. He closed his presentation by relating the story of Jen and Dawn's search for a preschool for McKinley. Denny explained that the impact of Iowa's marriage ban was not just to legitimize discrimination against same-sex couples but to communicate to their children that there was something wrong with their families of which they should feel ashamed.

McKinley and her sister Breeanna sat in the front row watching. McKinley was taking notes in a notebook. She had pressed Lisa and me many times for opportunities to speak up on behalf of her mothers and for ways that she, as a child, could play a role in advocating for her parents' freedom to marry. As Denny sat down after finishing his presentation, tears burned my eyes. I knew we had done everything within our power to vindicate the dignity of McKinley's family and the families of the other plaintiff couples.

Just four months later, much earlier than we expected a decision, Jim Bennett received a curious call from a supporter telling us that the Iowa Supreme Court had hired extra security personnel for their next "decision day"—that coming Friday. The supporter assumed, as did we, that this meant the Court intended to issue their decision in *Varnum v. Brien* on Friday, April 3, 2009. We also hoped the addition of security meant something positive for us, half-joking with each other that the Court couldn't possibly be worried about violence from *us*. We set up a phone tree and called our staff, plaintiffs, and allies around the country.

The next morning, the Iowa Supreme Court did indeed announce that it would issue *Varnum* on April 3. We all booked flights or drove to Des Moines for an emergency meeting on Thursday night. A member of the Gill team agreed to go personally to the Iowa Supreme Court and deliver the rest of us a paper copy of the decision, as we knew the Court's website was likely to crash at 9 a.m. when the decision was due. Then we dispersed so we could brief our plaintiffs and so the Gill team could prepare elected officials for what was to come. Each of us looked haggard and serious as we left the room in the hotel where we had met. We all had acted optimistic, but most of us were too nervous to sleep.

Each of the plaintiffs courageously agreed to relinquish their phones and other devices and remain sequestered in a room ignorant of the decision until a news conference, at which they would learn whether they had won or lost in front of television cameras broadcasting their reaction around the world. They understood that their reaction—whether tears of joy or grief—would educate the public about the stakes of our struggle and give their fight a human face.

Early on the morning of April 3, I huddled with Graciela and Ken as we read the decision. I first saw on the front page that Justice Cady had authored it, and my heart stopped. I assumed we had lost. Justice Cady was one of the most conservative members of the Court. I flipped to the end of the decision, shouting, "How many justices dissented, HOW MANY? DID WE GET ANYBODY?" Then, as I saw the relief granted to our plaintiffs on the last page of the opinion, and that there were no dissents or concurrences, I realized the extent of what we had accomplished. Not only had we won, but we had won unanimously! For the first time, a high court had ruled unanimously in favor of the freedom to marry for same-sex couples!

The press conference was gleeful. I have no poker face, so I could not help grinning as I walked to the microphone to announce the result to the families who sat in front of me, anxiously clutching their children and each other's hands. I practically yelled into the microphone, "We won! Not only that, it is unanimous! You are getting married!" Denny followed, telling them, "Go live the American dream! Live happily ever after!" I then said what we all knew to be true, even then, just minutes after the decision was issued: *Varnum* would "have a transformative effect on the nation."

I remember snapshots of tears, of Ingrid and Reva clutching Jason and Chuck, of Kate kissing Trish, and most of all, of McKinley raising her arms above her head with her eyes closed in an expression of victory and pure joy as her mothers briefly kissed each other in happiness and recognition of what they had accomplished. We had won. We had done it.

Varnum v. Brien marked a watershed for our movement. The decision's cultural impact was evident in the months immediately following, when legislatures in three New England states and the District of Columbia enacted marriage laws, more than doubling the number of jurisdictions where same-sex couples could marry. Cited more than a thousand times, the decision also served as cru-

Plaintiffs in Iowa, from the left, Trish Varnum, Kate Varnum, Jason Morgan, and Chuck Swaggerty. Photo Credit: COURTESY OF LAMBDA LEGAL

cial precedent in a snowballing series of marriage victories in state and federal courts over the next six years.

The lessons we learned from *Varnum*, in which the Iowa high court surveyed at length the social science evidence concerning lesbian and gay parenting, stuck with me after I became Lambda Legal's National Marriage Project director in 2010. We began submitting expert testimony routinely in marriage cases to combat junk science claims, and courts also began seeking out such testimony. We not only focused our own briefing on the harm to children from marriage discrimination, but actively sought out friend-of-the-court briefs from groups such as the Family Equality Council, which collected the words of children expressing, as McKinley had, the pain they felt upon learning that their government deemed their families unworthy of marriage. These briefs made a difference. During oral argument before the Seventh Circuit Court of Appeals in *Baskin v. Bogan*, Judge Posner castigated the lawyer defending Indiana's marriage ban for not being able to recall the Family Equality Council's brief, narrated a child's story from the brief at length, and described the harm experienced by such children as "harrowing."

In the wake of *Varnum*, courts shifted from viewing marriage discrimination as protective of children's interests to seeing such discrimination as harmful to children. Three years later, in *United States v. Windsor*, the Supreme Court focused on the harm to children as one of the justifications for striking down DOMA, the federal law denying recognition to same-sex couples' marriages. The Court wrote that DOMA "humiliates tens of thousands of children now being raised by same-sex couples," and "makes it even more difficult for the children to understand the integrity and closeness of their own family and its concord with other families in their community and in their daily lives." Federal appeals courts also cited this harm and struck down marriage bans in Utah, Oklahoma, Virginia, Indiana, Wisconsin, Idaho, and Nevada. And in finishing the job by striking down all remaining marriage bans in *Obergefell v. Hodges*, the Supreme Court described how such laws cause children to "suffer the stigma of knowing their families are somehow lesser." McKinley should be proud of how her story helped shape the national landscape and not only brought joy and security to countless loving couples, but lifted stigma from the shoulders of thousands of children.

IV. THE LONG, WINDING ROAD TO
MARRIAGE IN CALIFORNIA, 2004–13

CALIFORNIA DREAMING: WINNING MARRIAGE EQUALITY IN THE CALIFORNIA COURTS

———— ✸✸✸ ————

Shannon Minter is legal director of the National Center for Lesbian Rights (NCLR).

In hindsight, it is tempting to see the path to marriage equality in California as inevitable. For those of us who lived through those roller-coaster years, it seemed anything but. We poured countless hours of strategy, preparation, and collaboration into the fight. In the end, courageous individuals, astonishing events, and the sheer force of our community's aching, pent-up desire for freedom propelled us to the finish line more quickly than we had dreamed possible.

From the moment San Francisco Mayor Gavin Newsom began issuing marriage licenses to same-sex couples on February 12, 2004, the National Center for Lesbian Rights (NCLR) and our colleagues from Lambda Legal and the ACLU were embroiled in intense, ongoing litigation over the freedom to marry in California. From the beginning, we knew that if we prevailed, California might well tip the national balance toward marriage equality. And if we lost, we would likely delay that cherished goal for many years.

As 2003 drew to a close, the national movement for marriage equality was turning an historic corner. A decade earlier, the Hawai'i Supreme Court had appeared poised to strike down the state's marriage ban only to have the voters of Hawai'i strip that opportunity away, amending the Hawai'i Constitution to permit continued discrimination against same-sex couples. In 1999, in a case brought by private counsel and Gay & Lesbian Advocates & Defenders (GLAD), the Vermont Supreme Court had stopped short of mandating marriage equality, permitting the state to create the alternative status of "civil unions" for same-sex couples. Then in November 2003, in a case also brought by GLAD, Massachusetts finally broke through the barrier to full marriage equality, following a groundbreaking decision by the state's high court.

In California, the Massachusetts victory was thrilling. But, at least initially, California advocates were intent upon charting a different path. Faced with a conservative state supreme court and an easily amended state constitution, LGBT legal experts and leaders had met earlier that year, after months of research and preparation, to discuss the possibility of bringing a similar case to challenge California's marriage ban. After long discussion, most agreed that doing so in 2003 would be unwise. Not only was it uncertain whether the California Supreme Court would follow Massachusetts, but even if we won, there was little doubt that California voters would immediately amend the state Constitution to reinstate the ban. Only three years earlier, a huge majority of those voters had endorsed the existing statutory ban.

Instead, we agreed to redouble our efforts in the state legislature. Under the leadership of Geoffrey Kors, executive director of Equality California, we had begun to secure unprecedented legislative protections for same-sex couples and their families. If we could build on that progress, we reasoned, we could lay a strong foundation for a court case that would be easier to win and harder for the voters to undo, as they would be voting to take away protections enacted by the legislature rather than imposed by a court. Thus, in 2003, NCLR worked feverishly alongside our colleagues at Equality California, Lambda Legal, and the ACLU to expand California's domestic partnership law to provide the same rights and benefits provided to spouses under state law.

California had already made history when it enacted the first domestic partnership law in 1999, giving official statewide recognition to same-sex couples for the first time in our nation's history. Initially, however, the law included few substantive rights, providing only for a public registry, hospital visitation, and health insurance benefits for domestic partners of public employees. Then, in January 2001, Californians were shocked by the news that San Francisco resident Diane Alexis Whipple had been brutally attacked and killed by two dogs in the hallway of the apartment she shared with her domestic partner, Sharon Smith. Diane's death made headlines around the world. The story put a human face on the legal vulnerability of same-sex couples, and millions of people mourned with Diane's surviving partner, Sharon, as she not only grieved Diane's death but also faced unfair treatment as her partner.

In July of the same year, NCLR won a landmark case on Sharon's behalf, challenging California's exclusion of same-sex partners from the right to bring a wrongful death claim. For the first time in the country, a court held that a surviving same-sex partner must be treated the same as a surviving spouse. Although Sharon was an intensely private person who had never been involved in politics or activism of any kind, she forced herself to speak up for others after Diane's death, and the power of her voice was enormous. Later that year, after hearing emotional testimony from Sharon and other witnesses, the California legislature expanded the domestic partnership law substantially, adding eighteen additional rights.

In 2003, California took another giant leap forward with the introduction of the California Domestic Rights and Responsibilities Act. The bill marked a major shift in approach. Rather than providing domestic partners with specific, individually enumerated rights, the new bill created a presumption that domestic partners would have the same rights and responsibilities as spouses. The bill was drafted largely by Jon Davidson, the highly regarded legal director of Lambda Legal, and Jenny Pizer, now its Law and Policy director, with input from NCLR and the ACLU. In the legislature, majority support for the bill was razor thin. Equality California worked aggressively for every possible vote, calling on support from powerful allies such as the California NAACP and the United Farm Workers.

On September 3, the bill passed by a margin of 41 to 33, and with much fanfare, Governor Gray Davis signed the bill into law. That same year, the California legislature passed a record number of other landmark protections for the LGBT community, including a non-discrimination law for transgender workers, a similar law for LGBTQ foster youth, and the nation's first equal benefits in state contracting law, which required the State of California to enter into contracts only with businesses that provide equal benefits to their employees' domestic partners.

Enacting the new comprehensive domestic partnership law was a huge step forward, and yet scarcely before the ink on the new law was dry. State Senator William J. "Pete" Knight, the author of Proposition 22, the California ballot initiative that banned marriage by same-sex couples, challenged the law in court. In court papers filed in September 2003, Senator Knight's attorneys argued that the new law "would change the effect of [Prop 22] by providing to domestic partners a legal status so indistinguishable from marriage that the initiative statute would no longer have the effect of limiting the marital institution to opposite-sex spouses. Therefore, [the domestic partnership law] is unconstitutional under state law because it amends a voter-enacted initiative statute without the approval of the voters."

As the domestic partnership bill's primary sponsor, Equality California intervened in the litigation to help defend the bill, represented by NCLR, Lambda Legal, and Los Angeles attorney David Codell, who took the lead in briefing and arguing the case. The Superior Court in Sacramento upheld the new law, and the California Court of Appeal affirmed that decision on April 4, 2005, concluding that "[t]he numerous dissimilarities between the two types of unions disclose that the legislature has not created a 'same-sex marriage' under the guise of another name" by enacting the domestic partnership law. The California Supreme Court declined any further review, thus allowing the law to stand.

Even as we worked to defend the domestic partnership law, however, the pressure to win true marriage equality was increasing. Having tasted full equality for the first time in Massachusetts, same-sex couples across the country were becoming increasingly impatient with incremental progress and unwilling to settle for being relegated to a separate, inferior and stigmatizing status. Elected officials were also beginning to awaken to the injustice of discrimination against LGBT families and to see laws that undermined our dignity as deeply offensive and at odds with fundamental American values of fairness and equality.

Those emerging political allies included State Assemblyman Mark Leno, who announced in December 2003, shortly after the victory in Massachusetts, that he was introducing a bill to allow same-sex couples to marry in California. Gavin Newsom, San Francisco's dynamic new mayor, was also a strong proponent of LGBT equality. In January 2004, Mayor Newsom listened in sickened disbelief as then-President George W. Bush pledged to amend the federal Constitution to bar same-sex couples from marriage. Angered by the president's scapegoating of a vulnerable minority, Mayor Newsom called his staff and directed them to investigate whether San Francisco could begin issuing marriage licenses to same-sex couples.

Just days before moving forward with that plan, Mayor Newsom reached out for advice to NCLR's Executive Director Kate Kendell, who called me on a Friday night to share the stunning news: our mayor intended to start issuing marriage licenses to same-sex couples the following Monday. Kate had already briefed the mayor's office on the movement's existing strategies and plans and discussed potential concerns that the mayor's actions might alienate the California Supreme Court and thus damage our ultimate chance of success. At the same time, she understood that Mayor Newsom was acting from a place of deep moral principle and conviction. We shared his confidence that California's marriage ban was unconstitutional—and his impatience for change. Although sobered by the stakes, we were ready to do all we could to help defend the mayor's courageous actions. We spent the remainder of that weekend updating our senior legal staff and conferring with our colleagues, knowing full well that we were in the calm before the storm and that neither California, nor our movement, would likely ever be quite the same again.

Even as word of Mayor Newsom's action spread and the lines around City Hall began to swell with hundreds of couples eager to marry, opponents of the freedom to marry raced to launch legal challenges. On February 13, 2004, the day after San Francisco began issuing marriage licenses to same-sex couples, two anti-LGBT organizations, the Campaign for California Families and the Proposition 22 Legal Defense and Education Fund, filed lawsuits in the San Francisco Superior Court, asking for orders directing the city to stop issuing the licenses.

Within days after these first legal challenges were filed, NCLR, along with our colleagues at Lambda Legal and the ACLU, jumped in to defend the rights of same-sex couples and make the case that California's marriage ban for same-sex couples was unconstitutional. On behalf of five same-sex couples and Equality California, we moved to intervene in the two challenges and urged the Superior Court to allow the San Francisco marriages to continue. We argued that the state's marriage ban violated the California Constitution, and that Mayor Newsom and county officials had not only the right but the duty to issue marriage licenses to same-sex couples on equal terms with other couples.

Initially, we prevailed. The Superior Court permitted the marriages to continue, finding that the two anti-LGBT groups who sought to challenge city officials had no legal right to do so. Jubilant crowds of applicants continued to line up at City Hall, and couples from every corner of the country hastily made plans to come to San Francisco to fulfill their dreams of marrying.

Inside City Hall, a steady stream of couples celebrated their vows, clutching bouquets sent by complete strangers from around the world, and cheered on by their children, family, friends, city staffers, and others who had come simply to witness one of the most astonishing and beautiful moments in our movement's history. For those glorious weeks, to walk through San Francisco's streets was to be part of an elusive but unmistakable transformation, as families who had experienced so much stigma and shame felt the wonder and joy of equality.

Meanwhile, however, state officials were under mounting political pressure to take action. After the Superior Court declined to halt the marriages, Republican Governor Arnold Schwarzenegger urged California Attorney General Lockyer, a Democrat, "to take immediate steps" to "obtain a definitive judicial resolution" of whether San Francisco's actions were lawful. While expressing personal support for same-sex couples, Lockyer stated that his office had a duty to defend California's laws barring same-sex couples from marrying and "allow the courts to determine whether the city has acted illegally" by issuing the licenses.

As the month of February drew to a close, couples continued to marry in huge numbers in what became known as the "Winter of Love" in San Francisco. On

March 3, Attorney General Lockyer filed a petition in the California Supreme Court asking the Court to order San Francisco officials to stop issuing marriage licenses to same-sex couples and to invalidate the thousands of marriages that had already taken place.

On March 11, the California Supreme Court entered an interim order directing San Francisco officials to "refrain from issuing marriage licenses or certificates" to same-sex couples pending further judicial review. The Court was careful to make clear that it would not consider whether the marriage ban itself was unconstitutional, but only whether Mayor Newsom had the authority to order county officials to begin issuing marriage licenses to same-sex couples.

The Court's order brought the celebrations at San Francisco City Hall to an end—for the moment, at least. More than four thousand couples had married in the city from February 12 to March 11, 2004.

In August, the California Supreme Court ruled that Mayor Newsom and county officials had acted beyond their authority in issuing the licenses. Over the strong objections of some justices, it also invalidated all of the marriages that had taken place.

The California Supreme Court's August ruling was devastating to the thousands of couples who had married—and especially for those whose children had joined in their celebrations. But it was also clear that this ruling would not be the last word. The Court's earlier March order had included a critical sentence that its order did "not preclude the filing of a separate action in superior court raising a substantive constitutional challenge to the current marriage statutes." In effect, the Court was inviting a constitutional challenge to California's exclusion of same-sex couples from marriage.

It was a challenge we were happy to accept.

On March 12, the day after the California Supreme Court's initial order, we at NCLR, Lambda Legal, and the ACLU, along with pro bono counsel from the law firms Heller Ehrman LLP, Steefel, Levitt & Weiss, and the Law Office of David C. Codell, filed a new case in San Francisco Superior Court arguing that California's marriage ban for same-sex couples violated the California Constitution. Ultimately, the case was coordinated with other similar challenges into a single proceeding in San Francisco titled—accurately, if not poetically—In re Marriage Cases.

The same-sex couples who were our clients in the Marriage Cases reflected the racial and cultural diversity of California. They included government, academic, technology, and nonprofit workers; small business owners; retirees; and stay-at-home parents. Many were raising or had previously raised children together. Among others, the plaintiffs included Del Martin and Phyllis Lyon, legendary founders of the first national lesbian organization, the Daughters of

Bilitis, and beloved figures in the San Francisco LGBT community. Del and Phyllis had been together for more than fifty years and were the first couple married in the city in February 2004. The plaintiffs also included Equality California and Our Family Coalition, a Bay Area organization dedicated to promoting the well-being of families with LGBT members. All of the plaintiffs courageously agreed to stand in the spotlight and speak publicly about their relationships and the importance of marriage for their families.

On June 11, the coordinated Marriage Cases were assigned to Judge Richard Kramer of the San Francisco Superior Court who scheduled a hearing on the cases for December 22 and 23, 2004.

San Francisco Chief Deputy City Attorney Therese Stewart, now a justice on the California Court of Appeal, argued on behalf of the City and County of San Francisco, and I argued on behalf of the twelve couples in our case. California's new domestic partnership law was scheduled to go into effect on January 1, 2005, giving registered domestic partners most of the rights and benefits of marriage under state law. It was therefore critical for us to explain why domestic partnerships were not enough to make same-sex couples truly equal under the law or in the eyes of the community. I explained to Judge Kramer that "creating a separate class for same-sex couples necessarily sends the message that their relationships are less valuable and less deserving of respect." I quoted one of the plaintiffs, Stuart Gaffney, who had said in a statement filed with the court, "No member of our family has ever congratulated us for becoming domestic partners."

In defending the ban, the Attorney General's office could not argue—as state officials in other states had done—that children were harmed or disadvantaged by having same-sex parents. That argument had been foreclosed by the enactment of numerous California laws embracing same-sex parents and their children and treating them as equal. Acknowledging the consensus of decades of social science research, the Attorney General's office conceded that same-sex couples were capable and responsible parents who were just as fit to raise children as opposite-sex couples. Instead, the Attorney General's office argued that California had a right to retain the "traditional" definition of marriage and could choose to protect same-sex couples through a separate legal status.

After hearing arguments from counsel in all the coordinated cases, Judge Kramer issued his final decision on April 13, 2005: California's exclusion of same-sex couples from marriage violated the equal protection guarantee of the California Constitution. "The state's protracted denial of equal protection cannot be justified simply because such constitutional violation has become traditional," he wrote. He also rejected the idea that this constitutional violation could be cured by the state's creation of a system of domestic partnership that provides most of the same rights and benefits: "The idea that marriage-like rights without marriage is adequate smacks of a concept long-rejected by the courts: separate but equal."

Like all of our legal team, I was elated and thrilled to be part of such an important case. It was an honor to work with some of the most distinguished private litigators in the state, including David C. Codell and Heller Ehrman partners Stephen V. Bomse and Christopher F. Stoll, and with some of the most respected advocates in our movement, including Jon Davidson and Jennifer Pizer from Lambda Legal, Matt Coles and James Esseks from the ACLU, and Kate Kendell and Courtney Joslin from NCLR. Fittingly, given its tremendous national importance, the California case was staffed by a dream team of some of our nation's finest legal minds.

As a transgender man, I was also moved by Judge Kramer's decision in a very personal way. After transitioning from female to male, I had legally married my wife Robin in California in 2001, long before same-sex couples anywhere in the country were able to do so. Like millions of other LGBT people, I had never dreamed I would be able to marry or have a family. Growing up in a conservative farming community in rural Texas, I had struggled for years to accept my identity as a transgender person. As an adult I was estranged from my family and my cultural roots, which I felt as an anguished loss. Being able to marry had transformed my life in ways I never could have imagined. Not only did being married bring me great personal joy, it also enabled me to heal my relationship with my parents and extended family, who were able to understand my life for the first time.

Because of that experience, I knew firsthand the unique ability of marriage to change lives and to bring families and communities together. Now, from Massachusetts to California, courts were grasping that potential as well and helping to transform the place of LGBT people in our society. It was incredibly powerful to realize that, if we prevailed, future generations of LGBT children would not carry the same burdens of stigma and shame or be cut off from their families and cultures.

Victory, however, was far from certain. On October 5, 2006, the California Court of Appeal reversed Judge Kramer's ruling. In a 2–1 decision, the court upheld the marriage ban, holding that "it is rational for the Legislature to preserve the opposite-sex definition of marriage, which has existed throughout history and which continues to represent the common understanding of marriage in most other countries and states of our union, while at the same time providing equal rights and benefits to same-sex partners through a comprehensive domestic partnership system."

In a forceful dissent, Justice Anthony Kline criticized the majority's "indifference" to "the reasons the United States Supreme Court and the California Supreme Court have deemed marriage a fundamental constitutional right." "Though not its purpose," Justice Kline noted, "the inescapable effect of the analysis the majority adopts is to diminish the humanity of the lesbians and gay men whose rights are defeated."

Although the Court of Appeal's decision was a painful blow, our aim all along had been to get the cases to the state's highest court, which, despite its conservatism, had invited the suit and seemed ready to resolve the issue for the state. In addition, the Court was proving increasingly receptive to the claims of same-sex couples. In 2005, the Court issued a trio of groundbreaking decisions affirming the equality of same-sex parents. "We perceive no reason," the Court explained in one, "why both parents of a child cannot be women." With high hopes, we petitioned the California Supreme Court to review the Court of Appeal's decision, and on December 20, the Supreme Court unanimously granted review. After receiving the parties' initial briefs, the Court ordered all parties to respond in writing to four additional questions—a clear sign that the Court was treating the case with extraordinary care and attention to detail.

We welcomed the chance to address those new questions—especially one asking, in effect, why the freedom to marry is a fundamental right. Since 2004, when the case was filed, we had deepened our understanding of that question profoundly, in ways that were ultimately reflected in the *Obergefell* decision by the U.S. Supreme Court. As we had come to recognize, the most important aspects of marriage are not about legal benefits and rights, but about love, commitment, and equal dignity.

Just as most straight couples do not marry in order to gain legal protections, but in order to publicly join their lives together and to express their love and commitment, the same is true for most same-sex couples. Initially, our briefs had stressed the long list of legal rights and benefits that marriage brings and the inequality of denying those protections to committed same-sex couples. Over time, however, we shifted that focus significantly. While still noting the important legal rights provided by marriage, we put the primary emphasis not on the loss of specific legal benefits, but on the loss of dignity and autonomy in not being able to make such an important life choice. As the U.S. Supreme Court would ultimately put it in *Obergefell*: "Choices about marriage shape an individual's destiny."

In September, no less than thirty amicus briefs were submitted to the Court, representing scores of religious, civil rights, and child advocacy organizations, along with numerous California municipal governments, bar associations, and leading legal scholars. All urged the Court to put an end to state laws excluding same-sex couples from marriage. One of the most powerful came from students in the Civil Rights Clinic at Howard Law School in Washington, D.C., who

worked for months to draft a powerful brief comparing the historical justifications used to bar gay and interracial couples from marriage.

Presided over by Chief Justice Ronald George, the California Supreme Court
heard oral argument in the Marriage Cases on March 4, 2008. Appointed to the
bench by Republican Governor Pete Wilson, Chief Justice George was a well-
respected but conservative jurist. In 1998, he had authored a decision holding that
the Boy Scouts of America could exclude gay youth members. In 2005, however,
he had joined a decision holding that under California law, a country club could
not refuse to offer the same benefits to a same-sex couple in a registered domestic
partnership as it offered to married opposite-sex couples.

Those arguing on behalf of the freedom to marry included myself, Therese
Stewart, and private attorneys Michael Maroko and Waukeen McCoy. Attorneys representing the California governor and the California attorney general
argued in favor of the ban, as did counsel for two anti-LGBT amicus groups—
the Campaign for California Families and the Proposition 22 Legal Defense and
Education Fund.

During the argument, attorneys for those anti-LGBT groups repeatedly argued that permitting same-sex couples to marry would diminish the institution
of marriage, lessening its value to straight couples. In rebuttal, I urged the Court
to reject that offensive claim: "With apologies to Shakespeare, same-sex couples
are not here to bury marriage, but to praise it." Those arguments later played

NCLR Executive Director Kate Kendell reacting to winning the 2008 marriage decision in
California. Photo Credit: COURTESY OF NCLR

Los Angeles LGBT Pride 2009 with, clockwise from top, Lambda Legal National Legal Director Jon Davidson; then–San Francisco Chief Deputy City Attorney Therese Stewart, co-counsel in the California marriage cases; Jennifer Pizer, then–National Marriage Project director at Lambda Legal; and Stewart's wife, Atty. Carole Scagnetti. Photo Credit: COURTESY OF LAMBDA LEGAL

a prominent role in *Obergefell* as well, prompting Justice Kennedy to rebut the argument that "it would demean a timeless institution if the concept and lawful status of marriage were extended to two persons of the same sex." "Far from seeking to devalue marriage," he wrote, "the petitioners seek it for themselves because of their respect—and need—for its privileges and responsibilities."

On May 15, 2008, the California Supreme Court became the second state supreme court in the country to strike down a state marriage ban.

In a 4–3 decision, drafted by Chief Justice George, the Court ruled: "In light of the fundamental nature of the substantive rights embodied in the right to marry—and their central importance to an individual's opportunity to live a happy, meaningful, and satisfying life as a full member of society—the California Constitution properly must be interpreted to guarantee this basic civil right to all individuals and couples, without regard to their sexual orientation."

The Court's decision was the first to reject the constitutionality of an alternative status for same-sex couples, such as civil unions or domestic partnerships. It was also the first to hold that individuals who are discriminated against because of their sexual orientation must be given the same high level of constitutional protection as those discriminated against based on race or gender. "[I]n contrast to earlier times, our state now recognizes that an individual's capacity to establish a loving and long-term committed relationship with another person and responsibly to care for and raise children does not depend upon the individual's sexual orientation, and, more generally, that an individual's sexual orientation—like a person's race or gender—does not constitute a legitimate basis upon which to deny or withhold legal rights."

The California Supreme Court's ruling went into effect at 5:00 p.m. on June 16, 2008. At 5:01 p.m. that day, Del Martin and Phyllis Lyon, together now for fifty-eight years, again became the first couple legally married in San Francisco in a ceremony officiated by Mayor Newsom. In short order, both the Connecticut Supreme Court and the Iowa Supreme Court cited the California decision in striking down marriage bans in their states. After the California decision, our movement never lost another state marriage case. Over the next six months, until the devastating passage of Proposition 8, more than eighteen thousand same-sex couples married in California. These marriages propelled the movement forward, as the public saw firsthand that the joy and love marriage brought to millions of Americans was now being shared and respected by same-sex couples and their families. Over the next seven years there would be victories and defeats, ups and downs and delays, but the freedom to marry was on its way to becoming a lived reality for all.

PARALLEL JOURNEYS THROUGH DISCRIMINATION: ASIAN AMERICANS AND MODERN MARRIAGE EQUALITY

KARIN WANG

————— ∞ —————

Karin Wang is the vice president of Programs and Communications at Asian Americans Advancing Justice-Los Angeles and a founding member of API Equality-LA.

In February 2004, the City of San Francisco began issuing marriage licenses to same-sex couples, and hundreds of gays and lesbians lined up to legalize their committed relationships. This provoked a backlash from opponents of marriage equality, including lawsuits seeking to halt the marriages as well as protests and demonstrations. Among the latter were several anti-LGBT rallies organized by Chinese immigrant churches, which attracted thousands of Chinese Americans—and mainstream media attention—in San Francisco and Los Angeles.[1]

As an Asian American civil rights advocate and staff member at Asian Americans Advancing Justice-Los Angeles (the nation's largest Asian American legal organization), I was shocked and dismayed by the protests and feared they would be viewed as representing all Asian Americans. Desperate to raise an alternative voice, I helped to form API Equality-LA, a coalition of LGBT and allied individuals and organizations united by the common desire to demonstrate strong Asian American support for marriage equality.

Although API Equality-LA garnered strong initial support from respected voices in the Asian American community—such as elected officials, nonprofit heads, faith leaders, community activists, and even celebrities—we encountered significant hurdles in expanding Asian American support for marriage equality. Despite having personal one-on-one conversations at community events and placing positive stories of Asian American lesbians and gays in Asian-language newspapers, we found that many Asian Americans dismissed marriage equality and LGBT struggles as being wholly unrelated to their own experiences.

Meanwhile, the legal challenge to the San Francisco marriage licenses (In Re Marriage Cases) was working its way through the courts. At the same time, marriage equality opponents were seeking to qualify a state ballot initiative that would constitutionally prohibit marriage of same-sex couples (Proposition 8). The possibility of such an initiative added urgency to our public education and community organizing efforts.

In early 2007, as In Re Marriage Cases was headed to the California Supreme Court, API Equality-LA and Advancing Justice-LA, along with other Asian American LGBT and legal leaders, devised a community education and organizing strategy centered on the legal case. By filing an amicus (friend of the court) brief, which allows non-parties to a lawsuit to weigh in on a pending case, we thought we could leverage the intense media focus on the case to educate fellow Asian Americans and lay important groundwork for the likely battle looming at the ballot box.[2]

In particular, we wanted to lift up California's shameful history of racist marriage restrictions targeting Asian immigrants. We hoped that by highlighting how anti-miscegenation laws—along with governmental restrictions on immigration, citizenship, and other rights—had isolated and excluded Asian immigrants for decades from mainstream American society, more Asian Americans would understand and support the LGBT community's fight for the freedom to marry.

At the turn of the twentieth century, both state and federal anti-miscegenation laws prohibited interracial marriages, built on fears of integrating white and non-white groups. These laws were driven primarily by fear of black–white couplings. But in California, where Asian immigrants outnumbered African Americans in the early 1900s, the laws explicitly targeted Asians.[3] The California state law banning the issuance of marriage licenses between whites and non-whites specifically included "Mongolians,"[4] which referred to East Asians, and was later clarified to also include Filipinos or "Malays."[5]

In the nineteenth century, large groups of Asian immigrants, including Chinese, Japanese, Filipinos, and Asian Indians, were imported as laborers to build the West, working in mining, railroads, and agriculture.[6] Soon after these mostly male immigrants first began arriving in the 1800s, they became the targets of laws seeking to exclude or severely restrict them, including bans on immigration, citizenship, and marriage.[7] These laws undermined the formation of families and communities among these early Asian immigrants, creating isolated bachelor societies whose members had no hope of marrying, having families, or integrating into American society. Without families and children, Asian immigrant populations dwindled. For example, between the Chinese Exclusion Act and anti-miscegenation laws, the Chinese population declined rapidly from more than 107,000 in 1890 to less than 62,000 by 1920.[8]

The tactic of drawing parallels between the struggles of early Asian immigrants and those of modern same-sex couples proved effective. By the time we submitted the amicus brief to the California Supreme Court in September 2007, we had rallied sixty-three Asian American organizations in support of marriage equality.[9] The supporting groups included many of the largest and most prominent Asian American civil rights advocacy organizations, bar associations, social service providers, and community groups and represented the broad diversity of Asian America (e.g., Chinese, Filipino, Japanese, Korean, South Asian, and Southeast Asian).

Garnering the support of these groups advanced the issue of marriage equality within the Asian American community in several ways. First, focusing on the connection between Asian American and LGBT communities gave non-LGBT Asian American groups an opportunity to publicly "come out" in support of the LGBT community. Some organizations reached a decision to sign on relatively easily. For other groups, our request to support the amicus brief initiated complex conversations about the issue of marriage equality and the meaning of "civil rights" for an Asian American organization. Some who were not able to endorse the brief before it was filed did later voice public support for marriage equality, adding to the growing chorus of Asian American voices supporting the freedom to marry.[10]

Second, we successfully drew both mainstream and Asian-language media attention to our brief, expanding the influence of our message to a larger segment of the Asian American community. On the day we filed the brief, we held two simultaneous press conferences in San Francisco and Los Angeles, featuring diverse Asian American community leaders speaking eloquently about their support for marriage equality for same-sex couples.

In addition, the conversations that began with a simple request to endorse the amicus brief opened the door for many additional conversations with the organizations approached to endorse the brief. As the issue evolved—with the California Supreme Court ruling in favor of marriage equality in May 2008, and Proposition 8 ("Prop 8"), which challenged the basis for the ruling, qualifying for the November 2008 election—the groundwork laid by the amicus brief proved invaluable in subsequent marriage equality advocacy. In fall 2008, the relationships strengthened through the amicus brief helped line up dozens of Asian American groups in the campaign against Prop 8. After the measure passed on November 4, 2008, many of the groups that had joined our California Supreme Court amicus brief also joined amicus briefs in support of the legal challenge to the implementation of Prop 8.[11]

But the biggest legacy of the organizing in the Asian American community is the impact on views about marriage equality in the community. Prop 8 narrowly passed in 2008 (52 to 48 percent), and an exit poll conducted by Advancing Justice-LA found that Asian Americans in Southern California voted similarly to voters overall (54 to 46 percent for Prop 8).[12] However, in the years leading up to Prop 8, support for marriage equality shifted more rapidly in Asian American communities than in the general population.

In March 2000, California voters considered Proposition 22, an earlier ballot initiative to statutorily prohibit California from recognizing marriage between same-sex partners. Advancing Justice-LA's exit poll from that election showed that Asian American voters in Southern California supported Prop 22 by much wider margins than the general population, with 68 percent of Asian Americans in support of Prop 22 and only 32 percent opposed,[13] compared to 58 percent of voters overall in support and 43 percent opposed.

In the eight years between Prop 22 and Prop 8, the state of California made remarkable strides in building support for marriage equality, with the gulf between voters who supported and opposed marriage equality narrowing from fifteen points (58 vs. 43 percent) to only four points (52 vs. 48 percent)—a remarkable shift in less than a decade. But Asian Americans made an even greater shift during the same period of time—tumbling from a thirty-six-point margin (68 vs. 32 percent) to eight points (54 vs. 46 percent).

While many factors contributed to this change, I believe the organizing efforts of groups like API Equality-LA and Advancing Justice-LA had a clear impact. By drawing a direct line between the experiences of Asian immigrants a century earlier and modern-day gay and lesbian couples, we made a compelling argument for marriage equality that our community could not ignore. And when the U.S. Supreme Court ruled in favor of the freedom to marry in *Obergefell v. Hodges*, Asian Americans were among the most vocal and joyous celebrants, thrilled by the historic legal victory and the dismantling of a barrier to social integration that our own community knew too well.

TRANSLATING EQUALITY: ON THE ROLE OF LGBT LATINAS/OS IN THE MARRIAGE MOVEMENT

FRANCISCO DUEÑAS

———— ∞ ————

Francisco Dueñas is director of Diversity, Inclusion and Proyecto Igualdad for Lambda Legal.

I joined the Los Angeles office of Lambda Legal in January 2004. I was twenty-six and energized by the possibility of applying my organizing skills in the fight against homophobia. That winter was a roller coaster of emotions and possibilities. Within two months, the Massachusetts Supreme Court had ruled that same-sex couples had the right to marry there. In San Francisco, the mayor had ordered county clerks to issue marriage licenses. National change seemed imminent as I worked in New Mexico on Lambda Legal's behalf, seeking a local organizer and assessing the political landscape for a marriage case and campaign. I couldn't have been happier.

Back in Los Angeles, however, I was surprised by how tiny the marriage movement was. Consisting almost exclusively of LGBT organizations and mostly white faces, I questioned the lack of other progressive voices in the movement. Where were the HIV organizations? Where were California's various ethnic communities? Where was organized labor? The lessons of a 2000 California ballot initiative against marriage equality (Proposition 22) made it clear that more outreach and education was sorely needed. Latinas/os' support for Prop 22 was the highest of any ethnic group.[1]

At this time, there was only one Spanish support group for parents of LGBT children in the greater Los Angeles metro area, thirty-five miles south in Orange County.[2] This, in spite of the fact that the Latina/o population in the United States had doubled since 1990 and that half of all Latinas/os were in two states: California and Texas.[3] When I came out, I relied on a Spanish *telenovela* to help my parents understand what being gay meant. For me, that lack of racial diversity in the marriage movement, the high support against marriage equality, and the lack of support for my parents in Spanish were all related. This knot of oppression needed untangling.

The situation for LGBT Latinas/os was difficult. LGBT stereotypes and stigma abounded in Latina/o communities.[4] Being a gay man was still strongly associated with AIDS or dressing like a woman. LGBT Latinas/os were particularly harmed by anti-LGBT policies. For example, Don't Ask, Don't Tell (DADT) was more injurious to Latina lesbians, who reported six times the rate of military service than other women in the United States. The HIV immigration and travel ban, in effect until 2010, reinforced HIV and, by association, LGBT ostracism and shame. As a response to AIDS, many POC (people of color) LGBT activists had turned to HIV prevention and care and away from the general LGBT movement. Around the country, the few and vital Latina/o LGBT groups available were invariably volunteer-led and grassroots-funded. In many places, for better or worse, Latina/o HIV organizations were and continue to be the *de facto* Latina/o LGBT groups.[5]

This was the national context within which I was named coordinator of Lambda Legal's Latina/o outreach project, *Proyecto Igualdad*, possibly the first Latina/o outreach program of a national LGBT organization. Our goals were to translate educational information, build relationships with Latina/o organizations (LGBT and non-LGBT), advocate through the Spanish media, and have a presence at Latina/o conferences, fairs, and events. We wanted LGBT Latinas/os to know their rights and to help them safely come out. Coming out is the political *sine qua non* for marriage equality and LGBT rights, in general. I was very optimistic that Latinas/os could be ardent supporters for LGBT rights and marriage equality despite their past voting record. I began by focusing on our Latina/o plaintiffs and their stories.

One plaintiff, Lupita Benitez, a Mexican immigrant from California, had been fighting a denial of fertility treatments by her doctors, who claimed it was against their religious beliefs to treat her. The case was a precursor to the debates we are having today over religious exemptions. Other plaintiffs who helped highlight discrimination faced by LGBT Latinas/os in the United States included Jorge Soto Vega. He was told at his asylum hearing that he didn't look "gay enough" and could return to Mexico. Another plaintiff, Lydia Ramos, was fighting her deceased partner's family for custody of her daughters. Through these stories we were able to engage many Latina/o organizations and get our foot in the door. In the Benitez case, a few Latina/o organizations signed on to amicus briefs.

Additionally, research and demographic data on LGBT Latinas/os helped build our legitimacy with these organizations. From a study of the 2000 census by the National Gay and Lesbian Task Force (now National LGBTQ Task Force), we learned that Latina/o same-sex couples lived primarily in Latina/o communities and were as similarly disadvantaged as straight Latina/o households. It also made visible Latina/o same-sex couples living in Latina/o rural communities like California's central valley; Yakima, Washington; and along the U.S.–Mexico border in Texas. LGBT Latinas/os needed much of the same support as other Latina/o communities, but weren't sure if they were welcomed at non-LGBT Latina/o organizations.[6] Latina/o community leaders were surprised that Latina lesbians were raising children at almost similar rates as Latina/o straight couples. This data gave a relatable face to the victims of discrimination and helped to debunk stereotypes, a critical step in garnering support from Latina/o nonprofits.[7]

By 2005, an effort to certify a ballot initiative to amend California's Constitution to ban marriage for same-sex couples (Proposition 8) was a political certainty, but we were not sure when the effort might succeed in placing the question on the ballot. In response, what started as a Latina/o working group for the statewide marriage equality coalition turned into the Latino Coalition for Justice-LA, an effort to bring all the Latina/o LGBT, HIV, and allied organizations in Southern California under one advocacy umbrella. We named ourselves after a similar national effort[8] and mostly comprised Latina/o LGBT and HIV groups and LGBT organizations with Latina/o projects like Lambda Legal and GLAAD.

We convened Latina/o LGBT community leaders to brainstorm on what we wanted for the campaign, what we could each contribute, and what long-term opportunities were possible. United as a community, we wanted a say in how the Proposition 8 campaign engaged Latinas/os. We crafted messages we felt resonated with our communities. One suggested campaign commercial compared an undocumented immigrant trying to get a driver's license with a gay couple trying to get a marriage license, with the announcer saying, "Discrimination is discrimination."[9] I wanted a commercial that reminded Latina/o voters of the famous motto of a celebrated Mexican president: *El respeto al derecho ajeno es la paz* ("The respect for the rights of others is peace."). We thought Latinas/os would be roused by framing Prop 8 as discrimination. In this assessment, we incorrectly agreed with the LGBT conventional wisdom. Voters turned out to be swayed by arguments about love rather than equality. Still, we hoped to help secure Latina/o spokespeople, involve general Latina/o organizations, and identify compelling stories from the community. For the campaign, we wanted materials in Spanish, in print and on TV. The campaign was an opportunity as much as it was a threat. And while short-lived and modestly successful, the agenda this Latina/o LGBT coalition embarked on and the synergy that was created has had a lasting impact on Latina/o LGBT advocacy nationally.

The road to Election Day was a long one. Years passed while the official campaign went on hiatus, waiting for ballot initiative to qualify. During that time, the coalition continued our Latina/o LGBT advocacy but on other matters. As Election Day loomed closer, we refocused on marriage. We supported the campaign by helping with weekend canvasses and community forums, yet it seemed negligible. We were identifying supporters, but there were lots more "Yes on Prop 8" lawn signs than "No" ones in Latina/o communities.

As a coalition, we passed pro-LGBT resolutions at national Latina/o conferences. We knew Latina/o community leaders were with us, but we weren't sure about the Latina/o voter base. At our request, Oscar De La O, executive director of BIENESTAR, a Latina/o service organization known for their HIV work, joined the campaign executive team. Yet, we at the coalition still felt like outsiders to the campaign. A new Latina/o LGBT political action committee, HONOR PAC, opened its own campaign office in East Los Angeles to supplement the work (or lack thereof) of the central campaign in Latina/o communities. Ultimately, all these efforts were not enough to win Latinas/os that election night, although the numbers improved. Latinas/os supported Prop 8 by a 53 to 47 percent margin, down from 65 percent against marriage equality in 2000.[10]

In hindsight, we should have also educated LGBT Latinas/os on how to come out through authentic conversations, directly addressing the importance of marriage in our lives. We focused on Latina/o voters but not on their connections with us, the Latina/o LGBT community. In my case, for example, I never asked my parents how they would vote. I was too afraid to be disappointed by what I assumed was their lack of support. I thought my work on the campaign would make up for it. Ironically, it was the loss in Proposition 8 that spurred many LGBT Latinas/os and our allies to have intentional conversations about why they supported marriage.

While the Prop 8 campaign was on hiatus, the issue of immigration was galvanizing the Latina/o community in a way that few LGBT organizations recognized. Immigration turned out to be an entrée into marriage equality for many Latinas/os. Family unification is one of the central principles of U.S. immigration law, but married same-sex couples were not considered family for immigration purposes under the Defense of Marriage Act (DOMA). Unfair immigration laws led to highlighting the stories of same-sex binational couples and the need for marriage equality. Since many Latinas/os were intimately familiar with the country's immigration system, the coalition was eager to highlight the plight of binational same-sex couples, LGBT asylum seekers, and the realities of immigration detention for LGBT people. In July 2007, the death of Victoria Arellano, a transgender Latina in a local immigration detention center, further outraged the community after it was reported she had been denied her HIV medicines for weeks.[11]

That year, millions marched for humane immigration reform and against an anti-immigrant bill in Congress. Across the country, LGBT contingents were planned to join these May Day/Immigrant's Rights marches. In Los Angeles, in those first years, the LGBT contingent was not always noticed as such. Some marchers were not familiar with the rainbow flag that attracted LGBT people and allies along the way.[12] Many had never thought of LGBT people as immigrants, and few were aware of the lack of immigration benefits.

However, through our continual presence at immigrants' rights conferences and Latina/o community festivals, LGBT immigrants started to be visible in the larger immigration debate. In face-to-face conversations, we asked festivalgoers to support immigration benefits for married same-sex couples. Some immediately understood the injustice of marriage inequality. This strategy helped Latinas/os relate to LGBT people as part of their own community, increasing LGBT awareness and acceptance. An interesting corollary is how young LGBT undocumented youth, known as "undocuqueers," were inspired by the LGBT movement to come out and add their voice and leadership. Through these courageous individuals, many more LGBT allies were created in the Dream Act[13] movement. With the eventual demise of the HIV travel ban and DOMA, the U.S. immigration system, which affects the lives of so many Latinas/os, indirectly helped reduce HIV stigma, acknowledged the love of same-sex couples, and increased the support for marriage among Latinas/os.

As LGBT advocacy in the Latina/o community advanced, several new Latina/o LGBT organizations and projects developed with various areas of specialization.[14] At Lambda Legal, we targeted the Latina/o legal community. Latina/o lawyers, influential members of their communities, were a natural constituency for our Latina/o outreach. If Latina/o lawyers were not LGBT-friendly and knowledgeable, then LGBT Latinas/os, who mostly lived in Latina/o communities, were at a disadvantage when securing legal services and support.

By closely collaborating with national Latina/o legal defense organizations like MALDEF and Latino Justice/PRLDEF, their leadership recognized that LGBT Latinas/os were more vulnerable to discrimination, marginalized further by homophobia and transphobia. This shift was also a result of years of internal advocacy within these organizations, as Latina/o LGBT professionals had not always been welcomed. Lambda Legal sought the support of the Latina/o legal organizations for marriage cases as amici. Lambda Legal, in turn, joined as amici in several immigrant rights cases relevant to the LGBT movement. This collaboration was not always easy; Lambda Legal at times questioned whether immigration reform was an LGBT issue. However, through mutual education between these advocacy organizations, LGBT Latina/o rights were advanced. Prone to neglect from both LGBT and Latina/o communities, here LGBT Latinas/os were serving as a bridge, not a wedge community.

To further engage the Latina/o legal community, I started attending the conferences of the Hispanic National Bar Association (HNBA) in 2006 and received support for establishing a LGBT committee from then-HNBA president Jimmy Reyna. Support gained momentum for the LGBT committee with the election of the HNBA's first openly-gay president-elect, Victor Marquez. The 2007 annual convention was a coming out party for the LGBT members of the HNBA. I organized LGBT-related legal education (which was well-received), covering immigration, marriage, and workplace discrimination. A table at the gala was designated impromptu for the nascent LGBT section. Victor thanked his husband of many years and pointed at our table announcing the creation of the section to cheers and some puzzled looks from the crowd. Victor also announced the appointment of the first chair of the LGBT section, to that member's surprise, effectively outing him. But it was when same-sex couples took to the dance floor that longtime gay HNBA members were visibly moved. They related to me how they largely kept quiet about their sexual orientation. Many would not stay long at the gala but would rather head to the gay bars where they felt more acceptance. They marveled at the thought that they might no longer need to do that. Something began to change in the culture of that group. It was electrifying to witness and imagine the possibilities.

I have heard Victor talk about the homophobia he's encountered in his legal career, including at bar associations. I too have faced some pushback, but more often than not in my Latina/o outreach, I am told I am the first LGBT advocate to reach out. Today the HNBA is very LGBT-conscious and inclusive; the organization even moved their convention after the legislature in Arizona passed an anti-LGBT religious exemption law.

The story of Latinas/os and marriage equality is one of exclusion, tenacity, and missed opportunities. It is also a tale of a thousand reconciliations after so many rifts: between white people and people of color, between straight and LGBT Latinas/os, between marriage advocates and those who work on HIV, between this homeland and that former one. This work has been both enriching and, at times, lonely. I was one staff member to address the 54 million Latinas/os in the United States. In the past twelve years, I have witnessed the increased inclusion of LGBT Latinas/os and our issues, externally and also internally, within my organization and movement. Both the Latina/o and LGBT movements have changed, grown.

It is imperative for a minority like the LGBT community to build broad support across various sectors, especially in voter referendums, but even in the legal briefs. The fight for marriage equality has humanized same-sex couples and hastened the end of other anti-LGBT laws like DADT and the HIV travel ban. In turn, the removal of those discriminatory policies has helped more LGBT Latinas/os to come out. You were able to say to your *'Apa*, "HIV no longer disqualifies my partner from entering the country," or "The military doesn't care if I'm a lesbian, Mom." Today, Latinas/os are 63 percent in favor of civil marriage rights for same-sex couples.[15] I hope this support grows and translates into greater acceptance for LGBT Latinas/os within their families and communities and is not just a political belief in support of theoretical LGBT people. I hope today's marriage win will facilitate tomorrow's HIV- and homelessness-free LGBT generation and the realization of a more humane, sensible, and efficient immigration system. Yes, we can.

THIS CHANGES EVERYTHING:
PROPOSITION 8

KATE KENDELL

———— ⨯⨯⨯ ————

Kate Kendell is executive director of the National Center for Lesbian Rights (NCLR).

As I stood on the steps of the California Supreme Court on May 17, 2008, I thrust the just-issued marriage ruling above my head and thought, "This changes everything." In my mind we had not just won the freedom to marry in California. We had won a better future for every lesbian, gay, bisexual, and transgender person in the nation. I remember thinking, as I celebrated on that sunny spring morning, that in some small Southern town a gay teen would now feel that he mattered.

NCLR had been lead counsel, along with the City and County of San Francisco, in the marriage case in California. Our legal director, Shannon Minter, had argued the case before the Court. For four years, we had poured everything we had into the case. The case was litigated with co-counsel from our LGBT legal colleagues at the ACLU, Lambda Legal, the San Francisco City Attorney's office, and the private law firms and private counsel Heller Ehrman, Howard Rice, and David Codell. We had all pulled countless all-nighters at each critical stage of the litigation. It was the case of a lifetime.

The stakes had never been higher. A win in California, the most populous state in the country, would be a harbinger, a new high-water mark in our struggle to win the freedom to marry. To win marriage in California would be the pinnacle of my legal career and would mark a new chapter in the broader effort to win full equality and security for all LGBT people. So when we did win, when four years of unflagging effort resulted in a marriage victory, I was exultant. It now seemed to me that anything was possible.

This elation was short-lived.

Even as I stood on those steps on May 17, 2008, I felt the foreboding. Petitions were already circulating to overturn any court victory and to eliminate, by popular vote, our newly granted right to marry. On June 17, 2008, same-sex couples began marrying in California. Later that summer, Proposition 8 qualified for the November 5, 2008, ballot. I was both terrified and resolute. A loss was both likely and unthinkable. Up to that point we had lost on marriage in every ballot measure contest that had only asked about whether same-sex couples should be allowed to marry, and twenty-five states had passed constitutional amendments excluding recognition of our relationships. But this had to be different. Never before had voters eliminated the right to marry for same-sex couples. Never before had a court ruling in favor of marriage equality been nullified by voters.

From the beginning of the litigation in 2004, we knew if we won, a ballot measure to reverse the ruling was virtually certain. In California it is infamously easy to place a measure on the ballot. Proponents must collect a certain number of signatures (a percentage of the electorate in the most recent state-wide election) for a measure to be placed on the ballot.

We had already lost on marriage once at the ballot. In 2000, Proposition 22 was passed easily by a 61–39 percent margin. Prop 22 was an initiative, not a constitutional amendment, and its language was identical to Prop 8: "Only marriage between a man and a woman is valid or recognized in California." Prop 22 was placed on the ballot after several efforts to win passage of anti-marriage legislation had failed in the California legislature.

We did not take Prop 22 lying down. A campaign to defeat the proposition was formed, and I traversed the state as one of the key campaign spokespeople arguing for its defeat. The issue of the freedom to marry for same-sex couples was just beginning to be broadly debated. In no state could a same-sex couple marry, and few Americans had given the issue any consideration.

But when we faced Prop 8, the landscape had changed. Same-sex couples could marry in Massachusetts and, of course, California, where we had just won the freedom to marry. Surely, we thought, California voters would not eliminate this freedom.

Because of our experience with Prop 22, as early as 2005 we formed an executive committee and a much larger campaign committee to begin laying the groundwork for the organizing and messaging research we would need once a measure qualified for the ballot. The early Executive Committee included

NCLR and the leaders from Equality California, our state-wide political organization; the ACLU of Northern California; the Los Angeles LGBT Center;
the San Diego LGBT Center; Asian-Pacific Islander Equality; and Bienestar, a
grassroots Latino HIV service organization in Los Angeles.

The larger campaign committee brought together another forty or so organizations and grew to over eighty by 2008. We met every month to discuss messaging strategy, early organizing efforts, and fundraising. Raising resources for
this early work was exceedingly difficult. A hypothetical threat fails to galvanize
people. While we knew the threat was real, it was easy for many to deny or minimize that an actual constitutional amendment would materialize.

While this early work was never to the scale of the threat, it was nevertheless a huge benefit when Prop 8 became real. We were able to immediately pivot
from community organizing and engagement to a campaign to defeat Prop 8.
We had a structure, grassroots involvement, a campaign consultant (an essential
component of any California campaign), and dozens of organizations ready to
mobilize. We had more focus and attention than any previous ballot campaign
we had faced. And, most important, we had the expectation that we could and
should win.

This expectation was fueled by an early public opinion poll that reported Prop
8 would be defeated by a margin of 12 percent, even though support for marriage
equality among voters was still well below 50 percent. Although another early
Los Angeles Times poll had us losing by double digits, people focused on the positive poll and their belief that everyone shared the joy we felt in watching so many
same-sex couples marrying. Of course, polls of voters are only as good as the
screen for likely voters and the accuracy of the turnout model used.

Unfortunately, the public polling model was way off. Our own numbers from
our campaign pollster, which only included likely voters in July 2008, showed us
behind by 17 percent on Prop 8 and only polling in the low 40 percent in support
of the freedom to marry.

By the end of the summer, thanks to a multifaceted grassroots and
multimillion-dollar, media-driven public education campaign known as Let
California Ring, the gap closed significantly. Ads were placed in over eighty
ethnic newspapers and run in numerous languages on radio and in Spanish and
English on television. The television ads in the public education campaign used
new research that focused on feelings about marriage rather than rights. The ads
were highly effective: we closed the gap to a virtual tie of 47 percent "yes" and
47 percent "no" among likely voters in our internal polling. Many voters who
didn't yet support our right to marry were demonstrating a willingness to still
vote no and not take away this newfound right. We had a real chance of winning
if we could raise the money needed to convince enough voters who did not at that

time support marriage for same-sex couples to vote no. But getting that message out was a challenge at a time when we had less money than our opponents.

The early, widely reported and wildly optimistic numbers had the effect of diminishing both urgency and dollars, two elements our campaign to defeat Prop 8 badly needed. Not until the final weeks did we have the resources needed to mount the effort required to win a ballot campaign in California. And by then it was too late. This lack of resources undermined everything on our wish list, but the campaign also suffered in other ways. Despite several years of effort, we did not fully utilize and energize our own community. While we had a number of non-gay allies from a range of diverse communities engaged as spokespeople, most were underutilized. Many LGBT people of color felt that organizing communities of color was not the priority it should have been. Moreover, we did not deploy the thousands in our community who were eager to do something but not yet ready to participate in the phone banking or knocking on doors. The campaign ads, driven by focus groups and research, fell flat and failed to connect with voters.

I was deep in the middle of all of this, but like everyone else on the Executive Committee, I did not have the power to change the trajectory of the "No on 8" campaign. All major decisions around messaging and deployment of resources are made by the campaign consultants and their team—we hired some of the best in the business. Our campaign consultant, Steve Smith, had an impressive track record, particularly in convincing voters to vote "no" on a controversial social issue measure. But we were in uncharted waters here. While every state to face a marriage-specific ballot measure had lost, California was the first where the issue before voters was to eliminate the freedom to marry, rather than forbid such a right. We hoped that this crucial and significant difference might swing the odds. Winning any ballot measure campaign in California is a massive undertaking. Our number of registered voters alone is more than the entire population of most states. The only way to win a highly contested ballot measure in California is through very expensive and saturated paid media coverage. In smaller states, vigorous door-to-door canvassing, phone-banking, and a targeted, modest paid media campaign can be enough. This sort of effort does not work in California.

Ballot campaigns in California live and die by paid TV ads. Our experts insisted that the bulk of campaign resources must be spent on ads rather than on grassroots mobilization, community outreach, canvassing, or placing lawn signs. The ads were created based on poll and focus group tested messages. Too many voters in California in 2008 were still not comfortable with marriage for same-sex couples, and their responses in focus groups to the ads created by the campaign reflected this. Messages with non-LGBT spokespeople tested more effectively than ads with same-sex couples. But, by not including actual same-sex couples and our families and stories, we missed the chance to define our humanity and our lives, and angered many in our community who felt the campaign "buried the lead" by not featuring same-sex couples and LGBT-headed families. The "No on 8" campaign also did not have the benefit of the huge investment in messaging research that was developed after we lost. That research reinforced the lessons from the Let California Ring campaign: the best messaging for moving voters was to talk about our love and commitment as couples.

It was clear to me then and even more so now that the campaign should have featured same-sex couples and their family members who support them. If we had done that and invested more in community outreach and engagement, it would have left our community feeling that we had left everything on the floor in an effort to win. But to pour money into ads that were untested or in community organizing rather than TV spots was heresy. We wanted to win and believed we could win, just barely. This was not an environment conducive to taking risks. The campaign went with tried and true best practices.

This is actually the way it is supposed to be: the professionals run the campaign, and the activists raise the money and serve as spokespeople. But the "No on 8" campaign was not a usual campaign, and now, with the benefit of hindsight, I think I and everyone involved would have done things differently. But we still would have lost. I do not think it was possible to have defeated Prop 8, no matter what our messaging strategy. Too many voters had not had any real-life experience with our marriages, and it was all too easy for our opponents to peddle distortions and prey on voters' prejudices and fears.

The "Princess Ad" was a perfect example of this most cynical type of playing to bigotry. In the ad, an eight-year-old girl runs into the family kitchen exclaiming, "Mommy, mommy, guess what I learned in school today! A prince can marry a prince, and I can marry a princess!" The look of revulsion on the mother's face says it all. That image fades and is replaced by a suited man identified as a law professor who cautions voters that "this can happen here" if you do not vote "yes" on Prop 8.

The strategy of playing on the purported consequences of marriage on the children of California was brilliant. It struck fear into the hearts of millions of parents, while shielding them from having to face their own prejudices about LGBT people or same-sex couples. It was all about "protecting our children," not "harming same-sex couples." The day after we lost the Prop 8 campaign, I had a number of voicemail messages when I went to my office. Two were unexpected, from men I did not know whose messages were something like this: "I know and like gay people, but I felt forced to vote for Prop 8 to protect my kids. I'm sorry, but I really had no other choice."

There was a moment in the last month of the Prop 8 campaign where it seemed we might win. At the crack of dawn the morning after a Prop 8 fundraiser in L.A., I took a taxi to an industrial section of Los Angeles to a small satellite studio. I was a guest on a DC-based political show. Joining me on the show was Frank Schubert, the campaign consultant for the "Yes on 8" campaign. I had sparred with Schubert in the past, but this morning was different. He seemed particularly churlish and cold.

The back and forth lasted just a few minutes, but as we debated, I remember thinking: "He's losing." I called a "No on 8" campaign staffer and asked him what that day's tracking poll numbers were, and he told me Prop 8 was losing 51–49 percent. Three days later, the "Yes on 8" campaign issued a "Code Blue for Marriage" flyer. In it, Schubert pleaded:

> The institution of marriage is in cardiac arrest in California, and I am pleading with you to help save it. **Marriage as we know it is in a life or death moment.** Gay activists held a fundraiser on Tuesday night at billionaire liberal Ron Burkle's mansion in Beverly Hills where they raised an astonishing $3.9 million. Even as guests were being entertained by Barbra Streisand, Melissa Etheridge, and Mary J. Blige, **No on 8 operatives were busy launching a sneak attack on the institution of marriage.** They began dumping **an unbelievable $7 million on air time this week alone!**

He closed by saying, *"Unless we raise $3 million in the next week, we're going to lose."*

My impression of Schubert's desperation was correct. For the first time, it seemed we might actually win and defeat Prop 8. I had been told that in every campaign there is an "October surprise." Our October surprise came as we were gaining ground. As a result, our opponents went into opportunistic overdrive.

On October 10, the *San Francisco Chronicle* ran a front-page story about a first-grade class attending the wedding of their beloved teacher to her female partner. Generally, young students attending the wedding of their teacher would never make the paper, let alone the front page. The *Chronicle's* propaganda gift to the "Yes on 8" campaign resulted in an ad showing the children on the steps of San Francisco City Hall with an ominous voice-over: "Proposition 8 opponents claim gay marriage has nothing to do with school instruction. But then a public school took first-graders to a lesbian wedding calling it a teachable moment, and now a liberal politician claims schools aren't required to teach about marriage." Once this ad gained traction, our slim margin vanished.

As we headed into election night, November 4, 2008, I was still hopeful. Maybe the polls were wrong. Maybe we'd have a stronger LGBT and ally
turnout. Maybe folks on the fence would fall our way. I so wanted to believe in a
miracle. It was to be an historic night of course. All polls showed that we would
elect our first African American president, Barack Obama. I was hoping that
support for Obama would translate into support for the LGBT community, notwithstanding the fact that our soon-to-be president himself did not then publicly
support our right to marry.

Election night 2008 was brutal. Winning marriage was the zenith of my
career as an LGBT civil rights lawyer, and losing Prop 8 was the nadir. I, and
so many in our community and beyond, had worked day and night to maintain
our freedom to marry and turn back the unbroken string of losses at the ballot. I
had moved to the campaign headquarters in the final six weeks of the campaign.
NCLR and my family had hardly seen me. I knew there were hundreds like me,
who put their lives on hold doing all they could to defeat a measure that would,
in my mind, undo all the gains we had won.

When I finally crawled into bed at 2:00 a.m. at the hotel where we had hoped
to have our victory party, the outcome of Prop 8 had not been called. But we all
knew we had lost. Prop 8 had passed. President Obama had been elected, but
even that history-making moment could not quell my nausea and grief. I knew
Obama's election was historic and would portend great things. But all I could
keep thinking that sleepless night was how devastated I was.

Sandy, my wife, and I lay in bed fully awake, saying nothing. There was nothing to say. I got up at 6:00 a.m. and showered. When I came out of the bathroom,
Sandy and our kids, Julian, then age eleven, and Ariana, age six, were eating
breakfast. The effort to defeat Prop 8 had been a family affair. Julian and his
friends at school had made posters. He even designed me a "No on 8" T-shirt,
which is still tucked neatly in a drawer. My kids knew how important defeating
Prop 8 had been to me. I could see on their faces that Sandy had told them the sad
news. I forced myself to smile. I said that yes, Prop 8 had passed. But our family
was fine, Mommy and I were still and always would be married, and while this
was a hard day, it was not the end of the struggle. "That's right, Mom," said Julian, as he gave me a hug. "You just have to keep fighting and not give up." Julian
was right, and his simple exhortation helped. But I was still devastated.

The day after Prop 8 passed I attended a rally on the steps of San Francisco's
City Hall. It was a somber occasion. The speakers exhorted the crowd to keep
pressing for justice. The following morning, I was on a plane to Boston for a
panel I had long ago committed to attend. It was the last thing I wanted to do. I
wanted to curl up in a ball and sit in a corner. And that is what I was doing on the
inside. In my hotel room that evening I got a call from Sandy. I could barely hear

her over the noise in the background. She and the kids were at a demonstration in The Castro protesting the passage of Prop 8. She told me thousands of people were there. She said it was amazing, so many LGBT people, plus hundreds of non-gay families all united in protest against the insult that was Prop 8.

I went online and saw that there were dozens of such protests in cities across the country. The heaviness of the past couple of days began to recede just a bit. In the days after Prop 8 passed, a miracle did happen, but not the one I'd been hoping for on election night. Across the nation, tens of thousands took to the streets to protest the passage of Prop 8. While those of us inside the campaign might have known our chances of defeating Prop 8 were slim, most of the rest of the state and the country had thought we had it in the bag. Most had thought that in California, having just won marriage, the voters would not take that freedom away. The shock of the result turned to outrage, then to action.

While I can never say that the passage of Prop 8 was a good thing, what I will say is that its passage electrified a new movement of both our community and non-gay allies like nothing else could have. The passage of Prop 8, the later federal challenge to Prop 8, and the district court ruling striking down Prop 8 all paved the way for a wave of litigation, victories, visibility, conversation, and ballot box wins.

As I write this now, in the glow of having won marriage nationwide, it is clear to me that Prop 8 needed to happen for us to be at this current moment. This is the trajectory of every civil rights movement, electrifying victories and devastating setbacks. And we are still not done. But we've learned the hard lesson of never giving up.

RESTORING MARRIAGE TO CALIFORNIA: *HOLLINGSWORTH V. PERRY*

KRIS PERRY

———❧———

Kris Perry and her wife, Sandy Stier, were the named plaintiffs in Hollingsworth v. Perry, *the federal case that overturned California's ban on marriage for same-sex couples.*

THE LONG AND WINDING ROAD TO EQUALITY IN CALIFORNIA: OVERTURNING PROPOSITION 8

LISA HARDAWAY
LISA HARDAWAY IS DEPUTY DIRECTOR OF EDUCATION AND PUBLIC AFFAIRS FOR COMMUNICATIONS AT LAMBDA LEGAL.

In May 2008, the freedom to marry was won in the state courts in California in a thrilling victory (see page 145); then, in November 2008, it was lost in a heartbreaking defeat at the ballot box (see page 168); and then, on June 26, 2013, it was restored when the U.S. Supreme Court ruled that Proposition 8's proponents had no right to appeal a victorious judgment that had held the initiative unconstitutional. It took five years, multiple state and federal lawsuits, a pitched electoral campaign, dozens of lawyers, and thousands of activists to finally establish the freedom to marry in California.

In 2009, the American Foundation for Equal Rights (AFER) was founded by Chad Griffin, backed by a dedicated group of California activists and philanthropists. A seasoned communications and public relations professional,

Griffin was a gay man who was ready to take on a big fight. He had served on the Clinton White House communications team, the youngest staffer ever to serve in the West Wing, and had led successful ballot fights in California for clean energy and early childhood education.

AFER was founded to challenge the constitutionality of Proposition 8, in the hope of taking down all bans against marriage for same-sex couples. The foundation hired two private attorneys who came from opposite ends of the political spectrum: Theodore B. Olson, a well-known conservative, was a partner in the firm of Gibson, Dunn & Crutcher and had served as solicitor general of the United States from 2001–4, during the first term of President George W. Bush. David Boies, considered a friend to more liberal causes, was chairman of the firm of Boies, Schiller and Flexner LLP and had won major antitrust and consumer protection cases. In 2001, they had faced each other as legal adversaries in one of the most consequential Supreme Court cases of our time, *Bush v. Gore*.

They were an odd couple, and particularly unlikely advocates for the freedom for same-sex couples to marry. They poured their hearts and immense legal skills into the fight, speaking passionately in venues across the country about why the freedom to marry was a core American value protected by the Constitution. Olson, in particular, helped make the case among conservative people in America. In a December 6, 2010, interview with Nina Totenberg on National Public Radio, he said:

> We're talking about an effect upon millions of people and the way they live their everyday life and the way they're treated in their neighborhood, in their schools, in their jobs. If you are a conservative, how could you be against a relationship in which people who love one another want to publicly state their vows ... and engage in a household in which they are committed to one another and become part of the community and accepted like other people?

In *Hollingsworth v. Perry* (originally *Perry v. Schwarzenegger*), they won a powerful federal trial court victory on August 4, 2010—the first such marriage equality victory in a federal court. Multiple days of testimony powerfully demolished many of the arguments offered by the opponents of the freedom to marry. In fact, during the trial, David Blankenhorn, founder and president of the Institute for American Values, and a longtime opponent of the freedom to marry, was pushed under oath to say: "Gay marriage would be a victory for the worthy ideas of tolerance and inclusion. It would likely decrease the number of those in society who tend to be viewed warily as 'other' and increase the number who are accepted as part of 'us.' In that respect, gay marriage would be a victory for, and another key expansion of, the American idea."

Federal District Court Judge Vaughn Walker issued a 136-page ruling, declaring unconstitutional the amendment added to the California Constitution by Proposition 8:

> Because California has no interest in discriminating against gay men and lesbians, and because Proposition 8 prevents California from fulfilling its constitutional obligation to provide marriages on an equal basis, the court concludes that Proposition 8 is unconstitutional.

While the State of California, under both Governors Arnold Schwarzenegger and Jerry Brown, chose not to appeal this ruling, the decision was challenged by opponents of marriage equality and reached the U.S. Supreme Court in 2013, the same year the Court heard *Windsor v. United States* (see page 210) challenging the constitutionality of the so-called Defense of Marriage Act. Ted Olson stood before the justices of the U.S. Supreme Court, as he had so many times before; this time, he argued for the freedom to marry for same-sex couples.

On June 26, 2013, the U.S. Supreme Court ruled that those who had appealed the original Proposition 8 ruling lacked standing to do so, thus allowing the decision striking down Prop 8 to stand. This ruling allowed the freedom to marry to be finally restored to same-sex couples in California.

Lead plaintiff Kris Perry reflects, below, on what it meant to be part of this historic and momentous legal victory.

———— ∞ ————

Despite living for more than thirty years with the truth that I am a lesbian, I still referee an epic internal fight to feel equal to others. That internal fight nearly kept me from testifying effectively in the *Perry v. Schwarzenegger* trial. Despite years of education in psychology, sociology, and social work, I had yet to explore how profoundly I had been affected by a lifetime of homophobia, discriminatory policies, and institutionalized sexism.

At the seemingly mature age of forty-five, I reluctantly worked with our lawyers to chip away at years of "covering," Kenji Yoshino's term for muting the significance of one's identity. Over the course of many hours and long days, we peeled back the layers of emotional self-protectiveness I had carefully put in place. They asked me how it felt to be different, how being a lesbian affected my life, and if I was happy. We worked to uncover the feelings associated with shame over being a boyish girl, the embarrassment at being called a dyke by a group of boys at my high school, the sadness of my parents fearing I would never marry. We found the roots of the internal fight I still have over feeling worthy. We didn't rehearse questions or answers, or strategize the best way to describe the memories or feelings. We simply examined them together, in a law office in San Francisco. More than once I cried, but I never doubted that Ted Olson or our other lawyers would steer me in the right direction. I didn't know what I would say on the stand or even what Ted would ask, but I understood myself in a new though painful way. I was terrified but ready.

Our attorneys prepared the four of us for cross-examination, knowing the power and significance of our personal stories. They knew we could articulate for the Court the personal effects of discrimination and covering, and that our testimony would demonstrate real-life examples that would be underscored by evidence from expert witnesses in the fields of psychology, sociology, history, and political science. They prepared us to face humiliation, aggression, hostility. I thought defending my truth would be the hardest part, but the real pain came in simply acknowledging it and describing it to the Court in response to examination.

When asked why it was important for me to be married, I responded, "In some ways it's hard for me to grasp what it would even mean, but I do see other people who are married, and I—and I think what it looks like is that you are honored and respected by your family. Your children know what your relationship is. And when you leave your home and you go to work or you go out in the world, people know what your relationship means." The reality was that for most of my life I hadn't let myself want something so out of reach, focusing instead on what was attainable, building my family without the protections and supports most people took for granted.

Similarly, my wife, Sandy, testified: "Marriage is about making a public commitment to the world, to your partner and to . . . I hope is someday my wife, to our friends, our family, our society, our community, our parents. It's . . . the way we tell them and each other that this is a lifetime commitment. . . . We are not girlfriends. We are not partners. We are married." Sandy had been married to a man and had personally experienced the difference of acceptance and celebration between marriage and domestic partnership. For her, the difference had been stark and difficult.

As the parents of four boys, we represented tens of thousands of families raising children in California who were denied the right to marry. As a blended family we had to work through the complications that family formation brings. Holidays, vacations, discipline, household management, extended family—we had worked through so much. Before we entered the case, we asked each of our sons if they were comfortable with our involvement. Our four very unique boys were unanimous in their support for us, and for marriage equality. That's love; that's family.

I sat enthralled from the first through the last day of trial. Witnesses from both sides fought for an outcome they believed would either improve or destroy marriage in the largest state in the union. This was a critical public policy decision. Everyone who testified added to the volumes of legal documentation of the benefits of marriage and the harm of discrimination.

I left the courtroom on the last day, the words of witnesses from both sides ringing in my ears. My coping strategy for the past thirty years was no longer a mystery, and certainly not tolerable. Our family was closer in some ways, and more distant in other ways, than before. We could no longer ignore the homophobia we had tolerated—not from the world, and certainly not from the people we loved.

We had witnessed history—not just the historic nature of the trial, but the history of the lesbian and gay witnesses who had pulled back the defenses perfected to lay bare the scars of living in a state that would tell us our love isn't equal and neither were we.

During my testimony, I stated, "If Prop 8 were undone and kids like me growing up in Bakersfield right now could never know what this felt like, then I assume their entire lives would be on a higher arc. They would live with a higher sense of themselves that would improve their entire life." I spent my life finding myself, finding happiness, and working professionally to improve access to quality education for children in poverty. That higher arc meant something; and I do think kids born today will feel freer to be themselves and will benefit from seeing all kinds of couples and families celebrated and supported. Equality matters.

Participating in the trial was something like a rebirth. It was hard. It was wonderful. It was life changing. I felt lucky to have a seat at that table, but even more so to know myself better, to know Sandy better, and of course to eventually call her my wife.

V. HOPES RISE AND DOMA FALLS, 2007–15

NEW FRONTIERS: STATE LEGISLATIVE WINS AND FEDERAL DOMA CHALLENGES

MARY L. BONAUTO, GARY D. BUSECK, AND JANSON WU

———

Mary L. Bonauto is director of the Civil Rights Project at Gay & Lesbian Advocates & Defenders (GLAD).

Gary D. Buseck is legal director of Gay & Lesbian Advocates & Defenders (GLAD), where he served as executive director from 1997 to 2004.

Janson Wu is executive director of Gay & Lesbian Advocates & Defenders (GLAD).

Introduction

All three branches of government and the court of public opinion matter when seeking lasting social change. The Massachusetts legislature ended the debate about *Goodridge*, the case that legalized marriage for same-sex couples in the state, in 2007 by conclusively rejecting a citizen-initiated amendment to over-rule it. In early 2009, Gay & Lesbian Advocates & Defenders (GLAD) filed the first strategic challenge to the federal Defense of Marriage Act on behalf of married couples in Massachusetts, making the pivotal jump to federal court. The spring of 2009 also brought breakthroughs in state legislatures that built precious momentum in our movement. There were wins in Vermont, Maine, and New Hampshire in April, May, and June. Our opponents could no longer claim that only "activist courts" would vote for marriage.

At GLAD, we had already implemented an integrated strategy of federal litigation, media visibility, grassroots education, and state legislative advocacy to win "6 × 12"—our campaign to secure the freedom to marry in all six New England states by 2012—and to strike down the federal Defense of Marriage Act (DOMA). Each state had its own leaders and its own story, and each secured marriage before the Supreme Court's rulings on DOMA and California's Prop 8. Below is the story of how we all defended marriage in Massachusetts, how GLAD built a case against DOMA, and how we all won the freedom to marry in Maine.

Defending Marriage in Massachusetts

We felt great joy in Massachusetts, with over six thousand wedding celebrations in 2004 and over two thousand in 2005. Families and friends attended weddings, and a new understanding and acceptance settled in. At the same time, we felt intensely vulnerable during the five long years separating the *Goodridge* ruling in November 2003 from the California and Connecticut wins in 2008. Would Massachusetts stand strong as an island of marriage equality within the United States? Or would we eventually succumb to a constitutional ban, as had Hawai'i and so many other states? For most of that time, our opponents could assert that this "same-sex marriage experiment" would soon end. Before we could move ahead to secure marriage in other states, we had to defend it in Massachusetts.

Governor Mitt Romney pledged a million dollars of his own money to unseat marriage supporters in the 2004 elections. However, the campaign led by MassEquality, the state's marriage equality organization, returned every marriage supporter to the legislature, unseated an opponent with openly gay candidate Carl Sciortino, and won all of the vacated seats of opponents and supporters. This 100 percent-plus success rate was another first, and pushed back on the overblown claim that voting for marriage was a death knell for one's political career.

The Massachusetts legislature slowly but surely delivered a legislative triumph. Thousands of families contacted or met with their legislators. If the proposed citizen-initiated amendment secured the support of just a quarter of both the house and senate convened in two successive legislatures, then we would face an amendment at the ballot in November 2008. A lame duck legislature voted 62–132 on January 2, 2007, securing more than the one-fourth vote required. Our opponents won round one.

The Massachusetts-based groups like GLAD, led by MassEquality and with partners nationwide, as well as new levels of financial support, set out to turn around enough votes for us to defeat the second required vote. Governor Deval Patrick, elected in November 2006, was the first state executive to fully back our freedom to marry. His close relationship with MassEquality began in January

2007 with a phone call to Marc Solomon asking, "How can I help?" There is no doubt Governor Patrick's leadership against the amendment, his exhortations to focus on what unites us rather than divides us, his calming of the African American clergy, and his cajoling and persuading legislators were essential. Essential, too, was a shift in Senate and House leadership positions to marriage equality supporters.

The convention of the House and Senate convened on the afternoon of June 14, 2007. We had updates saying we would win, and others saying we would lose. Representing GLAD, Mary L. Bonauto sat with hundreds of others in the Gardiner Auditorium at the Massachusetts State House in Boston, where we watched Senate President Therese Murray open the session via closed-circuit television. Silence prevailed as the clerk called the roll, one by one. The "yay" and "nay" votes came quickly, and some had switched, but it was impossible to keep track of whether we would prevail. And then Senator Murray suddenly declared the vote: "Forty-five in favor, 151 opposed. The amendment fails." The cheering and crying that followed went on and on and on.

The 2007 vote was a turning point. As Governor Patrick stated that day, "In Massachusetts today, the freedom to marry is secure." The efforts to snuff out that beacon of equality were finished.

DOMA

The Defense of Marriage Act (DOMA) was the law that included a "federal definition" limiting marriage to the union of a man and a woman. As a practical matter, it meant that all of the married couples in Massachusetts were unmarried for all 1,138 federal laws and programs implicating married status.

DOMA was instantly a problem after couples started marrying. Nancy Gill, who later became our lead plaintiff in *Gill v. Office of Personnel Management et al.*, had married her longtime partner, Marcelle Letourneau, on a Friday, honeymooned over the weekend together with their children, and on returning to work Monday was told she could not place her spouse on her family health insurance plan with the United States Postal Service. Mary Ritchie, a state trooper and another plaintiff in *Gill*, sought to file her federal income taxes as married, only to learn that she was unmarried federally and would pay significantly more in income taxes as a result.

With the marriage issue now truly settled in Massachusetts, the stage was set for GLAD to challenge DOMA. To deliver the fatal blow, we looked at every federal statute implicating marital status and investigated how a great many programs work in practice before deciding to litigate several large federal programs that were well understood by the public. If we won on tax, social security, and employee benefits for federal employees, it would make it more likely or even inevitable that DOMA was unconstitutional across the board.

We assumed the Department of Justice would mount a vigorous defense and litigate every possible procedural angle to avoid the merits of our arguments. As a result, we spent three years to exhaust every possible administrative prerequisite, including pursuing a mini-trial for Dean Hara's request for pension and health benefits due to a surviving spouse of a long-serving member of Congress and multiple layers of appeal within the Social Security Administration.

Through comprehensive examination of how benefits were administered, we learned that the federal government's consistent, historical approach had been to recognize a state's determination that a couple was married. This powerful fact countered the expectation of a federal government role in determining the existence of a marriage for federal programs. DOMA had been considered untouchable and federal court too dangerous for a legal challenge. Would a federal judge say that the Congress lacked authority to define the terms relevant to federal programs? Even beyond the historical answer was the constitutional one: the equal protection clause limits how the Congress may define terms, even the term "marriage," just as it could not define the term "person" to embody gender or racial classifications. By relegating all marriages of same-sex couples to the category of non-marriages, DOMA treated married same-sex couples as second class. Never before had the federal government identified a class of state-certified marriages and explicitly nullified them for all federal purposes.

By the time we were close to filing in March 2009, we had two states allowing same-sex couples to marry: Massachusetts and Connecticut. A DOMA challenge might seem like a challenge to the laws of the other forty-eight states, since the justifications for DOMA were so close to those put forth to defend state-level marriage bans. The difference was we were challenging the *federal* government's disrespect of a couple's *existing marriage* and how such governmental disrespect rendered them second class, whereas the marriage cases brought up to that point had all challenged the *state*'s refusal to *allow same-sex couples to marry*. All the same, we were kicking a hornet's nest because a DOMA lawsuit was certainly a first cousin of a marriage lawsuit.

Despite the anxiety or even opposition from some movement colleagues, we filed the *Gill* lawsuit in March 2009 on behalf of seven couples and three widowers in federal court in Massachusetts. We had extraordinary assistance from Paul M. Smith, who had successfully argued *Lawrence v. Texas* in 2003, from other Jenner & Block attorneys, and from Foley Hoag and Sullivan & Worcester in Boston. Building on long-term educational efforts about DOMA, we rolled out a media-friendly "DOMA Story Book" describing DOMA's damage to ordinary people, including some of our plaintiffs. After argument in April 2010, Judge Joseph Tauro ruled in favor of our equal protection challenge on July 10. He likewise ruled in favor of the Commonwealth of Massachusetts, which had filed its own challenge to DOMA in July 2009 on both federalism and equal protection grounds.

Although some LGBT activists urged the Obama administration not to appeal, we actually wanted an appeal so we could get a ruling from a higher court that would apply throughout the states covered by the First Circuit Court of Appeals, bringing relief to other married same-sex couples and not just the plaintiffs. The administration appealed.

GLAD sought to keep up the pressure on DOMA. After the trial court victory in *Gill*, we filed an even broader challenge in the District of Connecticut with more plaintiffs and illustrations of DOMA's harms in November 2010. We added Horton, Shields & Knox to our already robust legal team. Once we learned of Roberta Kaplan's and the ACLU's imminent case on behalf of Edie Windsor in federal court in New York, we all agreed to file on the same day in the hopes of arriving at the Second Circuit Court of Appeals—where appeals from both Connecticut and New York cases go—together.

Kaplan, James Esseks (director of the ACLU LGBT & HIV Project), GLAD Legal Director Gary Buseck, and I were all on the phone in February 2011 when Tony West, the top official at the Department of Justice Civil Division, shockingly advised us that they would no longer defend DOMA in the Second Circuit. Soon we learned the DOJ would not defend DOMA at all, putting our First Circuit case on ice and delaying briefing and oral argument for over a year. In May 2012, that court held DOMA violated the equal protection guarantee, becoming the first court of appeals to do so. The House of Representatives, which had hired its own counsel, and the United States both filed a petition for certiorari in the U.S. Supreme Court.

By June 2012, Kaplan and the ACLU had won the *Windsor* case in the District Court, and seven weeks later we won our *Pedersen* case in Connecticut. The House appealed Edie Windsor's case immediately and agreed to fast-track it at the Second Circuit for reasons related to Windsor's health. The House did not agree to appeal the *Pedersen* case, leaving us in limbo in the Second Circuit. That court, applying heightened scrutiny, also unanimously ruled against DOMA in October 2012. As we discovered in due course, Justice Kagan was recused from our case, *Gill,* from her time as solicitor general, leaving *Windsor* as an excellent vehicle for Supreme Court review. And the rest is history! (See page 210 Esseks.)

Winning in Maine:
A Case Study in State Advocacy and Perseverance

On the fifth anniversary of the *Goodridge* decision and building on close partnerships with state advocates, GLAD announced its "6 × 12" Campaign. As then Executive Director Lee Swislow saw it, we had the opportunity to show progress in states and continue building toward a national resolution in the Supreme Court.

The states are small and close together in New England, influencing each other; and so an important précis to the Maine story is Vermont. Vermont Freedom to Marry worked tirelessly after 2000 to win marriage equality in the legislature. A legislative study committee in 2007–8 built on public hearings throughout the state and laid the basis for a 2009 marriage bill. That bill not only passed in April 2009 but was enacted by overriding the governor's veto.

Maine was full of dichotomies. It was the first New England state to pass a "mini-DOMA" in 1997. But the legislature also passed progressive laws about domestic partner health care coverage in 2001, and a domestic partner registry with important but limited protections for unmarried couples in 2004.

The primary struggle in Maine, we thought, was for non-discrimination protections pending since the 1970s. After several tries, we won a ballot fight in 2005 to defend the statewide non-discrimination law, which built confidence. We believed we could now address marriage and set ourselves the goal of highlighting LGB people as *families* and not *just* workers. In 2007, we linked the fairness ideas in the non-discrimination law with a bill expanding family medical leave to domestic partners. We also pursued second-parent adoption. In the state Supreme Court in 2007, we represented Ann Courtney and Marilyn Kirby, who had already fostered and adopted several older children but now refused to designate only one between themselves as a "forever parent" in the adoptions of their younger children. Together with other longtime advocates for our families, we won. When the first adoptions were granted in county courts all around the state, we made sure the media featured the happy families and put a human face on gay and lesbian parents and their children.

A longstanding partnership among GLAD, Equality Maine, the Maine ACLU, and the Maine Women's Lobby, along with longtime attorney Patricia Peard and later joined by Ben Dudley at Engage Maine, led the 2009 fight on marriage in Maine. Equality Maine, led by longtime Executive Director Betsy Smith, used its considerable field-organizing capacity to talk about marriage with voters year round, and particularly on primary and general election days in 2008. In November, one volunteer encountered an older gentleman wearing his Army uniform. "Do you want to sign a postcard in support of the freedom to marry?" she asked. Walking to her slowly, he answered, "What do you think our boys died for at Omaha Beach?" The growing support was palpable. Equality Maine had to scramble for more postcards. They ran out by noon.

After assessing the 2008 election results, we all agreed to move forward with a marriage bill in the 2009 legislative session. We had significant support in both chambers. Governor John Baldacci, however, supported civil unions. This was not a risk-free strategy. Some legislators favored civil unions, and such a bill would split our supporters. If civil unions were enacted, our community would be in the position of defending the inevitable referendum to repeal a bill we believed insufficient, but that still conferred important protections on same-sex couples.

In early January 2009, Democratic Senator Dennis Damon of Ellsworth introduced "An Act to End Discrimination in Civil Marriage and Affirm Religious Freedom." ACLU of Maine Executive Director Shenna Bellows partnered with GLAD on media events showcasing supporters from the business, religious, and child-welfare communities.

Equality Maine out-organized the opposition every step of the way. A critical milestone for the bill was the public hearing before the Joint Committee on the Judiciary on April 22, 2009. Held in a large arena, at least three thousand supporters outnumbered opponents by four to one. GLAD set the frame for the hearing with an objective of showcasing a level of content and emotion that normally forms the center of a legal case so we would win from both a head and heart perspective. Our core team and the larger coalition secured persuasive witnesses designed to move the ball forward and answer every concern—whether a Catholic Republican lawyer addressing concerns about religious liberty, or the founder of the NAACP in Maine making the case for civil rights of LGB people, or Massachusetts legislators who had voted for marriage and won reelection, or business leaders making an "equity in the workplace" case for marriage. Equally moving were the young people who spoke, like Gabriella do Amaral, who talked about her dream to fall in love with a woman and marry one day. Sam Putnam, a star athlete, simply wanted his moms to be able to marry.

We were ready for the opposition. A local pediatrician, testifying on behalf of the Maine chapter of the American Academy of Pediatricians, authoritatively debunked the "children need a mother and a father" claim, and noted the argument was "ignorant of the scientific literature" or was "misrepresenting it." We knew we would face a long line of individual clergy opposing the bill, so we prepared a joyful presentation of over seventy-five clergy of many denominations, who surrounded the Episcopal bishop as he testified for the bill. Even David Parker, a one-time resident of Lexington, Massachusetts, who sued its schools there for

providing a "diversity backpack" with the book "Who's in a Family," was effectively countered. As predicted, Mr. Parker tearfully recounted being handcuffed
and taken to jail simply for standing up for his children at school. But we had the
police report read aloud, which documented that Mr. Parker refused to leave the
building, well past its closing, telling police officers, "If I'm not arrested then
I'm not leaving." The obvious staging of the event totally deflated Mr. Parker's
persecution claims.

In every alternating half hour in which we could present witnesses to the
committee, we had couples, sometimes with children in tow, as well as surviving partners and sometimes their extended family members. Their presence required the debate to be about real people, not abstract issues. It was harder, for
example, to dismiss the claim for needed protections when Diane Sammer spoke
of waking up one morning to find that her partner of twenty-eight years had suffered a fatal heart attack overnight. And in the aftermath of that tragedy, she was
unable to make arrangements for her partner's final resting place despite having
the appropriate legal protections then authorized under Maine law.

A few days after that marathon eleven-hour public hearing, the Committee voted 11–2 that the bill should pass, and the Senate rejected a referendum
amendment to the bill. Then the Senate (20–15) and House (89–58) both approved of marriage on bipartisan votes. After final enactment in the Senate, Senate President Libby Mitchell walked the bill over to the governor. He signed
within minutes. "I have come to believe this is a question of fairness and of equal
protection under the law, and that a civil union is not equal to a civil marriage,"
he said in a written statement.

The "people's veto" repeal campaign, an extension of the legislative process,
came quickly. Stand for Marriage Maine (SFMM), led by the Roman Catholic Diocese, enlisted Brian Brown of the National Organization for Marriage
(NOM) to fundraise, and hired Schubert Flint for public relations, the same firm
that ran the Prop 8 campaign to amend California's Constitution to take away
the freedom to marry (see page 168 Kendell).

We knew it would be a big battle, and we talked to people about California.
Based on polling, we knew Mainers were committed to equality and named our
campaign "No on 1: Protect Maine Equality." We also thought Mainers wouldn't
be tricked into thinking their kids were going to learn about sex in kindergarten
just because the state licensed marriages of same-sex couples. Those of us who
worked the legislative campaign transitioned to the ballot campaign and were
joined by campaign veterans and consultants. With a solid set of identified voters with us already, the goal was to identify more voters based on a higher-than-
projected turnout and then get them to the polls.

We moved on TV first with a very positive, pro-Maine, pro-family educational ad in August called "Marriage for All Maine Families," and then with the first campaign ad. SFMM's first ad was spaghetti-style, throwing out everything to see what would stick: "homosexual marriage" would be taught in schools, churches would lose their tax-exempt status, and "traditional marriage" proponents would face a flood of lawsuits—the three themes of their campaign. Whether reframing and rebutting their attacks, or airing ads like "Grandma," with an older woman talking about her son, his partner, and their son, all seated by her, the race remained close. The hammer came in late October. A school counselor, supportive of the marriage law but unconnected with the campaign, filed a complaint with the social work ethics board against an anti-marriage colleague who had appeared in a television ad about the "gay agenda" behind "safe schools." Now SFMM's predictions seemed true. Another ad came: schools would "push" marriage on students, "just as they are trying to punish one of Maine's best educators for supporting traditional marriage."

By election night, we already knew we were in trouble. We had a strategy based on turning out our supporters, believing at the time that persuading new voters wasn't possible in the crucible of a campaign. Turnout was far higher than our already high projections. We didn't win with the margins we needed in places like Portland and the coastal communities. And so it was a night of death by a thousand cuts, as we lost small town after small town by twenty votes here, thirty-five there. The lead that had begun the evening slowly, steadily began to go. Around midnight, we had to share the news with our supporters that we had lost. Human Rights Campaign (HRC) Executive Director Joe Solmonese wondered whether it was possible for us to win anywhere in 2009. Rea Carey of the Task Force said they would be there for the next round. That night, we couldn't tell when that day would be.

Despite the setback in Maine, we had newly licensed marriages to look forward to in Maine's sister state of New Hampshire in January 2010. There, the law for gay people had evolved from awful in the 1980s to reasonably good in the 2000s. A legislative study commission in 2005 heard from the state's citizens, which ultimately led to a civil union law in 2008, followed by a whirlwind coalition campaign that brought marriage equality in June 2009. Even after a NOM-orchestrated effort to repeal the law and enact a constitutional amendment in 2011–2, large bipartisan majorities defeated those efforts. New England was one state closer to our "6 × 12" goal.

Losing at the ballot in Maine in 2009 was brutal. Our team knew we had to find a way forward. The post-election analysis showed that, despite extensive efforts, many of our identified supporters in 2009 did not vote, and many of those who did vote with us were persuaded to do so during the campaign. We also won the fight for votes of parents with children under age eighteen, a solid and promising proxy on the schools attacks. That analysis led to the adoption of the much more powerful—and successful—strategy of persuasion and building a significant majority in favor of marriage equality.

Donald Sussman, a donor to our well-executed 2009 campaign, wanted to help us figure out how to reach out to voters state-wide so we could win next time. In 2010 he committed a significant sum to our effort, promising support for research, testing, and outreach. GLAD hired MassEquality veteran Matt McTighe to lead this public education and research effort, and he turned to former colleagues Ryan Brown and Ian Grady.

Once on the ground in July 2010, Matt whipped around the state tornado-like, meeting everyone, getting on top of everything from the Maine voter file to connecting with the teams in Oregon and California, who were then contemplating a return to the ballot. With the help of consultant Amy Simon, we came to understand more about how voters felt about marriage and the 2009 campaign. Together with social psychologist Phyllis Watts, who often worked with Amy, we came to understand that a significant number of voters against us in 2009 could be reached if we focused on our shared values about why marriage matters. By 2011, Freedom to Marry had convened a weekly research call for the many entities focused on messaging, and that collaboration added even more value to the assessment of messages and messengers. Complementing this effort, trained volunteers from Equality Maine started face-to-face visits with voters at home in the spring of 2011, focusing on listening and discovering those shared values together.

The research also showed there was genuine fear about an imposition on churches and faith organizations if same-sex couples could marry. The Religious Coalition for the Freedom to Marry from 2009 ramped up its outreach. Pastor Michael Gray, a Methodist minister, and his wife reached out to support us. "I really struggled with the issue of same-sex marriage, but through study, prayer, and patience, I can gratefully say that my faith now informs me differently," Pastor Gray said repeatedly. He became the original signer on the draft initiative measure in 2011, which stated in plain language that clergy and religious institutions could refuse to perform or host marriages in accord with their religious beliefs, and that the refusal to do so would not be the basis of a lawsuit or affect the tax-exempt status of the refusers. Our opponents sought to change our proposed question and summary as though the religious protections were insignificant, but GLAD, together with attorneys Pat Peard and Kate Knox, and communications director David Farmer and deputy Ian Grady, successfully pushed back. After certification, and with renowned field expert Amy Mello on board at the start of 2011 with Equality Maine, volunteers gathered 105,000 signatures, far more than the required 57,000, from 450 cities, towns, and townships across the state. In all-day meetings in December 2011 and January 2012, we conferred with national partners, elected officials, funders, and other key stakeholders to assess whether to go forward and submit the signatures that would commit us to the ballot campaign. The assessment of GLAD's Executive Director Lee Swislow carried the day: where we had a good shot at winning, how could we hold back?

We launched our campaign in January 2012 with Matt as campaign manager, and a strong executive committee of the key Maine advocates and national partners like Marc Solomon of Freedom to Marry. After a statewide campaign kick-off to mark the official start of Mainers United for Marriage, the campaign was in full swing. President Obama endorsed marriage in July 2012, providing a critical boost, and our TV ads—the first of which launched on broadcast television on the night of the Olympic Opening Ceremonies—became the talk of the state. In "Harlan," we featured four generations of a family in Downeast Maine, seated at a dinner table presided over by the grandfather, a World War II veteran, and his wife of sixty years. He spoke of his service, and both spoke of wanting their lesbian granddaughter, seated there with her partner and their daughter, to be able to marry. In another ad, an Episcopal priest and his wife talked about their son who had just returned from duty in Iraq but did not enjoy the freedom to marry at home. In a third ad, a group of firefighters at a station house talked about their gay co-worker, their "brother," and how he, just like them, should have the same freedom to marry. We forcefully responded to the kinds of attacks we had heard in 2009, and reminded voters about the human consequences at stake—for the couples, for their children, and for their extended families and communities. Continuing with our tradition of unexpected spokespersons, the campaign featured a Republican lawmaker who had changed his mind on the

The crowd in Rhode Island for the signing of the bill legalizing marriage for same-sex couples.
Photo Credit: COURTESY OF GLAD

issue, a Christian photographer who was happy to have more weddings to shoot, and a teacher and her family and children talking about the key role parents play in educating their children about their family's values.

   On election night 2012, the team parsed the returns. We were winning towns we had lost before, and we lost by less in other places. When Matt, who had not slept for over two days, led our Executive Committee and consultants out to the stage, it was total victory. We had flipped the results from 2009, showed that voters could change their minds, and put wind in our sails nationally. Maryland and Washington successfully defended their measures at the ballot, too, and Minnesota defeated a constitutional amendment (see page 195). It was a phenomenal night.

New England: A Clean Sweep and a Big Lift

GLAD worked with amazing state leaders and national partners throughout New England, and the same was true in Rhode Island, where years of effort had both kept the state free of statutory and constitutional marriage bans and added incremental steps to protect LGB families. Finally, with a supportive Governor Lincoln Chaffee, who signed a civil union bill in 2011 (while noting its deficiencies), a final push for marriage equality was effectively organized by a broad coalition. With legislative approval and the governor's signature on May 2, 2012, Rhode Island became the eleventh jurisdiction and the tenth state in the country to approve marriage, completing GLAD's "6 × 12" campaign. We were proud to work with others and deliver the freedom to marry to so many loving couples across the region, and to have worked in the courts and on the ground to change hearts and the law. These victories provided a big lift, a surge of momentum to our movement, and sent a reassuring message as the U.S. Supreme Court was considering its rulings in the DOMA and California marriage cases that would be decided the following year.

TESTED AT THE BALLOT BOX IN 2012

MARC SOLOMON AND THALIA ZEPATOS

—— ∞∞ ——

Marc Solomon served as National Campaign director at Freedom to Marry.

Thalia Zepatos served as director of Research and Messaging at Freedom to Marry.

By 2009 the marriage movement had lost thirty statewide ballot[1] campaigns designed to limit marriage to "one man and one woman." In November 2004 alone (the year Massachusetts first began issuing marriage licenses to same-sex couples), Republican operatives used anti-marriage measures to galvanize support among social conservatives, driving efforts to put measures on the ballot in eleven states. Those measures were primarily in states where the marriage conversation had barely begun, and they passed by an average margin of 70 percent to 30 percent. Subsequent losses in California (2008) (see pages 145 and 168) and Maine (2009)—states we had hoped to win—were particularly devastating. Opponents of the freedom to marry taunted advocates that we could never win a vote of the people. We knew we had some serious challenges to address before marriage went back to the ballot.

The marriage movement's messaging challenges were clear. While we had hit majority support nationwide in 2011, those numbers were being driven by support in New England states, where marriage was legal. We were not making the case to "conflicted" voters in a persuasive way, and they were crucial to winning at the ballot box. Moreover, we were highly vulnerable to opposition attacks that raised fears that marriage for same-sex couples would be dangerous to children.

In January 2010, Freedom to Marry charted a path to confront and solve these challenges. We initiated a deep dive into previous research to find out what had worked and what had not, and enlisted pollster Lisa Grove to analyze all existing research data from the many state campaigns—over eighty-five data sets. We also organized a confidential research collaborative, which we called the Marriage Research Consortium (MRC), inviting leading national and state organizations (such as the Movement Advancement Project, Basic Rights Oregon, and Third Way) that were also investing in marriage message research to join. Determining how to bring new voters to our side was a challenge we had to solve together; we could not afford to duplicate efforts.

The analysis from Grove underscored what we had seen firsthand: previous messaging that focused on the rights and benefits of marriage and on the notion of equality and civil rights was effective with those we'd already enlisted to our cause, but was not persuading conflicted voters.

Voters who were conflicted on marriage often knew someone who was gay, lesbian, bisexual, or transgender. They wanted to be fair and supportive of LGBT people—yet they were not convinced that same-sex couples "deserved" marriage. For one thing, those voters felt that domestic partnership or civil union provided the rights and benefits that the LGBT community had been asking for. They also suspected that same-sex couples wanted to marry for "political reasons" rather than for the reasons they themselves had gotten married.

Step by step, through our partnership with Grove, we discovered the building blocks of a new message strategy: messages had to be in sync with conflicted voters'—and most same-sex couples'—understanding of what was central about marriage. Marriage, for these voters, was about love and commitment. To reach them and persuade them to vote in favor of marriage equality, advocates had to communicate that marriage mattered to gay and lesbian couples for the same reasons that it mattered to straight couples. Through research, we learned that these voters responded to the invocation of shared values: some responded to the Golden Rule, others to the value of freedom. Our challenge as advocates was to model the journey from unsure to accepting for voters who were truly conflicted. With careful analysis, we found out what messengers could be most persuasive, such as older parents speaking about their gay children, and both gay and straight veterans, and we identified a broad range of other important storytellers.

Telling the right stories to persuade conflicted voters was not enough, however; we also had to respond effectively to attacks. We devoted a year to determining how best to respond to opposition attacks, specifically ads that raised fears about harms to children from learning about marriage for same-sex couples in school (similar to arguments that we'd been fighting for decades about "gays" hurting children). Pollster Amy Simon helped craft a powerful approach to engaging voters who expressed faith-based concerns generated by religious attack ads. We found that "two-track messaging"—keeping our positive values-based messages before voters, while adding a second track of response ads, which also invoked those key values, to rebuff our opponents' attacks—was most effective.

We also employed multiple approaches for engaging voters. One-on-one conversations with undecided voters were tested rigorously and proven to be especially effective. Driving a narrative focused on personal stories and the harms of denial of marriage through social media, in print, and on television news kept the drumbeat going.

By 2012, we had a model and a strategy we believed would work:

- Early investment in public education campaigns to lay a solid foundation of support, placing compelling stories in newspapers and on radio and television and enlisting leaders to serve as messengers.

- Message testing and development to determine how to most effectively promote our cause and combat our opponents' most effective arguments over the airwaves.

- Immediate pushback to opposition attacks; fact-checking and calling out misinformation.

- Strong campaign structures, with boards of directors committed to raising funds and a proven campaign manager at the helm.

- A focus on raising early funds to ensure we could purchase sufficient television time to get our messages out.

- Recruiting people to share authentic stories, including both straight allies and same-sex couples talking about why marriage mattered to them and sharing stories of the personal journeys of those who had come around to support after years of inner conflict.

- Sharing stories of unexpected allies, especially Republicans talking about how their commitment to family and freedom led them to support the freedom to marry.

- Targeted approaches to reach key audiences of voters—Republicans, communities of color, people of faith, and others, using community-specific approaches adjusted state-by-state.

- Use of micro-targeting tools to ensure we made the case to the most persuadable voters using the most persuasive approaches.

- Robust field campaigns to engage voters in interactive conversations at the door and over the phone, followed by massive "get out the vote" efforts for Election Day.

That year, 2012, proved to be our big test, with four initiatives on the ballot: Maine, Maryland, Minnesota, and Washington. We thought we had the messaging down, but we also knew it would take more than words to prevail—we also had to organize effectively.

We began to enlist teams of advisors who could work across several states, and focused on building strong, well-organized campaign entities with talented campaign managers, tight campaign boards, and serious fundraising efforts in each state. We linked those managers together regularly so they could trade field and communications strategies, and Freedom to Marry provided centralized messaging, opposition research, political and legal coordination, and daily guidance to the campaign teams.

We knew it would be crucial to outspend our opponents. We raised early money, which allowed the pro-marriage campaigns to get on television early, set the terms of the debate, and lock in affordable rates for television throughout the campaign. This early investment enabled our campaigns to vastly outpace our opponents. Eventually, Freedom to Marry would raise and invest more than $5 million directly into state-level campaigns, becoming the largest out-of-state funder in three of the four states.

In each state, advocates built a campaign coalition with statewide LGBT advocacy groups, national organizations, and allies. State leaders and activists had spent years—often decades—building community and political support for LGBT equality. Our challenge as a movement was to build on these strengths, increase the resources, and focus the work in each of these states so we could finally break the political losing streak on marriage.

We also worked in other spheres to build national momentum. By the time Maine, Maryland, Minnesota, and Washington ended up on the November 2012 ballot, we had gained a Messenger-in-Chief. After working closely with—and pressuring—the White House, we were thrilled when President Obama came out in support of marriage for same-sex couples using the love and commitment and journey framework that was proving so effective. In a single day, the president modeled the journey for all Americans and gave permission to those who were most conflicted to join in support.

After a narrow defeat in 2009, marriage equality activists in Maine had mounted a two-year offensive to become the first state to place the freedom to marry on the ballot via initiative petition. Intensive public education included in-depth door-to-door conversations, with a special emphasis on engaging conflicted Christians. By Election Day, their talented field team organized 6,788 volunteers and conducted 260,000 conversations. With $3.3 million raised for public education and another $5 million for the ballot fight, Mainers United for Marriage won 52.6 percent of the vote.

In Washington, marriage was forced to the ballot by opponents after the legislature approved freedom-to-marry legislation. Voters had backed domestic partnership laws for same-sex couples only three years earlier, and the concern was whether voters would think that was good enough. Washington United for Marriage raised $1.5 million for public education and $13.9 million for the campaign, with 4,020 volunteers who took their case to the voters, and they won with 53.6 percent of the vote.

As in Washington State, marriage in Maryland was forced to the ballot by the opposition after the legislature affirmed the freedom to marry. With a strong champion in Governor O'Malley, a boost from the president's announcement, and an effective focus on African American voters, Marylanders for Marriage Equality raised $6 million and engaged 2,800 volunteers, winning with 52.4 percent of the vote.

Minnesota was the only one of the four state campaigns to fight a defensive battle in 2012 to defeat an anti-marriage constitutional amendment. Minnesotans United for All Families recruited and engaged a whopping 29,270 volunteers who conducted 420,000 in-depth phone conversations and spoke to 63,000 voters on their doorsteps. They raised just under $1 million for c3 public education and $13.6 million for the campaign, winning 52.6 percent of the vote, thereby setting the stage to build on their momentum and win marriage in the 2013 legislative session.

On Election Day, November 2012, marriage equality advocates swept the table in four distinct regions of the United States. This stunning clean sweep supercharged the momentum for marriage nationwide. Our movement was energized, politicians took note, our opponents were dejected, and, most importantly, Americans from coast to coast learned how much marriage really mattered to their gay and lesbian friends, neighbors, and family members. The political tide had turned.

PUTTING FAITH TO THE TEST: BLACK LEADERS AND THE MARYLAND VICTORY

Sharon Lettman-Hicks

———∞∞∞———

Sharon Lettman-Hicks is executive director and chief executive officer at the National Black Justice Coalition (NBJC).

I still pinch myself from time to time in disbelief when I remember that marriage equality is now the law of the land in our nation. As a full-time strategist and community engagement advocate since 2006, I have worked to build coalitions between people of diverse backgrounds, often with uncompromising and deeply rooted positions. The work of building a more equitable and fair nation for all people requires much persistence and boldness in the face of opposition—and the story of marriage equality in America fully epitomizes this truth.

In 2008, the most improbable, unimaginable political event of my lifetime happened with the election of Barack Obama as our nation's first African American president. As a child who grew up in the South, I've witnessed firsthand the unyielding stench of racism that has permeated the hearts of too many, while simultaneously limiting the possibilities of entire communities of color. In an instant, the world witnessed this unprecedented paradigm shift that ended centuries of the "Whites Only" occupancy of the Oval Office. However, this glorious moment was frozen in time when we learned that the voters of California had passed Proposition 8, banning marriage for same-sex couples in the state.

At the time, I was working on the front lines in California with people of faith, particularly within African American churches, to build bridges and frame the issue of marriage equality as a family issue that would strengthen the Black community, not harm it. When the results came back on election night 2008, I started to receive calls blaming the defeat entirely on Black voters. The political analysis in mainstream media confirmed this myth and labeled the entire Black community as homophobic. This unfounded, yet widely accepted opinion deeply impacted my work and challenged everything I knew and felt about political advocacy.

History will and has recounted that African Americans—like every other racial group in America at the turn of the twenty-first century—were in a process of evolution on the issue of marriage equality. Any proper analysis must take into account the effective strategy of President George W. Bush and other powerful conservative politicians in their push to utilize Black faith leaders as standard bearers in the fight to define marriage. This pervasive strategy polarized many African Americans, as the Black church has always wielded immense influence on our community. However, this narrative, in all of its prominence in the early 2000s, was dismantled in 2012 when the support of African American Marylanders—in strong numbers—pushed marriage equality over the finish line to extend this precious civil right to gay and lesbian couples in our state.

My personal story in the fight for marriage equality in Maryland began with my service at People for the American Way (PFAW), working directly to educate faith communities on the wedge issues of the time. My role was to initiate innovative and culturally competent engagement strategies within predominantly African American communities about the implications of their votes when issues like marriage equality were on the ballot.

This training became even more significant when I accepted the position of executive director and CEO at the National Black Justice Coalition (NBJC) in October 2009. NBJC was founded in 2003 by Black gay and lesbian advocates who were fed up with the homophobic rhetoric of some prominent Black ministers after the expansion of marriage to same-sex couples in Massachusetts. NBJC had built a reputation as a unique and critical civil rights organization that could bridge the gaps in the movements for racial justice and lesbian, gay, bisexual, and transgender (LGBT) equality. I was always intrigued with this group of Black LGBT leaders who knew the power they had in unapologetically living their truth, no matter the pressure to do otherwise. With such inspiring founders like Keith Boykin and Mandy Carter, NBJC worked from the outset to bring Black faces into the movement for LGBT rights. We have been fighting for over a decade to help LGBT African Americans live fully empowered, authentic lives.

The freedom to marry was seen by many in LGBT communities of color as an issue only important to elite, white people in the gay community. Issues like racial profiling, employment discrimination, and access to quality and affordable health care—bread and butter issues—were easily more imperative issues for Black LGBT people. However, many LGBT movement leaders and donors increasingly placed emphasis on marriage as the one all-consuming issue of importance to the LGBT movement's agenda. Black LGBT people found themselves having to choose between their multiple identities. On one hand, marriage was important to those who wanted it, but it evaded significant issues that confronted Black LGBT people daily.

As a married, heterosexual, Black woman, the work of NBJC has always been solidly in line with my mantra of "owning your power." Black LGBT people are simply Black people to me—folks I consider my brothers and sisters, culturally, and they should have the same rights and opportunities to live their most authentic lives in their truth as I do every day. It is not about being an ally for me. Instead, it is a deeply personal and social responsibility as a person of color with many unseen identities. I know firsthand how discrimination can hinder progress for marginalized communities. It can be crippling to the mind, body, and spirit—which is why I threw all of myself into the work of justice at NBJC when I took the helm of the organization in late 2009.

When I began this journey, it was essential to foster environments of affirmation for Black LGBT people, but also to meaningfully engage the Black church and other traditional African American institutions. This first mission was tested early in my tenure at NBJC when the movement for marriage equality reached our nation's capital.

Washington, D.C., also known as "Chocolate City," was the first battleground for marriage equality whose population was mostly Black—and it was the home and headquarters of NBJC. After much work by African American faith leaders, community organizers, and the Black LGBT community, the DC Council passed the Religious Freedom and Civil Marriage Equality Amendment Act of 2009. DC became the first jurisdiction below the Mason–Dixon Line to sanction the marriages of same-sex couples. Less than a year after the loss of Proposition 8, one of the nation's premier cities with a majority African American population and elected officials showed the nation that our community was not monolithic—and not as homophobic as many portrayed Black people to be.

History has shown us that when Black people lead movements for social justice, most of our community will rally behind that cause. In those early years of the fight for marriage in the courts, the media totally overlooked the implications of marriage on communities of color. The only faces to prominently represent the movement on television were those of white people who simply did not relate to African American families. When DC passed marriage for all, Black people—more specifically, Black LGBT people—were at the helm of the movement, and the media had no choice but to cover it. For the first time, the issue of marriage equality had deep and far-reaching implications for African Americans, because the stability of Black families headed by same-sex couples was the question before the public. Our reaction as a community was totally different from previous marriage fights because the Black LGBT community had a more visible role. This simple, intentional strategy to recruit Black folks, both LGBT and allies, to become the leaders and public face of the movement for marriage equality would once again be tested in the next popular vote on the issue of marriage in Maryland.

The state of Maryland has a distinctive role in the history of marriage equality. In 1973, it became the first state to define marriage in a statute as a union between a man and a woman, essentially banning same-sex couples from marrying. For nearly thirty years after this precedent was set, Maryland saw its share of organized efforts to expand marriage. In 2004, the ACLU and Equality Maryland filed a legal challenge to the ban (*Dean and Polyak v. Conaway*), at about the same time that similar challenges were filed in New York, New Jersey, and Washington. After winning at the trial court level, Maryland's highest court delivered a heartbreaking 4–3 decision on September 18, 2007, upholding the ban and continuing the exclusion of same-sex couples from marriage. We were determined to keep fighting.

In the aftermath of the marriage victory in DC and President Obama's instruction, in May 2012, to the U.S. Department of Justice—to no longer defend the constitutionality of the federal Defense of Marriage Act, the legal prohibition on federal recognition of marriages of same-sex couples—Maryland was now a prime state for advocates to target as their next major test.

At NBJC, the fight for marriage in Maryland was personal—as many of the staff, board members, and our membership called the state home. More importantly, we had preliminary data on Maryland highlighting the depth of the Black LGBT population and the power our community could have in the 2012 election if properly engaged. Because of the analytical work[1] of the Williams Institute at the University of California Los Angeles, we knew that Black LGBT individuals lived, for the most part, where other African Americans—not other members of the LGBT community—lived. The Williams Institute crunched the numbers from the U.S. Census, the Gallup Poll, and the American Community Survey and found that Black LGBT people could make the difference if marriage equality was put up for a popular vote in Maryland. According to these data, approximately 3.7 percent (more than one million) of all African Americans in the country identified as LGBT. Maryland had the second highest percentage of same-sex couples with African American householders, surpassed only by the District of Columbia.

The Maryland General Assembly first considered a bill to provide marriage equality, known as the Civil Marriage Protection Act, in early 2011, with support from Governor Martin O'Malley, who, like President Obama in 2008, had struggled to support the issue just a year earlier while running for reelection in the state. As part of our efforts at NBJC, I testified before the Assembly in favor of the bill. After a tenuous and dramatic debate, the bill passed the Senate, but ultimately died in the House of Delegates.

By mid-2011, after this setback, I had been deeply immersed in discussions with other LGBT equality and civil rights organizations about how to lay a foundation in Maryland to build support for the bill in the next session. From the beginning, we recognized that our success or failure would be determined by how African Americans came down on the issue of marriage. Most observers recognized that the only way to win in Maryland would be through effective engagement, resulting in a close-to-majority support of the African American community on the issue. Even though this was a daunting task, we were blessed by the examples of strength in Black leadership in DC's marriage fight and by having the president of the United States, a Black man, set the example for all African Americans to consider the issue affirmatively.

In the next year, we stuck to our wits and were able to move the new version of the act through both houses of the Maryland General Assembly. This time, the version of the bill contained even more explicit provisions protecting churches and other religious institutions from legal action if they refused to officiate marriages for same-sex couples as a matter of religious doctrine. On March 1, 2012, Governor O'Malley signed the bill into law. But the celebration was short-lived. One of the most disrespectful and inhumane actions that a so-called democracy can take is to place the question of human rights, especially those of minorities, up for popular vote. By the summer, those organizing to put the question up for popular vote had gained enough signatures to see it added to the November ballot.

In my first year as NBJC's executive director, Yoruba Richen, a young documentary film director, reached out to me. She had wanted to dissect the myth about Black people being inherently homophobic and to investigate the root cause of the ban on marriage for same-sex couples in California. As historic marriage-equality events unfolded, Richen's documentary had to take a new turn. These conversations and intense encounters out in the field, rallying the African American community to embrace marriage equality, formed the basis of her award-winning film, *The New Black*. It shows how the African American community grappled with marriage equality and ultimately evolved to a position of support by the end of the 2012 election.

Looking at the film now, I am reminded of the power of the conversations I had with local Black ministers, like Reverend Tony Lee, the senior pastor of Community of Hope African Methodist Episcopal Church in Temple Hills, Maryland. He challenged me to educate him about issues of importance to Black LGBT people in his congregation before asking him to support a loaded issue like marriage equality. Reverend Lee told me about another pastor who he felt was more evolved than most in Maryland on the issue of marriage equality— Dr. Delman Coates, the senior pastor of Mt. Ennon Baptist Church, an African American church with over eight thousand members in Prince George's County. As a married, Black heterosexual pastor of a "mega-church," Dr. Coates' public support of civil marriage for same-sex couples added momentum to the fight for marriage equality in Maryland.

There were a few other heroes and heroines on the front lines of the Maryland movement who made the ultimate victory there a reality. The Human Rights Campaign (HRC) had the great foresight to put some of the best Black LGBT activists and strategists on their staff to lead the campaign in Maryland. Three of the major players from HRC were Reverend MacArthur Flournoy, an openly gay minister who was essential to moving the legislation in the State Assembly with an amazing clergy outreach strategy; Donna Payne, a longtime grassroots organizer and also a founding member of NBJC, who directly and effectively engaged the Black population and Black civil rights organizations like the NAACP in Maryland; and Sultan Shakir, a senior field and political strategist. In addition, the voices and tireless efforts of many young Black LGBT people gave this movement the energy it needed to reach first-time voters and other Black voters not inclined to support Maryland's Question 6. Young activists like NBJC's Rodney Nickens and HRC's Karess Taylor-Hughes and Samantha Master were critical to the ground game to reach this population.

It is because of the collective leadership and dedication of many individuals, including the strong support of many Black voters, that on November 6, 2012, our nation reelected our first Black president and Maryland approved the referendum to expand marriage to same-sex couples by 52.4 percent of the popular vote. The persistent work of activists, learning from past defeats and working together to engage diverse communities, laid the groundwork and contributed to the progress toward the historic Supreme Court decision that expanded marriage nationwide on June 26, 2015 (my forty-seventh birthday!)

My life's work is a testament to the power of an organized, educated people— we can move mountains by working together. For the duration of my life, it is this hope that will continue to drive my passion and work: that our nation solidly addresses the unfinished business of freedom for all Black people. The work I do on behalf of the Black LGBT community is fueled by the fire in my belly to see Black people own their power. It takes collective work and authentic representation to reach the least engaged in our communities. It is when the political becomes personal that real progress happens.

"THE WORDS 'GAY' AND 'MARRIAGE' WERE NOT EVEN USED IN THE SAME SENTENCE."

PAT EWERT

Pat Ewert and Vernita Gray (1948–2014) were the first same-sex couple to marry in Illinois in 2013.

I was in a taxi coming home from the airport when I received the call. We had won the lawsuit for the freedom to marry in Illinois, which Lambda Legal had taken on, and which my partner Vernita Gray and I had joined. Vernita and I could get married immediately. We'd be the first same-sex couple to marry in Illinois. The taxi driver surprised me by saying he was very happy for me. But then I heard NPR on the radio: 'Longtime gay activist, Vernita Gray and her fiancée, Pat Ewert, will be allowed to get married before June 1 because Vernita Gray is dying of breast cancer."

Those words knocked the breath out of me. I started to cry. Would having those words said out loud make it real? I had to get used to it because the news of our marriage and Vernita's cancer was broadcast all over the world.

Vernita Gray was the best-dressed butch in the city of Chicago with a penchant for Cole Haan loafers and cashmere sweaters. She could pimp walk with the best of them and never passed up an opportunity to check herself out in a mirror. She had piercing brown eyes that laughed and danced. Incredibly gifted as a writer and orator, she had a strong sense of social justice and could move a room of people to their feet, inspired by her passion. She was a woman of strong opinions, compassionate without being a pushover, generous with her home, her time, her money, her

Vernita Gray and Pat Ewert celebrating their legal wedding in Illinois. Photo Credit:
COURTESY OF LAMBDA LEGAL

advice. She told gay youth, "Baby, you are a diva in training. Go show the
world how fabulous you are!"

Many of the things we take for granted in our community could be
traced directly back to Vernita's work—the Chicago Pride Parade, the
Center on Halsted (Chicago's LGBT Center), and the first lesbian and
gay presence in the Bud Billiken Parade, the oldest and largest African
American parade in the country.

Vernita was the Cook County LGBT liaison. She and I were introduced
by her boss, the Cook County state's attorney. Before meeting for the first
time, I googled her. There were nearly three hundred entries for Vernita
Gray. Very intimidating! It didn't occur to me that she would possibly be
interested in a newly out, old white chick. She was always surrounded by
an adoring throng, all the while texting and facebooking.

Then we were having a drink with some mutual friends when she
stopped and really looked at me for the first time. She said she liked my
smile, my laugh, my happy and easy way of talking with people, and, most
importantly, my shapely "badonk!"

Until the day I die I will never forget the first time Vernita reached her
hand out and touched me on the waist. I felt a jolt of electricity throughout my entire body. Later when I walked her to the elevator, she gave
me a little kiss on the lips, and I think I actually swooned. The next week
we went on our first date. We were pretty much inseparable from that
night on.

Vernita said that when she first came out over forty years ago, the words "gay" and "marriage" were not even used in the same sentence.

It's been nearly two years since Vernita passed, and about two and a half years since Vernita and I were joined in marriage. But she started fighting that fight about twenty years ago, without any idea that we would be the first to get married in the state. I feel so grateful for all of the amazing individuals and organizations that fought that fight with her. How blessed I was to have her love and to be able to share our story.

DON'T POSTPONE JOY: TAKING DOWN THE DEFENSE OF MARRIAGE ACT (DOMA)

James Esseks

———— ◦◦◦ ————

James Esseks is director of the ACLU Lesbian, Gay, Bisexual, Transgender & HIV Project.

"Don't postpone joy."

That was a guiding principle for Edie Windsor and Thea Spyer, who shared a life together for forty-four years. They met in the early 1960s in New York's Greenwich Village, at a bar that catered to lesbians, and danced all evening. In 1967, a few years after they became a couple, Thea proposed to Edie, not because they really thought they would be able to get legally married, but because that was the level of commitment and the kind of life they planned for each other. A traditional engagement ring would have raised unanswerable questions at Edie's job as a computer programmer at IBM, so Thea gave her a circular pin of small diamonds to mark their engagement.

Over the next forty years, Edie and Thea often found joy in their lives. They worked, traveled, entertained friends, and were advocates for LGBT equality. But they encountered challenges as well. In 1977, Thea was diagnosed with progressive multiple sclerosis, a degenerative neurological disorder for which there is no cure. Over the course of the next thirty years, Thea gradually lost her mobility, first resorting to a cane, then crutches, then a manual wheelchair, and finally an electric wheelchair that she could operate with her one working finger. Through all of this, Edie took care of Thea, and they kept dancing any way they could.

Edie and Thea had been watching hopefully as the movement for marriage equality grew through the early 2000s, and they had their heart set on getting married at home in New York. In 2007, Thea was told she likely had only a year to live, so they decided they couldn't wait for New York any longer, and went to Canada to marry. By that point, however, it wasn't so easy for Thea to travel, and they had to enlist friends to assemble and disassemble her wheelchair so she could get on the plane. After a forty-year engagement, still wearing her circular diamond pin, Edie married Thea.

Thea held on for two more years. Shortly after she died, Edie suffered a heart attack that the doctors diagnosed as "broken heart syndrome." When she got out of the hospital, she learned that the federal government was going to tax her simply because her spouse had been a woman rather than a man. Edie inherited Thea's portion of the joint possessions they had accumulated over the course of a lifetime, including the apartment they had lived in for decades. The so-called "Defense of Marriage Act" (DOMA) required the federal government to treat Edie and Thea as if they had never married. That meant that instead of facing an estate tax bill of $0, Edie had to come up with $363,000 for the IRS—just because she was a lesbian.

The problem Edie faced wasn't new. As soon as same-sex couples first started getting married in Massachusetts in the spring of 2004, they faced the reality that the federal government would not respect their marriages. That meant they were not recognized as spouses for purposes of Social Security survivor benefits, for veterans' benefits, for income taxes, and for family medical leave protections. And it meant that an American lesbian could not sponsor her foreign spouse for citizenship, the way different-sex couples could. The list went on and on.

Despite the stark clarity of the harms DOMA inflicted on married same-sex couples, there was a long debate among the LGBT legal groups about whether and when to file a constitutional challenge to DOMA. The reasons to file were as varied and compelling as the harms DOMA caused and the families it affected. The concern holding us back was primarily that it was too soon to put this constitutional equal protection question before the Supreme Court—we were seriously worried about losing. From 2004 until 2008, Massachusetts was the only state that allowed same-sex couples to marry, which wasn't the kind of national context that many advocates felt was needed to get the Supreme Court to rule in our favor. In 2008, Connecticut also recognized marriage equality, as did California for a while, but the numbers were still low. The argument in favor of filing suit was that, as explained below, a challenge to DOMA seemed easier to win than a federal challenge to other states' marriage bans and would not necessarily require courts to decide the ultimate question of whether all states must allow same-sex couples to marry. A DOMA ruling, we thought, would be a good interim step on the way to striking down all of the state bans on marriage for same-sex couples.

In March 2009, GLAD filed the first DOMA challenge, *Gill v. Office of Personnel Management*, in federal district court in Boston. GLAD had scoured Massachusetts for the most compelling stories and come up with a bumper crop of them. After his spouse and partner of over sixty years died, Herb Burtis was denied his husband's Social Security benefits because of DOMA. Nancy Gill, a postal worker, couldn't add her spouse, Marcelle Letourneau, to her health plan because of DOMA. And, if Kathy Bush's wife, police officer Mary Ritchie, were to die on the job, Kathy wouldn't qualify for the death and education benefits the federal government provides to the surviving spouses of public safety officers because, under DOMA, they weren't married.

Those stories proved quite persuasive to the federal trial judge, who struck down DOMA as unconstitutionally discriminatory in July 2010. That summer was quite a moment for the marriage movement, since the *Gill* ruling was followed closely by another groundbreaking court decision. This time, a federal court in San Francisco struck down Prop 8, the initiative that had taken marriage away from same-sex couples in California in 2008.

Both decisions were right, and both were transformative. But the two cases highlighted the difference between a case about the freedom to marry and a case about DOMA. The Prop 8 case asked whether all same-sex couples had the freedom to marry. A win in that case at the Supreme Court would require every state to let us marry. In 2010, when the Prop 8 trial court ruling came out, that would have overturned the law of forty-five states. The DOMA case, in contrast, asked only whether the federal government had to respect the marriages of same-sex couples who were already married under state law, just as it respected the marriages of other couples. A win there would not create even one new marriage state, but would simply require equal treatment of existing marriages. Many of us thought we had a much better chance of winning the DOMA issue and that it would be best for that narrower issue to get to the Court before Prop 8 got there.

So the race was on.

Soon after *Gill* was filed in 2009, I and other LGBT advocates started meeting with representatives of the Department of Justice (DOJ) in Washington, D.C., to flag for them the legal challenges that were headed their way. DOJ represents the federal government in court, including in cases like *Gill*, where federal statutes are challenged as unconstitutional. The usual practice at DOJ is to defend the constitutionality of those statutes, which is what it was doing in *Gill*. But there are limited circumstances where DOJ will tell a court that it cannot defend a statute because it's just too clearly unconstitutional. Our aim was to convince DOJ to drop its defense of DOMA in court.

We thought our best bet for convincing DOJ not to defend DOMA was to get them to agree that courts should consider government discrimination based on sexual orientation (which is what DOMA was) to be presumptively unconstitutional. We had long struggled under the reverse legal rule—that government discrimination against lesbians and gay men was presumed to be constitutional. Under that rule, called the "rational basis test," gay people complaining about the laws bore the burden of convincing courts that there was no possible rational reason for the differential treatment imposed by the law. It was really hard to strike down a law under that test. In contrast, under "heightened scrutiny," courts would presume that government discrimination based on sexual orientation was unconstitutional, and would require the government to come forward with a good reason for why it had to take sexual orientation into account in any given context. The difference in the presumption—the law being presumed constitutional under rational basis versus being presumed unconstitutional under heightened scrutiny—was the difference between night and day for lawyers. And if heightened scrutiny applied to government discrimination like DOMA, we hoped DOJ would agree that DOMA was simply indefensible.

One challenge for us was that DOJ had managed to hide from directly confronting this legal issue in court, and it clearly wanted to duck the issue as long as possible. Federal appeals courts in many parts of the country had old precedent saying clearly that the rational basis test applied to government discrimination based on sexual orientation. Those decisions were based on an old Supreme Court case that had since been overruled, and we thought they were just wrong. But right or wrong, DOJ could, and did, simply point to those decisions as binding on the appeals courts and trial courts in the circuit. That meant the DOJ didn't have to explain to the courts what it thought the right presumption was under the Constitution. The First Circuit Court of Appeals, which covered most of New England and was where the *Gill* appeal was pending, had already decided the presumption issue against us, holding that rational basis review applied.

But there was a place where DOJ couldn't hide from the presumption question: the Second Circuit Court of Appeals, covering New York, Connecticut, and Vermont, had never decided the issue. So the ACLU started looking for stories that would allow us to challenge DOMA in the Second Circuit. We were hopeful that GLAD would win its *Gill* lawsuit up in the First Circuit. But we needed a way to force DOJ to confront the constitutional question about antigay government discrimination head-on, and a case in the Second Circuit would do just that.

In September 2010, shortly after our second meeting with DOJ about DOMA and the presumptions issue, I stepped out of a meeting in DC to take a call from Robbie Kaplan. I had worked closely with Robbie years earlier, when the ACLU asked her and her law firm, Paul, Weiss, to be our co-counsel in a case in New York seeking the freedom to marry for same-sex couples under the state Constitution. She had clerked for the chief judge of New York's highest court and knew several of the other judges on that court, which meant that she, as an open lesbian, could make the marriage issue personal for them. Plus, she was a wicked smart and aggressive litigator. It was a wonderful partnership, but, after years of litigation, we lost that case in 2006.

Now Robbie was calling to return the favor and ask me to join her in a DOMA challenge representing Edie Windsor. I couldn't believe how perfect Edie's case was. Two things stood out for me: First, the love and commitment at the heart of their marriage. Recent messaging research had taught us that this was the kind of story that most moved public opinion. Second, Edie's case would be in New York, which is in the Second Circuit. Jackpot! I explained the DOJ dynamics to Robbie, and she got it immediately. I signed the ACLU on right away.

I met Edie a few days later, and my initial commitment to the case deepened. Here was a vibrant woman with a love story for the ages, one that the country could relate to, look up to, and embrace. She would be the perfect spokesperson for marriage!

We scrambled to get Edie's case, *Windsor v. United States*, ready, and filed it in November 2010, on the same day that GLAD filed a similar case, *Pedersen v. Office of Personnel Management*, in Connecticut. Connecticut is also in the Second Circuit, so *Pedersen* would also put DOJ to the test on the presumptions issue.

After filing Edie's case, LGBT advocates and I met again with DOJ to push them to drop their defense of DOMA in *Windsor* and *Pedersen* and to agree that express government discrimination should be presumed unconstitutional. They were non-committal, but it was clear they were having serious conversations internally. We were asking them to do something quite unusual, for which they would take serious political heat. But it was clear they knew we were right about the Constitution.

On February 23, 2011, just one day before the government's answer was due in *Windsor*, I got a call from Tony West, the assistant attorney general in charge of the Civil Division at DOJ. He had been a central player in our meetings with the agency. He connected Robbie Kaplan to the call and told us that Attorney General Holder was about to announce that DOJ would no longer defend the constitutionality of DOMA. I was floored. This is what we had been pushing for since 2009, but I hadn't quite believed it would happen.

After Tony hung up, Robbie and I, both amazed, talked about what a moment this was both for Edie's case and for the LGBT movement more broadly. We now had the most powerful ally we could possibly have in a case against the government—the government itself. Attorney General Holder's announcement made clear that DOJ agreed that state discrimination against lesbians and gay men should be presumed to be unconstitutional. With DOJ at our side, we knew that all the courts ahead of us, from the trial court right up to the Supreme Court should we make it that far, would take our constitutional arguments much more seriously. DOJ's switch of position transformed the prospects for Edie's case. It was a thrilling, overwhelming, unbelievable moment.

With DOJ no longer defending DOMA, the Republican leadership of the House of Representatives, through the so-called Bipartisan Legal Advisory Group, or BLAG, took over defense of the discriminatory statute in court. BLAG put us through our paces, raising profoundly antigay arguments. By September 2011, the case was submitted to Judge Barbara Jones of federal district court in Manhattan, and we could do nothing more but wait.

The following June brought great news on two fronts. The First Circuit appeals court ruled for the plaintiff couples in *Gill*. Shortly thereafter, Judge Jones struck down DOMA in Edie's case as well. Edie couldn't stop smiling at the press conference at the ACLU about her win.

Our legal team jumped into gear, eager to get Edie's case up on appeal quickly. As soon as BLAG filed its notice of appeal, we asked the Second Circuit to expedite the briefing and argument. To my surprise, the court gave us a crazy good schedule, with briefing completed by the end of August 2012 and oral argument in September. The panel assigned to the case initially gave us some pause because it was led by Chief Judge Dennis Jacobs, known as a conservative jurist. But at oral argument, the panel, and particularly Chief Judge Jacobs, seemed quite focused on the heightened scrutiny analysis that we and DOJ were both advocating. We started hoping for another win, one that would embrace the presumption of unconstitutionality we so desired.

A month later, we got just that decision from Chief Judge Jacobs, who was joined by Judge Droney. The Second Circuit said clearly that government discrimination based on sexual orientation should be presumptively unconstitutional. And, under that standard, it held that DOMA violated the Constitution.

Edie was elated. As a lawyer, so was I. This was the first federal appeals court decision in the country adopting heightened scrutiny for sexual orientation discrimination, and that by itself made the ruling a landmark in LGBT rights. But we didn't have time to celebrate. We were in a race to the Supreme Court.

Shortly after the appeals court ruling in Edie's case, DOJ asked the Supreme Court to take up the *Windsor* decision to decide once and for all the constitutionality of DOMA. Earlier in the year, DOJ had filed similar petitions asking the Court to take two other DOMA cases, GLAD's *Gill* case and *Golinski v. Office of Personnel Management*. *Golinski* was another DOMA challenge involving the denial of spousal health insurance benefits to a married, lesbian, federal court employee brought by Lambda Legal, in which a federal district court in San Francisco had held the core of DOMA unconstitutional. But with the Second Circuit's decision that heightened scrutiny applied to antigay discrimination, DOJ changed its mind and signaled to the Court that *Windsor* was the best vehicle.

The Prop 8 case had also progressed through the appeals court stage, where the Ninth Circuit Court of Appeals struck the measure down under equal protection. The proponents of Prop 8 filed a petition for Supreme Court review in the summer of 2012, so the Prop 8 petition and the petitions in four cases about DOMA—*Gill*, *Golinski*, *Pedersen*, and *Windsor*—were all pending at the same time.

On a mid-December Friday, Edie, Robbie, and I gathered with other team members to await word about whether the Court would take up *Windsor* or any of the other cases. Glued to SCOTUSblog, we joked and paced and tried to pass the time. Then the word came: "Prop 8 is granted, and so is *Windsor*." The room erupted! The country's Supreme Court marriage moment had arrived, with both DOMA and Prop 8 at center stage. I was thrilled that Edie and her story of love, commitment, and discrimination were headed to the Supreme Court. I saw first-hand how powerful her story was with both courts and the public, and I thought this was the perfect way to tee up the issues.

The next several months became a confusing blur of researching, strategizing, briefing, and debating. Pam Karlan of the Stanford Law School Supreme Court Litigation Clinic had joined the *Windsor* team a bit earlier, as soon as we started filing papers in the Supreme Court, and she brought brilliance and laughter to the work. And Mary Bonauto, lead counsel in GLAD's *Gill* case and the original architect of the DOMA challenges, now lent us her considerable talents as well, brilliantly coordinating the friend-of-the-court briefs, which brought the voices of Republicans, businesses, faith leaders, and retired military brass before the court, plus many others.

When argument day finally arrived in late March, I wasn't worried about Robbie, who had been grilled repeatedly through practice arguments and was super-prepared. Arguing before the Court was old hat for the solicitor general, Don Verrilli, who would also push for striking down DOMA. But I wasn't sure we had the five justices we needed to win. As the justices filed in, I remember standing at counsel table in disbelief that we were about to hear their thoughts about DOMA after having worked toward this moment for years.

One by one, the justices gave hints about where they likely stood on DOMA. The four more liberal justices all seemed on board with our arguments, but Justice Kennedy, whom everyone knew was likely a swing vote, kept asking questions focused on federalism. I left the argument thinking we probably did

The *U.S. v. Windsor* legal team gather to celebrate at the NY LGBT center on decision day: Donna Lieberman from the NY Civil Liberties Union; attorneys from the Paul, Weiss firm Julie Fink, Josh Kaye, and Roberta Kaplan, who successfully argued the case; Rose Saxe, ACLU LGBT & HIV Project; plaintiff Edie Windsor; James Esseks, ACLU LGBT & HIV Project director; Jaren Janghorbani and Alexia Koritz from Paul, Weiss. Photo Credit: MOLLY KAPLAN/ACLU

have Kennedy, but perhaps on a federalism theory that might be more limited in scope. And then the waiting began again.

The Supreme Court issues all of its decisions for the year by the end of June, with the higher-profile cases often coming right at the end. And, true to the pattern, *Windsor* was still outstanding when the Court announced that the last decision day of its term would be June 26, 2013. I remember walking to work that morning wondering if we were about to be in a world without DOMA.

Sitting in an office with my ACLU colleagues, connected by phone with Edie and Robbie in New York and Pam and her team in California, we watched SCOTUSblog for word of the decision. When the ruling came, we screamed and cried, hugged and high-fived. I was exultant, floating with happiness. I was amazed at the power of Edie and Thea's love affair to crystalize what was wrong about DOMA. And I was buoyed by the reaffirmation that our legal system can truly right profound wrongs.

Later that morning, in a jam-packed room at the New York LGBT Community Center, Edie addressed more TV cameras and microphones than I had ever seen before. When asked what Thea would say to her, Edie replied simply, "You did it, honey!" Indeed, she did. For all of us.

THE WAIT IS OVER: ELEVEN YEARS TO MARRIAGE IN NEW JERSEY

Hayley Gorenberg

Hayley Gorenberg is deputy legal director at Lambda Legal.

The plaintiffs in *Garden State Equality (GSE) v. Dow* had weathered everything from indignity to disaster. The painful irony is that bad situations for people can make good cases for courts, and our clients had the makings of a great case: a set of facts so bad that it was going to be very, very good.

GSE v. Dow was Lambda Legal's second and final litigation salvo over the course of eleven years to secure marriage equality in the Garden State. Our first New Jersey marriage case, *Lewis v. Harris*, was led by Lambda Legal's second Marriage Project Director, David Buckel. That case rose from filing in 2002 to the state's highest court in 2006,[1] as part of an early trickle that led to a torrent of constitutional litigation seeking access to marriage without discrimination based on sex or sexual orientation. When the New Jersey Supreme Court handed down its decision, the majority agreed with us that the New Jersey Constitution required access to the rights and protections of marriage but found that it did not necessarily mandate access to the *status* of marriage. Chief Justice Deborah Poritz, joined by Justices Virginia Long and James Zazzali, would have battered the barriers entirely:

> We must not underestimate the power of language. Labels set people apart as surely as physical separation on a bus or in school facilities.

Labels are used to perpetuate prejudice about differences that, in this case, are embedded in the law. By excluding same-sex couples from civil marriage, the State declares that it is legitimate to differentiate between their commitments and the commitments of heterosexual couples. Ultimately, the message is that what same-sex couples have is not as important or as significant as "real" marriage, that such lesser relationships cannot have the name of marriage. . . . I would extend the Court's mandate to require that same-sex couples have access to the "status" of marriage and all that the status of marriage entails.

But just as in Vermont in 1999, the majority punted to the state legislature to implement the decision. Lambda Legal worked closely with the statewide advocacy group Garden State Equality to advocate for marriage, but the New Jersey legislature, over a wave of objections from LGBT people and allies, hastily passed a civil union law purporting to give same-sex couples access to benefits equal to those of marriage. This latest experiment with supposed parallel systems was to be assessed by a Civil Union Review Commission that would collect evidence about whether this separate status could possibly be equal. In the years following the arrangement, many couples, variously referring to themselves as "civil-unioned," "civilly united," or even "unionized," raised their voices in hearings scattered across the state to complain of the consequences of their novel and oft-misunderstood and disrespected status. The Civil Union Review Commission unanimously reported that the parallel status failed to deliver equality, and disbanded—but many LGBT and allied community members, including the commission's vice chairman, the dynamo activist Steven Goldstein, continued to press for marriage without discrimination.

LGBT New Jerseyans compiled an extensive record of disturbing suffering due to unequal treatment. Lambda Legal, partnering again with Newark's Gibbons law firm, which had devoted countless hours of pro bono assistance in the *Lewis* case, returned directly to the New Jersey Supreme Court with an unusual plea on behalf of our original plaintiffs.[2] On March 18, 2010, we filed a "motion in aid of litigants' rights"—a common enforcement mechanism in a case concerning something like child support, where a litigant might directly complain that the court's money judgment had not reached the pocketbook. In this instance, however, we used the motion to complain that the measure of equality embodied in the top court's equality mandate had never enriched our clients' lives, as ordered.

We were not shocked when our creative effort, chosen because it was quick and direct, was denied. The Court indicated we should file again and put the limitations of civil unions on trial to test whether they violated constitutional guarantees. Only marriage would provide equality, and now we had to generate the record to prove it.

I criss-crossed the state of New Jersey with a Gibbons fellowship attorney, Eileen Connor, interviewing couples hurt and frustrated by their second-class status. Some were civil-unioned only; some had married elsewhere, but when they returned home, New Jersey law downgraded their entirely valid marriages to be regarded as civil unions only. This demotion happened courtesy of an attorney general opinion authored by Stuart Rabner, who had since become the chief justice of the New Jersey Supreme Court—which some viewed as cause for concern as we devised new litigation.

Plaintiffs Marsha Shapiro, a therapist, and Louise Walpin, a nurse, had married in New York after raising four children together. Their severely disabled son's tragic death became a further well of pain when the funeral home failed to recognize Louise's parental relationship. When Louise was called to jury duty, she was quizzed by the judge in front of all other jurors regarding her household members, forced to out herself as gay before strangers in a spotlight not of her choosing. As she explained, she did not know who in the courtroom might be hostile and waiting in the parking lot when she left that evening after doing her civic duty. When Louise was admitted to the hospital several times for a range of ailments, Marsha, who was always at her side, was identified variously as "partner," "friend," and "unknown." The records did not reflect their relationship, and Marsha and Louise feared an emergency in which doctors and nurses wouldn't understand their theoretical rights as civil union partners, a term which seemed to mystify medical staff.

Plaintiffs Danny Weiss and John Grant had lived precisely the medical nightmare the other plaintiff couples dreaded. Late one night in New York City, during a wild storm, John was hit by a car. Brought to Bellevue Hospital by ambulance, hemorrhaging into his brain, doctors doubted whether he would live. Danny was summoned when someone dialed the last number in John's mobile phone. But when Danny arrived, distraught at John's injuries, he faced a new crisis: hospital staff didn't understand the legal implications of civil union, and were not about to be taught on the spot. Danny frantically tried to explain the supposed equivalent. He showed how the band he wore on his left ring finger matched one John wore. The doctors were sympathetic and wanted to help, and asked if maybe he and John had "one of those Massachusetts marriages?" No? In that case, could Danny go out in the storm, return to New Jersey to get the civil union certificate and other medical paperwork, and return to New York City? Danny refused to leave John's side. The doctors wanted to perform a craniotomy and looked for an appropriate authorizing signature. So Danny was asked if he could please summon "a real relative." In the middle of the night,

John's sister drove from Delaware and cosigned the surgical authorization alongside Danny.

By a near-miracle and excellent medical care, John survived. As soon as he could safely travel, he and Danny drove to Connecticut to be married. Traumatized by their treatment around John's dreadful accident, Danny purchased multiple copies of their marriage certificate and never again traveled without copies of their marriage, civil union, and medical documentation on a flash drive attached to his key ring. At the news conference announcing our case filing, the mention of carrying papers at all times triggered knowing, pained looks and nods of acknowledgment. Everyone had papers, whether on flash drives or files carted around in their cars or in glove boxes. They navigated the world under what felt like actual or potential siege on their families at all times, whether in the emergency room, at their children's school, at the dentist, or even when queried in one instance by a tree surgeon, who showed up but hesitated to commence work. He stood in the doorway, puzzling out loud because one woman in the household had ordered the work done, and how exactly did this other individual at home today relate to her?

I met Keith Heimann and Tom Davidson in their home, lively with their two adopted daughters and multiple well-loved pets and festooned with crayoned drawings like the card for "Daddy and Papa." They had spent interminable hours trying to navigate what civil union meant for family insurance coverage, experiencing mounting aggravation over roadblocks and misunderstandings with bureaucrats.

Tevonda Hayes and Erica Bradshaw and their adorable infant son, Teverico Barack, joined the case after enduring confusion and delay when Tevonda was in active labor and Erica was held back from joining her because hospital security didn't understand their civil union. When Tevonda later spoke with their pediatrician's office, staff lacking words to navigate the unfamiliar technicality of civil unions referred to Erica not simply as "your wife," but rather as, "you know . . . the other one."

Also among our plaintiffs in the new case were two of our original *Lewis* couples: high school sweethearts Cindy Meneghin and Maureen Kilian, respectively a university Web services director and local church parish administrator, and Marcye and Karen Nicholson-McFadden, civil union partners who also partnered in running an executive search firm—walking illustrations of just one of the myriad ways the label "partner" failed to illuminate their life commitment to each other.

Homophobic critiques of gay parents had haunted early marriage advocacy, but we judged the time right to press forward with entire families as plaintiffs seeking equality. Lambda Legal had won a thrilling marriage victory in Iowa in

2009, asserting the importance of protecting the children of same-sex couples. Our New Jersey couples' young children joined Lambda Legal's new case as plaintiffs in their own right. With civil-unioned parents, they could become legal strangers on a road trip, traveling through a state that lacked any regard for New Jersey's novel formulation devised for same-sex couples only. Karen and Marcye's son, Kasey, reluctantly reported that his middle-school friend, entirely accepting of lesbian parents but perplexed that Kasey's mothers weren't married, had probed, "So, that means you're a bastard, right?" In his deposition conducted by the state's attorneys, he described his reaction: She must be right.

Finishing out the plaintiff pool was an organization, New Jersey's statewide equality group, Garden State Equality, helmed by Steven Goldstein. Steven had been organizing for marriage in New Jersey since 2002, dramatically increasing public and political support for equality. The stage was set.

The government quickly moved to dismiss our case, saying civil union on paper gave all that was necessary, and suggesting the plaintiffs ought to file individual complaints against every person, hospital, insurance company, or other entity that failed to comprehend that their rights should approximate marital status. Our responsive papers were comprehensive. We had even dug up a rarely cited Supreme Court case from 1964, *Anderson v. Martin*, concerning governmental responsibility for discrimination when Louisiana officials labeled candidates' race on ballots and voters rejected all Black candidates. The government protested that voters were independent, non-governmental actors. The Court saw through the contention and held the government responsible for what I analogized to tagging same-sex couples with a big "Kick me!" sign and then eschewing responsibility when voters acted on the invitation to discriminate.

On November 4, 2011, the trial court heard us argue the dismissal motion, and even in the hot seat, I enjoyed most of the argument. We had been reassigned to Judge Linda R. Feinberg, the judge from our original *Lewis* case. Faced with the suggestion that the plaintiffs should have filed individual complaints across the state against each of those who did not respect or understand New Jersey's special status for same-sex couples, she gestured to the plaintiffs and advised the government that the aggrieved families were, indeed, complaining! She understood that we sought to fight a government system that enmeshed health care workers and businesses and employers, as well as plaintiffs, by structuring discrimination throughout the state. She refused to dismiss our case, and we plunged into the swampy morass of discovery proceedings, papers, and depositions.

But then on June 26, 2013, as we neared completion of our trial preparations, the full sweep of DOMA challenges that we and sister organizations Gay & Lesbian Advocates & Defenders, the National Center for Lesbian Rights, and the

American Civil Liberties Union had launched blossomed into the United States Supreme Court's decision in the ACLU's *Windsor* case, striking Section 3 of the so-called "Defense of Marriage Act," which had to that point barred federal recognition of valid marriages of same-sex couples.

Windsor would topple discriminatory barriers to federal benefits and responsibilities like dominoes: family medical leave coverage, Medicare coverage, immigration sponsorship for a spouse, marital tax considerations, and more. All 1,138 references to marriage in federal provisions would apply to married couples regardless of sex or sexual orientation. But the rights, acknowledged in quick succession by interpretations issuing from the Obama administration, flowed pursuant to marriages only—not civil unions. We decided to move for summary judgment: an immediate decision on the law alone, foregoing the presentation of the reams of evidence of our plaintiffs' suffering we'd worked so hard to develop.

We moved with urgency and speed. On July 3, 2013, within a week of the Supreme Court's *Windsor* decision and with the ink still drying on those elite pages, we ditched our trial, opting for an effort that was instantaneous, sleek, targeted—and a calculated risk. We would rely on our ability to distill the essence of the injustice.

I was particularly proud that we were able to proceed quickly, without a struggle to amend our complaint at that date. We could do so because, with a mixture of outrage and optimism during the initial drafting, I had included paragraph 45, an arguably attenuated assertion that under New Jersey's law, our clients were

> hindered from engaging in marriage-based challenges to DOMA
> and its discriminatory effects, and will not gain the rights and bene-
> fits that will be available after the repeal or striking down of DOMA:
> under New Jersey law, they are not married spouses, but rather civil
> union partners, a term that has no established legal meaning in rela-
> tion to marriage-based federal benefits.

We needed no amendment and could barrel ahead!

We pelted the court with supplemental analyses of every federal agency decision in *Windsor*'s wake that allowed family protections, privileges, benefits, and responsibilities for those who were or could be married—but denied them to all others. We drew examples from Garden State Equality's membership, with binational couples and partners of federal employees denied basic rights simply through lack of access to marriage. For this second oral argument, after fighting off dismissal, it was Gibbons partner Larry Lustberg's turn. Judge Feinberg had retired, but Larry had appeared before our new judge, the Honorable Mary C. Jacobson, in past cases, and the argument sailed beautifully. (Larry would subsequently win a state bar award recognizing his pro bono work in the marriage cases.)

Lambda Legal's headquarters office tends to run quietly. So I remember with joyful self-consciousness the whoop I let out when word came on September 27, 2013, that we'd won. We had succeeded at this initial level. But even as congratulations flowed, the conviction loomed that we faced not only instantaneous appeal but an imminent judicial stay that would delay implementation of our success until the ultimate decision by the state's high court. Our cause was true but—all experience showed—would inevitably be delayed.

In no case up to that point had a marriage win been allowed to take effect prior to the final tussle at the top. The government argued there would be chaos if a win were ultimately retrenched on appeal. But what of the chaos and instability and mayhem for families together for decades, or with young children, or elderly partners, or ill people, all deprived of the ability to protect each other, when every passing day risked that such would be the case forever? In light of our powerful rationales, it was patently, desperately unfair, and had always been so. Yet the argument had never taken hold until now. We flipped the paradigm. The chaos and uncertainty, the harm and hurt, the risk (and the reward) were all squarely with our clients. The ineffable harm to the state was illusory. The emperor had no clothes.

The government moved for its stay. We opposed, with every reason we should win but never had. Well aware that stays were routine, as we dug into briefing to oppose, I experienced mounting outrage. The weight of logic and the balance of harms tilted in our favor. Haunted by Diane, our *Lewis* client who had lost her love, Marilyn, to Lou Gehrig's disease before they could marry, I became convinced we should press that every single day mattered. Especially with an organizational plaintiff representing thousands of members, someone could experience a tragic circumstance, death, or disability preventing competent and knowing entry into marriage, and be precluded for all time from ever protecting their family.

And then, on October 10, 2013, for the first time in a lower-court marriage win: stay denied!

We whipped through legal exchanges and made a successful pitch, from plaintiffs and defendants jointly, asking to take the unusual step of skipping the intermediate appellate court for a juggernaut to the New Jersey Supreme Court. In this we agreed with our opponents—the decision rested with the court of last resort.

I tend to feel that vote-counting is hubris, and I didn't dare. But the speculation streamed in: maybe this justice will find in your favor. Maybe another. Perhaps 4–3? And of course, the Court was now led by Stuart Rabner, the former

Plaintiffs in both New Jersey cases, Maureen Kilian and Cindy Meneghin, with son Joshua Kilian-Meneghin, at the NJ victory press conference and rally, October 18, 2013. Photo Credit: LESLIE VON PLESS/LAMBDA LEGAL

New Jersey attorney general whose reverse alchemy had transformed countless valid marriages to civil unions upon crossing the New Jersey state line.

The decision rolled in on October 18, 2013. We had won. Once again, the New Jersey Supreme Court was unanimous, but this time, building on all our work, it finally delivered equality:

> *Lewis* guarantees equal treatment under the law to same-sex couples. That constitutional guarantee is not being met. And the ongoing injury that plaintiffs face today cannot be repaired with an award of money damages at a later time. . . . Plaintiffs highlight a stark example to demonstrate the point: if a civil-union partner passes away while a stay is in place, his or her surviving partner and any children will forever be denied federal marital protections.

The high court had spoken (with Chief Justice Rabner authoring the opinion), and Governor Chris Christie, who had pledged to fight us to the New Jersey Supreme Court, accepted the loss. Finally, the people of New Jersey could marry free of discrimination.

The mood ran high, celebrating weddings in Newark City Hall a minute after midnight on October 21, 2013. Until that moment, then-Mayor Cory Booker, a staunch supporter of equality, had refused to use the power of his office to conduct weddings for any couples, saying, "I would not marry anybody until I could marry everybody."

I stood with a colorfully arrayed, festive assortment of clergy from diverse faiths, bearing witness to the buoyant ceremonies the mayor conducted, one after another. The crank who bellowed his dissent during the first ceremony, when Mayor Booker asked whether anyone present had reason to object, failed to crack the mood and was efficiently assisted from the rotunda by security. (He did manage to stir whispered consternation among the phalanx of clergy, several of whom hurriedly advised me that they *never* invite objections in their ceremonies!)

And when Cindy and Maureen finally married on October 26, 2013, after four decades together, their guests indulged in a history lesson as well as a richly deserved celebration. The anteroom before we entered for the ceremony was lined with their eleven years of scrapbooks, painstakingly detailing every effort and setback, documenting the entire New Jersey quest to marry. "Get your tissues handy," the news accounts urged, in enthusiastic anticipation. "They (finally) do!"

THE UNLIKELY DOMINO: *KITCHEN V. HERBERT*

PEGGY A. TOMSIC

───❦───

Peggy A. Tomsic is a partner at the law firm Magleby & Greenwood in Salt Lake City.

In 2004, Utah's legislature, in reaction to marriage cases in Hawai'i, Massachusetts, and Vermont, placed a proposed amendment to Utah's Constitution on the general election ballot, banning marriage by same-sex couples and legal recognition of same-sex couples' relationships ("Amendment 3"). The ban was one of the most draconian laws proposed by states in the backlash against legal recognition of relationships between gay and lesbian individuals:

1. Marriage consists only of the legal union between a man and a woman.
2. No other domestic union, however denominated, may be recognized as a marriage or given the same or substantially equivalent legal effect.

Amendment 3's proponents argued that the amendment was necessary to maintain "public morality, the justified preference for heterosexual marriage with its capacity to perpetuate the human race, and the importance of raising children in that preferred relationship." Amendment 3, they said, would ensure continuation of "the ideal relationship where men, women, and children thrive best, and that is an enduring natural marriage between a man and a woman."

While opponents of Amendment 3 knew they had an uphill battle given Utah's political and religious majority, we fought hard. We ran the "No on 3" campaign on television, radio, and in newspapers to educate our neighbors, showing same-sex couples wanted only the same security, protection, and dignity for their families as opposite-sex couples. The majority overpowered us with messages of morality and fear. Approximately 66 percent of Utah voters voted for Amendment 3, which became Article I, § 29, of the Utah Constitution effective January 1, 2005.

Amendment 3 remained unchallenged until March 2013.

In February 2013, Mark Lawrence, a Salt Lake City resident, was fed up that no one had challenged Amendment 3. Mark was not affiliated with any local or national LGBT organization, but he was determined to bring down the amendment. He organized a nonprofit organization, Restore Our Humanity, and searched for a lawyer.

After being turned away by national and local LGBT organizations and Salt Lake civil liberties lawyers, he took an unconventional approach. He went online to find a law firm known for being hard-nosed, successful civil litigators. He found Magleby & Greenwood. Jim Magleby, Jennifer Parrish, and I were and still are lawyers at that small litigation firm. Mark contacted Jim through the firm's website.

Mark could not have found a better choice. We have a reputation for fighting hard and winning. Mark had no way of knowing our personal beliefs, but all three of us are adamant supporters of fairness and equality. Jim and Jennifer have family members and friends who are gay. I am a lesbian. My partner and I had been together for fifteen years at that time, and she had adopted our son by herself because Utah law prohibited both of us from adopting him. But we would not take the case unless we believed we could win the constitutional challenges.

We met Mark, and he was passionate. He had a general understanding of the constitutional arguments and had possible plaintiffs. But he had no money. He thought he could raise the $1–$2 million necessary for the fees and costs. However, covering fees and costs was not our focus. The real question for us was whether we thought the constitutional challenge was strong and whether we could win. This is Utah—the reddest of red states, a bastion of conservatism, and home of the Church of Jesus Christ of Latter-Day Saints (the "LDS Church").

After carefully reviewing the major constitutional cases and briefs filed in the *Windsor* and *Perry* cases pending in the Supreme Court, I became convinced we could win—not just on equal protection grounds but on due process grounds, protecting the fundamental right to marry. Jim, Jennifer, and I had lengthy discussions about the legal issues, the makeup of the Utah District and Tenth Circuit benches, and the political and religious environment in Utah, and we agreed to take the case.

We knew we needed just the right plaintiffs. The case eventually would be high profile, and it would be the vehicle to educate Utah citizens, a responsibility that would fall to the plaintiffs, not the lawyers. We met the two couples Mark brought as potential plaintiffs and the couple who, upon hearing of the case, was interested. By luck or destiny, not by design, they proved to be the perfect plaintiffs.

The three sets of same-sex couples who became the *Kitchen* plaintiffs were in loving, committed relationships. They all adamantly believed in marriage equality and wanted to marry or have their already legal marriage recognized in their home state. They represented people in three different stages of relationships and generations. Derek Kitchen and Moudi Sbeity were young, in the throes of new love, and building a life and business together. While they were hesitant at first to take the risk of being plaintiffs, when they decided to be plaintiffs, Derek said, "If we are in, we want to be all in. I want my name to be the first name on the case." Hence the *Kitchen* case.

Kody Partridge and Laurie Wood were both English teachers who had taught thousands of Utah students. They had grown up in a very different world from Derek and Moudi. They both had come of age in a time when it wasn't particularly safe to let people know they were lesbians. They had kept much of their lives out of sight; but now, with age, maturity, and seniority, they were ready to take the risk of joining the *Kitchen* case.

Karen Archer was from an even older generation. She and her partner, Kate Call, had been legally married in Iowa, but Utah wouldn't recognize their marriage. They had suffered discrimination and ridicule. Kate had lost jobs because she was a lesbian. When they got married, Karen was suffering from a serious medical condition. Everyday life and end-of-life decisions made it important and essential for their marriage to be legally recognized. They agreed to become plaintiffs, hoping a win wouldn't come too late for them and others like them.

None of the couples knew the other couples before becoming plaintiffs in *Kitchen*. The case compelled them to become a family. They gathered to support each other during the tense and uncertain times in the case as well as to celebrate the victories. The case became their shared purpose of making a real difference.

We knew from the beginning that *Kitchen* should be a local case. It would benefit from plaintiffs who had set down roots to make Utah their home. The lawyers also had to be lawyers who lived and worked in Utah. They could not come from an organization like the ACLU—which is a four-letter word in conservative

Utah—or a national LGBT organization that would be seen as outsiders coming in and telling Utah citizens how to govern their state.

Many questioned our local strategy. The skeptics were sure we would lose because we were not a large national law firm or part of an organization that had a national marriage strategy. Utah was not part of that strategy, and they didn't want us to bring the case at all. We ignored the criticism and stuck with our local approach and plan to go through the Utah federal district court. The only exception was that Shannon Minter and David Codell from the National Center for Lesbian Rights (NCLR) had confidence in our local team and willingly gave us their seasoned insight for our summary judgment motion without requiring public recognition.

Contrary to conventional wisdom, the legal team also decided to lead with the due process argument instead of equal protection. For us, starting with the long-recognized liberty interest in the freedom to marry guaranteed by the Due Process Clause highlighted that the importance, characteristics, and constitutional basis for that right were not defined by who exercised it but by what the freedom to marry represented to all people, regardless of sexual orientation. Additionally, the due process argument set the stage for the equal protection argument. Given the *Kitchen* decisions in the Utah District court and Tenth Circuit, and ultimately the Supreme Court decision in *Obergefell*, our strategy proved to be correct.

In addition, we decided to file the case prior to oral argument in *Windsor* and *Perry* in March 2013. We believed the *Windsor* decision would provide a legal framework for winning, but the Supreme Court would not address the merits in *Perry* due to the number of states with marriage bans. So on March 25, 2013, we filed the *Kitchen* case without fanfare. Except for a short newspaper article, *Kitchen* seemed a non-event to most Utahans (and to the rest of the country). Only our plaintiffs, Restore Our Humanity, and the firm knew what we had set in motion.

Judge Robert Shelby, the Utah federal district court judge assigned to *Kitchen*, decided to adopt the state's adamant position on how to proceed with the case. Instead of setting a fact and expert discovery schedule, as is the usual process, the state argued that the case should be decided by the judge as a matter of law on the state's motion for summary judgment. Judge Shelby gave us the option to file a cross-motion for summary judgment, and then he set a rigorous briefing and argument schedule.

The oral argument before Judge Shelby was remarkable for several reasons. The fact that a Utah federal court would actually be hearing argument on whether to strike down Amendment 3 was remarkable in and of itself. The plaintiffs and attorneys' pride and confidence—as we walked bundled up and arm-in-arm to the courthouse on that cold December morning—made it seem like we were born for such a moment. The largest courtroom in the federal courthouse, where we argued, was filled to the brim with people supporting our case. Despite the seriousness of the occasion, I found room for humor. When asked by Judge Shelby if he would be the first federal judge since *Windsor* to decide that a state ban on marriage for same-sex couples is unconstitutional, I not only told him, "Yes," but, after a pregnant pause, added, "Congratulations." While we all expected an hour hearing, Judge Shelby gave each side the time it felt necessary to make its case—we were in court that day for almost three and a half hours.

We did not expect a decision until sometime in January 2014. But Judge Shelby surprised us.

On Friday afternoon, December 20, 2013, less than six months after *Windsor* was decided and just over two weeks since hearing arguments, Judge Shelby became the first federal judge to strike down a state law banning marriage for same-sex couples and refusing to recognize marriage for same-sex couples, stating: "All citizens, regardless of their sexual identity, have a fundamental right to liberty, and this right protects an individual's right to marry and the intimate choices a person makes about marriage and family." In Utah of all places.

Rachel Maddow on national news that evening, with the teasing caption "Snowball's Chance in Hell" and a backdrop saying "Do You Believe In Miracles" put it this way: "Does this just feel like a bigger deal than all the others because, forgive me, it's freaking Utah?!" It was a big deal. It soon became an even bigger deal locally and nationally.

Marriages of same-sex couples began immediately at the Salt Lake County Clerk's office. The state had not filed a motion to stay marriages by the time the decision was issued. Without a motion before him, Judge Shelby did not stay his decision. National and local news captured couple after couple saying "I do" in Utah. Lines formed around the three stories of the county building and out the door into the freezing late afternoon. Clerks worked furiously to process as many couples as possible, staying open until 8:00 p.m. so that officials, including the mayor of Salt Lake City, could continue presiding over marriages. You couldn't turn on a major news channel without seeing the joy Judge Shelby's decision brought to the young, the middle-aged, the old, families with children, and families without children. Never before had the people of Utah seen such images of love and families. We never thought marriage equality would happen in our lifetimes. But it did.

When the state finally filed a motion to stay, Judge Shelby denied the motion. The Tenth Circuit, a court considered to be very conservative, also denied the state's motion on Christmas Eve. What a Christmas present! Marriages continued for the next seventeen days until the Supreme Court granted the state's stay request. By that time, over three thousand same-sex couples had married in Utah.

The seventeen days of marriage triggered broad public awareness that helped turn the tide toward acceptance of marriage for same-sex couples. People in Utah began to realize same-sex couples were their friends, their co-workers, and their neighbors. The conversation over the freedom to marry began in living rooms, at kitchen tables, in churches, and at work. In private conversations and in talks and interviews with broader audiences, the plaintiffs represented our case for equality and fairness with compassion, love, and respect. Everyone worked to show that "love is love" and "How can you hate love?" By the time the Supreme Court took up *Obergefell*, 50 percent of Utahans supported the freedom of same-sex couples to marry, and over 60 percent of the nation supported it as well.

When the state appealed Judge Shelby's decision, the Tenth Circuit set an expedited briefing scheduling, with oral argument on April 10, 2014, only ten months after the *Windsor* decision. The courtroom and overflow courtroom at the Tenth Circuit were filled to capacity for the arguments. The air crackled with anticipation. At the end of the hour-plus of arguments, we felt our positions remained solid and unshaken, try as Judge Kelly might to bring them down and obtain concessions. We thought the state's arguments had become more extreme and speculative but didn't know if the judges agreed. Prediction as to how and when the Tenth Circuit would rule was impossible, and speculation ran all over the board. We were all nervous and impatient waiting for the decision.

On June 25, 2014, the day before the one-year anniversary of *Windsor*, the Tenth Circuit became the first federal appellate court to strike down a state law banning marriage by same-sex couples and recognition of their legal marriages on due process and equal protection grounds. We had won. We celebrated. But because the stay remained, we wondered what might be ahead. The state didn't have to allow further marriages. It could continue to challenge the marriages that had occurred during the seventeen days and could continue to deny second-parent adoptions. Everything was on hold. The consequences were real. There were terminally ill people who wanted to marry and could not. There were couples with children who needed two legal parents to protect their children. The uncertainty was unnerving, but we could only wait.

The state, on August 5, 2014, petitioned the Supreme Court to review *Kitchen*. Its petition became the first petition for review of a marriage equality ruling after *Windsor*. The issue for our legal team was how we should respond to the petition. After all, we had won. We decided to file an acquiescence brief in which we agreed that the Supreme Court should grant the petition but should uphold the Tenth Circuit decision. We did so because of the nationwide implications and because we believed *Kitchen* provided an appropriate vehicle for the Supreme Court

to consider these serious constitutional issues. Although all federal decisions after *Kitchen* had struck down the state marriage discrimination laws—hence no
split of federal circuit court decisions—we believed the Supreme Court might
still grant a petition given the importance of the constitutional issues and the
impact on U.S. citizens. We were very careful in our brief not to disparage the
other cases and lawyers who had filed petitions after Utah's. The common goal,
of course, was to have any petition granted and to help whoever was chosen to
write a winning brief and deliver a winning oral argument.

When the Supreme Court, on October 6, 2014, denied Utah's and all other
pending petitions, everyone was caught off guard and, quite frankly, shocked. I
have to admit that, for a moment, I was sad *Kitchen* wouldn't be the case to end
marriage discrimination in the United States. However, once the shock of denial
wore off, our overwhelming feeling of relief and exultation set in. *Kitchen* had
brought marriage equality to Utah and all the states in the Tenth Circuit. Same-
sex couples could marry if they chose. They could have normal courtships. They
could complete second-parent adoptions to protect their children.

While at the time we didn't realize it, the state's insistence in the district court
that *Kitchen* be decided on summary judgment motions made *Kitchen* the first
federal district court decision and first federal appellate court decision striking
down state laws banning marriage for same-sex couples after *Windsor*. It set in
motion, like falling dominoes, federal district and appellate court decision after decision striking down other states' marriage discrimination laws, all citing
Kitchen. *Kitchen*'s domino effect resulted in the legalization of marriage for same-
sex couples in thirty-six states.

What we were able to achieve after winning in the district court truly took a
village. All our filings and brief before the Tenth Circuit and the Supreme Court
were the result of thousands of hours of collaboration among numerous LGBT
organizations and committed supporters of this critical cause. They included
Shannon, David, Chris Stoll, and other members of the NCLR legal team; Mary
Bonauto and Gary Buseck of GLAD; Evan Wolfson of Freedom to Marry; and
many others too numerous to mention. In addition, after the state filed the petition with the Supreme Court seeking review of *Kitchen*, Neal K. Katyal and his
legal team from Hogan Lovells U.S. LLP provided guidance and input about the
proper response to the state's petition and our acquiescence brief.

When *Kitchen* was final and brought marriage equality to Utah, to our opponents' surprise, the sky did not fall. Life went on, but with the new fresh air
of equality and fairness. Utahans had been learning how to live side by side as
neighbors for almost a year. The Utah legislature for five years had refused to
pass an LGBT non-discrimination law, but now, after marriage equality became
the law because of *Kitchen*, it signed into law protections for its LGBT citizens

extending to housing and employment. The LDS Church supported passage of the law, which was a remarkable step forward in a state with such strongly held beliefs about both marriage and religion. What the Supreme Court would have seen in Utah, if indeed it had looked before deciding *Obergefell*, was that the freedom to marry was not only constitutionally mandated but that a greater segment of the public—even the religious and conservative majority—had accepted marriage equality. *Kitchen* was the only post-*Windsor* case striking down state marriage discrimination laws cited in *Obergefell*, which was decided one year and one day after the Tenth Circuit *Kitchen* decision.

HOOSIERS IN LOVE: INDIANA'S EXPRESS PATH TO EQUALITY

PAUL D. CASTILLO

———⟨⟩———

Paul D. Castillo is a staff attorney at Lambda Legal.

By February 2014, the demand to file a marriage lawsuit in Indiana was becoming increasingly difficult to resist. Hoosiers saw victories happening in the most unlikely of jurisdictions: Utah, Oklahoma, Ohio, Kentucky, and Virginia. But an ongoing battle at the Indiana statehouse required that we at Lambda Legal and our partners proceed cautiously and quietly until the end of the legislative session. Indiana, a conservative state controlled by Republicans, wanted to amend its Constitution to define marriage as between a man and a woman. We didn't want the announcement of a marriage equality lawsuit to galvanize legislators into rushing this process.

The state already prohibited marriage by same-sex couples under its laws. But many Indiana lawmakers had pushed for a state constitutional amendment since 2004. Having an amendment on the books would preclude another legal challenge under the state's Constitution (although it could still be subject to a challenge in federal court.) According to Indiana's law, a proposed constitutional amendment must be approved by two consecutive legislatures—elected in two different electoral cycles—before a statewide referendum could be put to a vote. However, the measure had already passed in 2011, and House Joint Resolution 3

(HJR-3) was widely expected to pass its second and final step to be placed on the ballot in November 2014.

Freedom Indiana, a grassroots statewide coalition opposing HJR-3, garnered enough support to remove a single sentence regarding prohibiting civil unions. Since the previous legislature approved different language, the clock reset and pushed any possible vote on the marriage amendment until at least 2016, if ever. Marriage-related legal challenges were percolating in all but eight states that didn't already have the freedom to marry. It was only a matter of time before one of those cases reached the U.S. Supreme Court.

Camilla Taylor, Lambda Legal's National Marriage Project director, held a staff meeting to discuss marriage cases across the country after *Windsor*. With our recent success in New Jersey and Illinois, she was already contemplating where we might reallocate resources to move our marriage work into other states. Several of my colleagues were actively litigating cases in Nevada, Virginia, and West Virginia. The legal department also recently approved filing a case in Arizona.

As the newest attorney on staff, I was eager to participate. After all, this was the reason I had left my prior job as a civil rights attorney with the federal government. When I contacted Camilla to offer an extra hand, she promptly suggested we focus on Indiana. I was honored to take on the case.

Jim Bennett, director of Lambda Legal's Midwest regional office, began to inform our partners and local stakeholders that Lambda Legal would be filing a lawsuit seeking the freedom to marry in Indiana. Timing was critical. We planned to avoid filing the case before the legislative session ended because of the possibility that a lawsuit might resurrect HJR-3 or cause other turmoil on issues that might affect the LGBT community. When the time was right to move forward with a suit, we had less than one month to assemble our legal team, interview and select plaintiff couples, and draft the complaint. A filing at the end of the session on March 14 was a tall order.

Camilla suggested we partner with attorney Jordan Heinz and his team at Kirkland & Ellis LLP, a Chicago firm. Jordan had considerable experience working with Lambda Legal, including the successful marriage lawsuits in Illinois. He immediately agreed to work with us, and we assembled a team to interview potential plaintiff couples from across Indiana. Erik Roldan, our public information officer, along with Graciela Gonzalez, Alex Kirschner, Cheryl Angelaccio, and Melinda McKew, our legal assistants, went to work narrowing our pool of couples. Within a week, we selected three same-sex couples who wanted to marry in their home state of Indiana.

Rae Baskin and Esther Fuller were residents of Whitestown, just outside Indianapolis. Together nearly twenty-four years, Rae and Esther were both warm and endearing. The retired seniors loved each other in a profound way, and you could see it in their eyes. But Rae was also a no-nonsense realist, keenly aware that the various legal documents they had assembled provided inadequate protection. Esther's medical scares, including breast cancer in 2008 and a broken hip in 2009, forced them to consider whether the state and other private actors would recognize Rae's control over Esther's medical affairs should the need arise.

Chesterton residents Bonnie Everly and Lyn Judkins had firsthand experience with medical professionals being quick to discount their thirteen-year relationship. Bonnie and Lyn, both active in their church, held a private religious ceremony in 2002. In the same year, their lives were altered suddenly when a drunk driver struck the two women, leaving both suffering from mobility impairments. Bonnie also faced additional medical issues resulting in frequent trips to the hospital. Their worst nightmare occurred in early 2014, when a nurse blocked Lyn from entering the intensive care unit to visit Bonnie. While the episode was quickly resolved, the situation would not have occurred if they were married.

Dawn Carver and Pam Eans were residing in the northwest Indiana town of Munster. They had been in a loving, committed relationship for seventeen years. Both of them were working as first responders in neighboring Illinois communities, Dawn as a patrol officer and Pam as a firefighter captain. In addition to the respect and dignity marriage afforded, they sought peace of mind should one of them get injured or killed in the line of duty.

The lawsuit was falling into place, and we were on pace to announce our case at the conclusion of the legislative session. On Friday, March 7, we learned that a private Kentucky law firm had filed the first marriage lawsuit in Indiana, *Love v. Pence*. Our legal team assembled within two hours and discussed options, carefully weighing the activity occurring at the Indiana statehouse. We agreed to file as soon as possible, but still needed counsel in Indiana.

We sought out Barbara J. Baird, an Indianapolis family law attorney who had worked on behalf of the LGBT community for more than two decades. She was a longtime champion of Lambda Legal and had worked with us on prior cases, including a 2006 case to establish law in the state permitting joint and second-parent adoptions for same-sex couples. Barbara jumped in immediately despite recovering from major back surgery. By the end of the weekend, she had been fully briefed, suggesting revisions to the complaint. She planned a pre-dawn excursion to the courthouse to file the case.

With one case already filed, we quietly filed *Baskin v. Bogan* on Monday, March 10, 2014. Unlike for many marriage cases across the country, we held no press event. It would be Wednesday before our lawsuit papers would make their way around the statehouse, and Thursday before the press learned a second case had been filed. The legislative session came to an end on Friday, without incident. The case for equality would now be made in federal court.

By the end of the week, three more marriage cases were filed in Indianapolis. ACLU of Indiana had filed *Fujii v. Commissioner*, and two other cases were initiated by private counsel, *Lee v. Abbott* and *Bowling v. Pence*. In total, five cases were filed within the span of a week—all seeking the freedom to marry, recognition of out-of-state marriages, or both. Combined, the cases demonstrated the wide array of harms imposed on same-sex couples across the state.

Although *Baskin* was filed, we continued interviewing plaintiff couples. We wanted to add one or two couples with young children. After all, the Supreme Court in *Windsor* highlighted the indignity the federal government imposed on lesbian and gay parents because of DOMA, as "it humiliates tens of thousands of children now being raised by same-sex couples" and that "it makes it even more difficult for the children to understand the integrity and closeness of their own family and its concord with other families in their community and their daily lives." In Indiana, we knew children were particularly important to *Baskin* because the state's sole justification for denying same-sex couples the freedom to marry had to do with "irresponsible procreation." The state claimed it wanted to "protect" children born by accident because preserving marriage for different-sex couples would encourage "irresponsible" parents to marry.

Henry Green and Glenn Funkhouser, along with their twelve-year-old son, Casey, exemplified the type of family Indiana was harming with its twisted, discriminatory logic. Henry and Glenn had spent years planning for and welcoming a child into their lives, but Indiana still denied them the ability to marry. Residents of Carmel, Henry and Glenn had been in a committed relationship for twenty-two years. They knew early in their relationship that they wanted to raise a child. They became licensed foster parents, and Indiana placed then-two-year-old Casey with them in 2004. They adopted him shortly thereafter.

Like same-sex couples across the country, Hoosiers had already waited too long for the freedom to marry. I had also told our clients that we would attempt to achieve a swift victory. But we had significant concerns that the sheer number of cases would slow down the notoriously snail-paced judicial process. How would we avoid getting bogged down in judicial molasses? Procedurally, the fastest way to get immediate relief from a court is a temporary restraining order (TRO). However, absent exigent circumstances, a court rarely grants them.

In the marriage context, there had been two occasions thus far where a court granted a TRO to same-sex couples. In both cases, a partner or spouse was suffering from a terminal illness, and time was of the essence. In Ohio, the TRO, secured by attorney Alphonse Gerhardstein, meant that the state would be required to recognize Jim Obergefell as the surviving spouse on the forthcoming death certificate of his husband, John Arthur, who was diagnosed with ALS. Lambda Legal secured the other TRO in Illinois, enabling longtime Chicago

LGBT activist Vernita Gray, who was fighting breast cancer, to marry Pat Ewert in November 2013, prior to the full implementation of marriage equality in the state.

In what was a pivotal moment for *Baskin*, Niki Quasney and Amy Sandler bravely stepped forward to tell their story. The women were residents of Munster, rearing their two young daughters, both under the age of four. After thirteen years together, they married in Massachusetts in August 2013. Amy was a full-time student attending the University of Chicago, and Niki was in the midst of a very intense and personal battle with Stage IV ovarian cancer. Despite everything going on their lives, they not only decided to join our marriage lawsuit; they decided to fight for immediate recognition of their marriage. Niki and Amy knew they were going to have to expose Niki's personal medical history to the public and that they were going to face intense scrutiny of their marriage and their family.

In order to secure an early victory, we had to focus the court's attention on the urgency of their situation. In 2009, when Niki was diagnosed with Stage IV ovarian cancer, her oncologist estimated a five-year median survival rate of 50 percent. Over the next four years, Niki chose an aggressive treatment regimen and remained optimistic, even while enduring years of chemotherapy and multiple surgeries to remove hundreds of tumors. With the five-year threshold on the horizon, Niki began to experience sharp abdominal pain in the days leading up to the first hearing. Tests confirmed that her tumor marker had increased significantly, indicating that the cancer had returned.

The gravity of the first hearing was weighing on my mind. There was much at stake, and I couldn't help but worry that time was running short for Niki. "Don't take this on yourself, my friend. You will be absolutely awesome at the hearing and will do her proud," Camilla said to me at precisely the right moment. "You can't save her. You can't stop her from dying. We can just help leave them a legacy. We have to give Niki, Amy, and their daughters a record they can point to, about what they did for love, for their daughters, and for each other."

Camilla was absolutely right. Maybe we would win, maybe not. Nothing was guaranteed, but we could help Niki and Amy feel like their sacrifice in putting everything on the line was well worth it. The hardest words I ever uttered to a court were spoken on the morning of April 10, 2014. "We are here so that a woman can die in dignity," I said to U.S. District Court Judge Richard L. Young. "And so that Niki, Amy, and their children will know what it feels like to be respected by the State of Indiana as part of a married family while she is still alive."

At the conclusion of the hearing, Chief Judge Young entered an order for the State of Indiana to respect their marriage as the case proceeded. The order recognized the incredible harm to Niki and Amy. Niki and Amy were elated about their victory. But their joy quickly dissipated when they learned the decision only applied to them. They didn't want to be Indiana's first family, standing alone in recognition of their marriage. Niki and Amy wanted all families to enjoy the legal respect they had.

While this early ruling foreshadowed where the judge might be leaning, Camilla and Jordan brilliantly closed the door on any remaining reservations the judge might have had when they argued on behalf of all same-sex couples a month later, urging swift and decisive action by the court.

Same-sex couples in Indiana did not have to wait long for their own vindication. On June 25, 2014, Chief Judge Young struck down Indiana's discriminatory ban on marriage for same-sex couples. "In time, Americans will look at marriages such as Plaintiffs, and simply refer to it as marriage—not a same-sex marriage," he wrote. "These couples, when gender and sexual orientation are taken away, are in all respects like the family down the street. The Constitution demands that we treat them as such." In the forty-eight hours following the ruling, hundreds of same-sex couples married within Indiana's borders.

Two days later, the Seventh Circuit, which covers Indiana, Illinois, and Wisconsin, suspended the decision after receiving a request from Indiana officials, effectively putting a hold on any new marriages by same-sex couples. By this time, it was not uncommon for appellate courts to place these rulings on hold, following the lead of the Supreme Court in the Utah marriage case. However, the same three-judge panel who imposed the stay at the Seventh Circuit also issued a separate decision requiring Indiana to continue to recognize Niki and Amy's marriage pending the appeal—something no other federal appellate court had done. The panel then expedited the appellate proceedings and consolidated *Baskin* with ACLU's marriage case in Wisconsin, *Wolf v. Walker*.

On August 26, 2014, the Seventh Circuit courtroom, located in Chicago, was filled to capacity. Judge Richard Posner, Judge Anne Claire Williams, and Judge David Hamilton presided before the oral arguments in *Baskin*. Camilla Taylor, Ken Falk of the ACLU of Indiana, and James Esseks of the national ACLU LGBT & HIV Project each argued in favor of marriage equality.

Judge Posner, a Republican-appointed judge, led the charge to expose the absurdity of the states' arguments. If Indiana really cared about the welfare of children, why deny children of same-sex couples the security and dignity that comes with allowing their parents to marry?

Not only did the panel understand the gravity of harm imposed on these families, but Judge Posner also drew a critical admission from the state that children benefit psychologically and economically from having married parents. The admission was fueled by a friend-of-the-court brief filed by the Family Equality

Council, an advocacy group for families led by same-sex couples, which high-lighted the stories of harms incurred by children whose parents were not allowed to marry.

Acting with unusual urgency, the Seventh Circuit issued its unanimous deci-sion a mere nine days later. In a scathing opinion written by Judge Posner, the court held the marriage bans violated the federal Constitution and that the states' strongest justification for excluding same-sex couples from marriage is "so full of holes that it cannot be taken seriously." Judge Posner eviscerated Indiana's core argument of encouraging straight couples to marry following "accidental births"—an argument that carried the day back in 2005 when the law was chal-lenged under Indiana's Constitution.

"In other words, Indiana's government thinks that straight couples tend to be sexually irresponsible, producing unwanted children by the carload, and so must be pressured . . . to marry, but that gay couples, unable as they are to produce children wanted or unwanted, are model parents—model citizens really—so have no need for marriage," Judge Posner wrote. "Heterosexuals get drunk and pregnant, producing unwanted children; their reward is to be allowed to marry. Homosexual couples do not produce unwanted children; their reward is to be denied the right to marry. Go figure." Paragraph after paragraph, the Seventh Circuit called out the law for what it was—invidious discrimination against les-bians and gay people.

The Seventh Circuit issued its decision in *Baskin* on September 4, 2014. We were elated at securing the only unanimous victory in a marriage case at the appellate level. The decision was powerful. And it could not have come at a better time. Just one day earlier, a district court judge from Louisiana had become the first in the country to uphold its state's discriminatory ban on marriage for same-sex couples, putting an end to the undefeated string of cases that had come out in favor of the freedom to marry since *Windsor*. Louisiana was a clear aberration, and the Seventh Circuit's decision in *Baskin* made us feel that we were one step closer to victory.

By then, the first cases calling into question the validity of the states' marriage bans in Utah, Oklahoma, and Virginia were already awaiting consideration at the U.S. Supreme Court. There was no question that Indiana would appeal the Seventh Circuit's decision in *Baskin*. The only question was whether Indiana would file, and we could respond to, its petition before the Supreme Court's deadline for submission—in just five days. Given the importance and urgency of settling this matter for our clients and all same-sex couples, we had to try.

On September 9, 2014, within hours of Indiana filing its request to the Su-preme Court, we submitted our response. *Baskin*, filed just six months earlier, was now awaiting consideration by nine U.S. Supreme Court justices.

To our surprise, the Supreme Court denied all marriage petitions for review on October 6, 2014. In effect, the high court handed us a complete and absolute win in every state within the Fourth, Seventh, and Tenth Circuits. The plaintiffs in *Baskin* had won at every stage, and the number of states with the freedom to marry jumped from nineteen to thirty, and soon to thirty-five following a positive ruling from the Ninth Circuit. The victory came sooner than we expected—and we were thrilled.

However, our opponents would not take the victory lying down. On March 26, 2015, in direct response, Indiana Governor Mike Pence signed a bill, Senate Bill 101 (SB101), to allow businesses, individuals, and organizations to discriminate against anyone in Indiana on religious grounds (see Jennifer C. Pizer's chapter, page 323). Lambda Legal and other advocates swung into action to shine a light on the harms this law would encourage and allow. But after receiving harsh criticism, Governor Pence appeared on ABC's *This Week* with George Stephanopoulos to defend SB101. He refused to answer questions about whether LGBT people should be protected from discrimination. Moreover, he deceived Hoosiers and the nation about the scope of the law because he insisted that it only applied to government actors, not private parties. The law established a license to discriminate.

The law prompted mass national outcry from grassroots supporters, faith leaders, businesses, civil rights organizations, and celebrities. Lambda Legal's Law and Policy Project Director Jennifer Pizer offered a way to improve the law by making it clear that it did not override antidiscrimination laws that were already in place. The growing national boycott of Indiana, costing the state millions of dollars, forced lawmakers to enact what amounted to a partial fix. Unfortunately, comprehensive antidiscrimination laws do not exist across the state, and LGBT Hoosiers statewide are still vulnerable to facing discrimination in every facet of life, including in housing, employment, and places of public accommodation.

While we continue to battle efforts to legalize discrimination under the guise of religious exceptions, marriage equality is the law the land. The battle in Indiana had to be fought with the same focus, care, and level of strategy as in other states. But the timing could not have been more fortuitous. *Baskin v. Bogan* benefited from the momentum that was sweeping the nation. The case lasted only two hundred and ten days from filing through final judgment after all appeals. Such a pace for any litigation is virtually unthinkable in the legal world. We were riding an express train, and we were among the first marriage cases to be considered for review by the United States Supreme Court.

Our client Niki Quasney passed away on February 5, 2015, after more than five years battling ovarian cancer. When our *Baskin* journey began, Niki told the court: "If my life is cut short because of ovarian cancer, I want our children to know that their parents were treated like other married couples in their home state, and to be proud of this. I want to know what it feels like to be a legally recognized family in our community, together with Amy and our daughters." And they did know. Not only was their family respected, Niki and Amy's bravery accelerated equality for all same-sex couples in Indiana. We owe them an enormous debt of gratitude.

This case was an incredible achievement for all of us at Lambda Legal, for all of our plaintiff families, and for all Hoosiers. We did our part to move Indiana and the country forward.

JUSTICE JUSTICE YOU SHALL PURSUE

AMY SANDLER

Amy Sandler and her wife, Niki Quasney (1976–2015), along with their two daughters, were plaintiffs in Baskin v. Bogan.

I was weeks away from giving birth to our second daughter, Maddox, in January 2013, while my wife, Niki, was fighting Stage IV ovarian cancer. She had been battling this awful disease for four years. Despite undergoing the most aggressive chemotherapy options available, Niki's cancer continued to outsmart the drugs. With Maddox on the way and the cancer on the run again, Niki's oncologist was concerned that if he tried a third major surgery, any minor mistake could result in Niki missing Maddox's birth. I was in tears as I told Niki and her doctor that this was not about the baby or me, this was about Niki. I was willing to switch my obstetrician to the University of Chicago and deliver Maddox there to be sure that if by chance Niki was hospitalized and I went into labor, Niki would be there for Maddox's birth. But Niki's doctor said, "You two have a baby on the way. Let's try a new chemotherapy and revisit this in a few months."

Our Massachusetts marriage held no legal weight in Indiana. In order for Niki's name to be on Maddox's birth certificate, I needed to deliver her in Illinois, where our 2011 Illinois civil union was recognized. Despite living in Indiana, Niki and I both drove across state borders for our medical care. I remember neighbors telling me that I was crazy to risk going into labor and driving thirty miles to Chicago in the middle of winter. What if there was a blizzard? I jokingly asked my obstetrician if we could move into her condominium as the delivery date came closer.

The heartbreaking part was that there is a reputable hospital just one mile from our home. But the hospital spokesperson was on record in 2011 stating that the hospital follows the state of Indiana's definition of

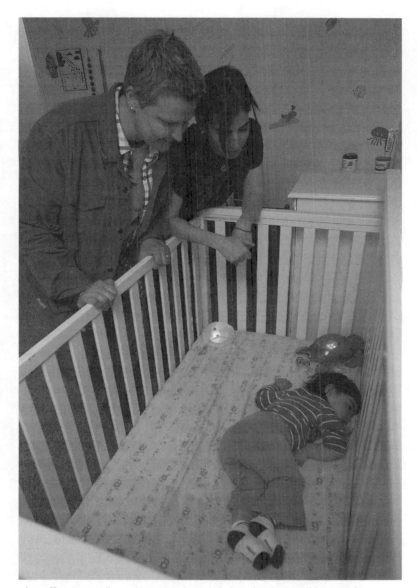

Plaintiffs Amy Sandler and Niki Quasney with their daughter Maddox in Indiana.
Photo Credit: COURTESY OF LAMBDA LEGAL

marriage, defining it as the union between one man and one woman. There was no way any of us was going there with that kind of statement. Not to deliver Maddox. Not to treat anyone in our family.

Niki's cancer was by far the most stressful part of our journey and the reason we filed the lawsuit against Indiana. Niki, who was born and raised in Indiana, never wanted anyone there or anywhere in the country to go through what we went through. She knew what it meant to find fulfillment in each precious moment, of treasuring every second with our children, with me, lighting Shabbat candles on Friday nights or jumping in the car for a road trip. It was a matter of the law catching up with us. Niki jumped on the emotional roller-coaster with the hope that others wouldn't have to endure the ride.

When we chose to join the lawsuit for the freedom to marry in Indiana, Niki and I had been together for fifteen years. Suing the state was the easy part. But no one could have prepared us for the emotional turmoil Indiana's government officials and our local media put us through. Niki's cancer was incurable. So of course she wanted to spend her good days living, biking, taking our daughters on adventures and vacations, and generating the laughter and thrills that had caused me to fall in love with her. Niki and I also promised each other that once we filed the lawsuit, we would not follow the media.

Soon after a federal district court judge granted a temporary restraining order for the state of Indiana to recognize our marriage, it was nearly impossible to avoid the public scrutiny. Niki walked into our local Starbucks, and right next to the cashier the local newspaper headlines read, "Gay marriage legalized for dying woman in Indiana." Niki came home that day in tears and said to me, "How can I ride my bike, mow the lawn, or walk the kids and dogs around the neighborhood while our neighbors are reading that I'm 'dying'? Did my doctor tell our lawyers I'm dying?" I called our lawyer and asked him. He assured me that no doctor gave him a specific time frame for Niki. What became apparent in our fight for the freedom to marry was that someone needed to die or be "dying" in order for the lesbian and gay community to garner the dignity and respect we knew in our hearts was guaranteed by the Constitution. But our state's leaders chose to fight us all the way to the United States Supreme Court. Thankfully, their callous appeal was denied, and marriage became legal in both Indiana and Wisconsin.

The Jewish tradition teaches "justice justice you shall pursue." The word "justice" appears twice. Maybe it is a reminder that if the original system of justice falls short, we have an obligation to engage justice, and fight for and secure it in each generation. Niki and I simply wanted the freedom to marry (for everyone in Indiana) and to have our marriage and family respected in our home state. Niki lived to see that day and realize that justice. Later in the afternoon on the day the Supreme Court made marriage for same-sex couples legal once and for all in Indiana, Niki said to me, "I think I'm going to stop chemo."

But after we finished reading and laughing with our three-year-old daughter, Asher, at bedtime, Niki apologized to me for her comment earlier and told me she wanted to keep fighting the cancer. There was no need for her to apologize. She fought for herself, for her family, and for the people of Indiana to be able to marry the person they love. We won that fight, and even though she is no longer physically with us, Niki won her fight against cancer, too, by how she lived.

A LONG BATTLE FINALLY WON: MARRIAGE IN FLORIDA

Nadine Smith

⸻⸎⸻

Nadine Smith is the co-founder and CEO of Equality Florida.

In 2005, when antigay forces brought their marriage ban crusade to Florida, our chances of stopping the looming ballot measure were already bleak. No strategy in other states had proven successful, and the steadily mounting losses had left our community deeply dispirited. And yet, a decade later, it is clear the moment had marked an inflection point in Florida. The resistance spurred by the constitutional amendment fight reshaped Florida into a leader in the South for LGBT protections. The strategies developed in this GOP-controlled state have become a vital part of the pro-equality road map in red states. And Florida's arrival in the marriage victory column ahead of the U.S. Supreme Court ruling helped to solidify the dawn of a new day in the third most populous state in the country. This is the story of a southern state's winding, harsh, amazing, and transformative path to marriage and beyond.

In 2006, John Stemberger, the leader of the Florida Coalition to Protect Marriage, let slip his mask of carefully calculated civility. As he rallied volunteers at a megachurch to help him embed antigay discrimination into Florida's Constitution, he invoked his favorite image of predatory gays endangering children.

"Now the picture is not two guys in holy matrimony, in bed together, so to speak. Now the picture is three little children sandwiched in between them.

What are two lesbian moms going to teach a little girl about how to love a man?"

The intensifying rhetoric reflected the frustration within the campaign, which had just failed to gather enough signatures to qualify for the 2006 ballot. The state of Florida, however, allowed signatures to remain in play for four years, so 2008 was possible, if they could fire up their network of churches to reach the 611,009 valid signatures required.

In their February 2005 press conference launching the campaign, antigay organizers had proclaimed that Florida's 1997 statute defining marriage as the union of one man and one woman was no longer sufficient to block the possibility of marriage equality.[1] They wanted this homophobic definition firmly ensconced in the state Constitution, away from the reach of the legislature or courts scrutinizing its constitutionality in Florida:

> Inasmuch as marriage is the legal union of only one man and one woman as husband and wife, no other legal union that is treated as marriage or the substantial equivalent thereof shall be valid or recognized.

And they had reason to be confident that they could win at the ballot box.

Nationwide, the 2004 elections had been a political massacre when it came to the rights of same-sex couples to marry. Voters in thirteen out of thirteen states amended their state constitutions to include marriage bans. Not even Oregon, the progressive stronghold with a history of blocking antigay ballot measures, could hold back the tide as 57 percent of voters gave their approval to the ban. The margins were even larger in the other states. Funders who had backed efforts to stem the antigay tide were disheartened by the losses and uninspired to give to campaigns that appeared doomed from the start. If Oregon could not win in 2004, Florida and the rest of the South had no chance.

But the South has a long history of carving out victories in hostile terrain and gaining ground until the impossible becomes inevitable. Those were the lessons we took to heart at Equality Florida. We knew the campaign to amend the state Constitution offered us the largest platform ever to tell our stories, to forge alliances, and to build our infrastructure. If we were going to lose, we would lose forward and ensure we were stronger on the other side.

Bracing for Impact

Facing the same overwhelming odds as us, a handful of state pro-equality organizers who expected ballot measures in 2006 or 2008 began connecting, eager to strategize. Those conversations led us to organize a national marriage strategy summit in early 2006. Soon, more than a dozen states answered our call, and national groups asked for time on the agenda.

State leaders fresh from ballot battles told similar stories. Not only had the campaigns to fight antigay initiatives lost but the defeat had left bitter divides. State organizations, typically sidelined when a new nationally funded campaign came, were left in worse shape than ever after the votes. When the machinery of the campaign was gone, along with the infusion of funding, state organizations were left to absorb the anger and disappointment with little infrastructure to show for the effort.

Out of those discussions with state and national leaders came the framework for our strategy. We would deliver messages that humanized our community. We would build an infrastructure that would outlast the campaign. And if suddenly an unexpected path to win materialized, we'd be ready to seize it.

Back in Florida, we named the campaign to fight back Fairness for All Families. With a roster of more than two hundred and fifty organizations and community leaders representing seniors, business leaders, consumer groups, and social justice organizations, it became the largest coalition in the state's history to step up on an LGBT issue. Julian Bond, an icon in the civil rights movement for nearly fifty years and longtime national chairman of the NAACP, became our honorary chair. When the membership of the Florida NAACP and the rank and file of the Florida Education Association voted at their annual meetings to join us in opposing the amendment, it was a huge boost that helped us grow the coalition and spark excitement. For the first time, I felt hopeful that we would not simply weather the storm but be strengthened by it.

We also figured out ways to use the organizing infrastructure to pass real and tangible policies at the local level. As our opposition used the 2006 primaries to gather signatures, we organized a day of action, with over five hundred volunteers blanketing 178 precincts across the state to educate voters about the amendment. By the time the campaign concluded, we had built a grassroots army of roughly three thousand volunteers. Team leaders emerged from the campaign who would later help us pass LGBT-inclusive local ordinances across the state.

A Glimmer of Hope

Two things happened in November 2006, sparking hope that the ballot measure could be defeated. Arizona activists blocked their ballot measure by a narrow margin, attacking it as a poorly crafted Pandora's box that would strip away domestic partnership protections and endanger a myriad of rights including health insurance, hospital visitation, and inheritance protections.[2]

This defeat was a first for an anti-marriage equality initiative, and it had happened in a state demographically and politically similar to Florida. The second potential game-changer was passage of an amendment in Florida, Amendment 2, that would now require 60 percent, not just a simple majority, to alter the state Constitution. Polling showed the ballot measure at that threshold. Could we nudge the needle just enough?

Now we had a slim but visible path to victory. We reached out to funders. A cadre of donors who had been similarly encouraged by the news in Arizona formed a separate organization, Florida Red and Blue. The existence of two campaigns to fight the amendment was far from ideal, but not uncommon in states that had faced ballot measures.

The Fairness for All Families Campaign focused on grassroots mobilization, progressive outreach, and organizing in communities of color. The Florida Red and Blue Campaign aimed to make the issue bipartisan by putting Republican leadership in the forefront. They focused on raising money for TV ads delivering the messaging that had been effective in Arizona: even if you don't support marriage for gay people, this goes too far in taking protections away from seniors and allowing the government to intrude.

When the campaign ended in 2008, polling showed the needle hadn't moved. Just over 60 percent of Florida voters chose to embed discrimination into the state Constitution. Election night was strange and bittersweet. Obama's victory and the hopeful note it signaled helped to soften the blow, but this thought burned in my head: six out of ten of our neighbors went to the polls to say we were less than them.

But there were silver linings. Every place we had field organizers on the ground, we held the vote below 60 percent, including in the majority black districts that our opponents said would carry the day for them. When armchair pundits publicly blamed black Obama supporters for pushing the ballot measure into the win column, it was months before researchers exposed that as a lie. University of Florida researchers showed that counties experiencing a high number of new black registrants were no more supportive of Florida's antigay marriage amendment than other counties. Their conclusions aligned with research on California's Prop 8 results that showed "party identification, ideology, religiosity, and age had a bigger impact than other voter characteristics, including race, on individuals' propensity to support the measure."[3] Yet that racial assumption and public blaming of black voters hardened into conventional wisdom that is still repeated today in mainstream and LGBT media. For me, it was the ugliest part of the campaign.

The Aftermath

As we prepared to fight the ballot measure, our colleagues who had been through the experience cautioned us not to neglect the fuller LGBT equality agenda in the midst of a ballot fight. This advice proved to be valuable. Because we had invested in building our infrastructure, we had a place for all the newly engaged volunteers, including those who had sat out the ballot fight but were now freshly in touch with their anger. As predicted, a whole new universe of straight allies was now eager to step forward on an array of issues, from employment protections to safe schools. Polling began to show a bounce in our direction, despite the loss, or perhaps because of it. It was as though the state had gone on a rampage and awoke slightly ashamed of itself. The marriage amendment was in place, but conversations about the rights of the LGBT community were intensifying. Florida Blue, a health insurance company, had been the first major employer in the state to speak out against Amendment 2. They became the anchor for a new program we launched called Equality Means Business, aimed at getting business leaders out front on our issues. The local campaign teams we had built around the ballot fight became lead organizers as we pushed domestic partnership protections, non-discrimination laws, and local anti-bullying policies that specifically included sexual orientation and gender identity. At the local level, our ability to pass non-discrimination ordinances was picking up speed. By 2014, more than half of Florida's population lived in communities with local sexual orientation and gender identity antidiscrimination protections.

Refuse to Lie

Just before tax time in 2012, we launched Refuse to Lie, a campaign to allow for individuals in same-sex relationships to challenge discrimination personally by identifying as married on their tax return. We created a website, RefuseToLie .org, which became a gathering place for same-sex couples to share their stories and for others to speak out in solidarity. The negative financial impact of marriage inequality had been well documented, but the Refuse to Lie movement was not spurred by same-sex couples looking for a bigger tax refund. In some cases, filing as married was more costly, but the principle was worth it.

The Refuse to Lie effort wasn't restricted to filing taxes. Increasingly, same-sex couples were pushing back against customs agents who required them to fill out separate forms rather than recognize them as family. The murky legal landscape had already begun tilting in favor of equal rights for married same-sex couples. We announced the Refuse to Lie campaign in the national media, gaining visibility in the *New York Times* and on MSNBC. We contacted the IRS and braced for the response. Nothing. My wife, Andrea Smith, and I filed as a family and began getting our tax refund like any other married couple.

Southern Momentum

By 2013, much had shifted nationally. Victories in Maine, Maryland, Minnesota, and Washington sent the message that the tide had fully turned. President Obama had declared his support for marriage equality in 2012. In Florida we were indeed stronger on the other side of the ballot fight. Our volunteer roster swelled, our donor base tripled, and our staff grew, covering much more territory in a massive state with more than 20 million residents and 97 million tourists.

Now that the states where marriage equality had been more easily achievable had been secured, new strategies needed to be employed to bring red and southern states up to speed.

A remarkable transformation was unfolding in Florida. But many of the equality report cards that grade a state based only on state laws had missed the local victories we had achieved. We needed to make these visible.

Along with our goal to secure marriage in Florida, we called on funders and national and state partners to recalibrate the expectation of what was possible in the South. As the Edie Windsor case and the Prop 8 lawsuit made their way to the Supreme Court in 2013, we began to craft a plan to secure marriage equality within three years, either through the courts or by the ballot, whichever path was quickest. Statistician Nate Silver's charts showed Florida as the leading Deep South state when it came to support for marriage equality. We would reach 60 percent support around 2020 by his projections, but he also acknowledged that positive rulings and additional victories could accelerate that shift.[4]

On June 19, 2013, just prior to the U.S. Supreme Court's decision in *Windsor*, Equality Florida, in partnership with Freedom to Marry, launched our marriage equality campaign, Get Engaged, a campaign to tell our love stories, to show why marriage mattered and how our families were harmed by discrimination. Simultaneously, Equality Florida issued a call for potential plaintiffs should it be determined that the most expedient path to marriage equality in Florida would be through the courts. Within forty-eight hours, more than five hundred couples throughout the state responded that they wanted to have all of the legal protections of other married couples in the state and were willing to be plaintiffs.

The Path Forward

On January 21, 2014, the National Center for Lesbian Rights (NCLR) in partnership with Equality Florida Institute, the law firm Carlton Fields, Jorden Burt, and local attorneys Elizabeth Schwartz and Mary Meek filed a lawsuit in state court with federal claims on behalf of six same-sex couples. The lawsuit argued that Florida's laws violated the U.S. Constitution's commitment to equal protection under the law. Raising federal constitutional claims in state court would allow us to challenge the ban but steer clear of the federal Eleventh Circuit, which had a history of antigay hostility.

The plaintiffs hailed from Miami and the surrounding area. They included:

- Catherina Pareto and Karla Arguello, together for fourteen years and raising a young son;
- Dr. Juan Carlos Rodriguez and David Price, together for eighteen years and raising young twins;
- Vanessa and Melanie Alenier, together for eight years and raising a child;
- Todd and Jeff Delmay, together for eleven years and raising a young son;
- Summer Greene and Pamela Faerber, grandparents, together for twenty-five years;
- and Don Price Johnston and Jorge Isaias Diaz, engaged.

Our lawsuit was the first specifically aimed at dismantling Amendment 2. Other suits and actions quickly followed:[5]

February 28, 2014: Private counsel filed *Brenner v. Scott* in federal court on behalf of James Brenner and Charles Jones of Tallahassee, who demanded that the state of Florida recognize their 2009 Canada marriage.

March 13, 2014: The ACLU of Florida filed *Grimsley and Albu v. Scott* in federal court on behalf of the local LGBT organization SAVE and eight married same-sex couples seeking respect for their marriages legally performed in other states.

March 18, 2014: Brenner and Jones' lawyers sued in federal court on behalf of Stephen Schlairet and Ozzie Russ, who wanted to obtain a marriage license in Washington County, Florida.

April 1, 2014: Two Key West men, Aaron Huntsman and William Lee Jones, sued Monroe County Clerk Amy Heavilin in state court for a marriage license.

April 30, 2014: In the *Grimsley* case, the ACLU of Florida filed a motion for preliminary injunction, asking the court to immediately stop enforcing laws barring legal respect for marriages between same-sex couples, adding a recently widowed Ft. Myers woman, Arlene Goldberg, as a plaintiff in the lawsuit. Goldberg had lost Social Security benefits that would have typically gone to other surviving spouses.

When the day for arguments arrived in the Equality Florida and NCLR marriage lawsuit, known as *Pareto v. Ruvin*, the Miami courtroom hit capacity, and an overflow room with a television had to be set up. The clerk's legal counsel and a representative of Attorney General Pam Bondi's office stood ready to argue against us. Judge Sarah Zabel had also granted permission to a far-right group to make a presentation after they argued that Bondi and Miami-Dade County Clerk Harvey Ruvin lacked motivation to vigorously defend the ban.

My frustration with the judge's appeasement diminished as the far-right attorney began to spew the same arguments that had already been discredited in courtrooms across the country, by judges of every political persuasion: that marriage was for procreation, and that legalizing it for same-sex couples would demean marriage in the eyes of different-sex couples and endanger the welfare of children. By the time the hearing was over, the steps of the courthouse were crowded with Christian Family Coalition protesters and our supporters. Our plaintiffs and lawyers walked through a gauntlet as we launched our press conference. In more than twenty years of activism, it was one of the ugliest encounters I had witnessed, and more than a few seasoned activists were shaken by the vitriol.

As the opponents shouted slurs and chanted, "Enough is enough," our side began our own chant that grew louder as passersby joined us. Slowly, as the ranks of our supporters grew, the only words that could be heard above the din were ones that would become the campaign's signature: "Love is louder! Love is louder!"

Soon the victories began rolling in.

By the end of July, both Judge Luis Garcia in Key West, in the *Huntsman v. Heavlin* case, and Judge Zabel in Miami, in *Pareto v. Ruvin*, had declared Florida's marriage ban a violation of the U.S. Constitution.

On August 4, 2014, Broward Circuit Judge Dale Cohen ruled the ban unconstitutional in *Brassner v. Lade*.

On August 5, 2014, Circuit Judge Diana Lewis became the first Florida judge to recognize the out-of-state marriage of a same-sex couple when she ordered that William Simpson be named the personal representative of his late husband Francis' estate.

Then, on August 21, U.S. District Judge Robert L. Hinkle declared Florida's marriage ban unconstitutional as well, in *Grimsley and Albu v. Scott*. In his decision, Judge Hinkle held that, by denying the plaintiffs their fundamental right to marry, Florida's marriage ban violated the due process and equal protection clauses of the U.S. Constitution. He also held that there was no justification for denying recognition of the marriages, stating that "[t]he undeniable truth is that the Florida ban on same-sex marriage stems entirely, or almost entirely, from moral disapproval of the practice," and that "moral disapproval alone cannot sustain" a ban restricting marriage to opposite-sex couples.

From the judge's decision: "Liberty, tolerance, and respect are not zero-sum concepts. Those who enter opposite-sex marriages are harmed not at all when others, including these plaintiffs, are given the liberty to choose their own life partners and are shown the respect that comes with formal marriage."

The Greenberg Traurig Memo

All the judges had stayed their decisions with the expectation that the state would appeal. But Hinkle gave his stay a time limit. In late December 2014, as everyone headed off for the holidays, it seemed clear that Attorney General Bondi had exhausted her options and that marriages were set to begin statewide on January 6, 2015, when the stay would expire.

That is when a memo to Florida clerks, from the legal firm Greenberg Traurig, sent everything into chaos. The law firm advised clerks that the decision did not herald marriage statewide, but applied only to the plaintiffs and only to the named clerk in Florida's Washington County. The memo went further and warned that any other clerk who used the ruling to justify issuing marriage licenses risked fine and imprisonment.

Clerks around the state began to issue statements that they would not follow Judge Hinkle's order. Even longtime allies on LGBT issues gave vague answers as to what they would do when the stay expired. Only one clerk issued a statement that he would follow Hinkle's order: Osceola Clerk of Court Armando Ramirez.

On December 23, 2014, NCLR and Equality Florida overnighted an urgent memorandum to all of Florida's county clerks explaining that they were required to issue marriage licenses to same-sex couples on January 6, 2015, based on Judge Hinkle's decision. The language was as hard-hitting as it was legally defensible. The issue became a question of which threat was more credible: the laughable idea that clerks would be arrested for following a federal judge's order, or our promise to sue any clerk that failed to do their job. We needed to make the

Florida married couple Jeff and Todd Delmay with their son. Photo Credit: COURTESY OF
EQUALITY FLORIDA WITH PERMISSION OF JEFF AND TODD DELMAY

clerks realize they were in danger of following Greenberg Traurig's legal advice
right off a cliff.

In the media, we repeated our threat to sue any clerk who refused the order
and made clear that they could be personally liable for court costs when they
inevitably lost. Soon, state attorneys across the state began publicly dismissing
the idea that a clerk would face charges for issuing marriage licenses to same-sex

couples. Then Washington County Clerk Lora Bell filed a motion with Judge Hinkle asking him to clarify his order. The Judge gave Bondi until December 29 to answer the clerk's question. Instead, Bondi told the judge that the court was "best situated to determine the reach of its own order."On December 29, 2014, NCLR submitted an amicus brief to judge Hinkle on behalf of Equality Florida, urging him to confirm the statewide scope of his earlier ruling.

On January 1, Judge Hinkle confirmed his marriage ruling in a new order. He stated that Florida's Constitution required clerks of all Florida counties to issue marriage licenses to same-sex couples after his stay ended on January 6. If they refused, they risked being sued and becoming liable for damages and attorneys' fees.

Miami Clerk Ruvin requested a hearing to clarify if Judge Zabel's stay in the *Pareto* state court case would remain in effect after January 6, given Judge Hinkle's federal ruling. The hearing took place on January 5. Judge Zabel lifted her stay on the spot, to a cheering courtroom. She even performed the first wedding, that of lead plaintiff couple Catherina Pareto and Karla Arguello, who had come dressed to wed just in case. By midnight, a handful of clerks' offices had opened their doors to perform weddings the moment Judge Hinkle's stay expired. I raced to Miami to perform the wedding of Equality Florida's deputy director, Stratton Pollitzer. I had been there eighteen years earlier when he and Christopher were "married by love" in the backyard of the family home in Stratton's hometown of Beaufort. Now they would be married by law in Florida and a rapidly growing number of states and nations.

Florida had secured marriage equality, not dragged forward by a U.S. Supreme Court order, but with court after court on our side and public opinion having shifted dramatically in our favor. We had marked the marriage equality map with a Deep South state. We were part of the momentum. The South and the country were ready for the freedom to marry.

VI. CLOSING ARGUMENTS, 2015

Gathered outside the United States Supreme Court, argument day, April 28, 2015. Photo Credit: LESLIE VON PLESS/LAMBDA LEGAL

10:02 ON TUESDAY MORNING: ARGUING *OBERGEFELL* BEFORE THE U.S. SUPREME COURT

MARY L. BONAUTO

Mary L. Bonauto is director of the Civil Rights Project at Gay & Lesbian Advocates & Defenders (GLAD).

I never expected to argue the marriage issue in the U.S. Supreme Court. I began helping the DeBoer team at the District Court and joined the Supreme Court solely to add what value I could. In fact, I had agreed to not seek that position. When the Court granted review in all of the cases from the Sixth Circuit on January 16, 2015—cases involving marriage licensing, marriage recognition, or both—the Michigan team hoped we could divide argument so an attorney from each state could argue before the Court.

All counsel joined in a motion to that effect, but the Court promptly denied our request. There would be one lawyer per question per side—plus a spot for the solicitor general of the United States. The many capable attorneys—from private firms, LGBT legal organizations, and even a law school Supreme Court Clinic—ultimately decided I should argue Question 1. This presented a highly compressed schedule, with just a month to write a reply brief and prepare for argument. It was daunting, but my colleagues all reassured me that I had been training for this day for more than twenty years.

Rigorous preparation is the rule for any appellate argument, and even more so when, after decades of work by millions of people, the final arbiters in our federal system would decide the issues. We already had superb merits briefing from the petitioners as well as comprehensive amici briefing by pre-eminent experts in their fields, reassuring me that nearly anything that could be asked had already been answered. Inspiration came from all quarters, from the petitioners themselves, to colleagues I've worked with over the years and, unexpectedly, from people across the country—the very people who were counting on a favorable decision. Throughout that whirlwind month, I had support from the DeBoer team, my GLAD colleagues, and the talented group of private and LGBT legal movement lawyers behind the respective cases. Solicitor General Donald Verrilli and his team, supporting our equality claims, were outstanding. For oral argument itself, WilmerHale attorneys Paul Wolfson, Alan Schoenfeld, Leah Litman, Dina Mishra, and others, some of whom had worked with GLAD on Circuit Court amici briefs, helped my preparation, as did other Supreme Court experts like Paul Smith of Jenner & Block, Jeffrey Fisher of the Stanford University Law Clinic, Steven Shapiro of the ACLU (both Jeff and Steve were on the Kentucky team), and Neal Katyal of Hogan Lovells. Leading lights Robbie Kaplan of Paul, Weiss, Rifkind, Wharton & Garrison and Evan Wolfson of Freedom to Marry provided sage counsel and encouragement. Particularly in the final two weeks, I worked closely with movement stalwarts like Jon Davidson and Susan Sommer of Lambda Legal, Shannon Minter and David Codell of NCLR, and James Esseks of the ACLU, along with Paul Smith and Jeff Fisher. Finally, I coordinated closely with Doug Hallward-Driemeier of Ropes & Gray, the phenomenal advocate who argued Question 2 on recognition to maximize every winning opportunity and avoid any trap that would pit the marriage and recognition questions against each other.

It was exactly 10:02 on Tuesday morning, April 28, 2015, when I was called by Chief Justice Roberts to begin the argument for the Question 1 petitioners. I wanted my opening to convey a visceral sense of what marriage bans meant for LGB people and the chasm between that treatment and our constitutional promises. In the fifty seconds before questioning began, I managed to get this out: the intimate and committed relationships of same-sex and different-sex couples provide mutual support and are the foundation of family life. Yet, marriage—a commitment, responsibility, and protection—is off limits to gay people as a class. The stain and second-class citizenship that consequently flows to individual gay people and same-sex couples, I argued, contravenes the Constitution's promise of equal dignity and the very purpose of the Fourteenth Amendment.

The intense questioning began, validating the prediction that most of the justices would have a lot to say given the dozens of marriage rulings since their *Windsor* decision. Whether the issue was the role of the democratic process or animus or how to ascertain when a "right" is protected by the promises of "liberty," the justices had already staked out that ground in other cases, and most recently in the 2013 rulings in *U.S. v. Windsor* and *Hollingsworth v. Perry*. While some of the dissents in the 2013 cases showed an unwillingness to vindicate a constitutional right to marry for same-sex couples, I assumed the justices had continued considering the issues. It made me feel like I was joining a long-standing, ongoing conversation, but one where I was out of the room at a crucial juncture.

Mary Bonauto on April 28, 2015, after her argument to the U.S. Supreme Court in *Obergefell v. Hodges*. Photo Credit: LESLIE VON PLESS/LAMBDA LEGAL

Like any lawyer arguing a case, I made lots of judgment calls on my feet, perhaps the most obvious being the exchanges centered on legal marriage for same-sex couples across millennia, including Ancient Greek and other distant civilizations. I held fast that the petitioners' liberty and equality claims were absolutely consistent with the spirit and judicial application of Fourteenth Amendment guarantees to new circumstances. Just as we had come to see race- and sex-based discrimination since ratification of the Amendment in 1868, so was it time to end different treatment in marriage for gay people and same-sex couples. At the same time, I sought to do no harm. Conceding that clergy would not be compelled to marry same-sex couples against their will, as I did in response to Justice Scalia, was an unexpected opportunity to underscore a helpful point.

After my argument, Solicitor General Verrilli delivered a stirring argument, telling the Court it was unacceptable for the petitioners and same-sex couples around the country to "wait and see" how the issue developed. The practical and dignitary harms visited on couples and the likelihood of a "house divided" required the Court to vindicate couples' claims, he argued. John Bursch, former solicitor general of Michigan, argued for the states. Mr. Bursch's argument that same-sex couples marrying could deter different-sex couples from marriage and thus increase non-marital birthrates fared poorly in questioning. I emphasized the absurdity of making that connection in my three-minute rebuttal. I argued that Michigan couldn't possibly be suggesting that everything about marriage comes down to biological procreation, and doing so was an "impoverished" view. After all, the State's brief claimed concern for stability for children. And at argument, Mr. Bursch conceded that the State "loves adoption" and specifically noted the petitioners in Michigan were good parents. The blatant contradictions between the ban and the State's policy goals, as in Vermont and Massachusetts long ago, demonstrated the absence of any justification. At precisely 11:32 a.m.—ninety minutes later—the Court took a brief recess before turning to Question 2 on recognition.

MY THIRTY-YEAR JOURNEY TO THE
OBERGEFELL CASE

ALPHONSE GERHARDSTEIN

―❧―

Alphonse Gerhardstein is a lawyer and a named partner in the firm Gerhardstein & Branch.

In 1985, many people were afraid of my brother. Jeffrey was gay. People thought he must have AIDS. He did not. Well, they thought, then at least his "lifestyle" must be contagious. It was not. Facts did not matter. Fear led even educated, otherwise welcoming people to shun gay friends, colleagues, and family. What a time to fall in love, but Jeffrey did. Bob brought great music and a wonderful laugh into our family. In 1985, I was eight years into my private civil rights practice, generally challenging unfair jail and prison conditions and seeking equal rights in the workplace for blacks and women. All of my clients were on the margins of economic life and power. The Constitution and civil rights laws were all we had to remedy their problems.

When Jeffrey and Bob called me that year, I was stumped. Bob taught music in a Catholic girls' school in Cleveland, Ohio. He was fired shortly after my brother moved in with him. I hate telling people who are obviously mistreated that they have no rights. I researched civil law and found no hook that would match justice with law. Very frustrating, but canon (church) law gave me some hope. We filed an appeal, and the Superintendent of Catholic Education for the Cleveland Archdiocese granted us a hearing. Through the window during that hearing we could see the protesters out on the sidewalk urging the Church to reinstate Bob.

My mom was out there standing with them. Very cool. Bob's parents also stood up publicly for their son. A candlelight vigil was covered in the *Cleveland Plain Dealer* and on local TV. The message was clear. It was OK to be gay. It was OK to love someone of the same sex. Those voices for equality and fairness were few. They were drowned out by those who clung to their fear. We lost the case, but the public witnessing and the obvious justice of our cause gave me hope.

That hope carried me through the case of a Presbyterian minister I represented in another ecclesiastical court when he was fired. I lost that one too—and all the cases of the gay workers fired from private work settings in the years that followed. Some I counseled on the phone. "No, I cannot help you," I was forced to say, not because I didn't want to, but because there were no laws on the books to protect them in the workplace. I pursued other claims relying on vague statements of fairness in employee handbooks, but I lost those too. When the LGBT community finally won passage of a human rights ordinance in Cincinnati, I thought we were making great progress. Then a city charter amendment repealed the measure and prohibited one from ever getting passed in the future. I joined with Lambda Legal and co-counsel Scott Greenwood to challenge the charter amendment. I lost that case too. Then Scott Greenwood was fired from his private law firm because he was gay. I sued to regain his job. Lost that too.

That hope I carried was dimming. When Evan Wolfson said we should focus on rights of same-sex couples to marry, I did not understand it all. How could we win marriage when I couldn't even win back anyone's job? My law partner Jennifer Branch and I made progress with public employees and cases on behalf of transgender inmates. But marriage equality for same-sex couples? Not in Cincinnati. Not in Ohio. And certainly not next on the agenda.

I saw the light when I read *Windsor*. Wow! The federal government had to recognize the marriages of same-sex couples from states where they were legal. Why not apply that to Ohio?

Soon after reading *Windsor*, I met a Cincinnati couple who had been together for two decades, John Arthur and Jim Obergefell. John was receiving hospice services in their immaculate downtown condo. He had ALS, and his prognosis was dire. John was dying. But Ohio would not let John and Jim marry. So with help from friends, John and Jim had flown in a medically equipped jet to Baltimore and legally married in Maryland. They were excited to be married after so many years together as a committed couple. But unless Ohio recognized their marriage, John's death certificate would incorrectly list John as single and leave blank the box for surviving spouse—the box that should be filled in with the name "Jim Obergefell." We filed suit against Ohio. The district court win was sweet, and Jim and John were thrilled. But the state appealed, and the loss in the Sixth Circuit Court of Appeals was very disappointing. John had passed away by

Lambda Legal Executive Director Kevin Cathcart and Atty. Susan Sommer, plaintiffs Pam Yorksmith and Nicole Yorksmith with children Grayden (five years old) and Orion (baby), and Atty. Al Gerhardstein standing in front of the U.S. Supreme Court on decision day, June 26, 2015. Photo Credit: LESLIE VON PLESS. LAMBDA LEGAL

then. But he always seemed close by in spirit as we pressed on with our fight. Jim knew he was finishing the struggle that he and John had jointly started.

By June 2015, thirty years had passed since my mom protested to demand justice for Bob and my brother Jeffrey. I was still litigating to secure LGBT rights. Nationwide, a new wave of protesters had added their voices to the clamor over the freedom to marry. Most hoped Jim would prevail in the Supreme Court. Many prayed we would fail. The case that would determine marriage equality for the nation carried Jim's name! By then we had met hundreds of married, committed, and loving couples seeking the right to marry and to have their marriages recognized. We also had worked with dozens of their lawyers, including Susan Sommer from Lambda Legal, James Esseks from the ACLU, and many other brilliant counsel from these organizations. The experience was humbling.

On June 26, 2015, I was at the Supreme Court to hear the decision. The hope I carried was stronger by then. Jim was also in the courtroom. John was in the air. Justice Kennedy spoke eloquently. Lawyers and longtime advocates surrounding me on all sides teared up as the significance of Justice Kennedy's words washed over us. Love won. Evan Wolfson was right. And hopefully, now, we will have an easier time protecting those jobs too.

OBERGEFELL V. HODGES—
A LEAP OF LOVE

SUSAN SOMMER

———⊗⊗⊗———

Susan Sommer is senior counsel and director of Constitutional Litigation at Lambda Legal.

On June 26, 2015, when Justice Kennedy announced from his seat on the Supreme Court in *Obergefell v. Hodges* that "the reasons marriage is fundamental under the Constitution apply with equal force to same-sex couples," our movement took an unprecedentedly giant leap forward. Finally, anywhere in this country, a lesbian, gay, bisexual, or transgender individual could turn to their loved one, say "will you marry me," and know that if the answer was "yes," they could marry in any state and receive full legal recognition for their marriage throughout the land. With the *Obergefell* ruling, the marriage equality movement finally entered the Promised Land.

After fifteen years at Lambda Legal working toward the freedom to marry, that day was truly one of the happiest of my life. Sitting in the front row of the Supreme Court's intimate yet grand courtroom as Justice Kennedy read the poetic words of his extraordinary ruling and history was being made, I could sense the joy and pride—as well as tears—overflowing from my lawyer colleagues by my side, from plaintiffs in the case sitting in the spectator section of the courtroom, and from the millions of Americans whose families and friends would celebrate one of our nation's finest days. From start to finish, the six lawsuits that were the vehicle for the Court's momentous ruling had taken less than two years to reach their landmark resolution, a rapid trajectory in our legal world. What a two years it had been.

Windsor Opens the Floodgates

Exactly two years before to the day, the Supreme Court announced another groundbreaking victory for same-sex spouses—*United States v. Windsor*, striking down Section 3 of the so-called Defense of Marriage Act (DOMA), which had denied federal recognition and benefits to the marriages of same-sex spouses. Then too, Justice Kennedy had authored an exceptionally lyrical majority opinion, replete with affirmations of the dignity and legal respect due same-sex couples, and expressing special solicitude for the children of families demeaned by governmental discrimination. *Windsor* built off the Court's two earlier gay rights landmarks, likewise authored by Justice Kennedy—*Lawrence v. Texas*, declaring bans on the sexual intimacy of same-sex partners unconstitutional on yet another June 26, exactly ten years earlier in 2003, and *Romer v. Evans*, striking down in 1996 a Colorado state constitutional amendment targeting LGBT people for discrimination. On the same day *Windsor* was announced, the Supreme Court also issued its narrow, jurisdiction-based ruling in the challenge to California's Proposition 8, avoiding the core question of the constitutionality of *state*—as opposed to *federal*—denial of marriage rights to same-sex couples. Although that ruling meant same-sex couples again could marry in California, it did not take the bigger step of requiring all other states to extend the freedom to marry.

Windsor, in addition to bringing critical federal protections and greater dignity to same-sex families, was read by many LGBT civil rights advocates as virtually an invitation to tee-up challenges to state bans for the Supreme Court to consider within the next several years. But regardless of what the professional civil rights advocates might have believed to be wise strategy, LGBT people around the country were fed up with being relegated to second-class status and the daily hardships inflicted on their families by marriage discrimination. Within weeks of *Windsor*, the floodgates opened, and what grew to a tidal wave of constitutional challenges, initiated by private attorneys and national marriage advocates alike, began.

The Cases That Climbed to the Supreme Court

One of the very first cases to hit the national stage was that of Jim Obergefell and his terminally ill spouse, John Arthur. Fittingly, Jim Obergefell later became the first named plaintiff in the Supreme Court proceedings, along with more than thirty other plaintiffs whose lawsuits spanned six cases and four states. What was perhaps most remarkable about all these plaintiffs was their very ordinariness. Like many in this country, their lives were defined by the day-in-and-day-out juggling of jobs, bill paying, and childrearing; by the inevitable crises arising in life's path; and by the sustenance they drew from their families. But unlike the great majority of people, they had been relegated by their states to a lesser caste and denied the myriad tangible and intangible protections of marriage. These quiet heroes had had enough. They were going to stand up for themselves and their children, and for many others like them, and insist that the discrimination end now.

Jim Obergefell and John Arthur, who had been a couple for over two decades, had an especially urgent reason to wed and demand respect as spouses. John was in the last phases of ALS (Lou Gehrig's disease). With just three months from his death, the couple had run out of time to wait for their home state, Ohio, to grant the freedom to marry. On July 11, 2013, just days after *Windsor*, Jim and John finally fulfilled their long-cherished dream, flying on a specially chartered medically equipped plane to marry on a Maryland tarmac. With John too ill even to leave the plane, the couple flew back that day to their Cincinnati home. While other newlyweds would have been welcomed back with open arms, from the moment the plane landed Ohio refused to recognize their marriage. The couple was horrified when Al Gerhardstein, a lion of the Ohio civil rights bar with whom they consulted, told them that Ohio would deny their marriage even on John's death certificate and would list him as "unmarried" without identifying Jim as his spouse.

As John's condition worsened, the couple determined to take a stand. With the help of Gerhardstein and other dedicated Ohio attorneys, they brought suit in federal district court in Cincinnati, challenging the Ohio laws that withheld recognition of their out-of-state marriage. Gerhardstein's team included, from his law firm, Jennifer Branch, Jaci Martin, and his soon-to-be-admitted attorney son Adam Gerhardstein, along with Ellen Essig and Lisa Meeks. Within days, federal District Court Judge Timothy Black granted the first of a series of orders in the couple's favor, ordering Ohio to issue a death certificate that would recognize their marriage. The couple's poignant story, and the district court's rulings suggesting that recognition bans like Ohio's are unconstitutional, made headlines around the country.

Similar lawsuits, in Ohio and throughout the nation, quickly followed. Lambda Legal became involved in the litigation that would eventually land in the Supreme Court after out-of-state married same-sex couples with Ohio-born children were denied birth certificates naming both adults as parents, even after the couples had received adoption decrees from their home states declaring them legal parents. Ohio's discrimination thus reached its tentacles well beyond its borders, even into more progressive states where same-sex couples were free to marry and jointly adopt children. We contacted Gerhardstein, with whom we had worked on other LGBT rights cases in Ohio over the years, about co-counseling with us. Gerhardstein likewise had been approached by married couples seeking dual-parent birth certificates, including several families due to give birth in Ohio hospitals within weeks. Gerhardstein's team quickly filed the *Henry v. Hodges* litigation before the same judge, and Lambda Legal joined the suit. By the time we reached the Supreme Court, Lambda Legal's team had grown to include myself as lead attorney, Legal Director Jon Davidson, Marriage Project Director Camilla Taylor, Currey Cook, Paul Castillo, and Omar Gonzalez-Pagan, with invaluable help from Law Fellow Keith Hammeran.

Our clients included three expecting married couples scheduled to deliver in Cincinnati hospitals—Brittani Henry and L.B. Rogers, Kelly Noe and Kelly McCracken (known as "the Kellies"), and Nicole and Pamela Yorksmith—and a fourth couple, two men, who had adopted their Ohio-born child in New York. Cooper, the adorable toddler son of New York couple Joe Vitale and Rob Talmas, would become the youngest plaintiff in the set of *Obergefell* Supreme Court cases. As babies arrived through the course of the litigation, our plaintiff families grew to include a total of five babies and preschoolers, making our gatherings raucous—and sticky—affairs.

Obergefell and *Henry* were fitting companion cases, demonstrating the cradle-to-grave harms inflicted on same-sex couples and their families. *Obergefell* tested the waters; buoyed by its initial success, we decided to pursue a more ambitious strategy in *Henry*. Instead of limiting our case to seeking birth certificates—the most pressing priority for our clients—similar to *Obergefell*'s request for death certificates, we asked the court to rule that Ohio's marriage recognition bans were unconstitutional on their face, and so could not be applied in *any way* to *anyone*.

When we appeared with our *Henry* clients for a court hearing in the spring of 2014, a number of the women present were obviously *very* pregnant. The visuals were powerful—the plaintiffs' babies were not going to wait to be born until some distant day when Ohio's voters might rescind the laws denigrating their families. We argued that these families needed the court's help to enforce their constitutional rights, and they needed it now. We were gratified when Judge Black, building off his *Obergefell* decision, quickly ruled in favor of the *Henry* plaintiffs, not only ordering the State to issue accurate birth certificates, but also declaring Ohio's non-recognition laws to be unconstitutional on their face. Although the judge stayed much of his ruling while the State appealed to the Sixth

Circuit, he required birth certificates to issue naming both parents without delay. In its grudging compliance, Ohio still marked these families for second-class status. After the babies arrived, although the birth certificates listed both spouses as parents, they also included the special asterisked notation that the certificates were issued pursuant to court order. That our clients' children were not mere "asterisk babies" became a rallying cry for our team.

As the cases progressed through the courts, the legal teams grew. The ACLU's National LGBT Rights Project co-counseled with Gerhardstein on *Obergefell*. Lambda Legal collaborated closely on the Ohio cases with extraordinary ACLU colleagues Steven Shapiro, James Esseks, Joshua Block, Chase Strangio, Louise Melling, Leslie Cooper, and Ria Tabacco Mar. ACLU of Ohio-affiliated attorneys also joined *Obergefell*, including law professor Susan Becker.

Similar cases that would eventually converge with the Ohio *Obergefell–Henry* duo were also proceeding in Tennessee, Michigan, and Kentucky, the other states that comprised the federal appellate Sixth Circuit. The Tennessee suit, filed in October 2013, *Tanco v. Haslam*, was co-counseled by the National Center for Lesbian Rights (NCLR), led by Shannon Minter, David Codell, and Chris Stoll. They were joined with a team of prominent Tennessee lawyers, including Abby Rubenfeld, a formidable veteran LGBT rights litigator and one-time legal director of Lambda Legal; skilled Sherrard & Roe attorneys led by the Atticus Finchesque Bill Harbison; Maureen Holland; and Regina Lambert. When *Tanco* reached the Supreme Court, the plaintiffs added Ropes & Gray, led by Supreme Court advocate Douglas Hallward-Driemeier. *Tanco*, like the Ohio pair of cases, sought only recognition of the existing out-of-state marriages for the plaintiff same-sex spouses, not the freedom to marry. Unlike the Ohio cases, its plaintiffs were exclusively couples who had been residents in the states where they married, later moving to Tennessee for work and other compelling reasons, and then finding their marriages disrespected by their new home state. *Tanco* presented strong facts, but could have yielded a narrow victory benefitting only transplant families, not the far more typical families who had briefly traveled to marriage jurisdictions to wed and returned home to discrimination.

The Michigan case, *DeBoer v. Snyder*, filed in 2012 before *Windsor* was even decided, similarly began not as a head-on challenge to that state's marriage ban. Instead, *DeBoer* started as a relatively more modest challenge to Michigan's laws prohibiting unmarried couples from adopting children. April DeBoer and Jayne Rowse, both nurses who had each adopted children with special needs, were doing a phenomenal job of raising them together. But these women could not enter into second-parent adoptions of each other's adopted children and provide their children the security of two legally recognized parents. Nor could they marry in Michigan to satisfy the state's adoption restrictions. Only when federal District

Court Judge Bernard Friedman asked the parties to address the broader issue of the constitutionality of the state's underlying marriage ban did *DeBoer* morph into a full-on marriage challenge. Following *Windsor*, the judge ordered a trial on the merits, a relatively unusual step in marriage cases, most of which were decided based on the legal arguments through procedural vehicles short of a full-blown trial. The Michigan lawyers in that case, Carole Stanyar, Ken Mogill, and Dana Nessel, poured great effort into the trial and also turned to the national LGBT groups for their expertise and assistance. Eventually, Mary L. Bonauto of GLAD joined *DeBoer* as co-counsel, and lawyers from the ACLU and Lambda Legal also assisted in the trial effort.

The plaintiffs' team mounted an overwhelming case about the fitness of same-sex couples to be spouses and parents—with DeBoer and Rowse themselves serving as inspiring examples of devoted and effective parenting for their special needs adopted children. In March 2014, the court issued its trial findings in favor of the couple, declaring Michigan's ban unconstitutional.

Another challenge to state marriage recognition bans was also underway in Kentucky. *Bourke v. Beshear* racked up yet another district court victory for the rights of same-sex couples in February 2014. Encouraged by that ruling, the *Bourke* lawyers promptly filed a complaint before the same judge, challenging Kentucky's refusal to allow same-sex couples to marry within the state. It was almost too good to be true that the surname of the lead plaintiff in that action was Love. The resulting case name, *Love v. Beshear* (Kentucky's governor), perfectly summed up the matter. It came as no surprise when *Love* prevailed. These two Kentucky cases were initially lawyered by Louisville attorneys Dan Cannon, Lauren Landenwich, Shannon Fauver, and Dawn Elliott. When the cases reached the Supreme Court, the Kentucky team was joined by ACLU Project attorneys, as well as by Jeffrey Fisher, head of Stanford Law School's Supreme Court Litigation Clinic. Fisher, a brilliant and generous star of the Supreme Court Bar, would make invaluable contributions as all the litigation teams collaborated in the high court.

The Sixth Circuit Loss, with a Silver Lining

The marriage equality movement was on an unprecedented winning streak, racking up straight victories in these six cases, as well as dozens of similar victories in others around the country. Appeals by defendants in other states made their way to the Fourth (*Bostic v. Schaefer*), Seventh (*Baskin v. Bogan*), Ninth (*Latta v. Otter*), and Tenth Circuits (*Kitchen v. Herbert*). Lambda Legal represented plaintiffs or filed amicus briefs in each of those appeals. In circuit after circuit, LGBT rights advocates scored rulings that state bans on the freedom to marry and recognition of existing marriages violate the Fourteenth Amendment of the U.S. Constitution. With only a couple of outlier lower court decisions against us, marriage equality seemed unstoppable.

Then came the Sixth Circuit. As expected, state defendants appealed all the pro-LGBT rulings we had won. The Sixth Circuit consolidated the six appeals for argument before a single three-judge panel, with one attorney on each side to argue from each state—eight in total. Not known to be populated with an abundance of progressive judges, the Sixth Circuit was a challenging forum for our cause. The fate of our cases—and the thousands of families whose rights hung in the balance—could depend on which three judges would be randomly assigned to the panel. We had cause for concern when we learned shortly before oral argument that our panel included not only progressive Clinton-appointee Judge Martha Craig Daughtrey, but also George W. Bush-appointees Judges Jeffrey Sutton and Deborah Cook. Judge Sutton, former law clerk to Supreme Court Justice Antonin Scalia, had a reputation as a conservative-leaning intellectual leader on the Sixth Circuit.

With the stakes mounting, the teams from Kentucky, Ohio, and Tennessee convened in Nashville for a moot practice argument session, where University of Louisville law professor Sam Marcosson, Esseks, and I played the roles of Sixth Circuit judges, for hours pummeling Gerhardstein, Harbison, and Landenwich, who were arguing for their states' plaintiffs, with the hardest questions we could imagine. Carole Stanyar prepared separately up in Michigan for her turn at the podium.

Days later, on August 6, 2014, we gathered in the Cincinnati Sixth Circuit courtroom for the real argument, along with dozens of plaintiffs from all the cases—and a few of their babies. One child not present, though, was New Yorker Cooper, whose fathers were afraid to step foot with him in Ohio so long as the state refused fully to recognize them both as his legal parents. They worried that if an emergency arose while Cooper was in Ohio, their rights as his parents might be questioned. Their fear was not without foundation. The Yorksmiths had had such an experience already. While the state's appeal in their case was pending, their baby fell ill with croup. Late one night, while Nicole remained home with their sleeping older child, Pam raced their baby to the same Cincinnati hospital where he had been born. But when she arrived, the hospital questioned her right to be there with her son, since only Nicole, the birth mother, was listed in the hospital records as a parent. Their ill baby had to wait to receive care while middle-of-the-night calls were made to Nicole to authorize treatment and vouch for Pam. This was just one example of the indignities and added stresses same-sex couples and their children had to bear every day, and a frightening reminder that far more than abstract principles were at stake for these families.

At oral argument, as in their written briefs, the states' lawyers labored to obscure these hard realities, instead casting the cases as about abstract virtues of majoritarian rule. They pressed the theme that whether to open marriage to same-sex couples should rest exclusively in the hands of the voters and the democratic process of each state, and should not be determined as a constitutional matter by federal judges. Some of the states' lawyers even claimed, with our many parent plaintiffs in the courtroom, that there was reason to believe same-sex couples made inferior parents. While Judge Daughtrey visibly scoffed at these arguments, Judges Sutton and Cook seemed receptive. After sitting through the states' offensive arguments and hearing the comments of Judges Sutton and Cook, many of the plaintiffs looked shaken. Despite the forceful presentations by the advocates on our side, I left the courtroom fearing a loss.

On November 6, 2014, our fears came true. The Sixth Circuit's 2–1 ruling against us, authored by Judge Sutton and with a strong dissent from Judge Daughtrey, was a paean to majoritarian rule. Judge Sutton argued that the rights of same-sex couples and their children must be decided by the voters, not by the courts. In Judge Sutton's words, the cases "come down to the same question: Who decides?" His answer: the legislators and voters who had enacted the discriminatory marriage bans targeting an unpopular minority and had done nothing since to rescind them. The Sixth Circuit's ruling was a painful splash of ice-cold water in what had otherwise been an almost unbroken stream of marriage equality victories.

But there was a silver lining to this loss. One month earlier, the Supreme Court had declined to take up for review the states' appeals from the Fourth, Seventh, and Tenth Circuit marriage victories, and had refused to stay the Ninth Circuit's pro-marriage ruling while the defendants petitioned, unsuccessfully, for review. These were startling developments, requiring all the states in those circuits to cease enforcement of their anti-marriage bans and to allow same-sex couples to marry. Almost overnight, the number of states in which same-sex couples could marry and have their marriages recognized more than doubled. The Supreme Court's refusal to review or stay the four circuit court decisions seemed a wonderful omen, portending that a majority of the Court agreed with those decisions. LGBT advocates sensed that the way had been paved to a Supreme Court ruling in favor of marriage rights. All that was needed was the right vehicle, a circuit court ruling *against* marriage rights, creating a split among the circuits on this important national question—the paradigmatic circumstances under which the Supreme Court was likeliest to accept review. The Sixth Circuit loss, and the division it brought to the circuits, was just the vehicle we needed.

Last Stop: The U.S. Supreme Court

Even before the Sixth Circuit ruling, we had done groundwork to prepare for a potential *cert.* petition. Within hours of receiving the Sixth Circuit decision, our plans for seeking *cert.* were well underway. The legal teams for all four states consulted over a course of conference calls in the days that followed. Meanwhile, I got to work drafting a joint *cert.* petition on behalf of both Ohio cases, *Henry* and *Obergefell*. Although our deadline to file a petition was nearly three months off, time was of the essence. Not only were the stakes high for the many families whose security and rights hung in the balance, but we wanted our cases decided by the end of the term in June 2015 by the current justices, at least five of whom we had strong reason to hope would rule in our favor.

The days following the Sixth Circuit's ruling coincided with Freshman Parents' Weekend at my daughter's university. She and I holed up together in her college library; she worked on an English paper, while I hammered out a draft of the *cert.* petition. Collaborating with Gerhardstein and the ACLU, we delivered the final petition to the printer within a week of the Sixth Circuit's ruling. By November 18, 2014, all the plaintiff teams had petitions on file. The states' responding briefs largely agreed that the patchwork division in the nation on the marriage question was untenable and that the Court should weigh in to resolve the issue once and for all. With the *cert.* briefing completed, the ball was in the Court's hands.

We did not have long to wait. On January 16, 2015, the Court announced it was granting *certiorari* in all six cases decided by the Sixth Circuit's ruling. The Court consolidated the cases, distilling what it would consider into two questions:

1. Does the Fourteenth Amendment require a state to license a marriage between two people of the same sex?

2. Does the Fourteenth Amendment require a state to recognize a marriage between two people of the same sex when their marriage was lawfully licensed and performed out-of-state?

The Michigan *DeBoer* and Kentucky *Love* cases raised the first question on the freedom to marry in-state; both Ohio cases and Kentucky's *Bourke* and Tennessee's *Tanco* cases exclusively raised the second question on recognition of out-of-state marriages. Together, these issues covered the marriage rights terrain.

The Court put us on a foreshortened briefing schedule, signaling its intent to slate the cases for oral argument before the end of the term, in time for a June

2015 decision. With our opening briefs due February 27, 2015, we had no time to lose. Not only were we going to write perhaps the most important briefs in our careers as civil rights advocates, but we also had a massive outpouring of amicus support to coordinate. In 2003 in *Lawrence,* sixteen amicus briefs were submitted on the LGBT rights side; by 2013 in *Windsor,* more than forty amicus briefs came in on our side. We expected even more in our six cases; ultimately, over eighty briefs supported our position.

The four national LGBT rights groups quickly formed a working group to field amicus queries, try to head off unnecessary duplication of briefs, and help ensure that the subjects likely to be of most interest to the Court were addressed by amici. The Court received forceful amicus briefs from prominent authorities on an array of subjects, with leading Supreme Court advocates appearing as counsel on many of the briefs. They ranged from deep dives in the social science, history, and hardships of marriage discrimination, to scholarly analysis of discrete issues of legal doctrine, to advocacy from leading national corporations, state governments, and members of Congress.

Perhaps the most important amicus brief came from the United States itself, by Solicitor General Donald Verrilli. The brief made strong Equal Protection arguments, urging heightened scrutiny for sexual-orientation–based governmental classifications. In past decades, it would have been unthinkable for the federal government to stand up for the constitutional rights of LGBT people in a challenge to state marriage discrimination. The solicitor general's participation on our side now was another sign of how far our movement had traveled.

Meanwhile, many of us were hard at work crafting the briefs that would be filed in the plaintiffs' opening and reply rounds. It was a challenge but also deeply fulfilling to distill years of thought on the constitutional issues, as well as what the freedom to marry means to same-sex couples and their children, into our painstakingly drafted briefs. I poured all I had learned and the passion I felt for this cause into those briefs, which likely would be the final chance we would have to make our case to these nine justices. And while we were certainly trying to speak to every justice on the Court, we were particularly focused on what might resonate with Justice Kennedy, often the swing vote on social justice issues. Justice Kennedy had been a stalwart supporter in past LGBT rights cases, but we could take nothing—and no one—for granted.

As in earlier phases of the litigation and past marriage equality cases, our core arguments centered on the fundamental right to marry that should protect the choice to wed the person you love whether of the same or a different sex, and the right to be treated with equality. Where the states again tried to justify their discrimination as the fruit of a noble process of democratic self-rule that should be permitted to unfold on its own timetable, we countered that, meanwhile,

same-sex partners were aging and dying and their children outgrowing childhood, and were still unconstitutionally denied the dignity and protections of
marriage.

The four plaintiffs' legal teams had another challenge—settling on which
two lawyers would represent our clients at the oral argument the Court had
scheduled for April 28, 2015. The Court had advised us that only one advocate
on each side could present argument on each of the two questions. That meant
we would have to select one person to argue the first question presented, on the
freedom to marry in-state, and one to argue the second question, on the right to
recognition of an out-of-state marriage. Whoever stood at that podium would
also be standing up for thousands of other families around the country; this
would be a career-defining oral argument. We were blessed with an abundance
of talented appellate advocates to choose from, any of whom would have done
a very fine job. In the end, two phenomenal lawyers argued on our side on
April 28, doing our cause proud.

It felt like destiny to have GLAD's Mary Bonauto, an architect of the modern
marriage equality movement who had earned the respect and affection of many
throughout the nation, the first to stand at the podium on April 28. Bonauto,
whose own wife and daughters were in the courtroom, was the very embodi-
ment of the dignity and grace with which LGBT people in this country led their
lives, cared for their families, and engaged their communities. She had toiled for
decades to bring us—and herself—to that day in April.

Representing us on question two was Doug Hallward-Driemeier, the impos-
ingly tall—and talented—Ropes & Gray partner, who stood more than a foot
above the diminutive Bonauto. Hallward-Driemeier had argued many times at
that podium; his Supreme Court seasoning and savvy complemented Bonauto's
steeping in the LGBT rights movement.

Many of us worked intensively in the weeks leading up to April 28 to help
prepare our two colleagues. We converged in Washington, D.C., for large,
formal moot courts, including ones at Howard and Georgetown Law Schools,
with "justices" comprised of law professors and prominent Supreme Court advocates, along with a side-trip for another at a Nashville law school. A core
of us, including Davidson, Esseks, Fisher, Codell, Minter, and a rotating cast
of others, spent hours hunkered down in conference rooms with Bonauto and
Hallward-Driemeier, researching and trying out responses to every question we
could imagine coming from the bench. By the morning of April 28, Bonauto and
Hallward-Driemeier could not have been better prepared.

In the days before that Tuesday morning, our clients and their children, as well
as the families of the other plaintiffs, descended on Washington to attend the argument. We were determined that every adult plaintiff in the collection of cases

Plaintiffs gathered in front of the U.S. Supreme Court, the day before arguments were heard in *Obergefell*. Photo Credit: LESLIE VON PLESS/LAMBDA LEGAL

would have their day in Court, present for at least part of the oral argument. With help from Supreme Court staff, we were able to obtain reserved seats in the public non-lawyer section so that two dozen plaintiffs could be present for at least one of the two argued questions.

On April 28, I woke at dawn to jog to the Washington mall so I could touch the steps of the Lincoln Memorial for good luck. Later that morning, I joined the plaintiffs and other attorneys as we were allowed through the security cordon rimming the Court and crossed the plaza leading to the building's entrance. As we proudly strode to the Court's iconic front stairs and the crowd below spontaneously roared their support, many of us were moved to tears. I sat in the front of the courtroom with the arguing attorneys and other lead lawyers in the cases, with many Lambda Legal colleagues and other prominent LGBT attorneys, including Freedom to Marry's Evan Wolfson, seated in the rows just behind. As the nine justices filed in promptly at 10:00 a.m., the tension in the hushed courtroom was palpable.

Up first, Bonauto faced a barrage of unfriendly questions from the more conservative justices. We had expected this; Bonauto was unfazed. But when Justice Kennedy remarked that in his thoughts about the institution of marriage he kept returning to the word "millennia," my stomach flipped uncomfortably; many others in the courtroom had similar reactions.

After Bonauto took her seat, we had another unpleasant moment. A man in the spectator section suddenly sprang to his feet shouting about "hell" and "abomination." He was rushed from the courtroom by marshals, but his ranting could still be heard ringing through the marble halls outside. One of the York-smith mothers who had been seated just in front of him fought back tears, worrying whether her children waiting in the cafeteria with their grandmother had heard those hateful words.

After this interruption, Solicitor General Verrilli took his turn at the podium, doing a masterful job conveying the urgency of this civil rights issue for our nation. He concluded: "Gay and lesbian people are equal. They deserve equal protection of the laws, and they deserve it *now*."

Hallward-Driemeier too made a star turn on the recognition question, hitting hard on the plight of married same-sex couples who feared their marriages would be disrespected on a routine trip across state lines, after a job transfer, or during an emergency hospital visit.

True to form, Michigan's and Tennessee's attorneys fell back on adherence to tradition and majoritarian will to justify discrimination. I could only hope that a majority of the justices found these arguments as unconvincing as I did.

"Justice Kennedy will announce the decision in Case 14-556"—Another June 26 for the History Books

That June, our vigil at the Supreme Court began. Commonly the Supreme Court issues its rulings on Mondays, but as term end approaches in late June, the Court often adds extra decision days. I was determined to be present in the courtroom when the *Obergefell* ruling was announced. On successive Mondays beginning in early June, and then on added days as the month progressed, I would show up outside the Court before 7:00 a.m. to be there when the doors opened and members of the Supreme Court Bar could line up inside. A hardy band of fellow LGBT rights colleagues would mill with me on those mornings, joined by lawyers awaiting decisions in other significant end-of-term cases. Jim Obergefell did not miss a day at Court, determined to be there with his beloved John present in spirit.

As the days passed and the likelihood grew that a decision in *Obergefell* would finally issue, the crowds of media and interested public outside the Court grew as well. A superstitious streak I had not even known I possessed also grew. I took to carrying tiny take-out packets of salt in my pockets, tossing grains over my shoulder when I heard someone predict the outcome of the case. Finally, with only two decision days left on the calendar, I was joined at the Court by Gerhardstein, Lambda Legal's Executive Director Kevin Cathcart, our Director of Communications Lisa Hardaway, and the Yorksmiths with their two young sons, along with many of the lawyers and plaintiffs in the other cases.

On Friday, June 26, the anniversary of *Lawrence* and *Windsor*, I was in the first row when Chief Justice Roberts said that Justice Kennedy would announce the decision in Case 14-556, a number I knew by heart. "That's us," I murmured to Cathcart. As Justice Kennedy began with a bland recitation of the procedural history of the case and we awaited some sign of the outcome, I found myself growing light-headed, and for the first time understood where the expression "waiting with bated breath" came from. Then came the Kennedy poetry, such passages as plaintiffs "seek not to denigrate marriage but rather to live their lives, or honor their spouses' memory, joined by its bond." As he read his beautiful elegy to the love and dignity shared by same-sex couples, to the solace and refuge marriage offers, and to the constitutional values that shelter us all, tears flowed throughout the courtroom. Justice Kennedy's description of the power of marriage in the lives of two people struck me as deeply personal and heartfelt, a love letter shared with the nation.

Chief Justice Roberts took the unusual step of reading from his dissent, concluding that, "[i]f you are among the many Americans—of whatever sexual orientation—who favor expanding same-sex marriage, by all means celebrate today's decision. Celebrate the achievement of a desired goal. Celebrate the opportunity for a new expression of commitment to a partner. Celebrate the availability of new benefits. But do not celebrate the Constitution. It had nothing to do with it."

As soon as Court broke, I headed out with our clients and colleagues, to the ecstatic crowd outside, to the joyous throng I addressed later that night in New York's Sheridan Square, to my own beaming spouse and children who joined me there, to an America that overnight had taken a giant step toward living up to its best ideals. I was convinced we had it *all* to celebrate—not least of all the Constitution that ensured we would reach that day.

DESPUÉS DE TREINTA Y NUEVE AÑOS, CASADAS ANTE LOS OJOS DE LA LEY

MARITZA LÓPEZ AVILÉS AND IRIS DELIA RIVERA RIVERA

⸙

Maritza López Avilés e Iris Delia Rivera Rivera fueron demandantes en el caso sobre el matrimonio que Lambda Legal llevó en Puerto Rico, Conde Vidal v. García Padilla.

Por 39 años soñamos con casarnos. Luego de años de lucha, amor, y apoyo continuo, de haber criado juntas a una maravillosa hija, y de momentos de ansiedad y separación debido al servicio militar de Iris, hemos logrado nuestro sueño de casarnos en nuestro hogar, en Puerto Rico. Nosotras nos conocimos en la escuela superior y desde la universidad hemos estado juntas. En 1978, debido a la importancia que el matrimonio tiene para nosotras y nuestras familias, nos comprometimos como pareja ante los ojos de Dios y le pedimos su bendición. El 16 de agosto de 2015 nos casamos ante los ojos de la ley en frente de familiares y amistades.

Nosotras nos unimos a la demanda por el matrimonio igualitario en Puerto Rico porque estábamos movidas por la inquietud en derechos que parejas como nosotras vivían día a día. Nos motivaron tanto los deseos que teníamos de formar un hogar con todos los derechos y privilegios que el gobierno le daba a otras parejas, tal como a que económicamente no podíamos viajar fuera de Puerto Rico para contraer matrimonio. Más aún, nos unimos a la demanda por nuestra hija.

Cuando el tribunal de distrito en Puerto Rico desestimó nuestra demanda, caímos en un proceso de incertidumbre, tristeza y devolución. Sin embargo, nuestros abogados siempre nos mantuvieron informadas y nos dieron la esperanza de que al final prevaleceríamos. Mientras nuestro

AFTER THIRTY-NINE YEARS, MARRIED UNDER THE LAW

MARITZA LÓPEZ AVILÉS AND IRIS DELIA RIVERA RIVERA

—— ⚭ ——

*Maritza López Avilés and Iris Delia Rivera Rivera were
plaintiffs in Lambda Legal's marriage case in Puerto Rico,*
Conde Vidal v. García Padilla.

For thirty-nine years we dreamed of getting married. After years of struggle, love, and constant support, of raising together our wonderful daughter,
of moments of anxiety and separation due to Iris's service in the military,
we have achieved our dream of getting married in our home, Puerto Rico.
We met in high school and have been together since college. In 1978, due
to the importance marriage has for us and our family, we committed to
each other under God and asked to be blessed. On August 16, 2015, we
married under the law, in front of our friends and family.

We joined the lawsuit for the freedom to marry in Puerto Rico because we were moved by the worry, in terms of rights, that couples like us
live day to day. We were motivated not only by our wish to make a home
with all the rights and privileges the government gave other couples, but
also because it wasn't economically feasible for us to travel outside of
Puerto Rico to get married. Even more so, we joined the lawsuit for our
daughter.

When the Puerto Rico District Court dismissed our case, we crashed
under a wave of uncertainty and sadness. Nevertheless, our lawyers always kept us informed and gave us hope that we would prevail in the end.
While our case was pending at the Court of Appeals for the First Circuit,
the Puerto Rico government changed course on March 20, 2015, and

caso estaba pendiente ante el Tribunal de Apelaciones para el Primer Circuito, el gobierno de Puerto Rico revirtió curso el 20 de marzo de 2015
y se allanó en nuestro caso. En su alegato ante el tribunal, el gobierno
finalmente coincidió en que la prohibición al matrimonio para parejas del
mismo sexo era inconstitucional, ya que infringía nuestro derecho fundamental al matrimonio y la igual protección de las leyes. Aún más, el gobierno se expresó contundentemente a favor de la igualdad de las personas
LGBTT. Y además expresó su acuerdo con nuestras alegaciones de que
las leyes que clasifican a base de la orientación sexual son presuntamente
inconstitucionales.

El 26 de junio de 2015 obtuvimos esa gran victoria por parte del Tribunal Supremo de Estados Unidos. Luego el primer circuito invalidó la ley
discriminatoria en Puerto Rico. Durante esos momentos, todas nuestras
emociones salieron de nuestros corazones y celebramos en grande. Ense-
guida llamamos a todos nuestros familiares y amistades para celebrar esa
gran victoria tan histórica para Puerto Rico. Muchos se nos acercaron
para decir lo orgullosos que estaban de nosotras. Hemos experimentado
una gran alegría junto a toda nuestra comunidad LGBTT. Nuestra feli-
cidad se completó durante nuestra boda, la cual esperamos con mucha
ansiedad.

Nosotras le damos gracias a la licenciada Ada Conde y su esposa que
fueron las pioneras en traer el caso de Puerto Rico. Gracias a Lambda Legal y todo nuestro equipo legal, en particular a Omar Gonzalez-Pagan, por
hacer que nuestro sueño de podernos casarnos en Puerto Rico y nuestra
dicha realidad. Mil gracias a nombre de nosotras y de la comunidad LG-
BTT porque las nuevas generaciones no van a pasar por el discrimen legal
que nosotras pasamos.

Sinceramente,

Maritza López Avilés
Iris Delia Rivera Rivera
Para nuestra hija ARB.

paved the way for our case. In their statement to the court, the government finally agreed that the ban against marriage for same-sex couples was unconstitutional, since it infringed equal protection under the law and our fundamental right to marry. Furthermore, the government expressed its overwhelming support for equality for LGBT people. It agreed with our argument that the laws that classify people by their sexual orientation are presumably unconstitutional.

On June 26, 2015, we won that huge victory at the U.S. Supreme Court. Then the First Circuit struck down Puerto Rico's discriminatory ban. During each of those moments, our hearts overflowed with emotion, and we celebrated enthusiastically. We called our families and friends immediately to celebrate such an historic win for Puerto Rico. Many approached us to tell us how proud of us they were. We have experienced great joy along with our entire LGBT community. Our happiness achieved full-circle during our wedding which we waited for anxiously.

We thank Attorney Ada Conde and her wife, who were pioneers in bringing up this case in Puerto Rico. Thanks to Lambda Legal and our entire legal team, particularly Omar Gonzalez-Pagan, for making our dream of marrying in Puerto Rico and our bliss into a reality. Thanks on our behalf and on behalf of the LGBT community because newer generations will not have to experience the legal discrimination we endured.

Sincerely,

Maritza López Avilés
Iris Delia Rivera Rivera
For our daughter, ARB.

(Above) Wedding day for Puerto Rico plaintiffs Maritza López Avilés and Iris Delia Rivera Rivera, with Lambda Legal Deputy Legal Director Hayley Gorenberg sharing in the celebration.

(Left top) Kevin Cathcart, Lambda Legal executive director; Kate Kendell, National Center for Lesbian Rights executive director; James Esseks, ACLU LGBT & HIV Project director; with attorneys who argued *Obergefell*, Douglas Hallward-Driemeier and GLAD's Mary Bonauto, after arguments, April 28, 2015. Photo credit: LESLIE VON PLESS/LAMBDA LEGAL

(Left bottom) Crowd gathers for victory celebration outside the historic Stonewall Inn in NYC after the decision, June 26, 2015. Courtesy of Lambda Legal. Photo credit: MAX GORDON/LAMBDA LEGAL

(Top) Plaintiffs Joseph Vitale and Robert Talmas with their son Cooper at the victory celebration outside the Stonewall Inn, with Lambda Legal attorney Susan Sommer, James Esseks, ACLU LGBT & HIV Project director, and Lambda Legal attorney Omar Gonzalez-Pagan, June 26, 2015. Courtesy of Lambda Legal. Photo credit: MAX GORDON/LAMBDA LEGAL

(Above left) Lambda Legal Director of Education and Public Affairs Leslie Gabel-Brett celebrates with her granddaughter Jasmine at the pride parade in New York City on Sunday, June 28, 2015, two days after the decision was announced. Photo credit: CAROLYN GABEL-BRETT

(Above right) Lambda Legal Executive Director Kevin Cathcart celebrates at the pride parade in New York City on Sunday, June 28, 2015, two days after the decision was announced. Photo credit: CAROLYN GABEL-BRETT

VII. LOOKING TO THE FUTURE

A GLASS ONLY HALF FULL: THE ONGOING STRUGGLE FOR LGBT RIGHTS

JON W. DAVIDSON

———— ✿✿✿ ————

Jon W. Davidson is national legal director and Eden/Rushing Chair at Lambda Legal.

The speed and sweeping nature of the changes in U.S. law and in our society's treatment of LGBT people has been breathtaking and is a testament to the courage, determination, and sweat of all who contributed to it. For those too young to remember, it may be hard to grasp just what life was like before the Stonewall Rebellion, when a few brave members of our community fought back against police oppression in 1969. At that time, laws criminalizing private, adult, same-sex intimacy existed in all states except for Illinois (which repealed its sodomy law in 1962). Publications urging our civil rights were seized by the postal service as obscene. Individuals could be arrested for appearing in public in clothing that traditionally was associated with a sex different than the sex they were assigned at birth, and gathering places serving our community were subject to closure if customers "flaunted" their queer identities. Homosexuality was classified as a mental illness, and gay people often were institutionalized and subjected to horrific "treatments" for our deviancy. We also were barred from immigrating into the United States, hounded from government jobs, declared ineligible for military service, universally denied protections against discrimination and bullying, and regularly subjected to loss of child custody and visitation.

Advances and reforms over the last four and a half decades have brought about
a new reality for many LGBT Americans. The American Psychiatric Association removed homosexuality from its list of mental disorders in 1973. Lambda
Legal's 2003 victory in *Lawrence v. Texas* ended the criminalization of same-sex
lovemaking across the nation. The immigration ban was repealed in 2000, and
the ban on immigrants living with HIV likewise was eliminated in 2010.

Approximately twenty years ago, in 1995, laws expressly barring sexual orientation discrimination in employment had been enacted in nine states and the
District of Columbia; only one state's law at that point covered gender identity
discrimination. Ten years ago, the totals had grown to sixteen states plus DC
that explicitly banned sexual orientation discrimination, and six plus DC that expressly protected transgender employees. Today, twenty-two states and DC expressly bar sexual orientation employment discrimination, and nineteen states and
DC explicitly extend protection against gender identity discrimination at work.

At the federal level, the repeal of the "Don't Ask, Don't Tell" policy in
2011 has been followed by the inclusion of sexual orientation in the military's
antidiscrimination regulations. The U.S. government now bars sexual orientation and gender identity discrimination in federal employment and by federal
government contractors. The federal Equal Employment Opportunity Commission and some federal courts also have begun to protect LGBT people against
workplace discrimination by private employers under the ban on sex discrimination contained in Title VII of the Civil Rights Act of 1964. Eighteen states and
the District of Columbia currently have enumerated anti-bullying laws that expressly cover harassment and violence against LGBT students. In addition, half
of all school campuses now have gay–straight alliances.

Laws governing parental rights, adoption, and foster parenting by LGBT
people likewise have improved dramatically in many parts of the country. In
nearly all states, sexual orientation and gender identity are no longer relevant
to custody or visitation determinations without concrete proof of likely harm
to the child. In addition, half of all state courts have invoked equitable parenting theories to allow non-biological, non-adoptive parents to seek visitation
or custody of the children they helped raise. In thirty-five states and the District of Columbia, LGBT parents can jointly petition for adoption. In fifteen
states and the District of Columbia, unmarried LGBT parents can petition for
second-parent adoptions statewide. Marriage equality brings with it the ability
of married, same-sex couples to obtain step-parent adoptions. Seven states have
non-discrimination policies that bar or restrict discrimination in adoption on the
basis of sexual orientation. Six have non-discrimination policies that bar or restrict discrimination in foster care on the basis of sexual orientation, and two of
those also bar discrimination based on gender identity.

Additionally, important progress has begun to be achieved with respect to the ability to obtain correct identity documents, appropriate access to sex-segregated spaces, and access to necessary health care for transgender people. Numerous states have made it easier to obtain an amended birth certificate reflecting one's current name and, in some cases, one's gender. A number of women's colleges now admit women who are transgender. Medicare and, in some states, Medicaid currently cover hormone treatment and sex confirmation surgeries for transgender patients. Private insurers in ten states and the District of Columbia have been barred from denying coverage relating to gender transition. Transgender patients are also protected against discrimination by federal health care programs and programs funded with federal support, pursuant to Section 1557 of the Affordable Care Act.

The Supreme Court held that people living with AIDS were protected against discrimination under federal disability laws in GLAD's *Bragdon v. Abbott* victory in 1998, and Congress made clear in 2008 that such protections extend to all people living with HIV, even if newly available medications suppressed viral loads and prevented the disease's progression.

We also have seen remarkable changes in the nation's courts. There are now scores of proud lesbian, gay, and bisexual members of the judiciary in the United States (although still only two openly transgender judges). There currently are seven openly lesbian or gay members of state high courts—including two on the Oregon Supreme Court and the first lesbian Latina on a state supreme court, in Colorado—as well as an openly lesbian Latina on the Puerto Rico Supreme Court. There are now ten openly lesbian and gay judges on the federal bench (ten times as many as in 2008), including six who are people of color and the first openly gay U.S. federal appellate judge in history. In addition, the federal Ninth Circuit Court of Appeals ruled in 2014 that prospective jurors cannot be subjected to peremptory challenges based on their sexual orientation.

And of course there are the incredible advances we have seen with respect to the law's treatment of same-sex relationships. The first state to pass a law recognizing same-sex couples was Hawai'i, which passed a reciprocal beneficiary law in 1997, followed by California, which passed the first state domestic partnership statute in 1999. It was only eleven years ago that same-sex couples became able to legally marry somewhere in the United States, when that became possible in Massachusetts on May 17, 2004 following the victory in *Goodridge*, a case won by GLAD. Just two years ago, same-sex couples could marry in only eight states and Washington, D.C. But, by the time the issue reached the Supreme Court this year, that number had more than quadrupled, with same-sex couples able to marry in thirty-six states and the District of Columbia. Now, after the victory in *Obergefell*, same-sex couples may marry anywhere in the United States, and that sweeping decision requires all government officials to treat the marriages of same-sex couples—wherever entered—the same as the marriages of different-sex couples, which already is bringing about important advances in family law and the issuance of proper birth certificates.

The ability to serve openly in the military, to be selected for jury service, and to marry are marks of equal citizenship in this country, and, at least for lesbians, gay men, and bisexuals, those badges of equality largely have been won. Most critically, the movement for marriage equality has dramatically helped humanize our community, telling relatable stories of love and commitment. It has dramatically shifted the nation's mental image of the lesbian and gay community as composed of promiscuous male predators and lonely lesbians living in the shadows to people who, like most others, fall in love and form families and deserve to have their commitment to their partners affirmed and celebrated. Likewise, the increasing visibility of transgender individuals in the media, in entertainment, in schools, and in the workforce has broadened the public's understanding of gender identity.

All of that is the glass half full. We indeed have come very far. But, make no mistake: the signs of progress described above are nearly all woefully incomplete, and our work is very far from done. There are still more states that do not have express sexual orientation and gender identity employment discrimination protections, that do not have anti-bullying laws expressly covering LGBT students, and that do not have bans on sexual orientation or gender identity discrimination in adoption and foster parenting than the number of states that do. Most states do not bar insurers from denying care necessary to transgender health. Police targeting of LGBT people and violence against members of our community continues at alarming rates. Indeed, we have become largely a nation divided, with states in New England, the Eastern Seaboard, and on the Pacific coast having come closest to equal treatment of LGBT people, and the southern and many Rust Belt and Rocky Mountain states still the furthest from providing equality under the law.

Many remain left behind by the progress that has been made, particularly LGBT people of color; working class, low income, and poor LGBT people; immigrants; those in rural communities; those who are incarcerated; couples who are not married; LGBT teens, young adults, and seniors; and those with non-binary sexual orientations and gender identities. Many of these individuals and communities face discrimination and oppression that is further compounded by the intersection of anti-LGBT bias and ongoing fears and myths about HIV with the impacts of racial prejudice and injustice, anti-immigrant sentiments, and economic disadvantage.

While the fight for marriage equality seized the media's attention in recent years and sometimes led to a myopic view that marriage equality was the end game, the LGBT movement has never been limited to that goal. Indeed, whoever might have thought the LGBT agenda was limited to achieving marriage equality could not have been paying close attention. To the contrary, the "To Do" list for our community has always been and remains quite a long one. There are at least ten major areas of work that remain imperative for our community to address.

I.   FIGHTING ANTI-LGBT DISCRIMINATION AND RELIGIOUS REFUSALS

According to the 2008 General Social Survey, 37 percent of lesbian and gay employees have experienced workplace harassment in the previous five years, and 12 percent lost a job because of their sexual orientation. In the largest survey of transgender people to date, a whopping 90 percent of respondents reported experiencing harassment or mistreatment at work, and 47 percent reported being denied a job, not getting a promotion, or being terminated based on their gender identity. Nonetheless, twenty-eight states still lack a law expressly barring sexual orientation discrimination in employment, housing, or public accommodations, and thirty-one still have no law explicitly barring gender identity discrimination. There likewise is still no federal law calling out anti-LGBT discrimination in such central areas of public life. As a result, obtaining explicit, comprehensive sexual orientation and gender identity antidiscrimination laws remains a top priority for our community.

Even when such laws have been adopted, those opposed to LGBT equality have sought to be exempted from their coverage. Having lost their hegemonic power to control the law, they now seek not to have it restrict *their* conduct. Emboldened by the Supreme Court's decision in the *Hobby Lobby* case, they have attempted to pass broad "religious freedom restoration acts" and other laws to allow them to use religiously based beliefs as grounds to deny equal treatment to LGBT people (and others) in employment, public accommodations, and adoption and foster care placement services. These religious refusal and "conscience" laws are among the most dangerous backlash we face against the progress we have made and the most serious barrier to our future progress. They falsely portray those engaged in discrimination as victims rather than perpetrators of harm, and they seek to use the law's power to immunize those most likely to engage in discrimination against being held responsible for the injuries they inflict. While, due to unprecedented business opposition, such efforts did not broadly succeed this past year, troubling laws nonetheless were passed in Arkansas, Indiana, Michigan, and North Carolina, and we are certain to see renewed efforts in legislative sessions to come that require the strongest opposition we can muster.

In addition, while there are signs of possible future change, service members discovered to be transgender remain at risk of discharge, and HIV-positive individuals are still barred from enlisting in the military. Through these laws and policies, our federal government, rather than being a model employer, continues to engage in unwarranted, blatant discrimination against members of our community. Ending these exclusions is essential to achieving equal employment opportunity in this country.

2.   MAKING THE WORLD SAFE FOR TRANSGENDER, INTERSEX, AND
     GENDER-NONCONFORMING PEOPLE

The problems faced by transgender, intersex, and gender-nonconforming people (including those with a non-binary gender identity or expression) alone belie any notion that our movement's work is anywhere close to being done. The level of violence, harassment, and discrimination against transgender individuals remains at staggeringly high levels. One tracking organization reported that 1,731 transgender people were murdered across the world between 2008 and 2014. In the United States, transgender women of color are at greatest risk, comprising more than half of all LGBT homicide victims in 2013. In addition, 78 percent of students who expressed a transgender identity or gender-nonconformity in grades K–12 reported being harassed on that basis at school (including 35 percent who were physically assaulted and 12 percent who were sexually assaulted), leading to 15 percent of these students leaving school.

Transgender people also are four times as likely as others to live in extreme poverty. They experience double the average rate of unemployment, and one-fifth have experienced homelessness at some point in their lives.

Transition-related care continues to be excluded from health care coverage provided by the Veterans Health Administration, in prisons, and by numerous government and private insurance plans. Nineteen percent of transgender people who were interviewed reported outright denials of medical care because of their gender identity or expression, and 28 percent reported harassment in medical settings. At the same time, the rate of HIV infection among transgender people is more than four times the national average.

Fifty-four percent of all transgender people further report being denied equal treatment or service in public accommodations, and 53 percent report harassment in businesses open to the public. Transgender people frequently continue to be denied access to bathrooms, locker rooms, and other sex-segregated spaces that are consistent with their gender identity, and bills to bar and even punish such access were introduced in 2015 in several legislatures.

Of those who have undergone transition in their gender expression, only one-fifth have been able to update all of their identity documents and records. More than 40 percent live without any identity documents matching their gender identity, compounding the likelihood that they will experience discrimination and harassment.

All of these problems contribute to the frightening 41 percent of transgender individuals who report attempting suicide, compared to 1.6 percent of the general population.

3. WORKING FOR A JUST CRIMINAL AND CIVIL JUSTICE SYSTEM

Lambda Legal conducted a survey in 2012 of the experiences of LGBT people and people living with HIV with police, prisons, courts, and school security. One-quarter of respondents with any recent police contact reported experiencing misconduct or harassment. Sixty percent of transgender or gender-nonconforming respondents who had recently been in prison or jail reported being placed in housing that conflicted with their gender identity. Nineteen percent of respondents who had been involved in the court system heard a judge, attorney, or court employee make negative comments in court about a person's sexual orientation, gender identity, or gender expression. Likewise, 23 percent of respondents between the ages of eighteen and twenty-four who had security personnel in their middle or high schools heard them use anti-LGBT language.

Clearly, the problems that gave rise to Stonewall have not disappeared. Police raids of LGBT gathering places continue in many parts of the country. Law enforcement officers regularly stop and search transgender and gender-nonconforming people—particularly transgender women of color—who were doing nothing wrong, sometimes accusing them of prostitution based solely on their appearance.

People with HIV have been subjected to criminal prosecution for engaging in sexual activity that was not likely to and did not transmit the virus, and incarcerated HIV-positive people often have been denied access to medications necessary to preserve their health. LGBT people in prison and jails likewise are commonly subjected to mistreatment, assault, and rape (by both other inmates and guards) with few or no consequences to perpetrators.

Reforms are needed throughout our criminal and civil justice system to ensure equal access to justice for LGBT people and people living with HIV, to further promote judicial diversity, and to rebuff efforts to intimidate judges against protecting our community's rights.

4. SECURING COMPREHENSIVE IMMIGRATION REFORM AND FIGHTING GLOBAL OPPRESSION OF LGBT PEOPLE

There are estimated to be approximately 267,000 LGBT-identified adults in the United States who are undocumented immigrants and 637,000 more who are documented. Many came to this country to escape persecution in their home countries. Our country's current restrictions on who can immigrate and who can obtain asylum, long delays in the immigration courts, and inhumane conditions in some immigration detention facilities all cry out for reform. We also cannot ignore the brutal treatment of LGBT people in numerous parts of the globe, including more than seventy-five countries that continue to criminalize homosexuality, some of which have increased their punishments at the encouragement of American anti-LGBT forces.

5.   PROTECTING LGBTQ CHILDREN, TEENS, AND YOUNG ADULTS

One measure of a just and equal society is how it treats its young people, and, on that scale as well, we have far to go. According to a 2013 survey, more than 74 percent of LGBT students were verbally harassed in the prior year because of their sexual orientation, and more than 55 percent suffered such harassment because of their gender expression. More than 36 percent had been pushed, shoved, or otherwise physically harassed at school based on their sexual orientation, and more than 22 percent because of their gender expression. Even more troubling, over 16 percent were physically assaulted (such as being punched, kicked, or injured with a weapon) because of their sexual orientation, and more than 11 percent because of their gender expression. It doesn't help that thirty-two states have no laws barring harassment at school or simply bar "bullying" without calling out its typical victims, and that eight states have enacted laws mandating that students be taught that being gay "is not a lifestyle acceptable to the general public," laws that forbid schools from portraying LGBT people in a positive light, or laws that bar any discussion of LGBT people.

Numerous studies also highlight the overrepresentation of LGBT children, teens, and young adults (and particularly young people of color) in foster care, juvenile justice, runaway and homeless youth systems, and among youth who have been trafficked or commercially sexually exploited, as well as the substandard treatment, discrimination, and harassment they often experience in programs that are supposed to help them. The "school to prison pipeline" that disproportionately treats minor disciplinary problems of students of color and gender-nonconforming students as cause for expulsion or referral to law enforcement feeds these problems.

These stressors take their toll in LGBT young people's increased rates of depression, substance use, and sexual behaviors that place them at risk for HIV and other sexually transmitted diseases. In addition, lesbian, gay, and bisexual adolescents in grades 7–12 are more than twice as likely to have attempted suicide as their heterosexual peers, and one study of transgender youth found that approximately 25 percent reported suicide attempts. Clearly, we must do more to protect the generations to come.

6.   SAFEGUARDING ALL OUR FAMILIES

While marriage equality will do much to equalize the families formed by married, same-sex couples, we need to continue to fight for same-sex couples who are not married, as well as their children. As I repeatedly have explained to my family and the family of my long-term non-marital partner, "we fought for the *freedom* to marry, not the *obligation* to do so."

Judges in numerous states continue to impose unjust custody and visitation restrictions on parents formerly in different-sex relationships. Moreover, many same-sex couples are not married, and numerous states still refuse to allow second-parent adoptions or to recognize the bonds formed by non-biological parents and the children they helped raise. Vigilance will be required to ensure that the presumption of parentage that protects families, even when a husband is known not to be a biological parent, is applied equally to lesbians married to women who give birth. We also need to fight refusals by insurance companies to cover assisted reproduction for lesbian couples and state bans on surrogacy that prevent gay men from having children biologically related to them.

7.   KEEPING LGBT PEOPLE HEALTHY

More than 50 percent of people diagnosed with HIV continue to be gay and bisexual men. Likewise, men who have sex with men still account for 63 percent of new HIV infections in the United States. Infection rates among young gay and bisexual men continue to climb, and the rates are even higher among those who are men of color. The federal Centers for Disease Control and Prevention reports that 44 percent of new infections are occurring among African Americans (although they make up only 12 percent of the U.S. population), and 21 percent of new infections are occurring among Latinos (although they comprise only 16 percent of the nation). Treatment saves lives and prevents infection, but insurers keep looking for new ways to deny coverage to those who are HIV-positive or to refuse to pay for necessary medications. Ongoing discrimination and backward penal laws also discourage people from getting tested and, if positive, into treatment. Efforts must continue to end other policies that also contribute to infection, like bans on needle exchange and its funding; the use of possession of condoms as evidence of prostitution; bans on condoms in prisons; and the lack of access to pre-exposure prophylaxis (PrEP), which is remarkably effective in keeping HIV-negative individuals uninfected.

LGBT people also face higher incidences of certain forms of cancer, and higher rates of high blood pressure, obesity, addiction, mental illness, and other conditions caused or exacerbated by chronic stress. Much remains to be done to end medical provider bias against LGBT people and to ensure cultural competency regarding LGBT people and their health care issues.

8. ENSURING THE RIGHTS OF AGING LGBT PEOPLE

How we treat our elderly is another marker of a civilized society. But LGBT seniors continue to face myriad challenges relating to their sexual orientation and gender identity, including denial of housing in retirement communities; unequal treatment at senior centers; discrimination by staff at nursing homes, assisted living facilities, and adult care facilities that runs the gamut from refusal of admission, unequal restrictions on visitation and shared rooms, denial of services, disrespect of gender identity, harassment, and even senior abuse. Enforcement of marriage duration requirements even for those who were barred from marrying in their home states continues to harm widows and widowers denied Social Security and V.A. spousal benefits. Our work on behalf of aging LGBT people is clearly far from done.

9. ADDRESSING RACISM, INSTITUTIONALIZED PREJUDICE, AND STRUCTURAL INEQUALITY

As noted above, one of the LGBT community's remaining key challenges is achieving not just formal equality, but justice and equality in the everyday lives of all members of our community, especially those who historically have been most marginalized and who face ongoing racism, xenophobia, and economic hardships. We have far to go in ending the reality that, for example, same-sex African American couples face poverty rates more than twice the rate of different-sex African American couples who are married. In addition, almost one in four children living with a male same-sex couple and nearly one in five living with a female same-sex couple are in poverty, compared to 12 percent of children living with married, different-sex couples. Our legal victories must be made accessible to those with less education and fewer economic resources. We need to tackle the ways in which multiple forms of discrimination and oppression interact, in order to truly create liberty and justice for all.

10. FIGHTING AGAINST ASSIMILATION AND COMPLACENCY

Perhaps our biggest challenge ahead will be fighting the misguided notion that we have achieved a post-LGBT status where no more needs to be done. The challenges outlined above show how far from true that is. One tool may be moving from having only or primarily an equality lens to examine and tackle the problems that continue to plague our community to one that encompasses the broad spectrum of human rights values of justice; dignity; protections of expression; and fair treatment at work, in school, in access to health care, and in how the government deals with LGBT and HIV-positive people.

Opponents to marriage equality frequently have cried out that if same-sex couples achieve the freedom to marry, the world as we know it will come to an end. It turns out they are right. The world as they know it indeed is coming to an end: it increasingly is no longer the case that the law treats LGBT people as criminals or as mentally ill, or ignores our existence altogether. But we won't make that fully a reality unless we continue to fight for it. A big agenda remains. If our past success is any indication, we are up to task. We can fill the glass if we press on.

MY LOVE–HATE RELATIONSHIP WITH MARRIAGE

BEVERLY TILLERY

—⊷∞⊶—

Beverly Tillery is executive director of the New York City Anti-Violence Project (AVP). From 2004 to 2015, she led community education at Lambda Legal, most recently as deputy director of Education and Public Affairs for Education, Advocacy, and Inclusion.

Since I joined the staff of Lambda Legal, marriage equality and I have had a tumultuous, love–hate relationship. When I started in 2004, marriage had just been won in Massachusetts. By June 2015, I was more than ready for a divorce. The Massachusetts victory was followed by multiple campaigns to win marriage equality across the country, state by state. A lot of effort went into determining which states were prime for a marriage equality win and to build the conditions in those states necessary to support and sustain a victory either in the courts or through the legislature. My staff team of community educators at Lambda Legal were an important part of this effort. Our work was to educate people about the importance of marriage equality, build diverse coalitions in support, identify ally organizations and individuals willing to stand up for marriage equality, and to elevate all those voices to further shape public opinion. Each state presented its own set of possibilities and challenges, but in each case, there was some tension between the work that was happening around marriage and other LGBT and social justice issues that needed time and attention. After supporting efforts in California, New Mexico, New York, New Jersey (twice for two different lawsuits), Washington, Iowa, Illinois, Georgia, and other states, I was weary of the marriage equality machine we had created.

I firmly believed in the fundamental right for same-sex couples who wanted to, to be able to marry, and have been willing to fight for that right. My partner and I had gotten engaged after the New York victory and were finally getting around to planning our own nuptials. But I never got comfortable with the way marriage equality was often put forth as "the civil rights fight of our era." What does that exactly mean when so many gay, lesbian, bisexual, transgender, queer, black, brown, poor, and other marginalized people in this country are under attack and fighting for survival? How many more black men would need to be incarcerated or killed senselessly by police before their lives become a priority? When would there be a public outcry about the violence against transgender women of color?

The months, even years, leading up to our trip to the *Obergefell* decision had been a difficult time to be a black person in the United States. Rarely a week went by without hearing about another tragic death. Whether by neighborhood vigilantes and police using "fear of black bodies" as justification, or by "crazies" attacking innocent church-goers, one thing was clear. Black people were under siege, and no one in a position to do anything about it was talking about the real problems: racism and anti-blackness. Our family had been having hard conversations about fairness, trust, safety, and discrimination. Along with thousands of others, we had marched, cried, and demanded justice, but was anybody listening? Like Eric Garner who was strangled in a choke hold by a New York police officer, and so many others who look like me who had been struck down too young, I was finding it harder and harder to breathe.

Sometimes it felt that as I became more acceptable as a lesbian, my blackness made me more of a threat. Victories for marriage equality became more commonplace, while the fights for transgender rights and racial justice had faced incredible setbacks. As a "gay for pay," an LGBT person working for LGBT rights, I sometimes felt as if I was expected to either check my blackness at the door or use that blackness as a bridge to bring together communities that struggled to speak the same language: LGBT and racial justice movements; white queer liberals and people of color radicals. I was excited about the successes, but my heart was heavy about the general state of justice in my country. As the Supreme Court decision day grew closer, I was afraid that if there was a victory, my LGB sisters and brothers who had been fighting so long and hard for marriage equality would not be prepared to fight the harder fight. I wondered if we had truly gained more acceptance of all of the wonderful ways we are different, or merely convinced mainstream America that we only wanted to be just like them.

So, while I was excited and anxious about the big day, I was relieved to be in another part of the world: Kenya, with my partner and our daughter. Being in Africa for the first time, particularly during a time when it is so hard to feel safe as a person of color in the United States, I welcomed being among a country of black people. I felt free and comfortable in my blackness in a way that I never had before. The trade-off was that I wasn't completely free as a lesbian. Most people assumed my partner and I were sisters, and every encounter involved a mental assessment of whether we should come out. I relished the escape from U.S. racism, but I was still holding out for a society that would fully embrace and celebrate me for all of who I am as a black lesbian and so much more. And I was still willing to fight for that reality in the United States.

On Friday, June 26, while the world's eyes were on Washington, D.C., waiting to see if the Supreme Court would be writing another chapter in the U.S. history books, I was making my own personal history. Even though I was not physically with my colleagues, I was with them in spirit, awaiting the decision. Thanks to hotel Wi-Fi, we saw the first messages appear on Facebook and Twitter. "We Won!" The Supreme Court had affirmed the right of same-sex couples to marry. I watched my social media feeds scroll by with congratulations and celebrations from all over. Our Kenyan friends joined us for a quick toast poolside, and in that moment, I realized that this victory matters not just for the LGBT community at home, but for our allies and our LGBT brothers and sisters around the world. It makes a difference in real people's lives, and it can give us hope about our ability to create the kind of change we need for everyone.

But even while celebrating, I still have questions about how much this victory really represents a significant shift in our society toward more acceptance and justice. When I finally got the chance to delve more into the actual decision, I read these words:

> No union is more profound than marriage, for it embodies the highest ideals of love, fidelity, devotion, sacrifice, and family. . . . Marriage is essential to our most profound hopes and aspirations.

While many point to these phrases from Justice Kennedy's decision as proof that LGBT people in this country are finally, fully respected for who we are, they give me pause. By reinforcing the belief that marriage is the ultimate way two people can show their connection and devotion to each other or build and create a union and family, have we convinced the rest of our country to respect all LGBT people for who we are, or have we just allowed those who more neatly fit into society's mainstream norms admittance into that club, and in doing so, have we pushed those who don't conform further into the margins? While we were fighting for marriage rights, did our community do enough to demand respect for those who do not believe marriage is the "most essential" and "profound" union, those who may never find someone they want to share that kind of bond with, and those who choose to or must live their lives differently?

I hope that we can build on this victory to bring together more communities of people to fight for even more than equality. My vision of justice includes demanding respect and rights for same-sex parents and families *at the same time* as single-parent families; insisting that LGBT people have equal protections on the job *and* working for a living wage for all; ensuring that queer students are not bullied and have equal access to education, while creating a school system in which *all children* can receive a quality education where they are safe and respected; calling for safety in our communities *while also* demanding that black and brown people are not over-policed and incarcerated *and* ensuring police are held accountable for the violence they commit.

My thoughts and emotions about the *Obergefell* decision are complicated, even conflicted. I am equally proud that our community has achieved such an incredible victory in our nation's highest court, and I am disappointed that the LGBT community has not been willing to fight for equality and justice for our most marginalized members and for others who are oppressed by the same institutions and systems that still deny us our rights. While I can celebrate, I will not fully be satisfied by a victory that is based primarily on acknowledging the ways we are the same and not accepting, and demanding, respect for our differences. For me and many others, our differences based on race, gender, nationality, sex, and ability and other parts of our identities are what make us unique and special, and we will only have achieved real justice when all the different ways we are and choose to live are honored, valued, respected, and celebrated.

GENDER IDENTITY DEFINES SEX: UPDATING THE LAW TO REFLECT MODERN MEDICAL SCIENCE IS KEY TO TRANSGENDER RIGHTS

M. Dru Levasseur

M. Dru Levasseur is the Transgender Rights Project director at Lambda Legal.

"At twenty-three I decided to live my life as a woman, full-time, in every way. A lot of people ask me, 'What is it like?' That's like trying to ask me to describe air. It just is for me. I can't really describe it to you because for me, it just is. But without it, I'm not me."

—*Donisha McShan, Lambda Legal client*

In October 2013, Donisha McShan, an African American transgender woman, was paroled to a halfway house in Marion, Illinois, to complete a federal prison sentence and be treated for substance abuse. Upon arrival, she informed the facility that she is a transgender woman, but the facility insisted on assigning her to a room shared with four men in the male-only unit, rather than the available female or co-ed units. Staff insisted on addressing her with male pronouns despite her protest, and forbade her from bringing feminine items into the facility. They repeatedly searched her living area and confiscated items they considered LGBT-related or remotely feminine. A staff member told Ms. McShan, in front of other residents, that she was a man and threatened to send her back to prison if she did not comply and live as male.

Ms. McShan contacted Lambda Legal's National Legal Help Desk, and Lambda Legal submitted a demand letter to the facility, outlining its obligations under state and federal law. The facility immediately took steps to rectify the situation by apologizing to Ms. McShan, moving her out of the room with men, referring to her with appropriate pronouns, and returning her personal items to her.

In a video about her experience, she said:

> They took all of my makeup, my favorite clothes, jewelry, bangles, earrings, necklaces, they even took my shower cap because it was pink. But the worst thing they took was my right to be myself. To have an advocacy group not only say that Donisha is right, but to say we stand behind her—it made me feel like I'm finally being heard. It was like I have been living my life on mute, singing, screaming, and yelling and somebody finally pressed the mute button and someone heard me.

Ms. McShan's experience of being stripped of her dignity because individuals or state actors did not acknowledge or respect her gender identity is not uncommon; the experience she had of receiving an apology and validation is. At the root of the widespread discrimination, harassment, and violence—both systemic and individual—that transgender people face is a lack of understanding or affirmation that transgender people are who they say they are. Widespread misunderstanding continues to exist in spite of the recent increase in transgender visibility in the media.

Justice for transgender people is linked to the validation of self-identity—you are who you know yourself to be. The source of much transphobia is a "fear of difference": cisgender (non-transgender) people and bodies are the "norm" from which transgender people differ, and the notion that transgender people are fraudulently being individuals they "biologically" are not. Transgender people are viewed as violating a "natural" or inherent boundary of fixed, binary sex. This simplistic understanding of sex as two fixed binary categories is medically, scientifically, and factually inaccurate but still broadly enforced by courts. For transgender people to be recognized as full human beings under the law, the legal system must make room for the existence of transgender people—not as boundary-crossers, but as people claiming their birthright as part of a natural variation of human sexual development.

In my experience as a transgender civil rights litigator, I have witnessed the deep confusion that courts, the general public, and even the LGBT community itself has faced in understanding transgender people. Even as they make strides inside mainstream culture, transgender people remain "strangers to the law." A transgender person could take all medically indicated steps for transition to affirm one's true self—including living in accordance with one's gender identity in all areas of life—and take all legal steps available to have one's gender identity recognized by the state and federal government on identity documents, yet still face the "legal horror" of a court of law that refuses to acknowledge or validate who they are.

When seeking legal recognition in the courts, transgender people have been dehumanized, have had their core, intimate aspect of their selves legally erased and their bodies publicly dissected for purported function and appearance. Transgender people have been judged defiant and worthy of punishment, immoral, fraudulent, mentally ill, delusional, medically wrong, or imaginary or nonexistent. Behind the courts' inability to accept and validate transgender people as full human beings is the courts' failure to embrace the medical understanding of sex, which gives primacy to gender identity when weighing the factors of sex.

For transgender people to be treated equally before the law and in the eyes of society, courts must use the latest medical science of determining sex. Segregating so-called "real" or tangible sex characteristics using coded language such as "physical," "anatomical," "biological," or "genetic" from so-called "imaginary" or intangible or psychological characteristics like "gender identity" or "self-identity" reflects a fundamental misunderstanding of sex. The etiology of sex reveals that it is a multi-faceted determination. There are unlimited ambiguities that may occur within each of the elements that comprise one's sex, such as chromosomal sex, gonadal sex, internal and external morphologic sex, hormonal sex, and gender identity and role. For most people, these factors are congruent. For transgender and intersex people, one or more of these categories vary. When any of these conflict, medical science places gender identity as the most important determinative component.

Understanding the importance of self-identity provides an avenue to liberation. Such framing provides necessary context to arguments for heightened scrutiny under the Constitution, shifting the concept of expressing oneself by choice to aligning oneself with a core, immutable trait.

While the range of cisgender bodies may be considered the most common bodies, they are not the only bodies, and certainly not the only bodies entitled to protection or respect under the law. At the moment, the U.S. legal system still requires everyone to fit into a binary category of male or female to enjoy the full rights and privileges of personhood under the law. There is actually no requirement that bodies look or function a certain way to be recognized as male or female—to qualify as "normal" or "enough." If that were the case, many cisgender people might fall outside of the categories due to say, size of breasts or size of penis. There must be room for the range of human variation that exists. Courts must refrain from privileging certain bodies over others by enforcing a cisgender standard as a "norm."

Transgender people deserve to have their identities affirmed by the law. They deserve to have their privacy respected, not their bodies dissected. While the general public may have miles to go in understanding the etiology of sex, the range of variations of each of the factors that comprise a determination of sex, how common variation is, and why gender identity is considered the core determinant of sex, courts must arrive there now. Courts do not have the leisure to rely on popular opinion of what constitutes sex and continue to ignore medical reality. The lives of many people, transgender and intersex, are at stake.

FROM LAVENDER SCARE TO RAINBOW HOUSE: THE ONGOING FIGHT FOR FULL FEDERAL EQUALITY

GAUTAM RAGHAVAN

Gautam Raghavan is vice president of Policy for the Gill Foundation; from 2011 to 2014, he served as President Obama's liaison to the LGBT community.

When President Barack Obama took office on January 20, 2009, no one—from activists to the president himself—could have predicted that advancing equality for the LGBT community would be one of his hallmark achievements and a defining element of his legacy. But two terms later, this fact is irrefutable: Barack Obama will forever be known as the U.S. president who championed LGBT equality.

We have come a long way. Sixty years ago, as the Cold War raged, the U.S. government engaged in an intentional and ruthless campaign—the "lavender scare"—to track down and fire gay federal employees. Thirty years ago, as tens of thousands died from AIDS, the Reagan Administration ignored the epidemic. Just over ten years ago, on the heels of the historic *Goodridge* decision that brought marriage equality to Massachusetts, President George W. Bush and Karl Rove tried to legislate against equality, using committed relationships and loving families as a wedge to divide the country and mobilize their base.

Given this history, it's not surprising that LGBT folks approached the Obama Administration with little trust and some apprehension. Then things started to happen. Congress passed and the president signed into law the repeal of "Don't Ask, Don't Tell" and a hate crimes statute bearing Matthew Shepard's name.

Federal agencies, led by strong allies in the President's Cabinet, took action to address LGBT discrimination in housing, health care, schools, and the armed forces. The president launched a National HIV/AIDS Strategy, issued a presidential memorandum on global LGBT human rights, signed an Executive Order prohibiting LGBT discrimination by federal contractors, and condemned the vile practice of conversion therapy. He began—and completed—his evolution on marriage, ultimately with the full backing of the Justice Department. And he used the power of symbols—the North Portico lit up in rainbows—and words—"Seneca Falls, Selma, and Stonewall"—to remind LGBT Americans that our stories are inextricably linked to the story of America.

President Obama's record on LGBT equality is unparalleled. It will be difficult for a future president to do more or better—but I sure hope she or he will try.

While we've seen significant change, there is so much more work to do. We must ensure that the federal government fully treats LGBT people, families, and communities with respect, dignity, and equality.

Most importantly, we need a comprehensive federal bill that explicitly protects LGBT people in employment, housing, and public accommodations. After decades of half-measures, such legislation has finally been introduced. Congress should pass this bill, and the president should sign it into law.

That said, we do not need to wait for a new law to extend sorely needed protections to LGBT individuals. Wherever possible, existing statutes prohibiting discrimination based on sex should be interpreted correctly and appropriately to include discrimination based on sexual orientation and gender identity. Several lower courts and federal agencies have already adopted this approach, and that work must continue, particularly in the absence of explicit federal protections.

The words "data collection" may make your eyes glaze over, but the fact is that we don't count unless we are counted. It is critically important that federal surveys—from the U.S. Census to agency-specific surveys on issues such as health, employment, and violence—fully include LGBT people and families. Until we have the information we need to paint a full picture of the lived experiences of LGBT people, we will be unable to take long-term action to meaningfully address the needs of our communities.

To be clear: federal data collection isn't about running regressions; it's about money. The philanthropic dollars that flow to LGBT causes today are a drop in the bucket compared to the vast federal funding opportunities that are open to other communities who have compelling evidence to back up their case. Without data, advocates are hamstrung in their ability to secure federal funding. For example, community health organizations focused on serving the LGBT community are unable to access federal grants and other federal funding streams due to a lack of sufficient data on the health disparities that impact their constituents, particularly those with low incomes. Members of the LGBT community need and deserve equal access to these funding streams.

At the same time, it's incumbent on us to advocate for a policy agenda that accurately reflects the needs of LGBT people across the country, particularly the most marginalized and vulnerable in our community: our young and elderly, transgender individuals, and people living with HIV/AIDS. Too often, we fall into a trap of narrowly defining our movement's interests. But in fact, the diversity of our community demands we show up for policy conversations on poverty and economic security, racial justice, affordable and medically necessary health care, decriminalizing HIV and expanding Medicaid, comprehensive immigration reform, policing and the criminal justice system, dignity and safety in aging, and voting rights.

In recent years, LGBT folks in America have become increasingly attuned to the dire situation faced by too many of our brothers and sisters around the world. The Obama Administration has taken a number of important first steps to contribute to the global conversation about equality. Whether through behind-the-scenes diplomacy or explicit conversations about foreign and military aid, that work must continue.

We have come a long way, and I am hopeful that the LGBT community will continue to be treated by the federal government like a partner, not as a political pawn or liability. The next president of the United States, regardless of partisan affiliation, should do what is required of the highest office in the land: to serve *all* the American people. I am optimistic that other executives—from governors to mayors—will follow suit and use their authority and bully pulpit to advocate for equal treatment.

But we cannot take anything for granted. We must be ready to protect the gains we've made, while employing new bold, creative tactics to fight for full federal equality. Yes, we need fierce activists who will employ direct action to call for big, sweeping change; but we also need savvy advocates who understand and can skillfully navigate the federal system. We need brave political leadership from the top, but we also need openly LGBT public servants and allies at every level of government. And we need sustained support by funders, ongoing mobilization by grassroots activists, and creative coalition building with unlikely allies from conservatives to chambers of commerce.

If we've learned anything from the movements for civil rights and social justice that came before us, it's that change—*even* change we can believe in—can be undone or rolled back. As we close out the most historic presidential administration on LGBT equality (thus far!), we should certainly celebrate our progress and recognize the leadership and strategies that got us here. But let's also pair hopeful hearts with cautious minds to continue our fight for the respect, dignity, and equality we have long been denied.

FIGHTING FOR AN AIDS-FREE GENERATION

Scott A. Schoettes

⸺ ⸢⸣ ⸺

Scott A. Schoettes is HIV Project director at Lambda Legal.

Some LGBT organizations remained focused on HIV as an important issue for the LGBT community even after combination therapies made it possible to turn it into a chronic, manageable condition in the mid-1990s; but HIV and AIDS have been largely eclipsed and overshadowed by the fight for marriage equality. The intense focus on marriage equality is certainly not the only reason HIV slipped off of our collective radar. A number of LGBTQ activists engaged in activism supporting racial justice have asked meaningfully if "black lives matter" to the LGBT community. Regardless of the various reasons the issues of HIV and AIDS have taken a backseat, it is well past time to retrain our focus on the foremost health issue affecting our community.

In the United States, the HIV/AIDS epidemic rages on. It is still largely a "gay disease"—and a bisexual disease, and a transgender disease. Sixty-five percent of the approximately fifty thousand new HIV infections every year are among gay and bisexual men, resulting in prevalence of about 20 percent within this group. Of particular concern are the rates of new infections among young gay and bisexual men of color—with black men between the ages of thirteen and twenty-four being the hardest hit. The numbers for transgender women are even more depressing, with prevalence estimated at 28 percent—and as high as

48 percent for black transgender women. While HIV has never been just a gay, bisexual, and transgender disease, the fact that nearly 70 percent of HIV diagnoses in the United States are within 4 percent of the population justifies its placement among the top priorities of the LGBT community.[1]

The question with respect to HIV is not so much "What's next?" as "Why haven't we already won?" Since the mid-1990s, we have had the medical biotechnology not only to restore people to relative health and extend life expectancy to near normal, but also to render a person with HIV non-infectious *and* to give HIV-negative individuals the option of medication that will prevent transmission in the event of exposure. In other words, we have a functional cure and a functional vaccine, so why aren't we approaching the "end of AIDS" in the United States?

While achieving that goal may seem a simple matter of resources, it will in fact take much more. We cannot forget that we are addressing what is primarily a sexually transmitted disease that first arose within—and continues to most dramatically impact—the GBT community and people who inject drugs. Initially shrouded by ignorance and legitimate fear of contagion, over time the epidemic has revealed additional intersections with race, poverty, gender, sex work, immigration status, and partisan politics over access to health care. While resources are important, they alone will not be sufficient to untangle the complicated knot that is HIV / AIDS in this country.

As a result of significant investments, medical science developed pharmaceuticals that are able to halt the inevitable progression toward death that once defined HIV / AIDS. Today, it is estimated that a twenty-year-old gay male in the United States who is diagnosed in a timely manner and provided with meaningful access to care and treatment has a life expectancy that is essentially the same as that of an HIV-negative twenty-year-old male.

Perhaps more important from a public health perspective, the same treatment that dramatically improves the health outcomes of a person living with HIV also reduces the possibility of onward transmission to near zero.[2] Several years ago, researchers learned that placing an HIV-negative person on two of the antiretrovirals used to treat HIV-positive people dramatically reduces the possibility of acquiring HIV. When these medications, known as pre-exposure prophylaxis or "PrEP," are taken consistently, they are nearly 100 percent effective at preventing HIV transmission. Scientists are not finished; they continue to work on additional and improved medications and prevention technologies, as well as an actual vaccine and cure.

Sadly, we are not even close to maximizing the benefits of these medical advances. Of the nearly 1.2 million people living with HIV in this country, only about 87 percent are aware of their status. There is a similar drop in the percentage of people with a diagnosis who are linked to care, another drop to those retained in care, another drop to those who are prescribed the medications—and at the end of this "continuum of care," or lack of access to it, only 30 percent of the people living with HIV achieve a suppressed viral load. This is an appallingly low figure for a resource-rich country, a damning indictment of the health care system in the United States. These numbers are even more disturbing when we take into account transmissions that are more likely because people are unaware of their status, or the impact on communities at highest risk, which are not reaping the full benefits of "treatment as prevention" or of PrEP.

What do we need to change these outcomes? In broad terms, the solution is twofold: 1) full and equal access to care; and 2) freedom from stigma and discrimination.

We have made progress on the first of those two fronts, but much remains to be accomplished. The Affordable Care Act has transformed the landscape of health care for people and communities most affected by HIV. However, the refusal to expand Medicaid in many states—particularly across the South, which is now the hardest hit in terms of new infections and poor health outcomes—will severely compromise promised improvements in HIV-related health. A significant number of people with HIV live below the poverty level, and a health care system that does not include them is never going to move us toward an AIDS-free generation. Furthermore, undocumented individuals are not eligible for Medicaid or the subsidies that make health insurance affordable. If we are serious about halting the epidemic, we must ensure that *everyone* living in this country has access to care.

We also must ensure that the health care provided through the ACA is both high quality and affordable. The United States retains a capitalistic health care system; insurance plans are incentivized to cut corners and to avoid insuring people with chronic health conditions through discriminatory benefit designs and marketing practices. We must use all of the tools at our disposal—including litigation, regulation, the media, consumer advocacy, and sometimes loud and angry protest—to ensure that people in communities affected by HIV are being treated fairly and given high quality care at a price they can afford. This includes not just people living with HIV but also people at high risk. If we are not making PrEP available to everyone who needs it, then we are not reaping the full benefit of this highly effective prevention method.

Universal access to health care means nothing if people are unwilling to utilize it—this is why the other major focus must be on reducing stigma. We have had a very accurate HIV test for thirty years, yet approximately 13 percent of people living with HIV in this country are undiagnosed. Of those who are diagnosed, less than half are engaged in care. Stigma is the greatest barrier to learning one's status and engaging in care; and not just HIV-related stigma, but also stigma associated with being gay or bisexual or transgender or engaging in sex work or using injection drugs or just being sexually active—all of the identities and activities correlated with a higher risk of transmission. If we are not addressing stigma at all of these levels, then we are not going to get people engaged in the care they need.

Unlike on the medical side, there is no "magic bullet"—no pill we can give people to eliminate stigma. It is a battle that must be fought on many fronts simultaneously, and with some degree of fervor, if we are to have any real shot at triumphing. Our state governments must stop using the criminal justice system to address a public health issue. Propped up by misperceptions, ignorance, denial, and fear, HIV criminalization laws serve only to exacerbate HIV-related stigma. The U.S. military—the biggest employer in the country—must reform its recruitment, enlistment, retention, and disciplinary policies to reflect the current medical understanding of HIV. There is not a single occupation—including doctor or soldier—that a person living with HIV cannot safely perform, and it is past time the federal government made that crystal clear. And we must convince the public health establishment that it cannot have it both ways when talking about HIV. Instead of fear-based policies and prevention messages, public health must adopt a sex-positive approach that includes stigma reduction strategies and helps to bring people living with HIV back into the mainstream of our communities.

I hope I am proven wrong, but I don't think HIV is going away any time soon. Since it appears it is going to be with us—and centered within GBT communities—for quite some time, let us take a lead role in advancing sensible health care related policies and in eliminating the stigma that has always swirled around this disease. As it once united our community, let fighting the HIV/AIDS epidemic solidify our alliances across the many communities affected—and together, let us achieve an AIDS-free generation.

A RETURN TO THE ROOT

———— ∞∞∞ ————

Andrea J. Ritchie is a Senior Soros Justice Fellow and co-author of Say Her Name: Resisting Police Brutality Against Black Women *and* Queer (In) Justice: The Criminalization of LGBT People in the United States.

Resistance to police harassment, profiling, brutality, and criminalization of LGBTQ people has been at the root of LGBTQ movements since long before Stonewall. While most mainstream LGBTQ organizations have focused a great deal of their efforts over the past quarter century on securing marriage equality, many grassroots LGBTQ groups—particularly those made up of and working with youth, queer, and transgender people of color, homeless and low-income people, and LGBTQ people in the sex trades—have continued to center organizing against police violence and criminalization, before and during the Stonewall uprising through the post-Ferguson rebellion.

The criminal legal system continues to be a site of ongoing, widespread, and often hidden discrimination and violence, both explicit and implicit, against LGBTQ people of color and low-income people. Indeed, it serves as a primary vehicle for ongoing denial of the "marks of citizenship," such as parental rights, and freedom from discrimination in housing and employment, won in recent years for LGBTQ people. As such, it remains a primary front in the struggle for queer liberation.

In fact, achievement of legal equality can bring into sharper relief ongoing discrimination at the hands of police. A transgender woman of color who consulted me about a strip search she had been subjected to by NYPD officers re-peatedly pointed out that she had been with her husband—her "for real," legal husband—at the time of the arrest which preceded the search. She even pulled out her marriage license to show me during the consultation. Her frustration at the disjuncture between the recognition of her relationship by the state and the violation she continued to experience in the criminal legal system was both pal-pable and poignant.

Lambda Legal's 2014 study *Protected and Served?* found that three-quarters of LGBTQ people and people living with HIV (PLWH) surveyed had face-to-face contact with police during the preceding five years.[1] Given ongoing patterns of enforcement and punishment driving mass incarceration of Black, Latinx (a non-gendered term in increasing use),[2] and Indigenous people in the United States, it is not surprising that the survey found contact with police to be highly concentrated among LGBTQ people and PLWH of color.

A quarter of respondents in the Lambda Legal study who had contact with police reported at least one type of misconduct or harassment, including pro-filing, false arrests, verbal or physical assault, or sexual harassment or assault. Transgender people and LGBTQ people of color, youth, and low-income people were much more likely to report at least one type of police misconduct.[3] Ad-ditionally, LGBTQ people of color respondents were five times more likely to be asked about their immigration status by law enforcement than white respon-dents.[4] These findings are consistent with research by academics,[5] anti-violence advocates,[6] policy organizations,[7] and grassroots groups,[8] and with investiga-tions of local police departments by the U.S. Department of Justice.[9]

Police targeting of people and communities branded as sexually and gender-nonconforming preceded, continued to operate alongside, and extends beyond the existence of laws explicitly targeting "sodomy," "deviate sexual conduct," and "crimes against nature."[10] Targeted raids of LGBTQ establishments, po-licing of queer sex in public and private spaces, profiling, false arrests, and dis-criminatory enforcement of prostitution laws and sexual offenses continue. So do demands for a "real" ID or name during stops of transgender and gender-nonconforming people, pervasive misgendering, homophobic and transphobic slurs, illegal and degrading searches conducted to assign gender based on anat-omy, arrests for using bathrooms and sex-segregated facilities consistent with gender identity. And so do sexual harassment, extortion, assault, and violence against LGBTQ people in police custody.

Legal challenges to discriminatory enforcement practices have been somewhat successful in limiting the impacts on white and affluent LGBTQ people. Law en-forcement agencies, however, have simply concentrated their focus on LGBTQ people of color and low-income people. And while *Lawrence v. Texas* struck down anti-sodomy laws, policing of public and commercial sex, where police discrimination and abuse against queers is pervasive, was explicitly side-stepped by privacy-based legal arguments and the Court's opinion. As arguments in favor of marriage equality narrowed discourse around the rights and dignity of LGBTQ people to state sanction of monogamous, private, non-commercial intimacy among adults, queers engaged in other sexual activity were too often left to face police harassment and abuse with impunity.

Post *Lawrence*, LGBTQ people continue to be criminalized for engaging in sex deemed "deviant" by virtue of being queer, commercial, or both. Prostitution laws consistently have been used as weapons of policing queer sex—as historian Joan Nestle wrote, "when the raids were on, prostitute or queer made no difference." Just months after the marriage equality decision, federal prosecutors and the Department of Homeland Security raided the headquarters of Rentboy.com and arrested many of its employees. Detailing at length the decidedly non-marital, non-heterosexual, and presumably non-desirable sexual practices they believed the website promoted, police and prosecutors offered no explanation for targeting a gay business that had operated openly for eighteen years beyond the fact that the site shamelessly promoted sex that was both queer and, in some instances, compensated. Perhaps now that the courts have decided one type of gay sex—private, in the context of monogamous, long-standing relationships based on love—is acceptable, they were emboldened to bring the hammer down on *this* type of gay sex—anonymous, non-monogamous, publicly and graphically described gay sex based on lust or money rather than love.

The tools of police harassment and criminalization of LGBTQ people are not limited to laws regulating sexual conduct. LGBTQ people continue to be disproportionately stopped, harassed, and ticketed under the "broken windows" policing paradigm, in which "quality of life" laws are discriminatorily enforced against people of color, homeless, and low-income people. A 2010 Queers for Economic Justice survey found that almost half of homeless and low-income LGBTQ people surveyed in New York City had been stopped, told to "move on," ticketed, or arrested. Almost 30 percent had been strip-searched; almost 20 percent physically and sexually assaulted. Rates of ticketing and arrest were as high as 62 percent among respondents who were currently or formerly homeless, and 70 percent among respondents who were transgender or Two Spirit.[11]

Laws that facilitate routine criminalization of LGBTQ people are not as easily pinpointed or challenged as sodomy laws or those denying marriage equality. Yet they are no less pernicious. Police officers make and enforce invidious classifications deeply rooted in homophobia and transphobia as well as racialized, gendered, transphobic, and heteronormative understandings of acceptable behavior and expression. The effects of unfettered discrimination and abuse of LGBTQ people in the criminal legal system are as profound and widespread as any denial of a marriage license.[12]

Over the past twenty-five years, grassroots groups like the Audre Lorde Project, FIERCE, Community United Against Violence, Queer to the Left, and the Transgender Law Center have challenged police brutality against people of color from New York City to Chicago to San Francisco—with far fewer resources than those devoted to the fight for marriage equality. Over thirty local and national organizations came together as the Get Yr Rights! network, launched by Streetwise and Safe (SAS) and BreakOUT! in 2014, to share resources, strategies, and support for local campaigns challenging policing and criminalization of LGBTQ people.

Thanks to these efforts, this is a time of unprecedented attention to LGBTQ experiences of policing. Amnesty International's groundbreaking 2005 report, *Stonewalled: Police Abuse and Misconduct Against LGBT People in the United States*, drew on the expertise of groups on the ground to document ongoing patterns of police profiling and violence against LGBTQ people across the country. Since 2011, the U.S. Department of Justice has recognized discriminatory policing of LGBTQ people in New Orleans and a growing number of jurisdictions.[13] New York City's recent campaign against the NYPD's discriminatory use of stop and frisk successfully highlighted experiences of LGBTQ youth and people of color, and resulted in passage, on the same day the *Windsor* decision was announced, of historic legislation creating the first enforceable ban on police profiling based on gender, gender identity, and sexual orientation, alongside race, religion, and other characteristics. Powerful personal testimony and leadership of queer youth and people of color, supported by a growing number of mainstream LGBTQ organizations, has ensured attention to these issues by legislators and policy makers on a local and national scale.

At the beginning of President Obama's second term, a group of advocates—including myself as coordinator of Streetwise and Safe (SAS); Urvashi Vaid, former policy director at the National LGBTQ Task Force; Dean Spade, founder of the Sylvia Rivera Law Project; former Lambda Legal attorney Catherine Hanssens, now director of the Center for HIV Law and Policy; and Aisha Moodie Mills, then of the Center for American Progress—convened a group of fifty LGBTQ, criminal justice, police accountability, and racial justice organizations to create a national criminal justice policy agenda that is both LGBTQ-specific and inclusive. The resulting federal LGBTQ Criminal Justice Working Group is working to advance *A Roadmap for Change: Federal Policy Recommendations to Address the Criminalization of LGBT People and People Living with HIV*.

Sustained advocacy by members of the Working Group led the Department of Justice to issue updated guidance for federal agents, and legislators to introduce an expanded version of the federal End Racial Profiling Act, both of which ban profiling based on sexual orientation, gender, and gender identity alongside race, religion, and other factors. In May 2015, the President's Task Force on 21st Century Policing released a report containing recommendations explicitly addressing the experiences of LGBTQ people and communities.

Intervention and ongoing engagement of grassroots groups has ensured that this work is accountable to LGBTQ groups who have focused on criminal justice issues, and to LGBTQ individuals directly affected by policing and punishment. As the original warriors at Stonewall were, we continue to be inspired by broader liberation movements challenging anti-Black racism and police violence.

Still, we are a long way from widespread understanding and adoption of policy responses that address the multiple ways in which LGBTQ people—and particularly LGBTQ people of color and transgender people—continue to be discriminated against, policed, and punished by the criminal legal system. The true challenge is to not just achieve cosmetic reform. We must secure changes that fundamentally eliminate the power of the criminal legal system to use race- and poverty-based policing practices to punish sexual and gender-nonconformity.

A radical reimagining of society and our approaches to violence and safety is necessary. The criminal legal system has failed to protect the lives of dozens of transgender women of color murdered in the past two years; of thousands of victims of hate crimes; and of Jihad Akbar, Marc Kajcs, Janisha Fonville, Mya Hall, Michelle Cusseaux, Jessie Hernandez, Kayla Moore—to name just a few LGBTQ people killed by police. As we celebrate victories, we must take responsibility for the empty promises of safety through the criminal legal system for transgender, gender-nonconforming, and queer people of color lost to brutal community, interpersonal, and state violence.

Long after wedding bells have rung, LGBTQ people will continue to face devastating discrimination and violence in the criminal legal system. Now is the time for the mainstream LGBTQ movement to fully invest in striking at one of the strongest roots of ongoing institutional and structural discrimination faced by LGBTQ people of color and low-income LGBTQ people. The struggle for LGBTQ liberation is not only for the right to love—in whatever way we choose—but also for the right to live, free of chains.

SHIELDS NOT INTO SWORDS: STOPPING THE MISUSE OF RELIGIOUS FREEDOM FOR DISCRIMINATION

JENNIFER C. PIZER

—⚬⚬⚬—

Jennifer C. Pizer is senior counsel and Law and Policy Project director at Lambda Legal.

Mike Pence deflected again. "There's been an avalanche of intolerance," he proclaimed. "It's a red herring. Just outrageous!"[1]

"Governor, it's a yes-or-no question. Will this law do as some of your supporters have said, and protect those who discriminate against gay couples?"

It was Sunday morning, March 29, 2015. Hosting *This Week* on ABC, George Stephanopoulos was determined.

"Does this mean it's now legal in Indiana for Christians to discriminate against gays and lesbians?"

Governor Mike Pence stuck to his talking point: Indiana's new Religious Freedom Restoration Act ("RFRA") was only for protecting Hoosiers from government overreach. The would-be Republican presidential nominee said he was proud he had signed the bill and was simply looking out for those who believe government is "impinging on their religious freedom." He demanded, "Isn't tolerance a two-way street?"

Stephanopoulos tried again. "Your supporters say it will protect discrimination. True or not?" Pence never answered, instead repeating that Bill Clinton had signed the original federal RFRA bill in 1993 and that Barack Obama had signed a similar bill when in the Illinois Senate. Stephanopoulos pushed back that Illinois has a civil rights law protecting gay people, unlike Indiana. He asked, "Will you push to add sexual orientation as a protected class?"

Pence was firm: "No. That is not part of my agenda."

Stephanopoulos pushed further: "What about this proposal from the Lambda Legal Defense Fund?" The screen then showed the language I had sent out the day before. The text had been tweeted and re-tweeted, posted and linked, and I had explained it to dozens of reporters during the weekend.

Squirming, Pence insisted, "We're not going to change this law."

Stephanopoulos tried a final time: "Yes or no? Do you think it should be legal to discriminate against gays or lesbians?"

Pence refused to answer, saying instead, "I stand by this law." With that inept, defensive tone, Indiana's governor effectively ended his presidential bid before launching it. He also showed why we had been sounding alarms about the bill since January.

I had been working with partners and colleagues for months, detailing why this type of RFRA legislation threatens everyone's basic rights, specifically including LGBT people. I had walked a stream of reporters through the Supreme Court's June 2014 *Hobby Lobby* decision, its radical reshaping of religious free exercise doctrine,[2] and the potential implications for LGBT people and women's reproductive health. Justice Alito's majority opinion had transformed the federal RFRA from a shield for minority faith practices into a potential sword for imposing religious beliefs and practices to others' detriment. As Justice Ginsburg's dissent made clear, it's not Bill Clinton's RFRA anymore. And, the sponsors of the Indiana RFRA had modeled SB 101 on *Hobby Lobby*'s assumptions while voicing their explicit anti-LGBT goals.

The new Indiana law had been designed to ensure that businesses could turn away same-sex couples. So, our proposal was simple:

> . . . add this to the new law: "This chapter does not establish or eliminate a defense to a claim under any federal, state, or local law protecting civil rights or preventing discrimination."

As the pace of our marriage wins accelerated in 2013 and 2014, so did our opponents' determination to secure religion-based rights to thwart our inclusion. In 2013, there were eight bills in state legislatures to create or expand religious rights to defy non-discrimination laws. Intense coalition efforts stopped six of them, but not the expanded RFRA bills in Kansas and Kentucky. In 2014, the number of bills surged to at least fifteen; we stopped fourteen, including Arizona's notorious SB 1062, but not the one in Mississippi. And in the spring of 2015, with the Supreme Court widely expected to make marriage equality the law of the land by July, the surge became a deluge, with at least eighty bills introduced in roughly half the states to expand religious rights or otherwise to facilitate discrimination against LGBT people. These included: (1) RFRAs with varied particulars; (2) rights to refuse marriage-related services, child welfare services, and health services; (3) rights for public school student groups to discriminate; (4) rights to receive public funding despite discriminating; and (5) preemption of local civil rights laws. And in state after state, bill sponsors' rhetoric made unmistakable the disdain for gay people that still permeated much of the country despite majoritarian support for marriage equality. These bills have been overt, preemptive attempts to secure rights to discriminate against same-sex couples, usually before adoption of basic non-discrimination protections for LGBT people. In 2015, eight such bills became law.

Indiana became 2015's highest profile state-legislative battleground for multiple reasons. First, Indianapolis hosts numerous major businesses with reputations for valuing diversity and having dynamic, forward-looking corporate cultures. Attentive business leaders in the state recognized the potential for a policy nightmare like the one that had erupted in Arizona the year before. Meanwhile, some members of the Indiana legislature remained furious at having failed to advance a state-constitutional marriage ban the year before. Our community's string of federal court marriage victories had followed. Angry legislators had promised passage of a RFRA as payback. And then there was the Final Four. The college basketball national championship, about to be played in Indianapolis, had the same effect as the Super Bowl had in Arizona the year before, riveting national attention and inviting protests and boycotts with the potential to inflict both economic and reputational damage on the state. The mix of sincerely held values and financial stakes created powerful motivation for business leaders to challenge Indiana's legislature as it had done in Phoenix.

Knowing that introduction of the RFRA bill was likely, Lambda Legal's Midwest Regional Director Jim Bennett had been preparing for the fight. In late 2014, he and our volunteer leaders in Indiana already were working overtime to engage civic and corporate leaders to speak out against this effort to use religion for antigay political goals. They connected with staunch supporters of the LGBT community at Cummins, Eli Lilly, and other major companies with bases in Indianapolis who had been instrumental in opposing the constitutional amendment. Most of them remained determined that Indiana not send a message and find itself paying the prices that Arizona has paid for its anti-LGBT and anti-immigrant policies.[3]

The Freedom Indiana campaign brought together resources and the passion of local volunteers, staff of national and local groups, and business leaders in a bipartisan effort that reflected public opinion. The coalition was led by the

ACLU of Indiana, with significant staff and financial investment from the Human Rights Campaign, Lambda Legal, and other advocacy groups, including
the American Unity Fund, a young organization of Republicans working for
LGBT equality. The campaign required a mix of principle and pragmatism, focused on the fact that many Republican legislators for years have embraced anti-
LGBT views reflexively, deferring routinely to ultra-conservative Christian
advocacy groups seen as having political power. Accordingly, Freedom Indiana
brought together progressive groups accustomed to opening eyes to the harms
of anti-LGBT discrimination and some who work with Republican elected officials. As we have been doing from our movement's earliest days, the goal was to
persuade people from all walks of life to reexamine their assumptions about gay
and transgender people, and about what religious liberty really means.

Two years prior, we had done well in a similar fight in Illinois. There, our
marriage bill was enacted by the state legislature, but not without a struggle
to limit damaging religious exemptions. The Illinois Catholic Conference had
made stopping the bill a priority. When it gained traction despite the bishops'
opposition, their demand became religious exemptions from the state's non-
discrimination and other laws. Jim Bennett, Lambda Legal attorneys Camilla
Taylor and Chris Clark, and I spent endless hours during the 2013 session doing
bill-language fire drills—emergency conference calls, overnight written analyses, and sprints to Springfield to testify—to explain the harmful consequences
of proposals from the Conference's lawyers. In the end, there was agreement
on a narrow "parish hall" exemption that accommodated the Church's central
concern while protecting those who receive social or medical services at religiously affiliated institutions. Our opponents deemed the law "the worst in the
country."[4]

The following year, our legal team had their hands full in Indiana, winning
the *Baskin v. Bogan* marriage case (see page 235 Castillo), then working with
Freedom Indiana to defeat attempts to amend the state Constitution. The fight
against the RFRA presented new challenges, however. The legal standards
can be confusing, especially because *Hobby Lobby* changed them in ambigu-
ous ways. We had to get legislators and other opinion leaders to recognize how
these RFRA rights likely would be used. One way to reveal threats is to propose
amendments that would negate specified harms and seek votes on them. Just as
Stephanopoulos' questions eventually unmasked Pence, we needed simple, clear
proposals on which House members would vote.

Camilla and I put heads together with the bipartisan national team of our
LGBT legal colleagues.[5] We developed a series of amendments that could lessen
the RFRA's potential to harm others. These included disallowing use of the religious rights (i) to excuse sexual or other abuse of a child; (ii) to authorize public

employees to refuse to perform their duties; (iii) to justify practices inconsistent with the standards of care or service applicable to licensed professionals; or (iv) to defend violation of a civil rights law.

While we crafted bill text, our engagement with business allies started paying off with top tech leaders speaking out first. Salesforce.com CEO Scott McCorkle sent a letter to Indiana lawmakers saying that the RFRA was discriminatory and must be opposed. Apple's openly gay CEO Tim Cook did an opinion piece in the *Washington Post* the Sunday before the House committee vote, calling for rejection of SB 101 and similar bills:

> There's something very dangerous happening in states across the country. A wave of legislation, introduced in more than two dozen states, would allow people to discriminate against their neighbors. . . . This isn't a political issue. It isn't a religious issue. This is about how we treat each other as human beings. Opposing discrimination takes courage. With the lives and dignity of so many people at stake, it's time for all of us to be courageous. [6]

To help House members understand the human impact of this discrimination, we asked one of our Indiana marriage plaintiffs, Amy Sandler, if she felt up to testifying. Our Indiana case had revolved in significant part around the additional hardships Amy and her wife, Niki Quasney, and their young children had faced the year before due to their family's uncertain legal status while Niki battled ovarian cancer (see page 244 Sandler; Castillo). Amy prepared her testimony about the stresses and heartache of discrimination while Niki was dying. She also explained how the religious rights to be expanded by the RFRA could be used against her nieces who likely would need hormonal birth control medication to reduce their own risk of the cancer that had taken Niki's life less than two months before. During the hearing, Amy's voice conveyed fresh grief and determination; she asked these legislators to consider how legal vulnerability had increased their family's pain. It was a wrenching account. Yet, when the House members considered each of our amendments in turn, they refused each one, and then approved the bill.[7] The House as a body passed it soon thereafter.

Governor Pence signed the bill in a private ceremony surrounded by ultra-conservative clergy and political leaders known for pushing extreme anti-LGBT proposals. They included Curt Smith of the Indiana Family Institute, who had helped write the bill (and has compared homosexuality to bestiality). All were smilingly captured by an official photographer; Pence's team apparently thought the image would aid his future campaign. It certainly undermined his later claims of moderate intentions.

The outcry grew. Bill Oesterle, former CEO of Angie's List, announced that the company was cancelling its plan for an office in Indianapolis. More corporate leaders with strong Indiana presence added their voices, including representatives of Gen Con (a $50 million annual gaming convention), Fortune 500-member Cummins, Eskenazi Health, Dow Agrosciences, Eli Lilly, and Roche Diagnostics. And more than three dozen tech company leaders came out against the RFRA in an open letter emphasizing that:

> No person should have to fear losing their job or be denied service or housing because of who they are or whom they love. . . . To ensure no one faces discrimination and ensure everyone preserves their right to live out their faith, we call on all legislatures to add sexual orientation and gender identity as protected classes to their civil rights laws and to explicitly forbid discrimination or denial of services to anyone.[8]

With the Final Four playoff games approaching, openly gay athletes Jason Collins and Greg Louganis joined the calls for a national boycott of the big events. The coaches of the four contending teams issued an unprecedented, joint statement condemning anti-LGBT discrimination.[9] Multiple states announced plans to forbid discretionary travel to Indiana. Local business leaders began insisting that their legislators "fix it."

We and our colleagues in Freedom Indiana insisted that more was needed than an amendment to prevent the new religious rights from being used for antigay discrimination. Because Indiana did not have state-level civil rights protections for LGBT people, those protections needed to be enacted along with amendments to limit how the new religious rights could be used to harm others. Following a whirlwind of drafting, conference calls, and public education, we offered a simple amendment to Indiana's civil rights laws to prevent discrimination based on sexual orientation or gender identity. It added one affirmative equal rights sentence to our prior amendment blocking use of RFRA-based rights to avoid non-discrimination rules.

Republican legislators were devising a less protective amendment. It added a civil rights carve out and exempted religious organizations; it also avoided thwarting of local non-discrimination ordinances, such as the one in Indianapolis. Our efforts to add state-level civil rights protections for LGBT people were rebuffed. So, too, were our intense efforts to get amendment language to prevent use of religious rights to harm others, such as by blocking access to reproductive or sexual health care, HIV-related care, or gender-confirmation care.

Looking ahead, the ongoing challenge is to educate the public and lawmakers about how RFRAs threaten basic rights and equality. For example, even when civil rights laws are "carved out," those laws sometimes are not seen to apply when goods or services are refused to everyone, not just to a targeted group; this often is the case even when only a disempowered group needs those goods or services. So when pharmacists object to filling prescriptions for contraceptives or HIV medications and when other health professionals withhold care related to gender transition, infertility, or mental health, vulnerable people are made to bear health risks and the humiliation of being refused necessary care based on others' religious beliefs. We all should be entitled to rely on state-licensed professionals to comply with the standards of care and service that govern their profession when doing their jobs. If they can't, they should select another field of work in which they won't be imposing the burdens of their own beliefs on others.

As another example, the civil rights amendment of Indiana's RFRA only applies to private businesses, leaving religiously affiliated hospitals, hospices, and other agencies free to discriminate against married same-sex couples, individual LGBT patients, women, people living with HIV, and anyone else whose medical needs may not match the beliefs of the agency. This includes exemptions for religiously affiliated hospitals and nursing homes that receive most of their revenue from the general public.

Also, the original text of the bill went further than the federal RFRA. It allows religious exemption demands if a burden on religion is "likely." It allows assertion of the religious rights in disputes between private parties, without government involvement. And it went beyond the U.S. Supreme Court's *Hobby Lobby* reinterpretation of the federal law, which now allows owners of closely held businesses to make religion claims. The Indiana RFRA goes further, including within the definition of a "person" with religious rights the full range of legal entities, including for-profit businesses and secular nonprofits, along with religious organizations and individuals. In other words, not all RFRAs are the same. And although the Indiana effort yielded improvement and had tremendous educational impact, the end result was only a partial victory.

The country had seen a similar drama the year before, in Arizona. There too, a handful of determined legislators had jammed the bill through on rails greased with the habit of deferring to religion and confusion about the actual legal standards. But, as in Indiana, the tide turned when business leaders joined the effort. Dozens of leading companies urged the governor to veto—from American Airlines and Delta Airlines; to Apple, Intel, and AT&T; to Hilton, Westin, and Marriott hotels; to the Arizona Hispanic Chamber of Commerce, the Greater

Phoenix Economic Council, and the Arizona Tech Council. And Governor Jan Brewer did veto the bill.

But no one should conclude that business leaders have become the reliable White Knights of the LGBT community. A couple of months after Governor Brewer's veto of SB 1062, there was no similar corporate rally against the RFRA bill advanced in Mississippi. There was no Super Bowl or Final Four looming. And, the local Chamber of Commerce merely arranged for an amendment to protect employers from religion claims by employees—the one change the Indiana legislature had accepted in its initial approval of SB 101.

The following year, angry social conservatives began to anticipate the Supreme Court's marriage ruling. As spring became early summer of 2015, and most state legislative sessions were coming to a close, some were in a frenzy over pending religion bills. Texas, for example, had a Texas-sized allotment of a dozen bills. They ranged from proposals to allow religious organizations (including Catholic hospitals) to refuse to recognize marriages inconsistent with their religious views (including for visitation and medical decision-making), to bills banning salary, benefits, and pensions to public employees who issued or processed marriage licenses for same-sex couples, even when required to do so by federal court orders. In part because many of the bills were blatantly unconstitutional, the skillful efforts of Equality Texas and allies succeeded in stopping all of them. The legislature in Michigan, on the other hand, resisted a RFRA bill all session, only to end by passing three separate bills to allow religiously affiliated child welfare agencies to discriminate, including when providing taxpayer-funded services to children in state custody.

Then, following the *Obergefell* decision in June 2015, a next act in the religious refusals drama opened, featuring public officials with law-enforcing roles choosing instead to grandstand against the law. The chief justice of the Alabama Supreme Court, Roy Moore, was among those in the headlines. His antigay position was clear. In 2002, he had authored a special concurring opinion contemptuously dismissing a lesbian mother's claim for custody against her physically abusive ex-husband, writing that "Homosexual conduct is . . . abhorrent, immoral, detestable, a crime against nature, and a violation of the laws of nature and of nature's God upon which this Nation and our laws are predicated. . . . That is enough under the law to allow a court to consider such activity harmful to a child."[10]

In early February 2015, after the Eleventh Circuit refused to put on hold the federal trial court's marriage equality ruling, Moore ordered all the probate judges in the state—those responsible for issuing marriage licenses—not to issue licenses to same-sex couples.[11] There was little doubt that, ultimately, the federal court orders enforcing the U.S. Constitution would trump administrative orders of a defiant state court judge. But Chief Justice Moore did encourage dereliction of duty by public officials and sent a message that the top figure of Alabama's justice system remained deeply hostile toward gay people.

And in Texas, state Attorney General Ken Paxton held the spotlight for much of the summer with his post-*Obergefell* proclamation that "Texas must speak with one voice against this lawlessness, and act on multiple levels to further protect religious liberties for all Texans, but most immediately do anything we can to help our County Clerks and public officials who now are forced with defending their religious beliefs against the Court's ruling."[12] He later instructed state officials not to issue birth certificates identifying same-sex parents of adopted children, or death certificates recognizing same-sex spouses of decedents. For two months, he caused heartache for Texas families and needless legal bills for the state. Only when facing jail time as a federal court contempt sanction did he stand down.

As summer turned to fall, the clerk of Rowan County, Kentucky, got her fifteen minutes of fame by instructing her staff not to issue marriage licenses to same-sex couples. Kim Davis claimed that her right to practice her Apostolic Christian faith entitled her to shut down the licensing function of the county to avoid having her name, as the county clerk, appear on licenses for same-sex couples. She served five days in jail for contempt of the federal court's order that she allow the licensing function of the county to resume. Some local community members and her lawyers at the radical Christian legal group Liberty Counsel hailed her as a martyr and likened her jail service to Dr. Martin Luther King Jr.'s time in the Birmingham jail. But many in the national press compared her instead to George Wallace—blocking the schoolhouse door to African American citizens attempting, pursuant to court orders, to exercise their rights.[13]

Davis' lawyers had asked for an accommodation that would allow her to disassociate from same-sex couples' licenses. They pointed to Utah and North Carolina for validation. That was misguided. In March 2015, Utah had added sexual orientation and gender identity protections to the state's employment and housing non-discrimination laws. At the same time, it amended the law governing public employees who issue marriage licenses or solemnize marriages. The amended law allows employees with a religious objection to marriage for same-sex couples to opt out of performing those duties for anyone, as long as others can perform those tasks without unfair burdens on those other employees or the public. North Carolina passed a similar law. Neither state permits public officials to pick and choose among members of the public, serving some and refusing others based on the officials' religious views. Nor could those or other states allow such discrimination without running afoul of the Equal Protection clause.

Social conservatives in Congress have proposed similar freedoms to discriminate against married same-sex couples. Utah Senator Mike Lee and Idaho Representative Raul Labrador introduced the First Amendment Defense Act ("FADA") just before the *Obergefell* decision. Like Indiana's SB 101 as introduced, it aims to ensure that employers, those operating businesses, and those receiving public funding may refuse jobs, housing, and services to married same-sex couples. It proposes similar license to fire and otherwise discriminate against anyone who engages in a sexual relationship outside of a heterosexual marriage. This is a clear threat to married same-sex couples, single mothers, and anyone shacking up without the boss's approval!

Meanwhile, the Equality Act was introduced in July 2015 to amend the 1964 Civil Rights Act to make explicit that sexual orientation and gender identity are included within the federal prohibitions on sex discrimination and to add such protections where they have been lacking for women over the past fifty years. The Equality Act had only Democratic sponsors in both chambers when introduced, and FADA had Republicans joined by only one House Democrat.

This is not to say that the country was evenly divided about whether anti-gay religious beliefs justify discrimination against married same-sex couples by public employees, businesses, employers, landlords, or others, let alone by service providers receiving public funding. Rather, national polling consistently has shown that strong majorities oppose religion-based discrimination by those conducting business, and even more so by those receiving taxpayer monies. So, the congressional line-up on these bills simply reflects the intensity of the radical religious groups who create headline-grabbing drama and drive groups of reliable primary voters. Kim Davis, Ken Paxton, and Roy Moore likewise are not representative. Although each has generated Twitter trends and adulation within particular constituencies, they stand out because they are so few. What matters is that they toss fuel on fires being lit state by state by the Christian extremists behind much of the anti-LGBT legislation, litigation, and other advocacy.

The courts' frequent rejection of religious-exemption arguments has not prompted our opponents to abandon their goals or arguments. Instead, we have seen vastly *increased* resources invested in a proliferation of ever-larger self-identified Christian legal groups seemingly determined to secure case law as well as statutes allowing religion-based rights to discriminate. It has been said that imitation is the sincerest form of flattery. If so, we at Lambda Legal are flattered indeed. Where once there were a couple of these Christian legal groups with opposition to LGBT equality among their top causes, now there are at least a dozen,[14] and their resources have ballooned. ADF, for example, currently has a staff of more than fifty attorneys and an annual budget of at least $40 million.[15]

We must continue to build the coordinated advocacy that has brought us great progress so far, including the freedom to marry. This requires policy reform, courtroom advocacy, and public education. First of all, unless we want America to tilt further toward theocracy, we must end the flood of religious refusal bills. We already have showed they are a misguided strategy in many places. We need to complete that reality check. Making our case in court also remains essential because, though we now are blessed with wonderful allies, LGBT people are a small minority and vulnerable in majoritarian votes. Litigation allows us to enforce core principles, while spotlighting injustices that show the need for change.

In the policy arena, more specifically, the work ahead should include:

- Resisting proposals for new religious rights at others' expense, such as for public employees to refuse to serve some members of the public, for refusals of medical or other services for people in need, or for discrimination against LGBT people in various public contexts.

- Pressing for explicit, comprehensive protections for LGBT people at all levels of government and without expanded religious exemptions.

- Amending the federal RFRA and similar laws of many states to confirm that the religious rights they protect may not be used against others.

- Restricting the ability of religiously affiliated institutions that provide state-licensed medical or social services to the public to refuse or otherwise to block access to important services on religious grounds, especially when receiving public funding.

In appropriate court cases, this work also should include:

- Enforcing non-discrimination rules, which means countering arguments for overly broad, judicially created religious exceptions or other reinterpretations of standards that weaken protections. It also means enforcing the Establishment Clause and its role in shielding government from religion, and religion from government.

- Helping courts delineate the constitutionally based "ministerial exception" to laws that burden religious organizations' freedom to select and supervise their clergy, while affirming the complementary principle that employees of religious organizations who perform no religious functions should have basic employment rights.

Freedom of religion always and rightly has been a core American value. Yet, our laws remain badly out of balance because LGBT people are legally vulnerable, and countless others also are at risk due to wrongful imposition of others' religious beliefs. Too many Americans are confused and conflicted about religious freedom. Some ignore their church's rules about premarital sex or divorce, while believing sincerely that they should shun a "sinful" gay co-worker. But, most would agree that the Orthodox Jewish rule against unmarried women and men interacting cannot apply the same way in business settings that it can in religious settings. Like when the pre-1978 Mormon Church taught that African Americans have no place in Heaven, religious beliefs are protected but cannot justify discrimination in the marketplace. For everyone, the shield—the protection for one's religious exercise—must not be turned into a sword—public rejection of those who are different.

NOTES

Introduction by Leslie J. Gabel-Brett and Kevin M. Cathcart

1. amfAR, The Foundation for AIDS Research, http://www.amfar.org/worldwide-aids-stats.

2. See, for example, Lillian Faderman, *Surpassing the Love of Men: Romantic Friendship and Love Between Women from the Renaissance to the Present*, 1981; John Boswell, *Christianity, Social Tolerance, and Homosexuality*, 1980: Martin Duberman, Martha Vicinus, and George Chauncey Jr., eds., *Hidden from History: Reclaiming the Gay and Lesbian Past*, 1989.

3. Peter Allen, Michael Callen, Marsha Malamet, "Love Don't Need a Reason," Warner Brothers Publishing, ASCAP.

4. "Beyond Same-Sex Marriage: A New Strategic Vision for All Our Families & Relationships" (July 26, 2006), http://www.beyondmarriage.org/BeyondMarriage.pdf.

5. "Senators reject both job-bias ban and gay marriage," Eric Schmitt, *New York Times*, September 11, 1996, p.16.

6. Brief of Historians of Marriage and the American Historical Association as *Amici Curiae* in Support of Petitioners, *Obergefell v. Hodges*, p. 6; citing Nancy F. Cott, *Public Vows: A History of Marriage and the Nation* (2000) pp. 2, 11–12, 52–53, 190–194, 221–224.

7. ACLU, GLAD, Lambda Legal, NCLR, the Equality Federation, Freedom to Marry, GLAAD, the Human Rights Campaign, and the Task Force.

The First Marriage Cases, 1970–74 by William N. Eskridge Jr.

1. Michael McConnell, "Marriage—My Childhood Dream Comes True" (November 2013), in The Tretter Collection, University of Minnesota, Michael McConnell Files, Box 20; Conversation with Michael McConnell, Minneapolis, MN, June 7, 2015.

2. Norman Human Rights Commission, "Community Attitudes on Homosexuality and About Homosexuals—A Report on the Environment in Norman, Oklahoma" (1978).

3. Conversation with Jack Baker, June 7, 2015.

4. McConnell, "Childhood Dream." See Ken Bronson, *A Quest for Full Equality*, 2–3 (2004).

5. Bronson, *Full Equality*, 4–5.

6. Memorandum from Hennepin County Attorney George C. Scott to Hennepin County District Court Clerk Gerald R. Nelson, May 22, 1970, in McConnell Files, Box 21.

7. E.g., E.B. Saunders, *Reformer's Choice: Marriage License or Just License?*, One, Inc., August 1953, 10–12.

8. Letter from Dr. Ward Pomeroy, Kinsey Institute, to Richard John Baker, May 25, 1970 (skeptical); Letter from Norman Dorsen, former ACLU president, to Matt Stark, former MCLU executive director, November 1, 2004 (recalling that the national ACLU was not enthusiastic about the Baker and McConnell lawsuit but congratulating the Minnesota chapter for supporting the case on appeal).

9. Letter from David Sails (aka "Becky Sue") to Michael McConnell, September 8, 1970, in McConnell Files, Box 29.

10. Letter from Jack Baker to [older brother] Bentley Baker, January 1, 1970, in McConnell Files, Box 20.

11. *McConnell v. Anderson*, 451 F.2d 193, 196 (Eighth Cir. 1971).

12. *Baker v. Nelson*, 191 N.W.2d 185, 186 (MN 1971), appeal dismissed, 409 U.S. 810 (1972).

13. Baker and McConnell's Blue Earth County license and related documents are in the McConnell Files, Box 31.

14. *Jury Halts Action on Gay Couple, Minneapolis Star*, March 28, 1972, in McConnell Files, Box 31 (grand jury rebuffed prosecutorial efforts to indict the minister or the couple for fraud).

15. Letter from Jack Baker to [his sister] Judith Della Baker Loferski, June 13, 1970, in McConnell Files, Box 20. For an earlier case for gay marriages, see Randy Lloyd, *Let's Push Homophile Marriage*, One, Inc., June 1963, 5–10.

16. Richard J. Baker and R. Michael Wetherbee, *Juris X: Homosexuality and the Law, Georgetown Law Weekly*, February 4, 1970, 1, 3–5.

17. *Two Milwaukee Women Fight for Marriage License, The Advocate*, December 8, 1971, 7.

18. *Black Lesbians' Wedding Crowded, The Advocate*, February 2, 1972, 5.

19. *Singer v. Hara*, 522 P.2d 1187, 1188 (Wash. App. 1974).

20. Conversation with Michael McConnell, Minneapolis, MN, June 9, 2015.

21. *The Homosexual Couple, Look*, January 26, 1971.

22. Kay Tobin and Randy Wicker, *The Gay Crusaders* 140 (1975) (interview of Baker and McConnell).

23. *Baker v. Nelson*, 191 N.W.2d at 186.

24. Catherine Fosl, *It Could Be Dangerous! Gay Liberation and Gay Marriage, Louisville, Kentucky, 1970*, 12 Ohio Valley Hist. 46, 56 (2012) (quoting Jones).

25. For the ways some early lawsuits were a collective effort at gay liberation strategy, see Michael Boucai, *Glorious Precedents: When Gay Marriage Was Radical*, 27 Yale J.L. & Hum. 1, 29–34 (Jones and Knight), 34–41 (Singer and Barwick) (2015).

26. *Jones v. Hallahan*, No. CR 140, 279 (Jefferson Cnty. Cir. Ct. February 19, 1971), *aff'd*, 501 S.W.2d 588 (KY 1973).

27. Plaintiffs' Memorandum in Support of Motion [Mandamus to the Clerk], Fourth Judicial District, *Baker v. Nelson*, No. 671379 (filed November 12, 1970), in McConnell Files, Box 15; Jurisdictional Statement, *Baker v. Nelson*, 409 U.S. 810 (1972) (No. 71–1027).

28. *Loving v. Virginia*, 388 U.S. 1 (1967).

29. Jurisdictional Statement, at 12, *Baker* (invoking *Loving*).

30. The Pandora's box analogy was raised by a Minnesota legislator debating Jack Baker. See Bronson, *Full Equality*, 18.

31. The premise of the argument is incorrect, as dozens of societies, including many Native American tribes, recognized marriage for same-sex couples. See William N. Eskridge Jr., *The Case for Same-Sex Marriage*, 37–54 (1996).

32. Jurisdictional Statement, 14–5, *Baker* (No. 71-1027).

The Hawai'i Marriage Case Launches the U.S. Freedom-to-Marry Movement for Equality by Evan Wolfson

1. Reprinted with permission. *Legal Recognition of Same-Sex Partnerships: A Study of National, European and International Law*, edited by Robert Wintemute and Mads Andenaes. Portland, OR: Hart Publishing, 2001.

2. See E. Wolfson, "Crossing the Threshold: Equal Marriage Rights for Lesbians and Gay Men and the Intra-Community Critique," (1994) 21, *New York University Review of Law and Social Change*, 567–8. On the history of discrimination and change in the institution of marriage, see W. Eskridge, *The Case for Same-Sex Marriage* (New York, NY, Free Press, 1996); E.J. Graff, *What Is Marriage For?* (Boston, MA, Beacon Press, 1999).

3. On the consequences of being denied the freedom to marry, see, e.g., J. Wriggins, "Marriage Law and Family Law: Autonomy, Interdependence, and Couples of the Same Gender," (2000) 41, *Boston College Law Review*, 265; C.W. Christensen, "If Not Marriage? On Securing Gay and Lesbian Family Values by a 'Simulacrum of Marriage,'" (1998), 66, *Fordham Law Review*, 1699; D.L. Chambers, "What If? The Legal Consequences of Marriage and the Legal Needs of Lesbian and Gay Male Couples," (1996), 95, *Michigan Law Review*, 447.

4. See Wolfson, *supra* n.2, 572–81.

5. *Baehr v. Lewin*, 852 P.2d 44, clarified on grant of reconsideration in part, 852 P.2d 74 (1993). For all the decisions in the *Baehr* case, see "Marriage Project," http://www.lambdalegal.org/cgi bin/pages/issues/record?record=9.

6. See Wolfson, *supra* n.2; "Marriage Project," ibid.

7. "Because marriage is a basic human right and an individual personal choice, RESOLVED, the state should not interfere with same-gender couples who choose to marry and share fully and equally in the rights, responsibilities, and commitment of civil marriage." See "Marriage Project," ibid. See also E. Wolfson, "Why We Should Fight for the Freedom to Marry: The Challenges and Opportunities That Will Follow a Win in Hawai'i," (1996), 1, *Journal of Gay, Lesbian and Bisexual Identity*, 79, 82–3; E. Wolfson, "How to Win the Freedom to Marry," [Fall 1997] *Harvard Gay and Lesbian Review*, 29.

8. For materials on the right's anti-marriage campaign and activities in the states, see "Marriage Project," *supra* n.5.

9. Codified as 1 United States Code section 7, 28 U.S.C.'s. 1738C. See Feldblum, chap. 3.

10. E. Wolfson and M. Melcher, "DOMA's House Divided: An Argument Against the 'Defense of Marriage Act,'" (1997), 44, *Federal Lawyer*, 31.

11. In a report prepared at the request of Congress six months after the vote to discriminate against gay people's marriages, Congress was informed that the federal anti-marriage law excluded same-sex couples from over 1049 ways in which federal law addresses marital status. Report No. OGC97-16 (January 31, 1997), http://www.gao.gov (GAO Reports, Find GAO Reports).

12. The Full Faith and Credit Clause, United States Constitution, Article 4, section 1, is a prime engine of federal unity and interstate comity, as well as a protection for the expectations of American citizens and couples as they travel or do business throughout the country. *Supra* n.10, 31–3.

13. On DOMA's unconstitutionality, see *supra* n.10; A. Koppelman, "Dumb and DOMA: Why the Defense of Marriage Act Is Unconstitutional," (1997), 83, *Iowa Law Review*, 1; L. Kramer, "Same-Sex Marriage, Conflict of Laws, and the Unconstitutional Public Policy Exception,"

(1997), 106, *Yale Law Journal*, 1965; M. Strasser, *Legally Wed: Same-Sex Marriage and the Constitution* (Ithaca, NY, Cornell University Press, 1997). Apart from the unconstitutionality of discrimination against lawfully married couples simply because they are gay, refusal to "recognize" couples' marriages as they travel from state to state "aconstitutionally" contravenes settled expectations and standard approaches toward interstate respect for marital status.

14. As of September 2000, thirty-three state legislatures had adopted anti-marriage measures. In three other states (Alaska, California, Hawai'i), voters had approved anti-marriage ballot measures or constitutional amendments. See "2000 Anti-Marriage Bills Status Report," http://www.lambdalegal.org/cgi-bin/pages/documents/record?record=578. On November 7, 2000, 70 percent of Nebraska voters ratified the most sweeping anti-marriage measure to date, Nebraska Constitution, Art. I, s. 29: "Only marriage between a man and a woman shall be valid or recognized in Nebraska. The uniting of two persons of the same sex in a civil union, domestic partnership, or other similar same-sex relationship shall not be valid or recognized in Nebraska."

15. See "Optimism Outduels Pessimism," *Wall Street Journal*, September 16, 1999, A10.

16. "Poll Is Mixed on Gay Marriage," *Newsday*, June 1, 2000. While showing only 51 percent opposition to equal marriage rights, the poll also reported that a majority support providing same-sex couples the components of marriage, such as inheritance, health insurance, and social security benefits. As in all such polls, young people were significantly more supportive of equality in marriage.

17. *Baehr v. Miike*, Civ, No. 91-1394, 1996 WL 694235 (Hawai'i Circuit Court, December 3, 1996). See also S.A. Marcosson, "The Lesson of the Same-Sex Marriage Trial: The Importance of Pushing Opponents of Lesbian and Gay Rights to Their 'Second Line of Defense,'" (1996–97) 35, *Journal of Family Law (University of Louisville)*, 721.

18. Following the landmark Hawai'i trial court ruling, a court in Alaska held that the choice of a life partner in marriage is fundamental, and therefore the state must show a compelling state interest in order to exclude same-sex couples from the freedom to marry. *Brause v. Bureau of Vital Statistics*, No. 3AN-95-0562 CL, 1998 WL 88743 (Alaska Superior Court, February 27, 1998), "Marriage Project," *supra* n.5. Before an appeal could be heard, right-wing groups pushed through a constitutional amendment, ratified by voters on November 3,1998, which blocked the courts' ability to hold the state to its obligation to show a reason before discriminating against gay people. See Alaska Constitution, Art. I, s. 25: "To be valid or recognized in this State, a marriage may exist only between one man and one woman." See also Wriggins, *supra* n.3, 291–2, n.176.

19. See State of Hawai'i, *Report of the Commission on Sexual Orientation and the Law* (1995), http://lrbhawaii.info/lrbrpts/95/sexor.pdf, (recommending that the legislature allow same-sex couples the freedom to marry, or "a universal comprehensive domestic partnership act that confers all the possible benefits and obligations of marriage for two people, regardless of gender"). The negotiations that led to the constitutional amendment also resulted in a 1997 law allowing same-sex couples, and other pairs legally prohibited from marrying, to register as "reciprocal beneficiaries" and receive some of the legal and economic protections and obligations of marriage (more than are accorded gay and lesbian couples in any other U.S. jurisdiction, except now Vermont). See Hawai'i Revised Statutes, e.g., section 572 C-4. See also B. Burnette, "Hawai'i's Reciprocal Beneficiaries Act," (1998–99), 37, *Brandeis Journal of Family Law*, 81.

20. *Baehr v. Miike*, 994 P.2d *566* (Table) (December 9, 1999). Even while declaring that it could no longer order the issuance of licenses, the Court did not foreclose litigation for the full and equal rights and benefits accompanying marriage (apart from the status itself). And in a pivotal footnote, the Court declared that sexual orientation discrimination warrants strict scrutiny under the Hawai'i Constitution. See Appendix to this chapter; "Marriage Project," *supra* n.5. The Court did not explain how the 1998 constitutional amendment, granting the legislature a power it had not exercised prior to the Court's decision, could retroactively validate the different-sex-only

marriage law. See M. Strasser, "*Baehr* Mysteries, Retroactivity and the Concept of Law," (2000), 41, *Santa Clara Law Review*, 161.

21. 198 P.2d 17 (1948). In *Perez*, a 4–3 majority made the California Supreme Court the first American court ever to strike down the long-standing prohibitions on interracial marriages—which, like same-sex couples' marriages, were condemned as contrary to the definition of marriage or divine will, likely to lead to a parade of horribles (i.e., bestiality, incest, polygamy, and the downfall of society), and best left to the mercy of legislatures rather than courts. It took another nineteen years following that breakthrough before the U.S. Supreme Court struck down race discrimination in marriage across the country, in the best named case ever, *Loving v. Virginia*, 388 U.S. 1 (1967). Just as we ended race discrimination in civil marriage, so will we see an end to sex discrimination in civil marriage, as more and more fair-minded people come to see that there is no good reason for excluding gay and lesbian couples from the commitment, responsibilities, and support we seek to share.

"Not tonight, dear—it's a felony": *Lawrence v. Texas* and the Path to Marriage Equality by Suzanne B. Goldberg

1. *Bowers v. Hardwick*, 478 U.S. 186, 194 (1986).

2. *Bottoms v. Bottoms*, 457 S.E.2d 102, 108 (1995) (citation omitted).

3. Katia Hetter, Focus on Cracker Barrel Hiring / Hevesi Opposes Anti-Gay Policy, Newsday, October 16, 1998, A67.

4. Edmund Reutter Jr., The Law of Public Education, Fourth Edition, 657 (New York Foundation Press, 1994).

5. See e.g., *Padula v. Webster*, 822 F.2d 97, 103 (DC Cir. 1987). "There can hardly be more palpable discrimination against a class than making the conduct that defines the class criminal."

6. For much more detail about the arrests, the legal proceedings, and the history and aftermath of the case in Houston, see Dale Carpenter, "Flagrant Conduct: The Story of *Lawrence v. Texas*" (2013).

7. *Romer v. Evans*, 517 U.S. 620, 635 (1996).

8. In 1958, the Court had reversed a lower court decision that declared a pro-gay magazine obscene and unmailable because of two stories and an advertisement for gay-oriented pulp fiction but did not issue an opinion in the case. The decision was *One v. Olesen*, 355 U.S. 371 (1958).

9. *Romer*, 517 U.S. 620, 635 (1996).

10. *Lawrence v. State*, 41 S.W.3d 349, 368 (Tex. App. 2001) (Anderson, J., dissenting), rev'd, 539 U.S. 558 (2003).

11. Ibid.

12. 539 U.S. 558, 578 (2003).

13. Ibid. at 574.

14. Ibid. at 585 (O'Connor, J., concurring).

15. Ibid. at 604 (Scalia, J., dissenting).

16. Ibid. at 604–5.

17. *Goodridge v. Dep't of Pub. Health*, 798 N.E.2d 941 (MA 2003).

18. *Windsor v. United States*, 133 S. Ct. 2675, 2694 (2013).

19. Ibid. at 2696 (Roberts, C.J., dissenting).

20. *Obergefell v. Hodges*, 2015 WL 2473451 (S. Ct. 2015).

21. Ibid. at *10 (citing *Lawrence v. Texas*).

22. Ibid. at *11 ("History and tradition guide and discipline this inquiry but do not set its outer boundaries.") (citing *Lawrence v. Texas*).

23. Ibid. at *12 (citing *Lawrence v. Texas*).

Movement + Strategy + Campaign: The Freedom to Marry Winning Combination by Evan Wolfson, with Adam Polaski

1. Evan Wolfson, Freedom to Marry's Ladder of Clarity: Lessons from a Winning Campaign (That Is Not Yet Won), *Columbia Journal of Gender and Law* 29.1, March 2015, pp. 236-242.

2. Freedom to Marry closed its doors in February 2016. The campaign's last public act was to launch a new, enduring legacy website—www.freedomtomarry.org—including our story of how marriage was won, videos, "how to" guides, and strategic campaign lessons that can be applied by other organizations, causes, and countries. See Amanda Terkel, "Freedom To Marry Shares Lessons From Victorious Equality Campaign," *Huffington Post*, January 16, 2016.

Parallel Journeys Through Discrimination: Asian Americans and Modern Marriage Equality by Karin Wang

1. Ulysses Torassa, Thousands Protest Legalizing Same-Sex Marriage—Asian Americans, Christians Rally in Sunset District, *San Francisco Chronicle*, April 26, 2004, at B1; Emanuel Parker, Group Protests Same-Sex Marriage, *San Gabriel Valley Tribune*, June 27, 2004, at A1.

2. See Robert S. Chang & Karin Wang, Democratizing the Courts: How an Amicus Brief Helped Organize the Asian American Community to Support Marriage Equality, 14 UCLA ASIAN PAC. AM. L. J. 22, 27–30 (2009).

3. All anti-miscegenation laws at the time explicitly prohibited white–black intermarriage; only seven states, almost all of them in the West, also targeted Asians. See http://racism.org /index.php?option=com_content&view=article&id=306:aspi0201&catid=64:asian-and-pacific -americans&Itemid=235.

4. 1880 Cal. Stat. Ch. 41, Sec. 1, p. 3.

5. See Roldan v. Los Angeles County, 129 Cal. App. 267 (2d Dist. 1933) (holding that a Filipino man was not subject to California's anti-miscegenation law because Filipinos were "Malay" and not "Mongolian"). The state legislature quickly remedied that oversight by amending the statute so that "Malays" also were covered. Acts effective Aug. 21, 1933, chs. 104–105, 1933 Cal. Stat. 561 (codified at Cal. Civ. Code, §§ 60, 69) (repealed 1959, 1969).

6. See Roger Daniels, *Asian America: Chinese and Japanese in the United States Since 1850*, (1988), p. 19.

7. *Immigration*. See, e.g., Page Act of 1875, ch. 141, 18 Stat. 477 (repealed 1974); Chinese Exclusion Acts of 1882 (ch. 126, 22 Stat. 58), 1884 (ch. 220, 23 Stat. 115), and 1892 (ch. 60, 27 Stat. 25) (repealed 1943). The Chinese Exclusion Act and subsequent exclusionary immigration laws were applied against most Asian immigrant groups and were not repealed until 1943 for Chinese, 1946 for Filipinos and South Asians (Indians), and 1952 for Japanese and Koreans. Pat K. Chew, *Asian Americans: The "Reticent" Minority and Their Paradoxes*, 36 Wm. & Mary L. Rev. 1, 17 n.59 (1994). It was not until 1965 that Asian Americans were allowed to immigrate into the United States in substantial numbers. See ibid. p. 18 n. 61. *Naturalization*. See *In re Ah Yup*, 1 F. Cas. 223 (C.C.D. Cal. 1878) (No. 104) (denying "the first application made by a native Chinaman for naturalization" because a "Mongolian" is not a "white person"); Chinese Exclusion Act of 1882. *Marriage*. Cal. Civ. Code, § 60 (adding "Mongolians" in 1905 to the list of groups barred from marrying "white persons"; such marriages were "illegal and void") (Deering 1949) (repealed 1959) and § 69 (prohibiting the issuance of a license authorizing the marriage of a white person with a Mongolian) (West 1957) (amended in 1959 to omit this prohibition).

8. See Robert S. Chang, *Disoriented: Asian Americans, Law, and the Nation-State*, 82–83 (1999). "Restrictions on marriage were an integral part of a broader system that excluded and isolated Chinese Americans, ultimately forcing many to repatriate." Chang and Wang, UCLA APALC, p. 507.

9. See Brief of Amici Curiae Asian American Bar Association of the Greater Bay Area & 62 Asian Pacific American Organizations in Support of Respondents Challenging the Marriage Exclusion, In re Marriage Cases, 183 P.3d 385 (Cal. 2008) (No. S147999).

10. For example, the Organization of Chinese Americans (OCA), a national Asian American civil rights organization, began discussing marriage equality after being approached to endorse the amicus brief. On October 20, 2007, the national board of OCA passed a resolution in support of marriage equality, entitled "Resolution in Support of Legal Protections of Family Relationships." Although OCA was unable to endorse the amicus brief, the passage of the resolution allowed California chapters of OCA to publicly support marriage equality.

11. Although there was no Asian American-specific brief filed in this litigation, at least forty Asian American organizations joined at least three different briefs that all articulated the same basic premise: that allowing Prop 8 to stand would contradict basic constitutional protections intended to protect unpopular minorities from the will of the majority. See Karin Wang, *The Real Threat of Prop 8 and Why It Must Be Overturned*, California Progress Report, March 3, 2009, available at http://www.californiaprogressreport.com/2009/03/the_real_threat.html.

12. *Asian Americans at the Ballot Box: The 2008 General Election in Los Angeles County*, Asian Pacific American Legal Center of Southern California and the Cyrus Chung Ying Tang Foundation (2009). Available at http://www.advancingjustice-la.org/sites/default/files/APALCBallotBoxLA2008FINAL.pdf.

13. Asian Pacific American Legal Center, *Exit Poll Data for March 2000 California Election* (March 2000), on file with Asian Americans Advancing Justice-Los Angeles.

Translating Equality: On the Role of LGBT Latinas/os in the Marriage Movement by Francisco Dueñas

1. *Diversity in Democracy: Minority Representation in the United States*, Gary M. Segura, Shaun Bowler, 2005.

2. Today, we are still far from meeting this need, as exemplified by the 40 percent of homeless youth that identify as LGBT, http://williamsinstitute.law.ucla.edu/wp-content/uploads/Durso-Gates-LGBT-Homeless-Youth-Survey-July-2012.pdf. Losing the support of family, especially parents, is the top problem Latino LGBT youth identify, and family acceptance and support the number one change they wish for, http://lulac.org/assets/pdfs/LGBT-LatinoYouthReport.pdf.

3. https://www.census.gov/prod/2001pubs/c2kbr01-3.pdf.

4. These stereotypes have historical and cultural roots. For example, the 1901 Mexico City police raid of a gay party among the bourgeoisie—half the men were dressed as women—caused a scandal. Inflamed by populist newspapers and political revolutionaries eager to denounce the ruling classes, the scandal, known as "Los 41," enshrined homophobia in the national psyche.

5. LLEGO, the national Latino LGBT organization, bridged this divide by working on both HIV prevention and LGBT rights from 1987 until 2004 when it ceased operations due to financial malfeasance. LLEGO also worked to provide a Latino voice against a proposed Federal Marriage Constitutional Amendment. Its closure was a great loss for the Latino LGBT community.

6. For example, few, if any, Latino LGBT organizations are part of larger national Latino coalitions or networks, like the National Council of La Raza's affiliate network.

7. Most recently, studies on family acceptance and undocumented LGBT communities has made it easier to seek allies and build campaigns, as well as prioritize and allocate funds. As social science illuminates the truth of our lives, our advocacy grows stronger. Unfortunately, there is

still much we don't know about LGBT demographics, and pressing research needs for LGBT people of color are often neglected.

8. The National Latino Coalition for Justice was a project of the national organization Freedom to Marry.

9. In Maryland, the 2012 campaigns for marriage equality and in-state tuition for undocumented students were jointly promoted with positive results.

10. *Diversity in Democracy: Minority Representation in the United States*, Gary M. Segura, Shaun Bowler, 2005.

11. http://www.lamag.com/longform/death-on-terminal-island/.

12. We also organized LGBT contingents for the Mexican and Central American Independence Parades in Los Angeles.

13. https://en.wikipedia.org/wiki/DREAM_Act.

14. These included groups like LULAC Rainbow Council 4871 in Dallas and the "A La Familia" Project, which focused on Latino Christians, a collaboration of UNID@S, National LGBTQ Task Force, and Human Rights Campaign.

15. http://www.freedomtomarry.org/resources/entry/marriage-polling.

Tested at the Ballot Box in 2012 by Marc Solomon and Thalia Zepatos

1. A thirty-first measure appeared on the ballot in Arizona in 2006. It would have outlawed marriage and civil unions of same-sex as well as opposite-sex couples. The constitutional amendment was defeated, largely by a campaign focusing on the impact on non-gay couples. The proponents returned to the ballot in 2008, passing a more narrow amendment that specifically banned marriage for same-sex couples.

Putting Faith to the Test: Black Leaders and the Maryland Victory
by Sharon Lettman-Hicks

1. LGBT African Americans and African American same-sex couples, http://williamsinstitute.law.ucla.edu/wp-content/uploads/Census-AFAMER-Oct-2013.pdf.

The Wait Is Over: Eleven Years to Marriage in New Jersey
by Hayley Gorenberg

1. We filed *Lewis v. Harris* on June 26, 2002, precisely one year—to the day—prior to our movement-rocking breakthrough in *Lawrence v. Texas*, eleven years—to the day—prior to the United States Supreme Court's decision in *Windsor*, and precisely thirteen years—again, to the day—before the SCOTUS decision in *Obergefell*. Contemplating this lineup, legal wonks among us may need to inaugurate a movement observance for these anniversaries!

2. In *Lewis*, Lambda Legal represented Mark Lewis and Dennis Winslow, Saundra Heath-Toby and Alicia Toby-Heath, Craig Hutchison and Chris Lodewycks, Maureen Kilian and Cindy Meneghin, Sarah and Suyin Lael, Karen and Marcye Nicholson-McFadden, and Marilyn Maneely and Diane Marini. Heartbreakingly, after the *Lewis* decision, Marilyn died of amyotrophic lateral sclerosis, leaving her life-partner, Diane, grieving without ever having been able to dignify their relationship through marriage.

A Long Battle Finally Won: Marriage in Florida by Nadine Smith

1. http://www.sptimes.com/2005/02/12/State/Group_seeks_gay_marri.shtml.

2. http://www.prnewswire.com/news-releases/hundreds-gathered-online-for-official
-arizona-together-campaign-rally-via-a-web-cast-55897027.html.

3. http://www.freedomtomarry.org/pdfs/SladeSmithObamatoBlame.pdf.

4. http://fivethirtyeight.blogs.nytimes.com/2013/03/26/how-opinion-on-same-sex-marriage
-is-changing-and-what-it-means/?_r=0.

5. Some of the information referenced on this timeline comes from Freedom to Marry's summary of legal cases in Florida, http://www.freedomtomarry.org/litigation/entry/florida.

Fighting for an AIDS-Free Generation by Scott A. Schoettes

1. HIV transmission via sexual contact between two women is rare, and the prevalence of HIV
among lesbians in the United States is lower than that of the general population. http://www
.gmhc.org/files/editor/file/GMHC_lap_whitepaper_0609.pdf, http://www.aidsmap.com/
Rare-case-of-lesbian-transmission-of-HIV-reported-in-US/page/2837236/.

2. While the HPTN 052 study interim results (published in 2011) postulated that infectiousness was reduced by 96 percent for those with a suppressed viral load, the final results (published in 2015) revealed no transmissions linked to the HIV-positive individuals in the study
who had reached full viral suppression, indicating the reduction in infectiousness may be nearly
100 percent.

A Return to the Root by Andrea J. Ritchie

1. Lambda Legal, *Protected and Served? A National Survey Exploring Discrimination by Police,
Courts, Prisons, and School Security Against Lesbian, Gay, Bisexual, Transgender (LGBT) People
Living with HIV in the United States* (2014), available at http://www.lambdalegal.org/protected
-and-served.

2. Latinx is a term developed by Latinx people to disrupt the gender binary inherent in the
terms Latino and Latina, referring to people of all gender identities.

3. Lambda Legal, *supra* n.1.

4. Ibid.

5. See Kathryn E.W. Himmelstein and Hannah Brückner, "Criminal-Justice and School Sanc-
tions Against Nonheterosexual Youth: A National Longitudinal Study," *Pediatrics* 127 (1) (2011):
49–57; see also Brett G. Stoudt, Michelle Fine, and Madeline Fox, *Growing Up Policed in the Age
of Aggressive Policing Policies*, 56 N.Y.L. Sch. L. Rev. 1331 (2011). (In the six months before the
study was conducted, LGBT youth were more likely to experience negative verbal, physical, and
legal contact with the police, and more than twice as likely to experience negative sexual contact).

6. National Coalition of Anti-Violence Programs, *Hate Violence Against Lesbian, Gay,
Bisexual, Transgender, Queer and HIV-Affected Communities in the United States in 2010,* (New
York: National Coalition of Anti-Violence Programs, 2011), available at http://www.avp.org/
storage/documents/Reports/2011_NCAVP_HV_Reports.pdf (law enforcement officers among
the top three categories of perpetrators of homophobic and transphobic violence against LGBT
people).

7. Jaime M. Grant, Lisa A. Mottet, and Justin Tanis, *Injustice at Every Turn: A Report of the
National Transgender Discrimination Survey* (Washington: National Center for Transgender
Equality and National Gay and Lesbian Task Force, 2011), available at http://www.thetaskforce
.org/static_html/downloads/reports/reports/ntds_full.pdf; "Stonewalled: Police Abuse and
Misconduct Against LGBT People in the United States" (Washington: Amnesty International,
2005), available at http://www.rfrresearchers.org/pdfs/Amnesty_Stonewalled-2.pdf.

8. See BreakOUT!, *We Deserve Better!* (2014), available at: http://www.youthbreakout.org
/sites/g/files/g189161/f/201410/WE%20DESERVE%20BETTER%20REPORT.pdf; Make

the Road New York, *Transgressive Policing: Police Abuse of LGBTQ Communities of Color in Jackson Heights*, (New York: Make the Road, 2012), available at http://www.maketheroad.org/pix_reports/MRNY_Transgressive_Policing_Full_Report_10.23.12B.pdf; Frank H. Galvan and Mohsen Bazargen, *Interactions of Latina Transgender Women with Law Enforcement* (Los Angeles: Bienestar, 2012), available at http://williamsinstitute.law.ucla.edu/wp-content/uploads/Galvan-Bazargan-Interactions-April-2012.pdf; Transgender Law Center and Ella Baker Center, *Walking While Trans* (2002).

9. U.S. Department of Justice, Civil Rights Division, *Investigation of the New Orleans Police Department*, March 16, 2011; U.S Department of Justice, Civil Rights Division, *Investigation of the Puerto Rico Police Department*, September 5, 2011; U.S. Department of Justice, Consent Decree, Albuquerque Police Department; U.S. Department of Justice, Consent Decree, Cleveland Police Department.

10. Joey L. Mogul, Andrea J. Ritchie, and Kay Whitlock, *Queer (In)Justice: The Criminalization of LGBT People in the United States* (2011).

11. Queers for Economic Justice, *A Fabulous Attitude: Low Income LGBTGNC People Surviving and Thriving on Love, Shelter, and Knowledge* (2010). Two Spirit is a term used by Indigenous people to refer to members of Indigenous communities whose sexual orientation or gender identity is non-heterosexual and/or nonbinary.

12. See generally Michelle Alexander, *The New Jim Crow: Mass Incarceration in the Age of Colorblindness* (2010); Joey L. Mogul, Andrea J. Ritchie, and Kay Whitlock, *Queer (In)Justice: The Criminalization of LGBT People in the United States* (2011).

13. *United States v. City of New Orleans*, 12civ1924, Consent Decree Regarding the New Orleans Police Department (Rec. Doc. 2) (July 24, 2012, E.D. La.); see also U.S. Department of Justice, Consent Decree, Albuquerque Police Department; U.S. Department of Justice, Consent Decree, Cleveland Police Department.

Shields Not into Swords: Stopping the Misuse of Religious Freedom for Discrimination by Jennifer C. Pizer

1. ABC News (March 29, 2015), https://www.youtube.com/watch?v=_-iOtRlDbzQ.

2. *Burwell v. Hobby Lobby*, 573 U.S. ___, 134 S. Ct. 2751 (2014). The case was one of at least three dozen similar cases brought by company owners claiming protected religious rights when doing business. Tom Ude, Camilla Taylor, and I had submitted amicus briefs explaining the potential implications for LGBT people in many of these cases at the appellate level. Justice Alito's 5–4 majority opinion allowed Hobby Lobby's owners to object to paying for birth control insurance in the health plans they must provide their employees because Hobby Lobby is so large. But, because the contraception is paid for instead by insurers and because Justice Alito disclaimed some other discriminatory consequences, the potential impacts remain unclear. See discussion in Jennifer C. Pizer, *Navigating the Minefield:* Hobby Lobby *and Religious Accommodation in the Age of Civil Rights*, 9 *Harv. L. & Pol. Rev.* 1 (2015), http://harvardlpr.com/wp-content/uploads/2015/04/9-1_Pizer.pdf.

3. In 2010, the Arizona legislature passed SB 1070, which many call the "papers please" law. Although substantial portions later were held unconstitutional, *Arizona v. United States*, 567 U.S. ___, 132 S. Ct. 2492 (2012), enforcement of the rest reinforced the state's reputation as hostile to immigrants and people of color generally. The legislature then passed SB 1062 with minimal debate in early 2014, causing another round of national protests and boycott threats.

4. See *Legal Experts Conclude Illinois Same-Sex Marriage Bill Worst in U.S. in Protecting Religious Liberty*, *Illinois Review* (May 29, 2013), http://illinoisreview.typepad.com/illinoisreview/2013/05/legal-experts-conclude-illinois-same-sex-marriage-bill-worst-in-us-in-protecting-religious-liberty.html. *Illinois Review* calls itself "the crossroads of the conservative commu-

nity," and the article cites lawyers from the Thomas More Society.

5. In addition to Camilla and me, the legal team consisted of the ACLU's Rose Saxe and Eunice Rho, HRC's Sarah Warbelow, AUF's Dale Carpenter, and NCLR's Shannon Minter and Chris Stoll, with lead roles varying some state by state.

6. Tim Cook, *Pro-discrimination 'religious freedom' laws are dangerous*, *Washington Post* (March 29, 2015), https://www.washingtonpost.com/opinions/pro-discrimination -religious-freedom-laws-are-dangerous-to-america/2015/03/29/bdb4ce9e-d66d-11e4-ba28 -f2a685dc7f89_story.html.

7. One proposal was accepted though—to prevent assertion of these religious rights by an employee or former employee against an employer.

8. Stephen Peters, *Update: More Tech Industry Leaders Make Unprecedented & Historic Joint Statement to Legislators* (April 1, 2015), http://www.hrc.org/blog/entry/tech-industry-leaders -make-unprecedented-historic-joint-statement-to-legisl. The statement further said:

> We believe it is critically important to speak out about proposed bills and existing laws that would put the rights of minorities at risk. The transparent and open economy of the future depends on it, and the values of this great nation are at stake. . . . Religious freedom, inclusion, and diversity can co-exist, and everyone including LGBT people and people of faith should be protected under their states' civil rights laws.

9. Kentucky's John Calipari, Duke's Mike Krzyzewski, Wisconsin's Bo Ryan, and Michigan State's Tom Izzo were the four head coaches of the 2015 Final Four. They said:

> Each of us strongly supports the positions of the NCAA and our respective institutions on the matter—that discrimination of any kind should not be tolerated. As a part of America's higher education system, college basketball plays an important role in diversity, equality, fairness, and inclusion and will continue to do so in the future.

Marissa Payne, *NCAA Final Four coaches release statement about Indiana's Religious Freedom Restoration Act*, *Washington Post* (April 1, 2015), https://www.washingtonpost.com/news/early -lead/wp/2015/04/01/ncaa-final-four-coaches-release-statement-about-indianas-religious -freedom-restoration-act/.

10. *Ex Parte H.H.*, 830 So. 2d 21, 26, 37 (AL 2002).

11. http://ftpcontent4.worldnow.com/waff/moore-order-samesex.pdf.

12. Attorney General Paxton, *Religious Liberties of Texas Public Officials Remain Constitutionally Protected After Obergefell v. Hodges* (June 28, 2015), https://www.texasattorneygeneral.gov /static/5144.html.

13. The discord of that comparison was all too poignant to many of us given the series of police killings of black men, and sometimes boys, without accountability. As the country marked the fiftieth anniversary of the Civil Rights Acts of 1964 and then the Voting Rights Act of 1965, the Black Lives Matter movement was calling out how far we have *not* come on the path toward a racially just society.

14. These include, among others, Alliance Defending Freedom (ADF), Liberty Counsel, Liberty Institute, Pacific Justice Foundation, Becket Fund for Religious Liberty, Thomas More Law Center, Christian Legal Society, American Center for Law and Justice, American Civil Rights Union, Institutional Religious Freedom Alliance, and Foundation for Free Expression.

15. I have encountered ADF's lawyers often as opposing counsel, including in our successful Arizona marriage case, *Majors v. Jeanes*, in which the State actually appointed them as special assistant attorneys general to defend the marriage ban.

INDEX